The McGraw-Hill World Wide Web Training Manual

The McGraw-Hill World Wide Web Training Manual

Ronald L. Wagner

Internet Home Page
http://www.marketing-coach.com/mh-web

McGraw-Hill

New York   San Francisco   Washington, D.C.   Auckland   Bogotá   Caracas   Lisbon   London   Madrid
Mexico City   Milan   Montreal   New Delhi   San Juan   Singapore   Sydney   Tokyo   Toronto

McGraw-Hill

A Division of The McGraw·Hill Companies

©1996 by **Ronald L Wagner**.
Published by the McGraw-Hill Companies, Inc.

pbk   1 2 3 4 5 6 7 8 9 BBC/BBC 9 0 0 9 8 7 6

Library of Congress Cataloging-in-Publication Data
Wagner, Ronald L.
    The McGraw-Hill World Wide Web training manual / by Ronald L. Wagner.
        p.   cm
    Includes index.
    ISBN 0-07-066938-4 (pbk.)
    1. World Wide Web (Information retrieval system)—Handbooks, manuals, etc.
I. Title
TK5105.888.W34 1996
025.04—DC20   96-28047
                                                                               CIP

Acquisitions editor: Brad Schepp
Editorial team: Robert E. Ostrander, Executive Editor
                Aaron G. Bittner, Book Editor
Production team: Katherine G. Brown, Director
                Rose McFarland, Desktop Operator
                Nancy Mickley, Proofreading
                Jodi L. Tyler, Indexer
Design team: Jaclyn J. Boone, Designer   0669384
            Kathryn Lukaszewicz, Associate Designer   TNG1

Dedications

To Lisa, Michael, Rich and Jamie, my everythings
(*www.citapei.com/family*)

Acknowledgments

Bill Adler, Jr., Adler and Robin Books (*www.adlerbks.com*)
Lisa Swayne, Adler and Robin Books (*www.adlerbks.com*)
Dick Connor, cmc (*www.marketing-coach.com*)
Jeff Davidson, cmc, The Breathing Space Institute (*www.brespace.com*)
Sidnie Feit, Yale University (*www.yale.edu*)
Orhan Onaran, Erol's Internet and Computers (*www.erols.com*)
Kevin Dugan, Erol's Internet and Computers (*www.erols.com*)
Alan Chung, Digiweb (*www.digiweb.com*)
Danny Tseng, Digiweb (*www.digiweb.com*)
Ed Lamb, Bell Atlantic (*www.bell-atl.com*)
Marty Melton, Bell Atlantic (*www.bell-atl.com*)
Vonda Majette, Bell Atlantic (*www.bell-atl.com*)
Jennie Svitaski, LNS Communications
Bob Clinton, Motorola (*www.motorola.com*)
Brad Templeton, ClariNet Communications (*www.clarinet.com*)
Kody Kline, D.T.P. Extreme (*www.ionet.net/~kkline*)
Michael J. Sullivan, Haywood & Sullivan (*www.hsdesign.com*)
Bea McKinney, askSam Systems (*www.asksam.com*)
Frank Zerbel, AMT Learning Solutions (*www.amtcorp.com*)
Chris Lofback, Clearwater Public Library (*snoopy.tblc.lib.fl.us/cpl*)
Jason Baer, Indirect, Inc. (*www.direct.net*)
Chris Anderson, JASC, Inc. (*www.jasc.com*)
Chris Cooper, Quote.Com (*www.Quote.Com*)
Megan Dixon, Qualcomm (*www.qualcomm.com*)
Mike Birdsall, Birdsall Designs (*www.birdsalldesigns.com*)
Swa Frantzen, Katholieke Universiteit Leuven (*route66.netvision.be*)
Kieran Gillett, Brooklyn North Software Works (*fox.nstn.ca/~harawitz*)
Harvey Kaufman, NetSpeak Corporation (*www.netspeak.com*)
Rick Holt, University of Virginia (*fmh6h@faraday. clas.virginia.edu*)
MMedia Research Corporation (*world.std.com/~mmedia*)

Contents

▶

▶

Introduction

Once a photograph of the Earth, taken from the outside, is available . . . a new idea as powerful as any in history will let loose.

Sir Fred Hoyle, 1948.

TWENTY YEARS after Sir Fred Hoyle made this prediction, we saw an earthrise for the first time when Apollo 8 orbited the moon on Christmas Eve, 1968. Many of the people who saw that earthrise were building a computer networking system that today brings you the World Wide Web.

Certainly the Web qualifies as Sir Hoyle's new idea. It is as powerful as any idea in history. It's no coincidence that the Internet was created by the first generation to see an earthrise. That moonrise illustrated the concept that we all are joined in global unity—and the Internet has turned that concept into reality.

Now the Internet is experiencing unprecedented growth. That growth has created in the computer book industry the same obsolescence problem that swept the music industry as it transitioned from vinyl records to CDs. One day all the record stores had a couple of aisles of CDs. Then a few months later, vinyl records vanished and everything had been transferred over to CD—even the golden oldies. And that's what's happened with the Internet. The World Wide Web is the CD of the Internet, and is quickly replacing the traditional methods that the Internet previously used to deliver information.

Many Internet books are about as useful as learning how to handle vinyl records and turntables. While you always will be able to play vinyl records, you'll have to settle for the golden oldies.

A book that tried to cover every detail of using the Internet would be out-of-date before it reached the store shelves. I've solved the obsolescence problem by leaving out material that quickly would go stale and including Internet links— both in this book and on-line at the book's Web site—that will ensure you stay up-to-date on any Internet topic you care about. This book, therefore, is but a starting point on what probably will be a lifelong journey of continuous learning in cyberspace. Each chapter closes with a module called Continuing Education—a listing of Internet sources that will keep you up-to-the-second informed on every topic. These sections will ensure that you stay abreast of the topics that affect your profession, your organization, and your personal hobbies and interests.

I've divided the book into three phases:

- Phase 1 gives you an introduction to the World Wide Web, and teaches you to surf the Net efficiently and productively.
- Phase 2 is a treasure trove of valuable Web sites and services that will help you get started right away.
- Phase 3 handles the "What next?" question by showing you what to do with the Internet tools and services you've learned to use.

I'll close with some helpful reference sources, including:

- A glossary of Internet, Web, and computer terms
- A guide to electronic copyright issues
- A guide for speeding your Internet connection with ISDN phone service.

Ron Wagner

http://www.marketing-coach.com/mh-web

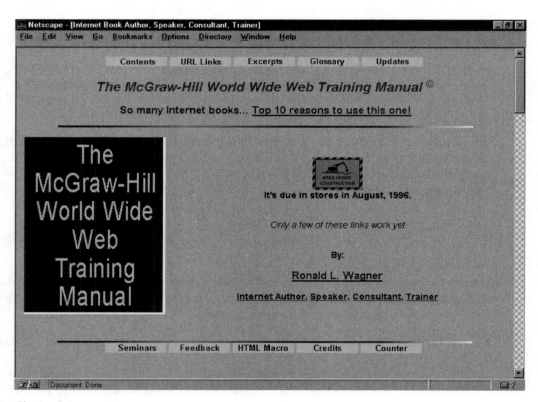

Figure I-1

PHASE 1
The basics

WINSTON CHURCHILL said "I love learning, but I hate being taught." Believing that you might agree with Churchill, I have strived in this book to create learning opportunities in which you can enjoy something you love—the pleasures of learning something new. This book is not constrained to the technical nuts and bolts. After all, volumes of technical computer tomes already crowd computer store bookshelves. Of course I'll give you plenty of technical material, but I'll do so in a way that will help you integrate your technical needs with your human needs.

Reading the first three chapters of this phase before going on-line will prepare you for the dramatic transformation that the Internet will bring to your life. The changes will be unprecedented.

- Chapter 1 will give you an Internet map and a quick tour of your new on-line environment so you'll know the lay of this new cyber-land before you jump in. Rather than being an in-depth technical report, it's an easy-reading overview that will introduce you to the basic technical aspects of the Internet.

- Chapter 2 will ease some of the stress that you will encounter whenever you face changes and new technology. Because the Web can overwhelm you—and me, too—I've given you this enlightening bonus that will prepare you for the onslaught of information that the Web can bring you. This chapter is a collaboration with Jeff Davidson of the Breathing Space Institute, who set the stage with his ground-breaking book *Breathing Space: Living and Working Comfortably in a Sped-Up Society*. If you don't need breathing space now, you soon will.

- Chapter 3 will help you understand the basics of turning your organization's Web site into a powerful, profitable business tool. There's way too much hype and gee-whiz technology on the Web so far. You, however, have a chance to help move the Web beyond gee whiz and into the world of valuable, professional business resources. This chapter will help you create the kind of Web site that your customers and clients will visit often and feel rewarded for the time they spend there.

- Chapter 4 presents the first Hands-On classroom training lesson in this book. I call it Windows Wide Open, because it will show you what I call the "advanced basics" of Windows. The advanced basics are the tools and techniques that few people learn in a basic Windows class, but they're the things that will ensure that you get top performance out of the software you use. Windows can be an incredibly powerful business tool, or just a really cool way to play Hearts by yourself.

- Chapter 5 is a Hands-On classroom training lesson that focuses on using Netscape. It goes beyond the mere basics of Web browsing, though, because it will show you how to tailor Netscape to be used aggressively. You're going to need these techniques to efficiently capitalize on the fabulous resources that you'll discover in Phase 2.

- Chapter 6 is a series of advanced Hands-On Netscape lessons. You'll discover that Netscape has a vast array of additions and extensions that can dramatically add to its abilities. I'll help you find out how to obtain the additions and how to implement the extensions. Netscape is changing rapidly, so this chapter closes with a treasure trove of resources that will help you stay abreast of the latest Netscape changes.

After you've finished these chapters, you'll be all set to explore the Web and learn how it can serve as a powerful enhancement to your daily work.

Quick tour and orientation

IN THIS CHAPTER you'll get a quick overview of how the Internet is laid out. You'll learn just enough of its origin, history, and current status to be comfortable, but I'll not burden you with a lot of details. After all, you probably have been driving for years without reading about how our interstate highway system was built. Of course, if you enjoy details, you can learn more about the Internet from the Internet itself. But let's not worry about details now; we're just out for a scenic drive to see the highlights.

The end of this chapter lists a wide selection of Internet sites that can help you peek under the hood of the Internet. There's no reason to include a lot of information in this book that's available on the Internet. So, I'll begin by defining one term important now, the term *internet* itself.

internet versus The Internet

There are internets and then there is The Internet. A small "i" internet could be any two computer *networks* that are interconnected so that users on both networks can share resources on either network. A network is at least two computers connected locally to each other—but some single networks have thousands of computers. An internet is at least two connected networks—regardless of the size of either one (see Figure 1-1).

If more networks are interconnected, they all might be directly connected to each other (see Figure 1-2). Notice that each network in Figure 1-2 has a direct connection to every other network on the internet.

It's easy to see that directly connecting each computer would severely limit the size and area that an internet could cover. Even if the numbers remained small, direct connections might be impractical, so they could be linked in series to limit the number of lines (see Figure 1-3).

If all networks on an internet are not directly connected, however, then communications between all networks only is possible if the middle networks act as relays for the outer-lying networks.

Figure 1-1

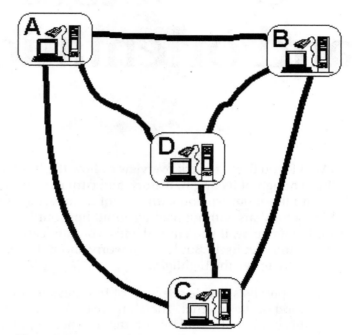

Figure 1-2

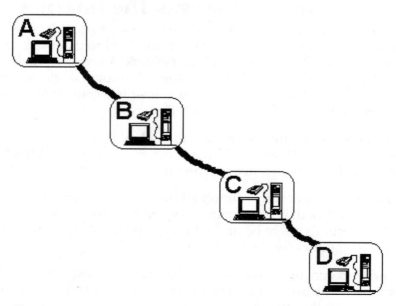

Figure 1-3

Networks that act as relays across an internet include devices called routers. In Figure 1-4, for example, Network B and Network E are not directly connected, so they can communicate only via the routers in intermediary networks. If Network A has a router, then communications could be routed from B through A to E. If Network A does not have routing capability, but Network C and Network D do, then Network B still could communicate with Network E through Networks C and D. Routers are what makes the global Internet possible.

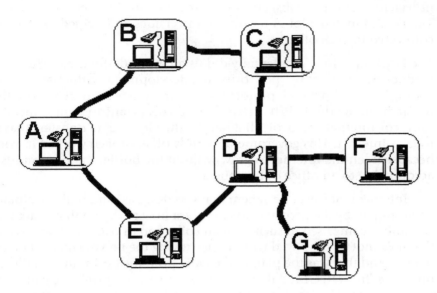

Figure 1-4

The Internet

The Internet is the master of all internets. It is growing explosively and has become practically a living entity. No one knows for sure how many networks the Internet interconnects. The number of computers connected via the Internet increases daily, approximately doubling every six months. I've encountered estimates that predict the number of Internet users could reach 100 million by 1998 and could reach 500 million by 2001.

Here's one example with some firm numbers. In October, 1995, *USA Today* reported that in the preceding three months approximately 24 million people had signed up for Internet service. That's approximately two million per week, which, if you do the math, is consistent with the estimates of 500 million by 2001.

Those figures could be off by a large margin in either direction. The bottom line is that the Internet is a vast, global internet of (literally) countless computers. If you really want to know the latest estimates, check out some of the addresses listed at the end of this chapter.

Imagine the network models depicted above if one of them grew to connect millions of computers around the world. That's the capital-I Internet.

No one owns the Internet. It has no central controlling authority. No one could control it if they tried. It's simply too large and too complex to be reined in by any single group or government. As you might be surprised to discover, however, it was planned that way.

How it got started

The Internet started at the U.S. Department of Defense (DoD). During the Cold War era, the DoD needed to create a research network to link computers in universities, research labs, and government control centers all across the country. The DoD donated a lot of money to universities and helped universities get connected to each other.

The DoD, therefore, accidentally did us all a wonderful favor. They planted the seed for the Internet by sponsoring the development of the basic "genetic-coding"—called network protocols—and then they set it free. From this early research sprang the TCP/IP network protocols (Transmission Control Protocol/Internet Protocol) that handle the global data transfers that race across today's Internet. This government's hands-off approach worked in your favor because it left the Internet to grow without the burdens and restraints of being accountable to an office of bureaucrats.

The Internet is at least one system that was designed and built in a totally free environment by the people who knew best how to design that system. It also is so vast and is comprised of such a varied collection of computers and connections that it cannot be destroyed without destroying the nerve centers of every developed nation. And that was the plan of the DoD from the beginning. I'll illustrate with a quotation from RFC1462 that says the Internet was born ". . . trying to connect together a U.S. Defense Department network called the ARPAnet and various other radio and satellite networks. The ARPAnet was an experimental network designed to support military research—in particular, research about how to build networks that could withstand partial outages (like bomb attacks) and still function."

So, while the U.S. government was the parent, no group ever has controlled the Internet. And now it's too big for anyone to even try to control it.

Why the Internet is so popular

Personal computers have been consumer products for more than 20 years, since the Apple II launched the PC revolution in 1974. During that time, most people have avoided computers completely. Many of those who use PCs do so because they're expected to use PCs at work—even though many of them would be delighted to never touch another PC. So why is it, after so much avoidance, that so many people today are racing to get on-line? I'll quote Albert Einstein:

A human being is a part of the whole, called by us "Universe", a part limited in time and space. We experience ourselves, our thoughts and our feelings as something separated from the rest—a kind of optical delusion of our consciousness. This delusion is a kind of prison for us, restricting us to our personal desires and to affection for a few persons nearest to us.

Our task must be to free ourselves from this prison by widening our circle of compassion to embrace all living creatures and the whole of nature in its beauty.

> Einstein understood that one day we would, collectively, begin to see through this optical delusion of separateness. The Internet is the first tangible evidence that humankind can truly be interconnected and can widen "our circle of compassion to embrace all living creatures." Cyberspace is the place in which we finally can see beyond the limitations of our personal desires and realize the vast benefits of global unity. I believe that we all—even if only subconsciously—feel this pull toward unity and that's what is pulling so many people on-line.

There's really no control?

That's right.

Practically speaking, of course, no complex system would function smoothly without some central coordination. But coordination is not control. The Internet's central coordination is provided by the Internet Architecture Board (IAB) that *ratifies* the communications standards on the Internet.

The IAB heads a group of volunteers called the Internet Society (ISOC) that fosters the Internet and promotes Internet usage. The ISOC is based in Reston, Virginia, has branch groups around the world, and hosts an annual, global conference (see Figure 1-5). The ISOC's first president, Dr. Vinton Cerf, is the co-creator of the TCP/IP that you will use as you cerf . . . I mean "surf" through cyberspace.

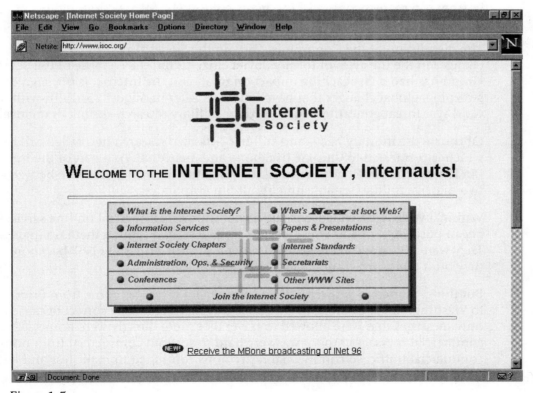

Figure 1-5

Another group of volunteers—no more groups after this, I promise—called the Internet Engineering Task Force (IETF) develops standards and resolves Internet technical and operational issues. The IETF functions as a public forum that organizes ad hoc workgroups that explore ways to keep the Internet abreast of technology changes.

How you got invited

During the Internet's first 20 years or so, the people who were building and using it did not allow any commercial usage. Its construction had been funded by a vast conglomeration of organizations and was used primarily for technical communications between the organizations that built it.

The first major step toward you being invited to the cyberspace party occurred in the late 1980s when the National Science Foundation (NSF) established a backbone, the NSFNET, to connect five supercomputers that it owned. The NSF became a key component of the Internet, which already included several very large nets that were linked together. At this time, people weren'e even commonly using the term "Internet."

Cyberspace

Cyberspace has become a generic term that represents the total universe of all interconnected computers. The term was created by science fiction author William Gibson. In Gibson's books, cyberspace is a computer network called "The Matrix". His books foretell of a cold and forbidding future that suffers from too many people and too many computers. Mere fiction, right?

The dissolution of the Communist Party in the Soviet Union triggered some vast changes in the lifestyles of former Soviet citizens. But the collapse of the Soviet Union has had a far-reaching impact on us all and the Internet is one sign of the sweeping, global changes that have followed. After in August 23, 1991, with the Cold War threat gone, the DoD's need for military research shrunk dramatically.

Of course the military had—and still has—its own research net, called MILNET, which is connected to the NSF backbone and, hence, still is a part of the Internet. But life on this planet changed and the potential for nuclear conflict between two massive military establishments all but evaporated.

Within a year of the collapse of the Soviet Union, commercial on-line services began pushing for commercial customers and started signing them up in droves. They were not supposed to send commercial traffic across the NSF backbone, so they built their own commercial switch in California.

But things started to get weird, with commercial messages going from Princeton to Washington via California. Of course this was technically correct because the only messages that were allowed to travel that route directly were non-commercial messages. And it was very hard to sort out commercial from non-commercial traffic, so commercial restrictions continued to make less and less sense.

Fortunately, the Clinton-Gore administration saw the wasteful lunacy in all the weird routing and the sorting of traffic, so it funded a new system that was separate from the NSF backbone. Then the government got out of the way.

Thus, commercial Internet traffic no longer was considered unacceptable or inappropriate and restrictions on Internet connection requirements were lifted. Commercial Internet service providers hooked up to one another and each covered as much territory as was economically feasible. And now, we've got a fully-functioning, commercial Internet.

Commercial online services

Where do the commercial online services—such as CompuServe, America Online, and Prodigy—fit into the Internet? You most likely have been bombarded by their advertising hype touting their Internet service. Many people ask me, "Isn't AOL the Internet?" Not exactly. Not even close. Let me illustrate.

I grew up in Tulsa, Oklahoma, about three houses away from Route 66. I loved that old television series *Route 66* with the two guys cruising the country in their Corvette convertible. Many years later I even did it myself. And now, the Route 66 TV series has become a good metaphor for the Internet: The Internet is to on-line services what Route 66 is to Disney World.

How so?

Picture walking through the front gate of a Disney theme park and picking up a nice, colorful map of what to do. You can read a schedule of events, locate safe places to eat and find the restrooms. Hey, the restrooms are even clean and there's not a gum wrapper in sight. Everything is laid out for you and there are plenty of ways to find organized, sanitized things to do.

That's an on-line service.

Now picture taking a road trip on Route 66 in a Corvette convertible. An entirely different experience, right? No one's going to show you where to go next. You don't know what will happen next. You have no idea what you'll see next. And nothing is organized or sanitized.

That's the Internet.

Oh sure, today, all of the on-line services have a special gate in them now that lets you exit onto Route 66. But you first have to drive your Corvette through a theme park just to get to the really fun stuff!

Of course many people enjoy the on-line theme parks. But if you've ever wanted to freely cruise top-down on the open highway, then you'll love the on-line version of Route 66.

By the way, Route 66 itself is on the Web (see Figure 1-6). In fact, it's an incredibly detailed and well-done Web site. Believe it or not, however, the Route 66 site was built and is maintained by Swa Frantzen, who lives in *Belgium*. The home page has a map of Route 66 and permits you to click on segments to zoom in to ever-increasingly detailed maps, and eventually down to photos taken along the way. I was thrilled to find a Web site in Belgium that had a photo taken two blocks from my childhood home in Tulsa. I guess that now "small world" and "Internet" are synonyms.

So, if you want to "get your own kicks on Route 66," you can visit *http://route66.netvision.be*. And the Corvette you'll need for the trip can be downloaded for free from Netscape. Now if I could just download a real Corvette . . .

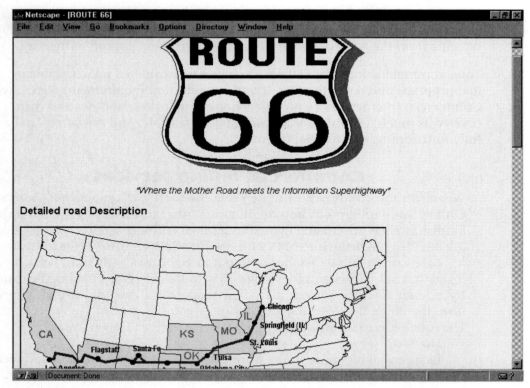

Figure 1-6

So, today, who is the Internet?

You are.

And *where* is the Internet?

It's your computer, every other computer connected to the Internet, plus millions of miles of copper wire, fiber optic cable, microwave channels and satellite links. It's similar to the air you breathe, no one owns it or controls it, and it's everywhere.

Isn't it wonderful that the Internet, with its roots tied to the DoD, has now become a thriving, open system? It seems to me to fulfill an ancient prophesy that said, "They will beat their swords into plowshares and their spears into pruning hooks." Well, that's a bit of a stretch because they were virtual swords and they've become virtual plowshares. But now it's yours, so jump into your virtual Corvette and hit the gas on for an exciting road trip!

What's out there for me?

You probably have heard a lot lately about the Internet. Most of what you've heard is about one aspect of the Internet that's called the World Wide Web. You'll often see it written in shorthand—Web, WWW, and W3. There are several other aspects to the Internet, but the importance of the others is waning rapidly. Here's a short rundown of each, beginning with the Web.

▶ *The basics*

World Wide Web (Web)

The World Wide Web has become more than anyone ever dreamed.

The Internet created the basic connections to join us all into a single interrelated system, but the Web was made possible by technology called *hypertext*. Hypertext as used on the Web makes the Internet user-friendly and almost universally accessible.

When information is written in hypertext, key words can be highlighted and linked to related text. The reader merely clicks on a highlighted word to jump to the linked, related text.

Think of the end of an article in an encyclopedia that has a listing of Related Topics. How many times have you actually dragged out all the additional volumes that would be required to see those related topics? How about never?

But in a hypertext encyclopedia (CD-ROM encyclopedias use hypertext), you simply click on the titles of the related topics to jump to the follow-on article. How many times will you actually click on a hypertext link to see a related topic? How about constantly? Hypertext is a charismatic attraction—it's an electronic black hole that can pull you ever deeper into interesting areas in cyberspace—and that attraction is why you may have heard so much about the Web.

E-mail

The bulk of Internet traffic is electronic mail (e-mail). E-mail enables you to swap messages with anyone on the Internet anywhere in the world. The best part is that e-mail essentially is free—there are no distance-based or per-message charges for e-mail. A few online services still charge a per-message rate, but usually only for those messages beyond a threshold number of messages included in their basic package. Whether it's free or very cheap, e-mail will completely change the way you conduct much of your communication.

Newsgroups

Newsgroups—sometimes referred to as the Usenet—are electronic discussion forums. Newsgroups are akin to community bulletin boards upon which people can post notices, but they serve the global community and have no formal membership requirements—anyone on the Internet can read and post messages. No one can accurately count their number, but estimates go as high as 15,600 public newsgroups. There also are private newsgroups, but counting them would be impossible.

FTP (File Transfer Protocol)

The title pretty much explains its usage—you can use the File Transfer Protocol (FTP) to transfer computer files between your computer and other computers on the Internet. You will use this mostly to transfer files into your computer from larger computer systems (download or receive), though you also can transfer files from your computer to others (upload or send). What can you get using FTP? Just about anything you can imagine that can be stored on a computer: software, documents, spreadsheets, maps, photos, a copy of the Constitution, audio sound clips, and even video clips. The Internet has thousands of FTP sites and millions of files. Perhaps you'll use the FTP directly sometime, but you primarily will encounter it as a hidden part of the Web.

Mailing lists

Here's a terrific tool to stay up-to-the-minute on a vast array of topics. The best feature about getting information from this system is that (unlike most of Internet) it comes to you. Instead of providing a repository of information that can be searched and downloaded, mailing lists send automated e-mail to users who subscribe to electronic publications.

When you subscribe to most mailing lists, you join an informal electronic community. The core of any mailing list is a software application called a *list server* that runs the list. When any member sends a message to the mailing list (actually to the designated list server), that message is redistributed to all members of the group. A large group with lots of traffic can fill the In box in your e-mail application in a few hours.

Some mailing lists are *moderated*, which means that someone reads the incoming messages and decides which ones to redistribute to the entire group. Depending on your point of view, you'll regard the moderator either as a meddling censor or as a thankless saint doing you an enormous favor.

Gopher (Gopher)

In 1991, a team of computer folks at the University of Minnesota developed a system that enables Internet users to "go fer" stuff all over cyberspace. Can it be merely coincidence, then, that the mascot of the University of Minnesota is a gopher? The name certainly fits, because this electronic rodent can burrow all over the Internet to find information you want. Once the mainstay of surfing the Net, most people now use Gopher only when it pops up on the Web.

There are Web-based Gopher searching tools, and you'll see some of these in the chapters in Phase 2. Sometimes a regular Web site—especially at universities and libraries—will take you to a Gopher page. Today's Web browsers handle Gopher pages so well that you might not even notice that you're not actually viewing a hypertext document.

Golden oldies

In the Introduction to this book, I told you that many aspects of the Internet already have become passé. That doesn't mean they're old—it just means that life in cyberspace moves pretty fast and yesterday's hot technology is today's "remember when." The vinyl records of the Internet are Veronica, Archie, Jughead, finger, Telnet, and WAIS. This book won't cover any of these; wait until you've gotten deeply involved with the Web to see if you are crying "More!" If you are, then investigate these tools.

Information that until recently only was available through these golden oldies is rapidly migrating to the Web. Depending on your field of interest, you might need some of these temporarily. Soon, however, you should be able to find everything you want without leaving your favorite Web browser. Because almost all of your Internet work will involve the Web, let's close your Internet tour by returning to the topic of the World Wide Web.

Web principles

While the World Wide Web is vast and it might seem complicated, the Web's underlying principles are surprisingly simple. The task of implementing those simple principles across a dizzying array of incompatible computer systems, however, has not been simple. I give a gold star to the people who invented and created the Web. It has required a lot of detailed planning and work, but the core principles remain simple.

The Web is built around computer documents. That basically is it. Using any Web browser on the Web is akin to loading documents into your word processor. As you most likely are aware, your Windows word processor can display embedded graphic images and play embedded sound files. So can Netscape. Netscape just can't edit the files it loads. So, you can think of Netscape as a read-only word processor.

Netscape Navigator Gold

Okay, things change. That's the nature of the Internet. Netscape has a Navigator Gold version that *does* let you edit Web pages. But the read-only principle still applies because you cannot edit the pages you see on the Web unless you download them to your local system and save them. Of course even then, you're not editing the original page, only a personal copy of the Web page. You cannot change the original page. So, for all practical purposes, you'll use Netscape as if it were a read-only word processor.

Why use a read-only word processor?

You'd have little use for a read-only word processor if all you ever loaded in it were files from your own computer. But what if you could connect your read-only word processor to a remote computer that held documents that contained information you could use? You might be interested in loading those files even if you couldn't edit them—especially if you could print them and save them so that you could edit them in your word processor.

Then we could connect your read-only word processor to thousands of remote computers—located all over the planet—that held millions of documents that contained just about every type of information you can imagine. Then we'll give you a wide variety of search tools to help you pinpoint information you need from among the millions of available documents.

Then we could include in these documents graphic images, photographs, sound files, video clips, and forms that let you submit applications and make credit card purchases. Then, we could cross-link all of these millions of documents so that when you locate a document that contains some information you want, it could link you to other documents on related topics merely by clicking a mouse. We'll call these links hypertext, because they hyper-accelerate your ability to find what you need from among millions of pages of text.

Finally, we could give you the ability to put your own information on this system so that anyone connected to it could find your information by topical index or by a keyword search, and give you the ability to cross-link your information to other documents on related topics. If this sounds valuable to you, then you'll find the Web to be an exciting tool that will revolutionize the way you think about the world.

Hypertext

If you are becoming confused by the term hypertext, don't be dismayed. It's not your fault, because hypertext is not hypertext anymore.

The term was created as a definition for a word or phrase within a text document that provides a link to other text documents. In an electronic encyclopedia, for example, you merely click on any of the Related Topics and you see the related article—that's hypertext.

Your first exposure to using hypertext, however, might be to click on a graphic image that jumps to another graphic image. Or you might click on a graphic image that downloads a sound file. Why, you might ask, is a button called *hypertext*?

Sorry about the confusion. But a long, long time ago—way back in 1991—no one had any idea that hypertext would become what it is today. Obviously the people who coined the term hypertext were better computer programmers than seers. That's not a complaint, though, because no one saw this coming. If the term were to be coined today, it might be called hyperlink.

The bottom line is that hypertext is on-screen magic. It has revolutionized communication. You'll be able to click on words, buttons, or graphic images and be swept off to any region within cyberspace that the author wanted you to see—other documents, images, sound clips, video clips, forms, software, and tables of data. And you easily will be able to create your own hyperlinked documents, thus being able to jump your readers off to any region within cyberspace that you'd like them to see.

We all are one

We all want to be connected—it's a natural part of human nature because, truly, we all are one. The hyperlinks on the World Wide Web are rapidly creating a physical manifestation of our longing for unity—to become one.

> *In a real sense all life is interrelated. All persons are caught in an inescapable network of mutuality, tied in a single garment of destiny. Whatever affects one directly, affects all indirectly . . . I can never be what I ought to be until you are what you ought to be, and you can never be what you ought to be until I am what I ought to be. This is the interrelated structure of reality.*

Martin Luther King, Jr.

King probably wasn't thinking of the Internet when he wrote about "the network of mutuality," but it's possible—the Internet had been born. Whether or not he knew it then, today we have an unsurpassed network of mutuality that will have joined together everyone on this planet by the end of 1996. As I write this book, the World Bank is completing its Web presence in Africa, the last populated continent to get Internet connectivity. Thus, global Internet service soon will be in place and the planet will be able to act as a unit.

The World Wide Web has given us the ability to transform humanity into a single living organism. Think of it on a personal level first, then on a planetary level.

If you get a splinter in your finger, your whole body rallies to help the tiny area that's affected. Similarly, the World Wide Web has given us the ability to direct our energies toward even tiny areas that need the help of the entire system. Such an intense focus will help us all, because it will prevent small problems from festering into much larger ones that could harm the global population.

For example, if we all had had the benefit of splinter-like communication when the HIV virus first was discovered in monkeys, there likely would be no global epidemic today. Unfortunately, the parts of humanity that had the ability to stop the problem while it was only a splinter did not feel a oneness with such a small affliction. We still were suffering under the delusion that we all are separate. But the Web can help us prevent future splinters in the body of humanity from festering into serious, harmful problems. I hope that as you learn to use the Web, you'll bear in mind its unprecedented ability to join us as we always have been meant to be joined.

About all that jargon

The glossary at the end of this book gives you the basic jargon you need. It is brief because I only need to introduce you to terms you'll need for your hands-on training.

This glossary is available online as well. You can use your Web browser to search the online version and jump directly to terms you want to learn. Also, the online version is constantly updated and will be more comprehensive than the one in this book.

I've used in this book as few technical terms as I could, but the Internet involves a lot of technical jargon. Learning it can bewilder an Internet beginner. In fact, there's even jargon for an Internet beginner. The term is newbie, and, as you soon shall see in the Continuing Education section at the end of this chapter, there's a whole Internet site dedicated to helping newbies.

Jargon is an integral part of the Internet, so please learn the essential jargon before the hands-on lessons. Jargon is useful, of course, because once you understand the terms, its shorthand will save time when communicating about the Internet. Besides, you're going to see it everywhere, so you might as well learn it now.

What about other, more technical terms? You can find all you need and more than you'll ever want in a variety of places using the Internet itself. Here's a listing that includes some sites that can put the definition of every Internet jargon term at your fingertips.

Continuing Education

The McGraw-Hill World Wide Web Training Manual
http://www.marketing-coach.com/mh-web

This URL is the book's home page, where you'll find a link to the Glossary. It also is indexed in most of the online search engines such as Yahoo and Lycos. You can check out other glossary listings by searching these services for Internet Glossary, and I've provided a button on the Glossary home page that automatically searches Yahoo for other glossaries. Of course the results list will include this book's entry, too. The same glossary also can be found at the Web site for my last book, *The McGraw-Hill Internet Training Manual* (see Figure 1-7).

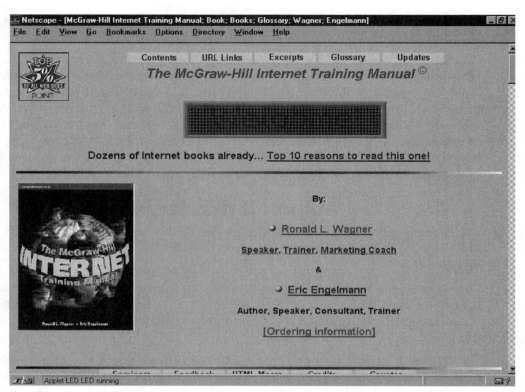

Figure 1-7

Cyber Course
http://www.newbie.net/CyberCourse

Here's a permanent, ongoing training site on the Web, designed especially for new Internet users (newbies). It's an extremely well-done treasure trove of information and it's free. It uses the Netscape 2.0 frames feature, so it will work best for you if you have Navigator 2.0 or later (see Figure 1-8).

It includes a section called Cyber Course and another called Newbie Newz. The course has several sections that can walk you through learning Internet basics. The Newbie Newz is a mailing list that will help you learn about the Internet.

The smiley FAQ
http://www.newbie.net/JumpStations/SmileyFAQ.html

Because you can't see the person who is sending you electronic mail, you are sometimes uncertain whether they are serious or just joking with you. About 14 years ago, Scott Fahlman, of Carnegie Mellon University, devised a scheme for encoding and conveying one's feelings as small text glyphs to overcome this frustration. These glyphs are called smileys (or emoticons), and this Web site includes a listing of the most commonly used smileys and their definitions.

The Internet Society
http://www.isoc.org

The Internet Society (ISOC) is the nongovernmental international organization for global cooperation and coordination for the Internet and its internetworking

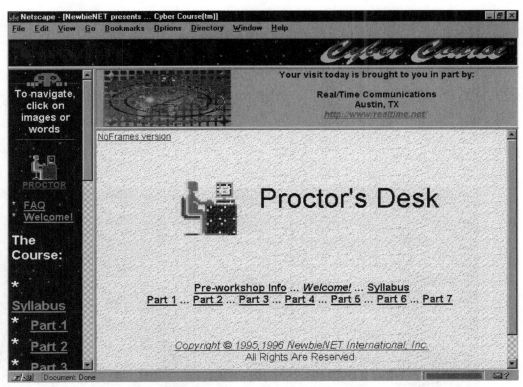

Figure 1-8

technologies and applications. Its members, both individual and organizational, have a common goal of maintaining the viability and the global scaling of the Internet.

For individual membership:

membership@isoc.org

For organization membership:

org-membership@isoc.org

Fax: 703-648-9887

Voice: 703-648-9888 (or 800-468-9507 in the USA only)

12020 Sunrise Valley Drive
Suite 270
Reston, VA 22091, USA.

Internet literacy consultants

http://www.matisse.net/files/glossary.html

The home page of the Internet Literacy Consultants (ILC) includes a jump to the Internet Glossary, an alternative glossary to this book's service. It's comprehensive, but lacks an alphabetical index you can use to quickly locate terms. A nice touch is that many definitions that contain other technical terms are cross-linked so you can look it up.

Boardwatch Magazine

http://www.boardwatch.com

Originally a magazine for the Bulletin Board System (BBS) community, *Boardwatch* magazine (see Figure 1-9) now covers the Internet and commercial online services as well. This Web site has the full text of back issues, dating back to October 1994. The articles deal with trends, legal and social issues, and technology. Luckily, they avoid much of the hype I've warned you to expect on the Internet. I recommend this site highly if you want to stay abreast of Internet developments.

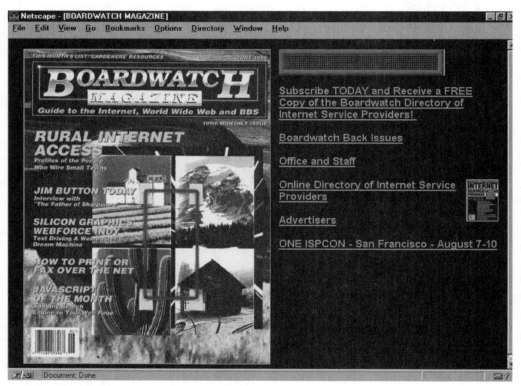

Figure 1-9

Racal-Datacom

http://www.racal.com/rdg

From the ISDN User's Guide to the Cell-Relay (ATM) Archives, Don Joslyn's Data Communications's page surveys the Networking resources of the Net. Don is a software engineer at Racal-Datacom, which hosts the page. The page has an especially good collection of links to other specialized collections of links.

Computing oriented abbreviation and acronyms

http://crl.nmsu.edu/lists/Babel.html

This is New Mexico State University's search interface to the Babel Computing Oriented Abbreviation and Acronyms database. If you're ever stumped by gibberish like RISC, COBOL, VRAM, VDT, IMTV, or OEM, this is a good place to visit.

Computer Literacy Bookshops home page

http://www.clbooks.com

Here's a good example of a Web page that was designed with functionality, not glitz, as the highest priority. It serves its purpose well and you won't waste time downloading unnecessary graphics. Use their search feature to locate books by topic or by author. You even can use this page to order more copies of this book for your colleagues who aren't lucky enough to have their own copy!

Useless Web pages

http://www.primus.com/staff/paulp/useless.html

There's more to the Web than value, business and commercialism. Need a break? Then check out America's Funniest Home Hypermedia. This site has been rated by Wired magazine as a waste of electrons; but don't confuse this with bad Web pages. Useless isn't necessarily bad, it's just useless. Sometimes that means you'll see some very good Web pages—depending on your point of view and sense of humor. Be forewarned, though: This page can lead you into the deepest, darkest side of the Web. Sit back and waste some electrons, Internet bandwidth, and time.

Internet joke book

http://www.clarinet.com:80/inetjoke.html

The Internet isn't all a bunch of boring computers, computer networks and computer nerds. It has its funny moments. Check out this page to order an Internet joke book—although you might need to be a computer nerd to get the jokes. It's edited by Brad Templeton, the founder and editor of the ClariNet Communications Corporation that publishes the Internet's first and largest electronic newspaper (now with 1,200,000 paid subscribers). Just in case going online has made you and your coworkers a bit edgy, remember this book and see if you can use it to find some humor out there in cyberspace.

Dear Emily Postnews

http://www.clarinet.com:80/brad/emily.html

Another Brad Templeton creation. This guy is very versatile. He also is featured in the appendix of this book, where I've reprinted his Top 10 Copyright Myths. Here's everything you always wanted to know about netiquette, but were afraid you already knew it. You do, but this puts it in perspective and is far more effective than reading a guilt-oriented plea to be kind to your neighbors.

Breathing space for cyberspace

Life goes by pretty fast. If you don't slow down, you might miss it.

THAT'S FROM the 1986 movie *Ferris Bueller's Day Off*. Ferris Bueller's advice made sense then—before anyone had heard the term information superhighway and when the Internet still was a closed system—but today Ferris' advice is a sound business principle.

The volume of information that spewed forth to spawn the term Information Age is dwarfed by what the Internet brings to us today. You now live in the Over-Information Age and the Internet is bringing it into your life faster than ever.

The volume of new knowledge disseminated in every field is enormous and easily exceeds anyone's ability to keep pace. As a result, everyone today fears that he/she is increasingly underinformed despite absorbing an unprecedented volume of information.

One big blur of information

Before they were 24, your grandparents probably had acquired enough knowledge or training to make a good living their entire lives. Such a deal is not available to you.

You ain't seen nothin' yet

In the spring of 1996, researchers pushed the top rate for transmitting information to the rate of 1 trillion bits per second. This speed required an optical fiber cable, so it won't be coming into your home at that speed next week, but eventually it will. It was no fluke, because three separate research teams achieved that speed, including AT&T Research and Lucent Technologies, both of which were formerly parts of Bell Laboratories.

So what does that speed mean in terms of stuff you have to read? It's the equivalent of sending the information in 300 years' worth of a daily newspaper in a single second. It's approximately one thousand times faster than current cable television systems. So, instead of being limited to only 120 channels, maybe someday your cable system will have the capacity for 120,000 channels. If they allocate enough of that capacity for cable access channels, we all can start our own talk show.

Be sure to check out the tailored news services featured in chapter 8, that let you create your own newspaper by filtering out everything you *don't* need to see.

In this Over-Information Age, you have so much information competing for your time and attention that nearly everything is becoming one big blur. When more things compete for your attention, you feel as if the time in your life is passing by more quickly. In this chapter I will show you that, ironically, you'll have to slow down before you can keep up. Let me put in perspective the size of the tidal waves of information from the Internet ocean that are crashing on your personal shores.

Information

- A *single* Sunday edition of the *New York Times* contains more information than your great-grandparents may have encountered in a *lifetime*.
- Every *five years* (and dropping) half the world's technological information is replaced.
- On average, 3000 books are published *each week* just in the U.S.—the global total is more than 2000 new books *every day*!
- In 1970, there were three TV networks in the U.S. Now there are more than 350 full-powered networks and independent stations—and cable systems now are gearing up to bring a total of 500 or more channels into your home.
- A single Internet Web search service has indexed more than *100 million* records, including more than ten million books and tens of millions of journal articles.

Paper generation

- With the advent of computers, we expected the paperless office; but we now consume *three times* the paper that we did in 1980!
- In the 1980s, *growth* in junk mail was 13 times faster than the *growth* in population.
- In the United States, each adult annually consumes 700 pounds of paper. That's a *55-foot-high* stack of regular (8.5×11) paper. Where do you store yours?

And you wonder why you barely seem able to remain abreast of changes in your own field? Add in the increasing amount of time you spend on-line with the Internet, and you might be missing a life—yours.

Can you feel how the pace of your life has increased in the last five years? Do you fear that you are not going to be able to keep up? And you're just starting to use the Internet! But, wait, you're not alone: Nobody is keeping up! The good news is that you don't have to keep up with most of it.

Cyberlock

With the increasing number of people going on-line to tap into the vast cache of information on the Internet, combined with the inability of the service providers to meet the increased demand, you'll be facing gridlock on the information superhighway. Jeff Davidson, author of *Breathing Space: Living and Working at a Comfortable Pace in a Sped-up Society*, calls it *cyberlock*.

As Jeff notes, cyberlock is in full swing. Lengthy waits for on-line connections are common—and that just gets you connected so you can begin waiting to download information. Often—especially during business hours—you won't even be able to log on to a favorite Web site. Cyberlock could become a long-term phenomenon as even more people go on-line for longer periods of time, sending and downloading ever-larger volumes of information.

The information superhighway of today is but a dirt road winding past an old farm compared to what you'll see in cyberspace by the year 2001, and cyberlock isn't going to disappear.

You need an information switchboard

Adding up all the factors competing for our time and attention, we are the most distracted generation in history. We're a generation that grew up with the notion "Take in more—there's no harm." The harm already has shown up, however, in our perception that our lives are racing by.

The Internet is going to put at your fingertips more information than you probably have imagined existed. You will become more acutely aware of an ever-increasing number of topics and areas in which you cannot keep up. Fortunately, you need not become a victim of the Over-Information Age—unless you choose to be. Here are two keys to restoring control over the information that bombards your life.

- The sooner you quit trying to keep up, the better you will feel.
- Carefully choose where you give your time and attention.

Your goal is relearning how to live with relative grace and ease. Remember the days when we all left work on time, got work done on time, did our taxes on time? You have to simplify. The quality of your life—for the rest of your life—depends on it. You can surf the Net for two hours, but you pay a price. Are the things you do on the Internet worth the price you pay?

Micro-niching

For at least the past decade, scores of business books have touted the concept of niches. The idea was that the business world has become too complex for anyone to be a jack-of-all-trades; the secret to success was picking one crucial niche in which to excel, and becoming an expert in it.

Today, confining your interests to a single, crucial niche is not nearly narrow enough. Suppose you had picked science—marine biology—as your niche and have ignored developments in all other fields. That won't work anymore. Within the scientific world alone, more than 40,000 journals publish more than 1,000,000 articles annually!

While most of those articles aren't directly focused on marine biology, what humankind learns about the ice age, fossil fuels, sun spots, tectonic plates, and a host of other areas might impact your understanding of marine biology. The Internet makes nearly all of these findings instantly available. Soon, merely counting new journals could be a full-time job.

Today you cannot effectively handle more than a tiny *micro-niche*. The good news is that the Internet—while massive and growing explosively—has the tools to make you an expert in the micro-niche you need while screening out what everybody else needs.

Consider the days of horse-and-buggy travel, when drivers placed blinders on their horses to keep them from being startled by things they didn't need to see. Similarly, you can choose to travel the information superhighway wearing electronic blinders that enable you to see only the information that affects your micro-niche.

Watch carefully in this book for tips on how to apply kill files that can block unwanted e-mail messages or screen bothersome newsgroup files. Be sure you understand how to set bookmarks so you easily can return to crucial information without browsing all over cyberspace. Learn to set up in your e-mail application an address book with nicknames. And, absolutely, learn Windows well enough to quickly use Cut, Copy, and Paste and to jump back and forth between Windows applications so you'll never retype anything that Windows can let you transfer.

You will need to carefully choose where you're going to give your time and attention; your time will, indeed, run out one day. Paradoxically, you can spend all the time remaining in your life logged onto the Internet and still be farther behind than you are today.

Spend time with friends. Make time for hobbies and the things you want to do. Most of all, be able to drop back at any time, take a long deep breath, and renew your spirit.

How can you do that?

Become your own information switchboard. Simply turn off your information receptors for several hours each day. Do not let new information invade your being if it doesn't promise immediate benefit to you, your family, your community, your organization, or any area of your life, or if it comes after hours. Choose to acquire only knowledge that benefits or truly interests you, not that you simply happen to ingest, or think you must ingest.

Most importantly, at all points, recognize that there is but one party who controls the volume, rate, and frequency of information to which you're exposed: You. The notion of keeping up is illusory, self-defeating, and harmful. The sooner you give it up, the better you will feel.

Just-in-time education

The information available on the Internet is going to reduce and perhaps eliminate your need for much of the knowledge you acquire in traditional education. We already have seen computers bring a similar transformation to many manufacturing industries.

Factories traditionally stockpiled parts needed to feed their assembly lines. Today, however, computers and improved transportation systems have enabled them to switch to a far more efficient system that uses the just-in-time principle. Instead of stockpiling every necessary part, efficient factories today receive needed parts just in time. This saves on storage costs, handling costs, inventory tracking costs, and on interest paid on idle parts awaiting use. These costs were necessary until it became possible to deliver the parts just-in-time.

The Internet is going to enable you to stop stockpiling information for eventual use, because you'll be able to get what you need just-in-time. Connections today are too slow, costly, and undependable to rely on to supply everything you need just-in-time, but that's changing rapidly. One day we will rely on it routinely. Already the principle of just-in-time education is seen in use weekly on television in Star Trek episodes. A Star Trek crewmember might say "Computer . . . what was the name of that crude twentieth-century computer networking system on the planet Earth?"

And the unseen, omnipresent computer would reply "The Internet."

The rise of misinformation

Unfortunately, when you do choose to absorb new information, it's difficult to ascertain what is accurate information. You see, along with the wealth of information we may tap into also comes voluminous amounts of *misinformation*. There is no easy way to say this. We have a society in which, too often, generated information is false. The Internet increases this phenomenon to extreme levels. Because of our vast capabilities for disseminating such information, the truth rarely catches up with the falsehoods. Here's an example:

> In his book, *Agents of Influence*, author Pat Choate debunks the myth that the Japanese as a whole contribute to the development of innovation and technology as evidenced by their annual lead in the number of U.S. patents they file for and obtain. As Choate explains, in a dramatic example of the way the Japanese tilt the economic playing field, they practice the ruthless art of patent flooding.

> When a U.S. firm, for example, applies for a patent representing an innovation on which the Japanese would like to capitalize, Japanese firms will issue a flurry of patent applications that surround the technology in question. This technique can tie up an invention in the courts simply because of nuisance patents for a component or contributing element to the major patent.

> Yet most of us have heard—and fear—that the Japanese are far out-pacing U.S. firms in technological advances; and most people already are working at a feverish pace. Misinformation about Japanese patent practices has hoodwinked us into believing our technology seriously lags behind the Japanese.

In *Backlash*, author Susan Faludi points out how pop market forecasters make a fortune by reviewing popular media such as newspapers, television, movies, and so forth, and then concluding what trends are looming in America. The extreme fallacy with this method of forecasting, Faludi notes, is that it tends to promulgate that which only a handful of editors, publishers, and directors believe or perpetrate. Hard data supports few of these forecasts. Similarly, vast stores of information on the Internet are but the opinion of someone who posted a Web page.

We rely on information in our lives, and very often it is not valid information. We, as managers, career professionals, and employees—in addition to bearing the burden of the Over-Information Age—must ensure that we act only upon quality information.

You need accurate sources

So, how do you use the Internet in a way that recognizes the informational realities we've introduced so far?

Always confirm information you've encountered on the Internet before making any decision that can impact the underpinnings of your company. Go to original sources whenever you use statistics or data. Send e-mail back to the source asking for verification. Check informational headers in on-line documents. You'll learn how to implement these techniques in later chapters. For now, beware that the Internet is teeming with misinformation called *spoof data*.

Spoof data is information that is a joke or an intentional deception. Why does spoof data abound? Until very recently, the majority of Internet users have been male college students. Did you watch the movie *National Lampoon's Animal House*? Of course Animal House was a hyper-exaggerated parody, but it's a good reminder that a few college students with an immature sense of humor can cut a huge swath of confusion and ruin.

Spoof data, of course, can come from any source. A clever junior-high student can generate spoof data that appears to emanate from the White House. Spoof data is not difficult to create, and a few people think it's hilariously funny. Don't give them the satisfaction of seeing their handiwork do its intended dirty work. Always check your sources before acting!

Conditioning your environments

In addition to controlling the amount and quality of information to which you're exposed, you need to *condition your environments*. Most people do this some of the time, but people who don't do this often say it takes too much work. It takes work to get off mailing lists. It takes work to learn new computer software. Sure it does, but when you take time to condition your environment, when you take time out to set up your world for the way you work and live, the payoff comes over and over again. Let's consider some specific examples.

Condition your work environment

One of the great paradoxes of our society is that to accommodate the pace of the sped-up society in which we live, sometimes—as Ferris Bueller said—we do have to slow down. Often, that doesn't feel good, but to help you practice this principle, our first hands-on lesson (covering the advanced basics of using Windows) will slow you down to speed you up.

It might not feel good to spend the time I'll ask you to take to complete the Windows lesson. In fact, most people whom I've encountered in my role as a computer trainer believe they cannot afford the time to complete a lesson on Windows. Actually, the reverse is true. The more time-pressed you are, the more you need to be a whiz with Windows. If you're going to work all day in a Windows environment, you might as well master that environment.

Go through your file drawers—studies show that four out of five papers stuffed in files are never used again. Toss out everything you don't need to retain. Do the same on your computer. We have no studies to back it up, but we imagine that the four out of five data files stored on computer hard drives are never used again. The Internet actually can lessen your own storage burden because so much now is available electronically, which means that other people store it on their computers.

Condition your personal environment

One goal worth pursuing is getting a good night's sleep. Stanford University's Center for Sleep Research conducted a study and concluded that the typical American no longer has any idea what it means to be fully awake and alert! The Internet has had an enormously negative impact on the sleep habits of countless entranced computer users. Cyberspace is a powerfully engaging world that has a charismatic attraction for most people. An all-nighter can seem like a couple of hours.

Fortunately, you have the ever-present option to make new goals, such as the number of hours you sleep, health foods you eat, great novels you read, and so on. These are just a few examples of the kinds of goals that we ignore or short-change in our fast-paced lives.

As you begin to condition your environment, you see that it's possible to choose other types of goals instead of traditional ones, such as how much money you'll make, or how big a house you want. A conditioned environment also will increase your success with other types of goals, such as reducing your weight or blood pressure, or finding time to meditate.

Managing the beforehand

Managing the beforehand is related to conditioning your environments. It involves looking at forthcoming events in your life and deciding what you can handle in advance. Such a method enables you to be more rested and better prepared to encounter what enters your life—and since you're pulling onto the global information superhighway, we know that huge volumes of information soon will be pouring into your life.

Creating ad hoc piles of information you receive and don't know where to file is simply dealing with the aftermath of living in an over-information society. Creating space in anticipation of new information is managing the beforehand. How can you manage the beforehand electronically?

- Before you encounter mounds of new information, eliminate what you already have that is not useful to you. Throw away outdated paper documents and delete unnecessary files from your computer system.
- Create a default download directory on your hard drive or on the network, and specify this directory in the preferences sections of your favorite Internet

software. This way, you always will know where to find freshly downloaded files instead of having to search your computer system.

- Create directories into which you'll transfer important files from your default download directory—after you've confirmed their long-term usefulness to you.
- Download from the Internet only the information that truly will support you. Instead of downloading a file you might use only occasionally, record its Internet address and leave the information on the Internet.
- Knowing that you'll be saving Internet addresses, create a computer file for storing and organizing them. A sidebar in the next chapter, Windows Wide-Open, details the steps for implementing this technique.

It takes a little more work to condition your environment and manage the beforehand. But once you begin practicing the techniques, the payoffs are so tremendous that you can't *not* do them anymore. Sure, you already are inundated with rules, guidelines, and checklists without us adding to them. These aren't rules, however, they are *ways of being.*

Remember: *More is going to compete for your time and attention than you ever will be able to absorb.* To keep from being overwhelmed with over-information, you must take new approaches. You could read all the best time management books and follow the best advice and still feel farther behind. Why? Because everything's changed, even if your perceptions haven't caught up.

Questions that can ease the crush

Ask yourself "What would it take for me to feel good about ending work today at 5:00?" Not every day, but today. You'll strike a bargain with yourself; you'll get the most important work done in exchange for getting out of the office on time.

Next, ask yourself "By the end of the work week, what do I want to have accomplished, so I can feel good about the weekend?"

How many times do you take a minute—just one minute—after lunch to take a deep breath and get yourself focused? Or do you just get your lunch and jump right back to your desk? You can take that minute, can't you? In the Western world, we're caught in a trap in which we *act* like everything's important; we substitute motion and activity for results. Yet, if you're the president of a company, for example, it would be helpful to sometimes stare out your office window and just think about the direction in which you want to take the company.

Practice living and working with grace and ease, because that's when your greatest decisions and breakthroughs will come. Charles Osgood once said that we've become hostage to our busy-ness. The way to reclaim time in your life is not through some personal revelation or cataclysmic change. The changes you need to implement can be subtle, even piecemeal, and they'll be just fine. The most important factor is to begin today.

Once you begin to adopt some of these measures, you'll see a cascading effect. One or two months from now, you'll begin to change in ways that are natural and comfortable for you. It won't be because of some set of rules; it will be because you acknowledge that there are too many choices and too much information, and it always will be that way.

The Over-Information Age is enough to give anyone a brain cramp—don't let it cramp your health, too. If computers and the Internet are adversely affecting your body as well as your mind, check out these sites for a world of information about computer ergonomics. So put down this book for a moment and relax. After all, you deserve a little Breathing Space!

 *Continuing Education*

Breathing Space Institute

http://www.brespace.com

The material in this chapter was derived from a variety of resources produced by Jeff Davidson, the Executive Director of the Breathing Space Institute (see Figure 2-1), and has been used with his permission and cooperation. Jeff is a popular speaker and the award-winning author of 18 books, including *Breathing Space: Living and Working at a Comfortable Pace in a Sped-up Society* (MasterMedia, $10.95) and *The Complete Idiot's Guide to Managing Your Time* (Alpha Books).

Jeff offers presentations that present critical survival tools for almost anyone who is involved in business on the Internet. His *Marketing in Complex Times* presentation helps companies integrate the five mega-realities of our era: information, media growth, population, paper, and an overabundance of choices. Jeff's *Managing the Pace With Grace* seminar teaches space-, time-, and stress-handling techniques most people have never considered, and offers progressive methods for daily effectiveness that anyone can master.

This Web site features catalogs of books, videos, and tapes, as well as information on Jeff's availability to speak to your group. You also can e-mail Jeff directly at jeff@brespace.com, or fax a message to 919-932-9982.

Netsurf: the reading list

http://www.seas.upenn.edu/~mengwong/netsurf/contents.html

Here's a reading list of publications that can help you make sense of the onslaught of over-information brought to you through cyberspace. For a nice overview of the long-term implications, check out the topic titled Social Psychology of Media Effects.

Intentional communities

http://www.well.com/user/cmty

Now that you're working on the Internet, do you still need to live in a major city and commute to work in a glass-walled high-rise tower? Intentional communities (see Figure 2-2) have for many centuries been places where idealists have come together to create a better world. There are thousands of intentional communities in existence today and many others in the formative stages. This Web site is increasing public awareness of existing and newly forming communities. It offers information and referrals for those who are actively seeking, or simply curious about, alternate lifestyles for themselves and their families.

Figure 2-1

Communities come in all shapes and sizes, and share many similar challenges—such as defining membership, succeeding financially, distributing resources, making decisions, raising children, dividing work equitably, and choosing a standard of living. Many wrestle with questions about right livelihood, spiritual expression, land use, and the role of service in our lives. At the same time, there is limited awareness of what others are doing to meet these challenges—and much to gain through sharing information and experiences with others exploring similar paths.

University of Virginia
http://www.virginia.edu/~enhealth/ERGONOMICS/toc.html

This home page (see Figure 2-3) is titled "Avoiding a Painful Desk Job!!!" You'll find links that lead to educational hypermedia and information about defining and evaluating ergonomic risks, creating ergonomically appropriate video-display terminal (VDT) workstations, and preventing work-related musculoskeletal disorders (CTDs). Be sure and click on the link titled "Stretch Breaks" for a series of graphic images that depict stretching exercises designed for computer users.

University of California, San Francisco and Berkeley
http://www.me.berkeley.edu/ergo

The home page of this site describes its vision as being "To understand the mechanisms leading to upper extremity musculoskeletal disorders, such as tendonitis and carpal tunnel syndrome, and identify and evaluate equipment designs and work practices that reduce excessive stresses on tissues in order to prevent these disorders from developing."

▶ *The basics*

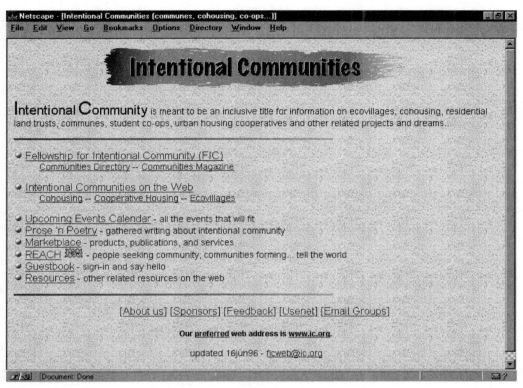

Figure 2-2

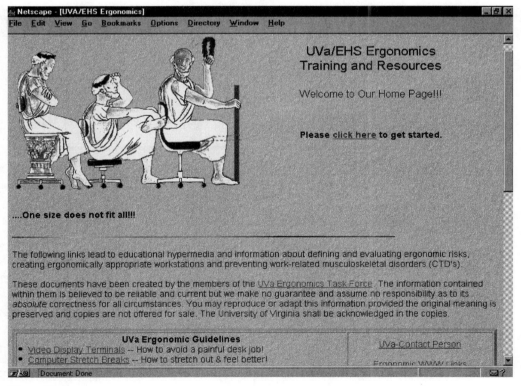

Figure 2-3

Typing injury/keyboard alternative archive

http://alumni.caltech.edu/~dank/typing-archive.html

This site specializes in Carpal Tunnel Syndrome, Repetitive Stress Injury, Cumulative Trauma Disorder, and such innovations as DragonDictate, a voice-activated computer command system that enables you to issue WordPerfect for Windows commands by speaking them. For example, to save a document, you could say "File, Save."

Typing injury FAQs

http://www.cs.princeton.edu/~dwallach/tifaq

This is the home page for the Typing Injury FAQ and Typing Injury Archive. Clicking below should lead you to all kinds of documents and resources. One feature is titled "Keyboard Alternatives" and includes more than 30 alternatives to regular keyboards—some obscure and expensive, others surprisingly affordable. Another feature profiles furniture information and proves that specially designed desks and chairs can increase comfort and boost productivity.

Computer-related repetitive strain injury (RSI)

http://engr-www.unl.edu/ee/eeshop/rsi.html

This site defines RSI, lists symptoms for which you can be on guard, doles out prevention advice, and can help you if you already are suffering from the effects of RSI (see Figure 2-4). This site includes a slew of MPEG desktop exercise videos courtesy of David Brown & the New Zealand Occupational Safety and Health Service as well as references to several good books on RSI afflictions.

Figure 2-4

Computer-related health issues

http://www-penninfo.upenn.edu:1962/tiserve.mit.edu/9000/25203.html

This site has hyperjumps to several important ergonomic sources that address these topics: *Access Technologies for Hands-Free Computing, Are Computers Hazardous to Your Health?, Eye Problems—Coming to a Screen Near You?,* and *Tendonitis, Anyone?* It also offers a searchable index so you can locate health topics in which you're interested by doing a keyword search for pertinent articles.

Client-centered Interneting

THE INTERNET was designed to be an information distribution system. Today it sparkles with stunning graphics, it sings with audio, and it's alive with animated JavaScripts. But underneath all the razzle-dazzle, everyone wants the same thing from the Internet: valuable information at their fingertips. After all, that's what the Internet was designed to do. Unfortunately, too much of the Internet is focused on the gee whiz of technology rather than on the gee whiz of the information it can deliver.

Fortunately, the Web gives you the leverage to deliver value faster and better than ever before, but only if your Web site focuses on your clients and customers, and not on making your organization feel good about itself. When your Internet site becomes a focal point and distribution system for valuable information, Internet users will find it, use it, return to it, and tell others about it.

All the buzz these days about audio, video, and action-packed JavaScripts can distract you from your organization's core strategic goals for the Internet, which are to:

- Create a Web site and systems for distributing and delivering information that your customers and clients will regard as valuable. To paraphrase a popular slogan, your Web site needs to be the gift that keeps on giving to its visitors.
- Continuously increase the promotion and delivery of perceived and acknowledged value to your key clients, customers, and targeted prospects. Remember that value always is defined by the client, never by you.

Dick Connor, CMC

I have partnered with Dick Connor, Certified Management Consultant (cmc), to jointly develop strategies for making a Web site more user-centered. Dick has specialized for 30 years in assisting his clients in developing and delivering value to their clients through a system that he founded that's known as Client-centered Marketing. To meet the marketing demands of clients who wish to market on the Internet, we have created a cyberspace version of Client-centered Marketing that we call Client-centered Interneting.

The principles behind Client-centered Interneting (CCI) are derived from Dick's lifelong work that laid the foundation for CCI before the Internet was born. Dick, one of only 2500 Certified Management Consultants in the world, also is the author of three marketing books published by John Wiley and Sons: *Marketing Your Consulting and Professional Services, Getting New Clients,* and *Increasing Revenue.* These books have helped thousands of professionals use Client-centered Marketing (CCM) techniques to serve their clients and customers. You can learn more about CCI, CCM, and these books through the Your Marketing Coach Web site at *http://www.marketing-coach.com.*

In this chapter, Dick and I give you some key principles and action ideas that will help you apply Client-centered Interneting principles to your organization's Web site.

Client-centered Interneting

The marketing task has changed from pushing your firm and services to pulling your clients into value-adding opportunities that you provide. This change is profound. It's analogous to going from checkers to chess; the play and strategy are different and more complex. In fact, it's even more of a change than that, because you don't even use the same old board in this new game.

As you learn to use the Internet in the Hands-On phase of this book, you will find a few examples that illustrate Client-centered Interneting principles. Unfortunately, you'll see far more examples that illustrate the severe lack of such user-oriented principles. Too much of the Web is self-serving hype about the Web itself. There are a lot of people who want to prove to everyone that they know how to use Java.

Java is a fabulous technology and it eventually is going to increase the speed and the value of the Internet. But the gee whiz has worn off the early Java demonstration sites, and now it's time to move the focus from Web technology to delivering value. Remember, that's your core strategic goal.

HYPERJUMP

Value
Value is the worth your service adds to the existing information and knowledge base of your clients and customers, as well as to their organizations and their markets. Satisfying today's clients and customers means adding more value than ever, more knowledge than ever, more experience than ever, and more solutions than ever.

Value is a function of a need being met in ways that meet or exceed the client's expectations. In other words, your clients must feel that they earn a suitable return on their investment in visiting your Web site. You get about 5 to 10 seconds to convince visitors that you offer value in return for their time.

Ban the hype

At times it seems that the Web is a last-chance outlet for press releases that otherwise never would be seen by a single public eye. Press releases are news, and they rarely create value for your clients and customers.

Sure, your press release might announce a major new product or service that is going to bring tremendous value to all of your clients. But is posting a press release at the top of your Web site the best way to inform your best clients? No. They will expect that you'll notify them directly and that the notification will be tailored to help them understand the value they'll be getting. New products and services are no better than the value they deliver, so announce them with that core strategic principle in mind.

Business consultant Marcus Bogue says ". . . it doesn't matter how good you are; it only matters how relatively good you are." If someone else is better than you are, it doesn't matter how good *you* are. Web site visitors don't care about how good a press release says you are—they'll judge your site based on how it delivers perceived value. You might put one short pull-quote from your press release on the home page and include a link to the full text. But always remember that people will sell themselves based on how much your Web site improves their lives or their business.

The attributes of value

Even if you haven't started surfing the Net, you probably have heard about its amazing abilities to deliver previously obscure or hard-to-locate information. The prime goal for your Web site is to help your clients and customers find information that consistently will add value to their organizations. Consistently adding value to your clients requires answering two key questions: At this time, what defines value for my clients and customers? How can I deliver this client-defined value to them more conveniently, consistently, and compellingly than any other source?

Your next step is to consider some client-sided value attributes:

- **Client-defined** Value always is defined by the recipient, never by the provider. Value is in the eyes and emotions of recipients and always is founded on their personal and organizational needs.
- **Benefits** Distribute information that enhances performance, improves profits or improves the client's working environment. Value-added solutions are the tangible and intangible benefits that your service delivers.
- **Hope** Clients don't purchase your services and products; they buy the hope that you will help them create a more favorable future, as they define it.
- **Justification** Value is perceived in the heart. You might believe we all work in a cold, impersonal business world, but even in cyberspace people make most decisions by intuition. They then justify a buy/no-buy decision to themselves and to others by the use of such things as competitive proposals and testimonials that support their decision.
- **Other resources** Track and recommend resources that can help your clients when they have needs that you cannot meet. Remember, when someone in search of a solution visits your Web site, you need to make sure that your site provided what they wanted. Even if you do not directly profit from the solution, they'll remember you as a value-added provider.

Quantity and quality are not value-adders

Clients are not satisfied by your quantity or quality—how much you put on your Web site or how good it looks—but by the value they perceive during the delivery and after using the information you provide. Your Web site is a source of potential value that must be translated and made visible for your clients on their terms.

At best, quality is only an entry fee to play the game. An ingenious, humorous, or attractive Web site might draw a slew of first-time curiosity seekers, but no one will return often if they discover no perceived value for them at your site.

Build a gift that keeps on giving

How about a quick example of a value-added Web service? Subscribe to a stock market reporting service such as Quote.Com at *http://www.quote.com* (see Figure 3-1). With Quote.Com, you can track an unlimited number of stocks, commodities, mutual funds, and news pages. You do not need to own stocks to track them. Instead, you can use Quote.com's reporting features to create a value-added service for clients and customers by tracking stocks and market news reports that affect their industry and their competitors.

- **Portfolio quotes** Retrieve quotes for any programmed basket of stocks with one command, using e-mail or the Web. Use this to stay abreast of your clients and customers and their competitors, as well as your own competitors. Quote.Com will deliver this stock report to you at the end of each business day, along with a list of any articles related that contain news affecting the stocks you track.
- **Alarms** You can set upper and lower trigger points for each item in your portfolio. Quote.Com will monitor your trigger points during the trading day and send you an e-mail notice if the alarms are triggered. Wouldn't your clients and customers like to know that your Web site will help them understand the meaning behind a dramatic swing in a prime competitor's stock?
- **News alerts** Subscribe to MarketScope, BusinessWire, PR Newswire, or S&P News and they automatically will send you financial news items that impact the industries you track for your clients and customers.

Once you receive any of these reports, you immediately can write a value-added analysis and put up the analysis on your Web site. You could e-mail key clients to alert them to the updated news on your Web site.

Regularly update your Web site

Valuable information often is extremely time-sensitive. The value visitors find today might be worthless next week. Of course that's not always true, but let's consider both cases.

If the information you provide on the Internet is static, then you can put it up and nearly forget about it. For example, the documents you need to file a request for information with the federal government under the Freedom Of Information Act (FOIA) are available on-line. Because these forms remain unchanged for years, that aspect of the federal government's Internet site requires little oversight.

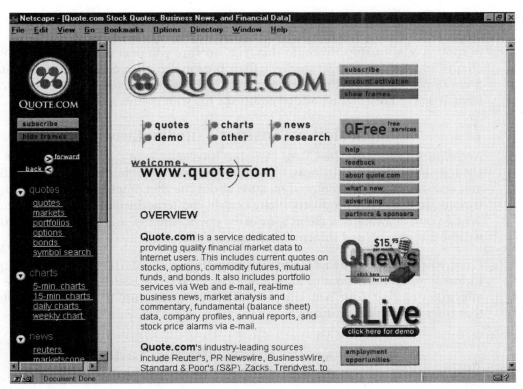

Figure 3-1

You rarely will have that luxury. Government reporting forms are static; your industry likely is not. Much of the information that makes your organization valuable to its clients and customers has a short shelf-life. Make sure every client and customer knows that you are a source for fresh information that's been repackaged in a way that brings them value.

Users who find exciting information on their first visit to your site likely will return in a week or two. If they find the same information on the second visit, most still will visit again. But three visits to the same old page probably is your limit, and you might lose a prospect forever. Perhaps some users may give you another look in a few months, but maybe not.

Relationship development

Client-centered Interneting essentially is relationship development. The relationship is based on both technical and personal factors that create interdependence—you need your clients and customers, and they need your Web site.

Professionals who are effective marketers have learned to develop special relationships—called strategic alliances—both with organizations and individuals with whom they jointly serve the needs of clients and customers. On the Web, this means cross-linking with related sites. Once the special, cross-linked relationships are established, the primary task is jointly to sense, sell, serve, and satisfy the needs and expectations of mutual clients and customers in ways that are mutually profitable.

The cultivation of a satisfied Internet client requires much more than an eye-stopping Web site. Satisfying clients and customers requires building a value-perceived relationship. To build this relationship, you need to understand your clients' industry and target markets, their business goals, needs, restraints, and areas of potential growth in their markets. Then you need to use this specialized knowledge to create value-added solutions for your clients and customers.

Develop an insider's understanding

An important tool for the Client-centered Interneter is to possess an Insider's Understanding of the business, environments and expectations of your clients and customers. Client-centered insights about the dynamics of surviving and thriving in the client's industry niche enable you to add value to their operations. When you are aware of a client's industry, environments, and technology, you will be a highly valued information source.

Once you have an Insider's Understanding of your clients' industry, you can raise industry issues that demand their attention, even if the issue will not directly affect them today. Your Web site can raise these issues and include links to sites that offer or discuss solutions.

Build an Insider's Understanding

To develop an Insider's Understanding of your clients' and customers' industries, you need to track industry developments, both within your own industry and within their industry. You also need to track their competitors as well as your own.

An information service such as Farcast can give you and your clients and customers the competitive advantage you need. Farcast is an agent-based, personal news and information service (see Figure 3-2), available at *www.farcast.com*. Farcast lets you browse and search its collection of news, press releases, and reference material.

Farcast is available interactively 24 hours a day, or you can contract with Farcast to automatically send you news articles from a wide range of topics. You also can create your own information robots (Droids) that search more than 5000 articles daily to retrieve news that will help you build an Insider's Understanding within targeted industry niches.

Be sure you subscribe to newsgroups and mailing lists that affect the industries of your clients and customers. A good place to start on this quest is with the DejaNews search engine at *www.dejanews.com*. Be sure you constantly check out your customers' Web sites as well as the Web sites of their competitors. Your clients and customers need to know that you know their industry as well as they do.

Save visitors from the over-information crunch

New Internet users universally report they are stunned by the amount of raw, unfiltered information that the Internet makes available. The impact on people of such an avalanche of over-information is serious enough that we devoted a chapter on handling its effects. Be sure you didn't skip chapter 2, "Breathing space for cyberspace."

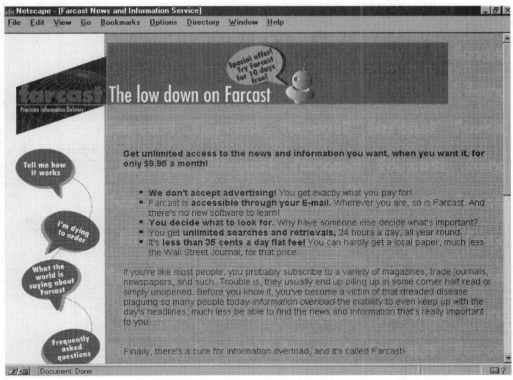

Figure 3-2

The effects that the Over-Information Age has on people actually can work in favor of your business. You can provide a valuable service to your Web site visitors merely by sorting and repackaging information, and then providing links to the information they most need to see.

You now have an opportunity to rescue your clients and customers from under the electronic avalanche by giving them a safe haven where they quickly can tap into that minuscule portion of information that they find valuable. The key to your success lies in a feature of today Web browsers: the Bookmark List (see Netscape's Bookmark feature in Figure 3-3).

How to know when you've become a Client-centered Interneter

As a marketer you need to understand the significance of the Netscape Bookmark feature. When Internet users encounter an exciting or valuable site, they can (with a couple of mouse clicks) add that site to their Bookmark List. Think of this as similar to television remote controls that have a favorite channel feature. Bookmarks enable users to return with a couple of mouse clicks—no matter how deeply they've strayed into unfriendly cyberspace—to a comfortable, favorite site.

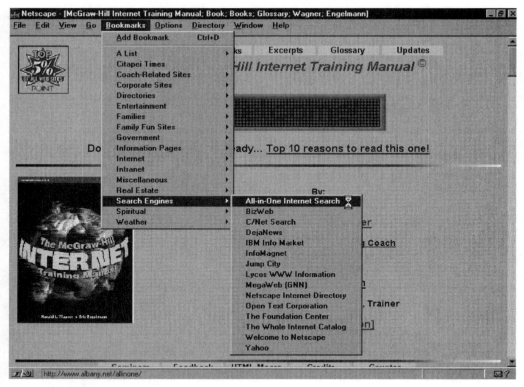

Figure 3-3

Make your site easy to find

Until they put your site on their bookmark list, clients and customers may have difficulty locating your site. Don't make them work hard to find your organization. Here's a couple of tips that can help:

Structure your Web site for search engines

You can schedule your own URLs for exploration by Lycos—this alerts the Lycos web explorer to your home page so it can add your Web text to its search index.

Lycos scores words by how far into the document they appear. Thus keyword hits in the title or first paragraph are scored higher. For each document it indexes Lycos keeps the title, headings, subheadings, links, the 100 highest-weighted words, and the first 20 lines. Make sure your title and opening paragraph contain the keywords upon which you expect people to search when trying to find your site.

Most Web sites waste the title on something generic, such as "Welcome!" No one is going to locate your service because they searched Lycos or Yahoo! for sites with *welcome* in the title. Fill the title with keywords that are likely to be used by potential visitors when they're using a search engine. This is your one shot—don't waste it by making your title read "Our Home Page." Be sure and read the Continuing Education at the end of this chapter for some Web sites that can help you register your URLs with the major Web searching engines.

Register your own domain name

Using your own domain name is an important factor in helping your clients and customers find and remember your Web site. For example, Dick Connor and I established a Web site for our Client-centered Interneting, which is based on a software application called Your Marketing Coach. An Internet service provider (Digiweb at *www.digiweb.com*) registered the domain name of *marketing-coach.com* for us. The Yahoo! Web search engine lets users search for strings in URLs, so that URL makes marketing a sure hit for our site.

When your clients and customers see your site and click **Bookmark, Add Bookmark**, then you'll know that you've embodied Client-centered Interneting. If your Web site gets assigned to lots of bookmark lists, then your organization is cruising in an express lane on the information superhighway.

Of course once you're in that fast lane, you can't slow down. People can change lanes pretty quickly. It only takes a couple of mouse clicks to remove a bookmark. If you've let your information go stale, then when a client finds another hot site and notices that his or her bookmark list is getting full, you can get bumped.

Tips for staying on the bookmark list

Update your Web information at least weekly, but don't expect your clients and customers to return out of curiosity. Your Web page needs to tell visitors that you update the page regularly and when they can expect new material. Television channels and movie theaters announce what's coming next and when it will be available. Part of maintaining a Client-centered Web site is providing previews—your current information may not interest them, but your site might make someone's bookmark list because they want to return for one of your Coming Attractions.

Don't try to impress Web visitors with a lot of breathless hype about your products and services. Most consumers today are well-informed, and have long ago learned to ignore the hard sell. In other words, what visitors find on your site must appear to benefit them first.

If visitors perceive your site as valuable, your clients and customers will do some of your sales work for you. People want to be well-informed, and your organization's on-line presence can let them learn exactly what they want to know—and to learn it on their terms.

I'll repeat the Winston Churchill quotation I used at the beginning of Phase 1: "I love learning, but I hate being taught." Your clients and customers will love learning from a site with depth, but they don't want to be taught by hyped-up press releases.

Less fun is more

It's a good idea to make your site fun to visit as well as valuable. But be careful. Another challenge for you is to make your site something that an employee could use during business hours without fearing that the boss will walk in and catch them on your site. Be wary of providing "cool stuff" links as an enticement to attract visitors. You might poll some of your clients and customers about this concept. If your site passes the boss test, then it most likely is client-centered.

Top 10 ways to build a successful Web site

I'll close this chapter with a Top 10 list of some of the best things Dick and I have found for leveraging your Web site. Remember, the design focus must be Client-centered—never technology-centered. Create value through depth, avoid hype, and let visitors discover for themselves the value your site provides.

10. Keep visitors from getting lost

Make sure that every page on your site includes multiple links that take them back to your home page, to the previous page, or to another value-packed page. If visitors get lost or side-tracked while exploring your site, you don't want them to move on to another site out of frustration. Make sure they quickly can return to something familiar and comfortable, or move forward to something that appears as though it's going to bring them value.

9. Go easy on the graphics

Thousands of Web sites truly are works of art by master graphic artists. But during peak business hours, bandwidth limitations might actually make it impossible for some people to access your site. Millions of people work in home-based offices and are limited to analog telephone modems. Because they're working from a home office, they might rely upon your site to keep them in touch with their industry. At a minimum, use interlaced graphics and offer a text-only hyperlink at the top of the document so visitors quickly can select a faster option if they are not willing to wait for your art to download.

8. Include multiple contact links

What a waste of your time and resources if a visitor decides to contact you and can't locate the necessary information. I've seen some highly professional-looking sites that contain no personal contact links. People want direct, personal contact, and cyberspace hasn't changed that. In fact, a personal touch on your site might heighten people's interest. Even giant Microsoft has been bombarded with requests to add personal replies to its technical support Web site, and they currently are testing a system that can fulfill those requests. Your site should contain frequent and obvious links that point visitors to personal contact information within your organization—e-mail, fax, snail mail addresses, and phone numbers, if appropriate.

7. Test it personally

Test your site regularly to see how it looks and feels to clients. Check it out using different settings (toolbars and directory buttons on and off); different hours (peak and off-peak); different modems (try slow and fast); different browsers (Netscape for Windows, Microsoft Explorer, and Macintosh, for example); and different screen resolutions. I've got a 128kbps ISDN connection and a blazing-fast Pentium PC with a top-of-the-line graphics accelerator card. I can test a site with this setup and be very happy with its performance. Then I see the site on an older, slower PC with a 14.4kbps modem, and realize that many visitors are going to have a completely different experience.

6. Build it with professional designers

You don't have to hire a consultant if your organization has design and advertising professionals on staff. If not, however, investing in a professional designer and ad copywriters might be some of the best money you ever invest in your business. Don't clutter up the open screen with a wall of text about your organization's philosophy. Have you ever read that stuff? You know it's going to sound wonderful or they wouldn't have put it there. But what you want is links, links, and more links that will fill your screen with information you value. The same goes for visitors who see your site.

5. Submit it to indexers and directories

Contact every Web indexer. Make sure they've got your URL and make sure you've placed keywords high in your document. And don't waste that valuable title text on "Welcome to our Home Page!"

4. Link, link, link

Cut deals with everyone you can whose site relates to your business. Get your link on as many other pages as possible. Of course you will reciprocate. Multiple links make your site more valuable, because your clients will know that you are a source for fresh, valuable, related sites from all over the Web.

3. Preview regularly scheduled updates

The movie theaters do it. The cable movie channels do it. Television stations do it. Even magazines do it. You simply must include on your site a preview listing of upcoming topics. You never know when a visitor might find nothing at your site today, but notices something important in the preview that will bring him back next week.

How do I update my site if my visitors don't need news tips?

So you don't need the information services we've profiled earlier? Your clients and customers need in-depth research instead? Then try the most comprehensive information on the Internet: NLightN at *www.nlightn.com* (see Figure 3-4).

If you think Lycos is comprehensive, prepare to be dazzled—or overwhelmed. NLightN is so vast that Lycos provides only about five percent of the information resources that NLightN has indexed. The NlightN index lets you search a universal index that's 20 times as large as Lycos! It includes 10 million books; 1 million dissertations; 1 million patents; hundreds of thousands of wire service records from more than 20 wire services; tens of millions of journal articles; book, movie and audiovisual reviews; and informal and formal searches of the full-text of encyclopedias, dictionaries, and standard reference works.

This is a fee-based service and you'll have to sign up for a membership, but prices start at only 10 cents. Take a trial run at this site and then brainstorm ways you can use it to put value-added services on your Web site—you're sure to find something here that your clients and customers will appreciate finding on your Web site.

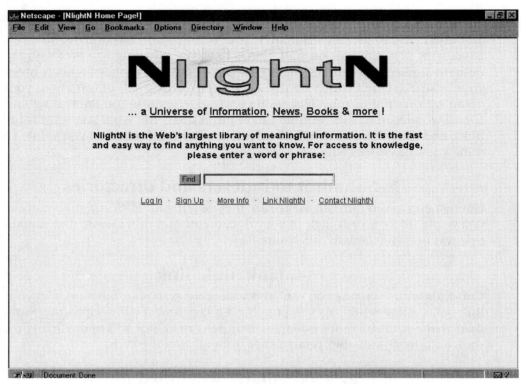

Figure 3-4

2. Start *now* and grow

You probably already have seen some Web sites that are under construction. Don't be shy about applying this caveat to your own site (see Figure 3-5). If you've got valuable information, get it out there right away. Any moderately advanced user of WordPerfect for Windows or Microsoft Word quickly can create some basic web pages. Get the site up and running and let the search engines start indexing your keywords. Actually, your site needs to constantly offer new features and information anyway (see Item #3), so why wait until you think it's done?

1. Make it Client-centered

And the number one factor in a successful, business-oriented Web site is to focus on the needs of others. Provide value that rewards your visitors and they will reward you. I've been amazed at the number of people who've consulted me about Web sites that had the home page filled with photos of the organization's top officers. No one *wants* to wait for personal photos to download on a site's home page, unless it's a Helen Hunt fan club. Make sure that your most valuable information has the most direct access with the fewest graphics.

A closing example

Here's an example of how *not* to do a Web site. I consulted on a Web site for a government agency that provided natural resource statistics to users in the field. They expected that most visitors would access their site using notebook

The basics

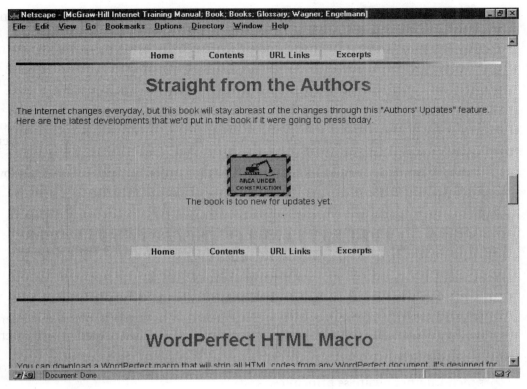

Figure 3-5

computers with 14.4kbps modems and poor phone service in remote areas; yet the two top directors of this agency had decreed that the home page must feature their photos. So, each day, the users in the field had to begin their quest for the daily resource statistics by first spending about two minutes to watch two photos meander down onto their screens, as well as a huge graphic of the agency's logo.

Remember, your clients and customers are being crushed under the onslaught of the Over-Information Age—make your site a safe haven for them. Give them easy access to what they want.

From there, users had to scroll past several paragraphs of text about the agency's philosophy and mission. (I'm certain that it said something about putting its clients first.) Beyond these paragraphs lay three links to regional pages. Guess what? Clicking those links launched a three-minute download of an organizational chart that contained about a dozen photos of the regional office's top officers. Then came a personal message from the regional director—yes, it was all about service. Scrolling past all of that hype finally unveiled the magic buttons—links to download the daily statistics.

Thus a user, going through the normal chain on this agency's Web site, would consume about five or six minutes each day just getting to the links he or she needed. How many times did he or she need to see those photos? Of course a savvy user would capture the actual URL of the statistics page and put it on a bookmark. But your visitors shouldn't have to resort to work-arounds—and if you've got competitors, they might just skip your site altogether.

I recommended a redesign of the Web page with a thumbnail logo and a menu of links at the top of the first screen—including links to download photos of all the directors if anyone wanted to take the time. This would have enabled users to start downloading their information within seconds each day. I say "would have" because the site's webmaster said that the directors would never approve a home page that didn't have their photos at the top and the links buried under. Sad.

So, unless your organization has no competition, then keep in mind the lesson in this chapter. But, hey, even if you don't have competition, you can use Client-centered Interneting principles just because people will appreciate it. Then, someday, someone might look up those photos to see the nice folks who provide such a value-driven Web site.

 Continuing Education

Internet Business Guide
http://www.intuitive.com/taylor

Here's a site that includes a sample chapter from a business book on the Internet by Dave Taylor, the founder of the Internet Mall. Dave has posted this chapter in the hope that you'll buy the book. Here's a chance to sample a book at your leisure before you buy. The full, printed version of the book has a wealth of top-notch Internet business principles.

Small and home-based businesses
http://www.ro.com/small_business/homebased.html

The fastest growing segment of our economy is the home-based business (see Figure 3-6). Downsizing and outsourcing is creating a revolution in home-based businesses. Here's a Web site that can help you serve the needs of this booming market niche or help you create new marketing ideas to sell the services of your clients and customers to home-based businesses. Here's what this site says about itself, small and home-based business info: small and home-based franchises, business opportunities, small business reference material, information to help run and market your small or home-based business, small and home-based newsgroups, searching tools, services for small business, just about anything related to small and home-based business can be found in these links. Enjoy!

Internet marketing discussion list archives
http://www.popco.com

This site is a source both for information you can use as well as for information you can repackage after putting your industry-specific spin on it for clients and customers. It discusses appropriate marketing of services, ideas, and items to and on the Internet. Currently more than 4500 people and sites—involved in all aspects of marketing, sales, programming, journalism, and other fields—were active in this forum. This site is a good source both for organizations that want to create Web sites, market products and goods electronically, develop payment systems, or write about industry developments.

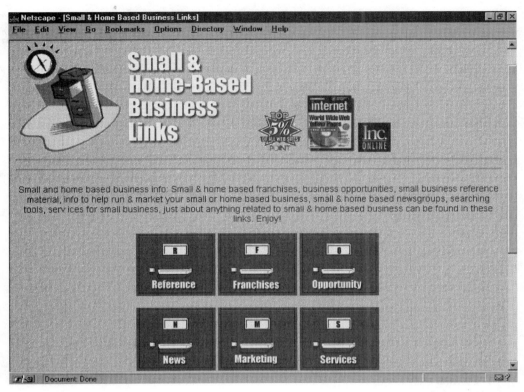

Figure 3-6

Digiweb
http://www.digiweb.com

Here's the fastest-responding Web services provider I've found (see Figure 3-7). Digiweb registers your unique domain name, sets up a Web site (up to 25 megabytes, plus 10 megabytes of e-mail), forwards mail to your new domain to an existing e-mail address, and provides FTP service for unlimited updates. As of the spring of 1996, Digiweb charged only $25 for setup and $20 per month for all of this, and the site was up in hours—other providers I've tried haven't come close. At those rates, even a sole proprietorship can afford a personalized domain name and a Web site.

Direct FTP uploading of your own Web pages is a must—never contract with a Web service that promises to transfer your updates soon after you send them in. Any delays by your provider will prevent you from offering some of the Client-centered Interneting features I profiled in this chapter.

World Wide Web yellow pages free listing
http://www.yellow.com/cgi-bin/online

Check out this URL right away! For a limited time, they're giving away yellow page listings. Fill in the on-screen form and provide the URL to your own home page. World Wide Yellow Pages is a trademark of Home Pages, Inc.

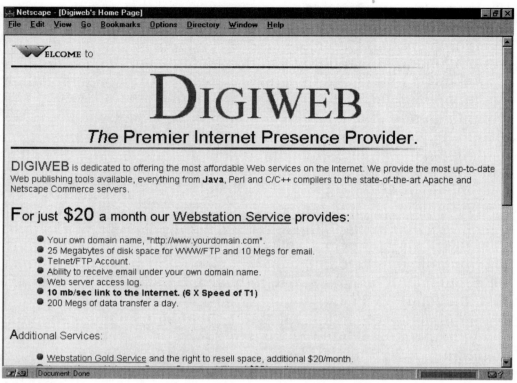

Figure 3-7

Internet size

http://www.netrex.com/business/basics.html

The Internet connects some 35 million users (the figure is debatable) and is the fastest-growing communication resource on the planet. Based on these figures, the number of Internet hosts will hit 100 million by 1999. The links on this page may help you determine for yourself the potential size of your markets and your demographics in cyberspace.

Windows wide open—advanced basics

IN CYBERSPACE you will encounter a bewildering assortment of windows all over your screen. To work efficiently, you're going to need to know how to quickly and easily transfer information between any two windows. This hands-on lesson will provide a foundation for everything you do on the Internet.

Without knowing the principles in this lesson, you might constantly be scribbling notes on the side and doing a lot of retyping. Many people do that. With the expertise this lesson can give you, however, you might never need to retype anything that you can see on your screen.

Windows wide-open

Most race cars have their windows wide open all the time to help drivers be intimately engaged with their cars. Open windows help them hear and even feel every sound. They can hear the tires biting into the track in the corners. A lot of information comes through those open windows. A lot of information can come through *your* Windows if you really open them up, and enjoy full contact with and control over your computer. I'll help you think of Windows controls and techniques generically. When you regard them as general principles that apply to all the Windows software you use, you'll be ready for anything.

Simplifying your computer work

Windows brings the same philosophy to the controls in software that you've experienced in using the controls in cars. You probably have rented cars and have noticed that while the controls vary a bit from one car to the next, the basic functions remain common. When you rent a car, you look for the common controls. The heater controls in a rental car are not exactly the same as the ones in your car, but you know that you'll find controls that adjust the temperature, select heat, defrost, or vent, and select a fan speed.

Windows has a term for this design philosophy. It's called Common User Access (CUA). CUA is the principle under which all Windows programs provide common user access by using common user controls. Apply to your Windows software the principle of operating its common controls and you will be an expert Windows user. When using Windows software, focus on the commonality, not on the differences.

Advanced basics

Over the rest of this chapter, I'm going to cover what I call advanced basics. I'll cover features that I have found to be basic, but that usually are overlooked. The tips presented here have been proven to be important productivity-enhancing tools. Some people have used Windows for years without knowing these advanced basics. They have paid—usually many times over—for the time it would have taken to learn the features when they first learned Windows.

Window types

You and your computer communicate constantly. You communicate what you want, and the computer tells you what it's doing. When you use Windows, all communications with your computer pass through a window. There are three basic types: Application Windows, Document Windows, and Dialog Boxes. For this lesson, start Windows on your computer. We'll begin with the Program Manager.

Application window

Every application runs inside its own window. Netscape is an example of an application. The easiest way to identify an application window is by the icon in the upper left corner. Application windows use the same icon as the icon that you used to start the application (see the arrow in Figure 4-1).

Most application windows can cover your entire screen. There are exceptions; but remember, we are focusing on common principles.

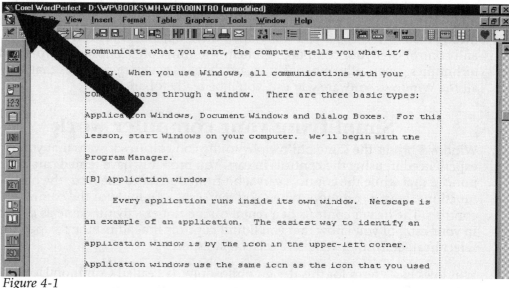

Figure 4-1

The basics

Shortly, we'll show you how to access all of your open applications windows and give you a variety of ways to switch between them, enabling you to easily run multiple applications. Running multiple applications is called multitasking. Windows 95 has some powerful new multitasking features, yet retains some of the best ones from Windows 3.1.

All application windows can be closed by pressing **ALT+F4** or by double-clicking on the application icon in the upper-left corner.

Document window

Many applications have windows within them that are called document windows, though they are not always for documents. Spreadsheet applications, for example, use document windows for individual spreadsheets. Internet e-mail applications such as Eudora use document windows for their In box, Out box, Trash, etc.

The icon in the upper-left corner of a document window is different from the main application window icon. Document windows cannot cover the entire screen because they are limited to filling the maximum amount of screen space being used by their parent application window. You cannot place a document window on your Windows 95 desktop because you cannot drag a document window out of the borders of its parent application window.

Document windows can be closed by pressing **CTRL+F4** or by double-clicking on their icon (see the arrow in Figure 4-2).

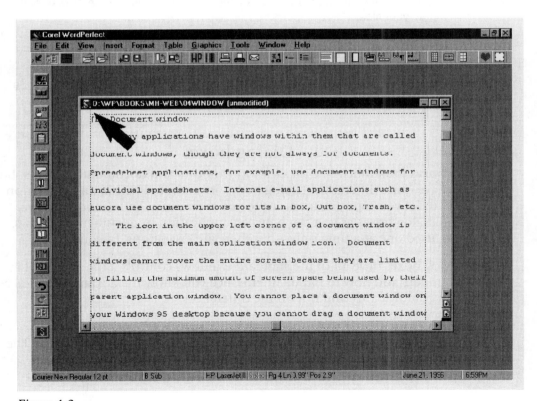

Figure 4-2

If an application uses document windows, it lists them on the menu bar under the Window menu item. You can use this list to switch to any document window within the current application window. Using this list makes it impossible to ever again lose a window, because even if you cannot see the window, its title will be listed under the Window menu item.

HYPERJUMP

Start Button

Just in case you've missed all the Microsoft commercials, I'll define a term that will be used throughout this chapter: the Start Button. It might be visible now on your screen in the lower-left corner. If so, then click on it when you see the command: Activate the Start Button. If not, then moving your mouse pointer to the bottom of the screen will display the Start Button by activating a new feature called the Taskbar—the Start Button is on it.

Hands On

Objective: Activate a window.

❑ Activate the **Start Button**.

❑ Click **Run**.

❑ Type *c:\windows\progman.exe* and press **ENTER**.

    This will be a reunion with an old friend: the Program Manager. If your Program Manager is in another directory or on another drive, you can use the browse button to navigate your files.

❑ Click **Window** on your Program Manager.

❑ Click any window on the list that you cannot see open.

    The menu windows only can display nine document windows at once. If your application has more than nine document windows, the last item on this list will be More Windows . . .

Dialog boxes

Dialog boxes look much like application windows and document windows, but they behave quite differently. Dialog boxes are activated within an application window to let you input instructions to your computer. You cannot switch between dialog boxes as you can between application or document windows. They are used one at a time only—but there are exceptions, of course.

Few dialog boxes have all of the standard windows controls. Still, usually it is easy to understand how to handle them once you know the advanced basics, and focus on commonality and not on the differences.

I'll give you four simple techniques that are easy to learn and can increase productivity, yet are overlooked by legions of experienced Windows users. The first lesson is for dialog boxes that have text entry boxes (see Figure 4-3).

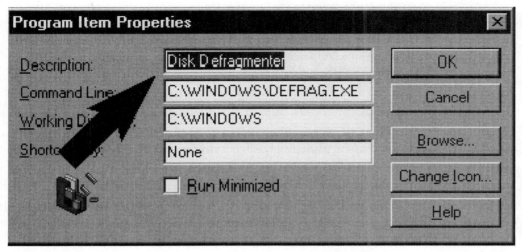

Figure 4-3

Hands On

Objective: Improve speed when typing within text entry boxes.

❏ Click on any application icon on the Program Manager.

Remember the title shown under this icon.

❏ Press **ALT+ENTER**.

The highlighted text on the top line means that your cursor is on that line. Also, you're in a special, momentary state that will behave differently depending on your next keystroke. Don't waste your time using the mouse to position your cursor when you see this state; the cursor is already in the text entry box.

❏ Press **END**.

The highlight will disappear and you can edit the existing text. (Actually, any cursor movement key will set the text in this box.)

❏ Press **ENTER**.

❏ Press **ALT+ENTER**.

Again, don't waste time using the mouse, because the first non-cursor-moving keystroke clears the text box.

❏ Type the original title.

❏ Press **ENTER**.

The next two lessons will enable you to make dialog box selections more quickly using the keyboard instead of the mouse.

Hands On

Objective: Improve speed when using any dialog box.

❏ Press **ALT+ENTER**.

❏ Press **ALT+I**.

The letter I on the Change Icon button is underlined. When you see an underlined letter on a button label, you can press **ALT** plus the letter instead of interrupting your workflow by picking up the mouse.

Windows wide open—advanced basics ◀

❑ Press **ENTER** twice to return to the Program Manager.

    If the dialog box does not have any text boxes, you don't need to hold down **ALT** to activate a button. Let's demonstrate that principle.

❑ Open the Accessories group and double-click on Notepad.

❑ Press **F5** to enter the date and time.

❑ Press **ALT+F4** to close Notepad.

    You will be asked if you want to save the changes. Again, spare yourself picking up the mouse.

❑ Press **N** to say No.

    You will exit Notepad immediately without saving.

❑ Minimize the Accessories group.

Using these keystroke techniques can save you a lot of time over the years. They also will reduce physical stress by eliminating unnecessary mouse use. I've got more exercises that demonstrate simple, time-saving keystroke techniques.

Hands On

Objective: Quickly jump to a specific, known listing.

❑ Open the Main group by pressing **ALT+W**, then press the number on the line that says Main.

❑ Use your arrow keys to highlight Control Panel.

❑ Press **ENTER**.

❑ Use the arrow keys to highlight Regional Settings (see Figure 4-4).

❑ Press **ENTER**.

    Most likely English (United States) is highlighted.

❑ Press **S**.

    Notice that the list jumps to Spanish.

❑ Press **S** repeatedly and check the list each time.

    You will scroll through all the language options that begin with s. Eventually, pressing the letter will cycle you back to the first option that begins with that letter. Most users make changes on lists such as this one by using the mouse to click on the drop arrow at the end of the list and then using the scroll arrows to meander to the desired entry, then they click on it, then they move their mouse pointer over and click on OK. Whew!

❑ Press **ESCAPE** to dismiss the dialog box.

    Pressing **ESCAPE** works for most dialog boxes and is much faster than clicking on **Cancel**.

❑ Press **ENTER** to bring back Regional Settings.

❑ Press **UP ARROW**.

    The list will scroll through the options.

❑ Press **DOWN ARROW** repeatedly until you return to English (United States).

❑ Press **ENTER** to close the dialog box.

    This works for most dialog boxes and is much faster than clicking on **OK**.

❑ Press **ALT+F4** to close the Control Panel.

    You now will be back to the Program Manager—and you did all of that without the mouse.

Using keystrokes is not always faster than using the mouse. When you already have the mouse in hand, you can save time by continuing to use it. Still, you can increase speed overall by using keystrokes and your mouse together, depending on which is faster for the task at hand. Later you'll see more keystroke examples, including some that will give you access to some crucial Windows commands even when they're not available on a visible menu.

▶ *The basics*

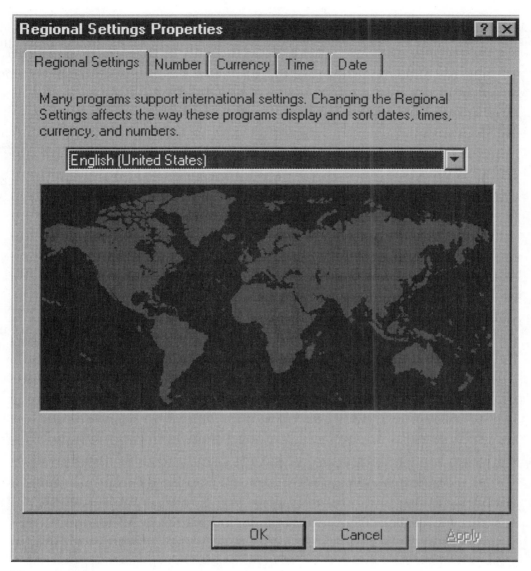

Figure 4-4

Window controls

When you learned basic Windows techniques, you learned how to use the icons in the upper right corner of a window to maximize the window and to restore it to its previous size. When you get deeply into Internet software, you might have windows all over your screen and you will not always be able to see the maximize and restore buttons on all of them. Instead of dragging a window around to bring these icons into view, you can double-click anywhere on the window's title bar to maximize it. Or, if a window already is maximized, double-clicking on its title bar will restore it.

Hands On

Objective: **Learn a shortcut to maximizing a window.**

❏ Double-click Main again to open it.

❏ Double-click anywhere along its title bar to maximize it.

Windows wide open—advanced basics

◀

While we're here, let's go over a few important points.

Notice that the Main window covers all of the other windows in this application. This state often happens accidentally when users inadvertently double-click on a title bar. At this point, they fear that their other windows are lost, but that won't happen to you once you've completed this next lesson.

Hands On

Objective: Learn how to switch document windows.
❑ Click on **Window**. (Click on any window other than Main.)
❑ Click on **Window**.
❑ Click on **Main**.

> None of the other document windows were gone; they just were hidden by one maximized document window. Even in this state, you still have full access to every window. Of course, these windows don't contain documents, but the document windows in your word processor will behave exactly the same, so you can use this technique to manage multiple documents or spreadsheets.

While we're in this state, let's make one more important observation. Notice the title bar no longer says Program Manager. It now says Program Manager - [Main]. That's because a document window can never fill the screen. A maximized document window cannot extend outside of its parent application window, so it must share the title bar with its parent.

Look for this state when you're experimenting with new applications, or when it seems that you've lost something. If you see two titles on the title bar, here's the interpretation:
● The first title is the application window title.
● The second title (in square brackets) is a maximized document window.

If any document windows seem to be missing, they simply are being covered by this one maximized document window and you can switch to them via the Window menu. Now let's see a couple of quick ways to make all of your document windows visible again.

Hands On

Objective: Learn to use Cascade and Tile to find lost windows.
❑ Click **Window**, **Tile** to Tile the document windows.
❑ Click **Window**, **Cascade** to Cascade the document windows.
❑ Press **ALT+W**, then press **T** to Tile the document windows.
❑ Press **ALT+W**, then press **C** to Cascade the document windows.
❑ Press **SHIFT+F4** to Tile the document windows.
❑ Press **SHIFT+F5** to Cascade the document windows.

Every open document window now has been neatly cascaded down from the top of the application window, and all minimized document windows have been arranged at the bottom of the application window. These principles often are essential to successfully using Internet applications, especially a mail program that might use dozens of document windows for its mail boxes.

▶ *The basics*

Whenever anything seems to be missing, click **Window**, **Cascade** (or press **SHIFT+F5**) and you'll get your bearings again.

Miscellaneous keystrokes

Next I'll present some keystroke tidbits that can help speed your work in Windows 95. One even might bail you out sometime when it appears that you need to reboot your computer.

The **ENTER** key

On most dialog boxes, pressing **ENTER** is the same as clicking on the highlighted button. I can't tell you how many times I've watched users pop up a dialog box that needs a single line of text entry, then pick up the mouse to click in the box (when the cursor is already in place), then put down the mouse, then type the text, then stop, pick up the mouse, move the pointer over to a button that already is highlighted, and then click. Spare yourself the agony; usually you merely need to type the line and hit **ENTER**!

Of course, you've got to make sure that the highlighted button represents the action you want to take, but it almost always does.

There are exceptions, of course. Some text boxes allow multiple-line entries. In many of these, pressing **ENTER** will start a new line of text. The basic principles still apply, though, because if you'll notice carefully, you'll see that there are no highlighted buttons on this type of dialog box. Thus, pressing **ENTER** can't activate a highlighted button because there isn't one.

Some multiline text boxes use another key to make new lines, such as **CTRL+ENTER**. Your clue will be to check whether or not any dialog box button is highlighted. If one is, then pressing **ENTER** *will* be the same as clicking on that highlighted button, and you'll have to find out what other key is used to create new lines in the text entry box within the dialog.

The **TAB** key

Closely related to the current subject, the **TAB** key can save you a lot of time. **TAB** moves the focus within a dialog box from item to item. It's much faster than using the mouse. I'll show you a quick example, but you'll see it's something that will be a major benefit within large dialog boxes that have more entries than are used in this exercise.

Hands On

Objective: Learn to speed your work using TAB.
❑ Open any group on the Program Manager.
❑ Press **ALT+F**.
❑ Press **ENTER** twice.
    This dialog box will let you add a new application to the Program Manager. You'll add one, then delete it. First, notice that the cursor is in the top text box.
❑ Type *Solitaire*.
❑ Press **TAB**.
❑ Type *sol.exe*.

❑ Press **ENTER**.

❑ Press **ENTER** again to start solitaire.

❑ Press **ALT+F4** to exit solitaire.

That was quick, wasn't it? Your hands never left the keyboard.

Millions of users would have clicked in the first window, then typed *Solitaire*, then stopped typing and then picked up the mouse, moved it over the second text box and clicked, then put down the mouse and typed *sol.exe*, then stopped typing and then picked up the mouse and moved it over and clicked on **OK**. You're going to fill in lots of forms on the Internet, and you can blaze through them if you'll type, press **TAB**, type again, press **TAB**, type again, press **TAB**, then press ENTER when you're done. Avoid the mouse when completing forms.

One more note. Using **SHIFT+TAB** will cycle backward through the available items on a dialog box in case you need to return to a previous entry.

A final quick lesson while you're here:

Hands On

***Objective:* Learn how to delete an application icon.**

❑ Make sure the Solitaire icon still is highlighted.

❑ Press **DELETE** to delete the icon.

❑ Press **ENTER** to confirm the deletion.

> Don't confuse this with eliminating a program, because this only deletes the icon. The application itself still occupies space on your hard disk. To completely eliminate most programs, you'll need an uninstall program. Windows 95 can uninstall any programs that you added through the new Add/Remove Programs feature.

The **ALT** key

You've already seen how to activate menu items by holding down **ALT** and pressing the underlined letter. But **ALT** has a broader effect than that. Pressing **ALT** always activates the menu system, whether or not you press a letter while holding it down. You can tap and release either **ALT** key, then press any underlined menu letter.

This is a critical property of Windows to remember. Most likely, you sometimes will tap an **ALT** key by mistake. Many Windows 3.x users who did not know this principle have rebooted their systems after inadvertently pressing an **ALT** key. Once the menu system has been activated with **ALT**, Windows is waiting for you to hit one of the underlined letters. Under Windows 3.x, this gave users the impression that their system had frozen. Fortunately under Windows 95, only the first keystroke counts and if it's not a valid menu letter, the menu system is deactivated until you press **ALT** again. Try it yourself, using the Program Manager.

Hands On

Objective: Learn to activate the Windows menu system.

❑ Continue to use the Program Manager.

❑ Press and release either **ALT** key.

    The menu item **File** will be highlighted.

❑ Type **X**.

    Your computer will beep, but **File** no longer will be highlighted. In Windows 3.x, this condition persisted until you pressed **ALT** again or hit a valid letter.

The **PRINTSCREEN** key

You can copy an image of the entire screen or of any active window into your clipboard. This sometimes is a great help when you find something on the Web that you want to transfer to your word processor. **PRINTSCREEN** captures the entire screen and **ALT+PRINTSCREEN** captures the active window. Let's do a quick demonstration of both, again using the Program Manager.

Hands On

Objective: Learn to capture screen images.

❑ Continue to use the Program Manager.

❑ Press **PRINTSCREEN**.

❑ Open your Accessories group.

❑ Double-click on **WordPad**.

❑ Press **CTRL+V** to Paste the screen image into WordPad.

    You might want to use the images handles to resize this for a better look, but you'll see that you've captured the entire screen.

❑ Press **CTRL+N** to start a new document.

    You'll see a dialog box asking you to specify the new document type. You'll capture just this dialog box to the clipboard and Paste it into the new document.

❑ Press **ALT+PRINTSCREEN** to capture the New dialog box.

❑ Press **ENTER**, then press **N** to close WordPad without saving.

❑ Press **CTRL+V** to paste the image of the dialog box.

    You might find countless uses for this as you surf the Net. It can be a wonderful tool. Of course if you don't have a dialog box active, then even **ALT+PRINTSCREEN** will capture the entire screen.

❑ Press **ALT+F4** again to exit.

❑ Press **N** to confirm you don't want to save.

Switching windows

This lesson will make sure you know how to use the full power of Windows. Remember, Windows is plural. You can have a lot of them open at once, but you can only work with one at a time, so you need to know how to switch between them to activate the one you want. The techniques are different for switching between document windows and application windows.

Switching document windows

You already have seen this principle, so this will be only a reminder. Remember, document windows only can exist under the control of an applications window. If your application window can support multiple windows, it will have **Window** on the menu bar. Here's a summary of some of the methods you can use to switch document windows:

Hands On

Objective: **Learn to switch between open Windows application document windows.**
- ❏ Click on any visible document window.
- ❏ Click **Window**, then the name of the window you want.
- ❏ Click **Window**, **Cascade**.
- ❏ Click **Window**, **Tile**.
- ❏ Press **SHIFT+F5** to Cascade.
- ❏ Press **SHIFT+F4** to Tile.
- ❏ Press **ALT+HYPHEN**, then press **T** to cycle to the next available document window.
- ❏ Press **CTRL+F6** to cycle through all available document windows.

Switching application windows

Here are the key principles to truly becoming a Windows expert. Without them, you don't have a chance of keeping up with the Internet. You cannot afford to run one application at a time and exit each one before starting another. First, let's start several applications so you can practice using these methods.

Hands On

Objective: **Learn to switch between open Windows applications.**
- ❏ Use the Accessories group that is still open from the last lesson.
- ❏ Double-click on **WordPad**.
- ❏ Click on any blank space on the Program Manager.
- ❏ Double-click on **Calculator**.
- ❏ Click on any blank space on the Program Manager.
- ❏ Double-click on **Paint**.
- ❏ Minimize Paint.
- ❏ Click on any blank space on the Program Manager.
- ❏ Double-click on **Clock**.

   You now have five applications open, so let's learn to switch back and forth between them.
- ❏ Move your mouse pointer to the bottom of the screen.

This activates the Taskbar that shows every active application.

❑ Click on **WordPad** on the Taskbar.

❑ Move your mouse pointer to the bottom of the screen.

❑ Click on **Clock**.

You get the idea. Now we'll learn another technique that doesn't require use of the mouse.

❑ Hold down either **ALT** key.

❑ Keep holding down **ALT** while pressing **TAB**.

Use this **ALT+TAB** method until an application you want is highlighted, then release **ALT**. Pressing **ALT+TAB** once returns you to your last application, thus you can use **ALT+TAB** to jump back and forth between your Web browser and your word processor—a big time-saver if you frequently switch between them.

Now we'll summarize the methods you can use to switch application windows. Most were covered in the exercise, but there are others you might want to test. Choose whichever method you prefer. Here's the summary:

❑ Click on any visible application window to make it active.

❑ Activate the **Taskbar** and click on the desired application.

❑ Use **ALT+TAB** to cycle through all open applications, and release **ALT** when the desired application appears.

❑ Use **SHIFT+ALT+TAB** to cycle backward through all open applications and release **ALT** when the desired application appears.

❑ Press **ALT+ESC** to cycle between all open applications.

This is not as direct as **ALT+TAB** and you might have to cycle through a lot of windows to get to the one you want. It always cycles through in order, in contrast to **ALT+TAB**, which starts with your most recently used application.

Hiding the Taskbar

If you are hooked on using the mouse but tired of giving up screen space to the Taskbar, you might want to do the next Hands-On exercise. I'll show you how to reconfigure the Taskbar so it will be hidden until you need it.

Hands On

***Objective:* Learn to hide the Taskbar.**

❑ Position your cursor on a blank area of the Taskbar.

The next step won't work correctly if your mouse is over any of the buttons on the Taskbar.

❑ Click the right mouse button on a blank area on the Taskbar.

❑ Click **Properties**.

❑ Make sure **Always on top** is checked.

❑ Make sure **Auto hide** is checked.

❑ Check **Show Clock**. (optional, but why not?)

❑ Click **OK**.

The Taskbar now has been reduced to a thin line at the bottom of the screen. You probably can't see it, because it's gray and the status bar on your current application is gray. With some applications, though, you'll notice the line.

❑ Move your mouse pointer to the very bottom of the screen.

This activates the Taskbar so you now can use it normally.

❑ Click on **Program Manager**.

Modifying the Taskbar

Once you've hidden the Taskbar, there's no need to limit it to its normal narrow width. You might prefer it somewhere other than at the bottom of your screen.

You can widen the Taskbar simply by dragging its border as you would with any window. Figure 4-5 shows the Taskbar at the bottom of the screen, but widened to three rows. If you open a lot of applications at once, their Taskbar buttons get too small to read. Widening the Taskbar can keep all of your buttons full-size, but you definitely will need to activate the Auto Hide feature outlined in the previous Hands-On exercise.

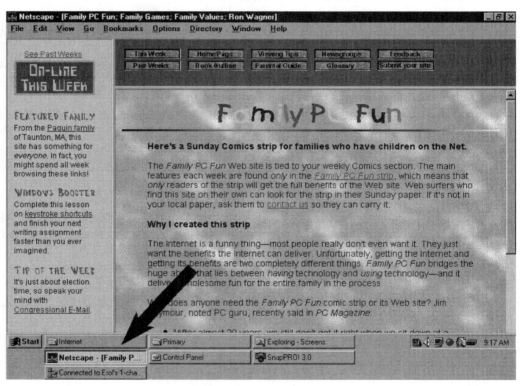

Figure 4-5

The Taskbar can be positioned to any edge of the screen. To move the Taskbar, activate it, grab it someplace other than on a button, and drag it to the desired side. It will remain there for future Windows sessions until you move it again. Figure 4-6 shows the Taskbar moved to the left edge of the screen and stretched out wide enough to display the full name of all the buttons. This configuration actually makes more sense than the default, because after you click **Start**, **Shut Down** is at the bottom of the list, where you're unlikely to choose it accidentally.

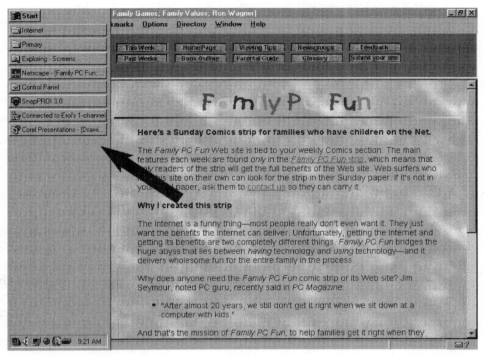

Figure 4-6

Window-switching exceptions

As you might expect, there are exceptions to the methods I've shown here for switching between windows. A popular example is Netscape's bookmark window. Netscape also has the **Window** menu item on its menu bar; you would expect that each of the features under **Window** would appear in document windows. But here's the exception: Each feature under the Netscape application window actually is a separate application and runs in its own application window. Yet, you can use **Window** to switch between these different Netscape applications.

That's something that you only would expect to be able to do using application-switching techniques such as the **Taskbar** or **ALT+TAB**. Of course those techniques do work, and you can use them in addition to the **Window** menu item.

And, even though they appear under the **Window** menu, these windows are closed with **ALT+F4** instead of with **CTRL+F4** as you would expect. Thus, you can see that without understanding the difference between document windows and application windows, you might get confused. Let's see Netscape's exception in action.

Hands On

***Objective:* To see an application window that you might expect to be a document window.**

❑ Start Netscape.

❑ Click **Bookmarks, Go to Bookmarks . . .**

This window is an application window, even though you might have expected it to be a document window. Let's see more.

❑ Press **ALT+TAB.**
    You now see an extra icon on this list, next to the Netscape icon.
❑ Press **TAB** until you've cycled back to Netscape, then release **ALT.**
❑ Click the icon on the Netscape Bookmarks window.
    Note that the keystroke to close it is **ALT+F4** and not **CTRL+F4.**
❑ Click on **Close** to close the Bookmarks window.

If you can't do this exercise now, keep these principles in mind, because you will encounter windows that do not behave normally. Knowing these principles will keep you from being stymied by oddly behaved windows.

Boosting your productivity

I've shown you how to quickly switch between document windows, but quick switching-methods are no match for not having to switch at all. So now I'll help you set up your Windows for maximum productivity. You can greatly increase your Windows productivity by grouping your most frequently used icons into a single, primary folder on the Windows 95 desktop. Once you've created this new folder, you'll keep all other folders closed because you rarely will need them. Here's a good example of a primary folder (see Figure 4-7).

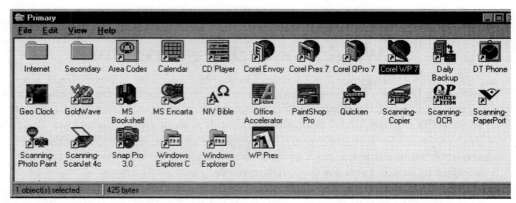

Figure 4-7

Create a primary folder

Follow these steps to create your Primary folder on the Windows 95 desktop. Most users find this folder to be a tremendous productivity enhancement.

Hands On

***Objective:* Add a Primary folder.**
❑ Move the mouse to the Taskbar and click the right mouse button.
❑ Click **Minimize All Windows**.
❑ Right-click the desktop.
❑ Click **New, Folder**.
❑ Type *Primary* and press **ENTER**.
    You now have created a new folder.

Add your productivity icons

Now that your Primary folder has been created, it's time to add your most frequently used icons. Using the Internet aggressively will have you running lots of multiple applications, so you'll want them available for speedy access. Adding icons to your Primary folder won't be any harder than playing Solitaire, so let's do it.

Hands On

Objective: **Add your best productivity-enhancing icons.**

❑ Open the folder that contains your word processor.

> You only need one icon in this group, so we'll copy that one to Primary.

❑ Use the right mouse button to drag and drop your word processor's icon into Primary.

❑ Click **Copy Here** to copy the icon into Primary.

❑ Close your word processor folder.

❑ Open the group that contains your Internet icons.

> You might need several of these icons, or you might need several different folders. Use the right-button drag-and-drop method to copy all of your frequently used icons into Primary. As a minimum you will want your primary Internet connection icon (Netscape, for example) and your e-mail icon (Eudora, for example).

Adding icons to your primary folder

Look at the example pictured earlier for ideas about which icons to include in your Primary folder. Here are a few suggestions:

- File Manager, Print Manager.
- Calculator, Notepad, WordPad.
- Others: Word processor, Netscape, Eudora, Usenet reader, Network e-mail, Calendar/Scheduler, Contact Manager, Spreadsheet, Graphics Drawing Package, Database Application, File viewer, Backups, Scanning Application.

When all of your Primary applications are in one folder, you won't waste time hunting down the right folder or browsing through multi-level menus on the Windows 95 Start button. As long as you never close your Primary folder (always use Minimize instead), the Taskbar will have Primary on it. And you'll be able to use **ALT+TAB** to return to Primary quickly to start any of your favorite applications.

Of course, the Windows 95 desktop lets you create a folder for any application and put it on the desktop; but a single primary folder reduces desktop clutter, and lets you find your most important applications with the mouse or with **ALT+TAB**.

You might find that you have a second tier of applications that you need regularly, but not daily. If so, create a folder entitled Secondary and copy the icons you want into that folder. You probably will keep Secondary minimized instead of closing it, so that it, too, will be visible on your Taskbar.

Fitting in more icons

You can get more icons inside each group if you'll change the icon spacing within Windows. The examples listed in the next exercise work well with a screen resolution of 800×600. While this is a common setting, yours might be different and you might need to experiment with different settings. Consider these icon-spacing numbers as starting points.

Hands On

Objective: **Get more icons in a group by changing icon spacing.**

❏ Right-click the desktop.

❏ Click **Properties, Appearance**.

❏ Click the **Item** drop list, click **Icon Spacing (Horizontal)**.

❏ Change the number to **36** (or whatever you want to try).

> See the accompanying sidebar for more information about the effect of screen resolution on the numbers you enter here.

❏ Click the **Item** drop list, click **Icon Spacing (Vertical)**.

❏ Change the number to **42** (or whatever you want to try).

❏ Click **OK**.

❏ Open your new **Primary** folder.

> You will NOT notice any changes. It's a little quirk of Windows 95. To put the new spacing into effect, follow the remaining steps.

❏ Right-click the folder.

❏ Click **Arrange Icons, by Name**.

Windows screen resolution

The example of a Primary group shown here uses a screen resolution of 800×600 pixels. Pixels are dots on the screen. As the number of pixels in your resolution increases, the image quality improves and you can get more information on your screen. There are, however, two trade-offs.

First, if the resolution gets too high, the text and icons will be too small to use. The ideal solution to that problem is to get a 21″ monitor. Because a 21″ monitor alone costs more than an entire PC with a 15″ monitor, few people have them. You probably won't want to go above 640×480 on a 14″ monitor. Most people are happy with 800×600 on a 15″ or 17″ monitor. With a 17″ monitor, you might even go up to 1024×768. The highest resolution in common use today, 1280×1024, makes the text too small for most users on any monitor that is smaller than 19″.

The second trade-off against the joys of increasing screen resolution is a penalty in computer memory. The high resolutions require lots of memory and can render some systems inoperable. The 800×600 setting is a good balance among resolution, readability, and computer memory resources.

Menu fonts

While we're on the subject of screen appearance, I'll give you a little-used tip that your eyes might appreciate very much. You can change the font face, font size, and font attributes on your Windows 95 menus. One of the options, applying bold to the menu words, is especially nice. Here's a short Hands-On that will walk you through making your menu words bold and, while you're there, you can make other changes as well.

Hands On

Objective: **Change fonts for Windows 95 menus.**

❑ Right-click the desktop.

❑ Click **Properties, Appearance**.

❑ Click the **Item** drop list and select **Menu**.

❑ Click the **Bold** button on the **Font** line.

> You now can make any other changes you might desire. You can change the font face, font size, and font color.

❑ Click **OK** to accept the changes.

> Alternatively, if you're undecided, you can click **Apply** to see the changes take effect now and then make other changes if desired. The **Cancel** button, however, will not undo any changes you make if you have pressed **Apply**.

Displaying all open applications

Windows 95 lets you see all of your open applications at a glance. You can Cascade or Tile every open application to get an overview of everything that's running. Windows 3.x also had the same feature, but Windows 95 has a bonus: After seeing the applications, you can Undo the Cascade or Tile action and restore all windows to their previous state. In Windows 3.x, you had to restore each one individually, which was a lot of work.

Hands On

Objective: **Learn how to see all open applications at a glance.**

❑ Right-click the Taskbar.

❑ Click **Cascade**.

❑ Right-click the Taskbar.

❑ Click **Undo Cascade** to restore all windows.

❑ Right-click the Taskbar.

❑ Click **Tile Horizontally**.

❑ Right-click the Taskbar.

❑ Click **Undo Tile** to restore all windows.

NET TIP

Exiting Windows Never turn off your computer or reboot it when Windows is running unless it has frozen and there is no other way to recover. Windows does a lot of cleanup work when it closes down. When you turn off your computer while Windows is running, you can end up wasting a lot of hard disk space with stray files. Even worse: It's possible for Windows to become corrupted and require reinstallation. Always use the Taskbar to click **Start**, click **Shut Down**, then click **Yes** or press **Y** to confirm. Then wait for a message to tell you it's safe to turn off your computer.

Special switching techniques

As you might imagine, there are many other ways to start and switch applications. The switching techniques we've shown you so far are generic and will work with all copies of Windows. Because starting and switching applications is so important when you work on the Internet, we'll show you some specialized alternatives.

Windows resources

When you begin freely using **ALT+TAB**, you will begin to run your Windows with a lot of applications open simultaneously. If you're using Windows 3.x, you might begin to encounter system problems such as hangups that you never before have experienced.

One way to keep Windows running reliably is to keep an eye on the system resources. Here's how you can check system resources at any time:

Hands On

Objective: Learn how to check system resources rapidly.

❑ Activate the Taskbar and click **Start**.

❑ Click **Settings, Control Panel**.

❑ Double-click **System**.

❑ Click **Performance**.

❑ Click **OK**, or press **ENTER** to dismiss the dialog box.

❑ Close **Control Panel**.

Unlike Windows 3.x, Windows 95 does not suffer from serious resource limitations. You can expect to simultaneously run five major applications without any problems.

Check your system resources sometime immediately after you have turned on your computer and started Windows. They should be above 80 percent. If not, then you probably have a lot of fonts loaded or some out-of-date drivers. Check with the manufacturers of some of your computer's components, especially your video display card, and make sure you have the latest driver. I've seen some quirky, unreliable systems become stable simply by updating the display driver.

For example, one computer had serious problems hanging up when using WordPerfect for Windows. The owner blamed it on a recent WordPerfect upgrade. But the problem was with the video display driver that was designed long before the manufacturer knew about Windows 95. Installing an updated video display driver restored the system's reliability.

Microsoft Windows key

New keyboards today are sporting a couple of new keys designed specifically for Windows 95. Hopefully you got a new computer with your Windows 95 and it has the new keys. If not, you'll find that a new keyboard is inexpensive and even can help decrease physical stress. Microsoft makes one of the best ones, the Microsoft Natural Keyboard. I wrote my last book, the *McGraw-Hill Internet Training Manual*, entirely on one. I now have switched to another brand that includes a Glide-Point mouse pad and mouse buttons. Choose the one that feels best to you; just make sure it has the Windows logo on a couple of its keys.

Pressing either Windows key activates the Start button. In Windows 3.x, this key performs the same function as the **CTRL+ESC** keystroke. Once the Start button menu is activated, you can press **ESC** or either **ALT** key to cancel it.

Most Windows keyboards also have another new key. It's got a menu icon on it because it is designed to activate context-sensitive menus within applications. Within true Windows 95 applications, it performs the same function as right-clicking the mouse. In Windows 3.x applications, the results are unpredictable.

CUA keystroke summary

Here's a summary of some of the keystrokes that will help you the most when you're working on the Internet. Having every one of these techniques in your repertoire will make you a maestro of the Internet and you'll be able to direct it to new heights of productivity.

The **SHIFT** key with the mouse

You also can use the **SHIFT** key with your mouse to quickly select multiple items on a list. From earlier Hands-On exercises in this book, you should still have the Program Manager open. We'll use that again for examples.

Hands On

Objective: **Learn to select a series of items on a list.**

❑ Click **Window, Main** to open the **Main** group.

❑ Double-click **File Manager**.

❑ Select any directory with a long list of filenames.

❑ Click on one file near the top of the list.

❑ Hold down **SHIFT** while you click an item near the bottom.

    All files between and including the two on which you clicked will be selected.

❑ Click on one file near the top of the list.

❑ Hold down **SHIFT** while you press the **DOWN ARROW** key.

    This, too, will highlight files in sequence.

The **CTRL** key with the mouse

You can select a random assortment of files on any list using the **CTRL** key with your mouse.

Hands On

Objective: **Learn to randomly select multiple items on a list.**

❏ Use the same list you used in the previous lesson.

❏ Click on any file.

❏ Hold down the **CTRL** key while you click on another item.

 Every click adds another item to the selection. Almost any file function you perform will be performed on this entire group of selected files (see Figure 4-8).

❏ Continue holding down **CTRL** while you click on more items.

❏ If you want to deselect a selected item, click on it again while holding down the **CTRL** key.

❏ Click on any item without holding down **CTRL**.

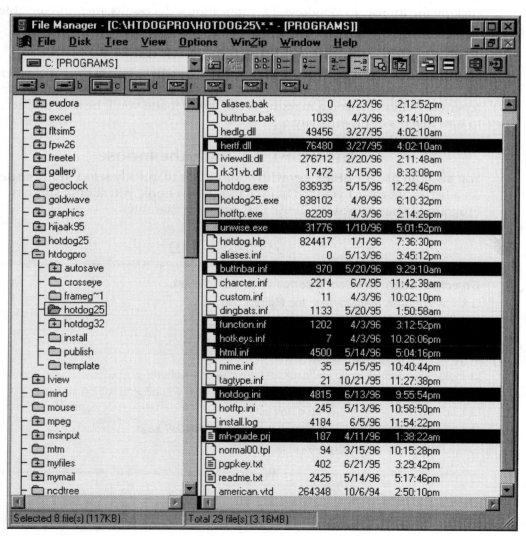

Figure 4-8

The **SHIFT** key with cursor movement keys

Here's one of the best Windows tricks of all. It's hard to imagine using the Internet without this feature: Any cursor movement key selects text if **SHIFT** is depressed.

Here are a couple of examples that will greatly boost your speed. To see this in action, it will be best if you open a file with some text. The exercise begins with you opening a document you can use to practice these keystrokes. I'll have you continue to use the Program Manager icons.

Hands On

***Objective:* Learn to quickly select text using keystrokes.**

❏ Click **Window, Accessories** to open the group.

❏ Double-click **WordPad**.

❏ Click **File, Open** or click the **Open** icon.

❏ Navigate to the Windows directory.

This typically is **c:\windows**, but might be different on your system.

❏ Double-click the file **Exchange.txt**.

❏ Move to the bottom of the document with **CTRL+END**.

❏ Hold down **SHIFT** and press **CTRL+HOME** to move to the top of the document.

This selects all the text in any document with but two keystrokes: **CTRL+END**, **SHIFT+CTRL+HOME**. This is a time-saving, valuable trick on the Internet and an excellent way to capture entire documents. You'll use it often.

❏ Press any cursor movement key to deselect the text.

Try a couple more examples to reinforce the concept.

❏ Press **CTRL+HOME** to jump to the top of the document.

❏ Press **DOWN ARROW** to go to the first line of hyphens.

❏ Hold down **SHIFT** then press **DOWN+ARROW** four times.

This will select the entire title heading at the top of the document. You now could perform any number of operations on this text, just as if you had selected it with your mouse.

❏ Press **DOWN+ARROW** to deselect it and move to the copyright line.

❏ Hold down **SHIFT** then press **END**.

This selects the entire line. You can do this in either direction. Let's try it now.

❏ Press **END** to deselect the line.

❏ Hold down **SHIFT** and press **HOME**.

❏ Press **DOWN ARROW** to deselect the line.

❏ Hold down **SHIFT** and press **CTRL+END**.

This selects from the current cursor position to the end of the document.

❏ Press **CTRL+HOME**.

This deselects the text and positions you back at the top of the document for the next exercise.

Using the **SHIFT** key to select text is especially important when copying URLs and addresses. Try this with your cursor in a single-line text entry window. I'll have you copy a line of text into the clipboard and then Paste it into this document.

Hands On

Objective: **Learn to copy the contents of a text entry box.**

❑ Continue to use WordPad.

❑ Click **File, Save As . . .**

> The text in the Filename box already is selected, so you could copy it now, but let's not so we can see how to do it if the text is not selected.

❑ Press **END** to move to the beginning of the line.

❑ Press **SHIFT+HOME** to select all the text on that line.

> This is an improvement over the frustrating method of trying to drag your mouse across the entire line without missing the first or last character. Even if you use the mouse to click in the text entry box, finishing with the keystrokes might be quicker.

❑ Click at the far right of the text entry box.

❑ Press **CTRL+C** to copy it to your clipboard.

❑ Press **ESC** to cancel the Save As dialog box.

❑ Press **CTRL+V** to Paste the filename into the current document.

> You'll use this principle countless times on the Internet as you copy URLs and paste them to other applications or locations.

❑ Press **ENTER** to start a new line for the next exercise.

Bold, italics, and underline

Nearly every windows application uses the same keystrokes to emphasize text with bold, italics, and underline. Let's practice this, using the same document you used in the previous lesson.

Hands On

Objective: **Learn the keystrokes for bold, italics, and underline.**

> Use the same document as above. Don't worry about the mess we're having you make of this document. When we're through we simply will exit without saving.

❑ Press **CTRL+B** to turn on Bold.

❑ Type some bolded text.

❑ Press **CTRL+B** to turn off Bold.

❑ Press **CTRL+I** to turn on Italics.

❑ Type some italicized text.

❑ Press **CTRL+I** to turn off Italics.

❑ Press **CTRL+U** to turn on Underline.

❑ Type some underlined text.

❑ Press **CTRL+U** to turn off Underline.

❑ Select the title header again using **SHIFT+DOWN ARROW**.

❑ Press **CTRL+B** to bold the existing text.

❑ Press **CTRL+I** to italicize the existing text.

❑ Press **CTRL+U** to underline the existing text.

The basics

❑ Press any arrow key to deselect the title header.

> All three of these font attribute keystrokes are toggles. That means that if the associated attribute is off, the keystroke will activate it; if it's on, the keystroke will deactivate it.

❑ Press **ENTER** to start a new line.

> Using these keystrokes will be much faster than interrupting your typing to grab the mouse, find a button, click, put down the mouse, and then return to the keyboard.

Cut, Copy, and Paste

These keystrokes will enable you to freely move text between any two Windows applications. Practice these and remember them; they will be a major factor in productivity success using Windows on the Internet. They use the universal Windows clipboard to move and copy text and graphics between any two locations within Windows.

Hands On

Objective: **Learn to use keystrokes for Cut, Copy, and Paste.**

❑ Select the copyright line.

❑ Press **CTRL+C** to Copy these words into the clipboard.

❑ Use **ALT+TAB** to return to Program Manager.

❑ Double-click **Notepad**.

> This could be any Windows application, from e-mail to WordPerfect to an HTML editor.

❑ Press **CTRL+V**.

> This will paste the copyright line into Notepad. Using Paste does not affect the clipboard contents. You can repeatedly Paste the same text until you change the clipboard contents with Cut or Copy. Let's demonstrate.

❑ Press **CTRL+V** two more times to see the clipboard is preserved.

❑ Use **ALT+TAB** to return to WordPad.

❑ Select an entire paragraph of text.

❑ Press **CTRL+X** to Cut it from the document.

❑ Move your insertion point to another spot in the document.

❑ Press **CTRL+V** to Paste the paragraph to the new spot.

Using Cut, Copy, and Paste in conjunction with application switching (such as **ALT+TAB**) is the key to working quickly, easily, and powerfully on the Internet with Windows. For example, transferring text from your Web browser to your word processor will be a snap. Simply use your mouse to select the desired text right on the Web page, press **CTRL+C** to Copy it to your clipboard, press **ALT+TAB** to jump to your word processor, press **CTRL+V** to Paste the text into a document, then press **ALT+TAB** again to return to the Internet for more text. Of course you can reverse the process to transfer information from your word processor to an Internet application.

The next two lessons are on Netscape Navigator and the Eudora for Windows mail application. Both Netscape and Internet mail programs can stifle your productivity by making you write down and retype lots of annoying little text

Windows wide open—advanced basics

strings. Or, you can cruise the Information Superhighway with your Windows Wide Open.

Saving URLs

Here's an optional hands-on exercise that will prevent you from losing track of important information sites around the Internet. You're going to create a new icon for your Primary folder that will use the Windows WordPad to save a file of important URLs along with a brief note on each. You then will be able to get to your URL list merely by double-clicking on this new icon, which always will be available in your Primary folder.

Hands On

Objective: **Create an icon that provides instant access to important Internet URLs.**

❑ Open your Primary folder.

❑ Click **File, New, Shortcut** to create a new icon in Primary.

❑ Type *write.exe c:\internet.wri* and press **ENTER**.

❑ Type *URLs* and press **ENTER**.

> You now have created an icon that will instantly open a file containing all of your URLs, but the file does not yet exist. The first time you activate this icon, you'll get an error message, so let's do it now.

❑ Double-click your new **URLs** icon.

> A dialog box will warn you that the file does not exist, but the file will pop up instantly after this exercise.

❑ Click **OK**.

❑ Click **File, Save** to save the file.

❑ Type *c:\internet.wri* and press **ENTER**.

> The file now exists, so you can exit.

Anytime you discover a valuable URL on the Internet, highlight it, press **CTRL+C** to copy it to the clipboard, use **ALT+TAB** to switch to your Primary folder or use the Taskbar to open the Primary folder. Then double-click your **URLs** icon, then use **CTRL+V** to paste in the URL. You then can use **ALT+TAB** to go back to your Internet application and copy some text to paste in here for a brief reminder or you can type it in from scratch. Keep each URL on a separate line with the descriptive paragraph immediately under it. The Find feature (**Edit**, **Find** or **CTRL+F**) will enable you to quickly locate URLs by searching for key words in the description that you wrote.

New techniques for Windows 95

Windows 95 has many new features for managing files and folders. For example, you can place the URL file itself on your desktop and then double-click it to activate WordPad. And you could maintain on your desktop several of these URL files to organize your URLs into categories.

If you access the Internet from more than one computer, you might want to check out the new Windows 95 Briefcase feature to use for your URLs. A URL Briefcase can store all of your URLs and enable you to easily copy them to a notebook or to a floppy disk. And if you update any of your URL files while you're using your notebook, the Briefcase feature can synchronize the two separate collections of files so that your desktop computer will be updated with the changes.

The techniques presented in this chapter are, of course, not the only ways to save URLs. Windows 95 is rich with powerful features that can help you organize files. You might discover some on your own or you might learn them from other users. Ask around, read other books, read the Windows 95 help files or manual, and be open to using new techniques and features.

You also will find that Internet browsers have a built-in bookmark feature that stores your best URLs. This bookmark list might quickly become full or you might find URLs you want to remember that do not merit a bookmark slot. That's when you'll appreciate your URLs file.

Wrap-up

Here's the final Hands-On exercise to close all the Windows you've opened and clean up your desktop.

Hands On

Objective: Close all the extra open applications.

❑ Activate the Taskbar and right-click **Calculator**.

❑ Click **Close**.

❑ Activate the Taskbar and right-click **WordPad**.

❑ Click **Close** and don't save the changes we made.

 Continue to close all open applications you no longer need to use now. Or, if you're through for now, you can:

❑ Click **Start**.

❑ Click **Shut Down**.

❑ Click **Yes** to shut down Windows.

Congratulations on sticking with me through this long lesson. It seemed like a lot of work, didn't it? You soon are going to see, however, a payoff for that work when you start browsing the Web in the next chapter. The techniques you've learned here will serve you for many years as you trek through the vast reaches of cyberspace. Now that you've completed the Windows lessons, let's move on to the next chapter to learn about the vehicle that will transport you through cyberspace: the Netscape Navigator.

Continuing Education

Frank's Windows 95 page

http://www.conitech.com/windows

Frank says that this site is a collection of useful news, resources, and tips about Microsoft's newest version of Windows. I try to keep it as up to date as possible, and much of my information comes from you, so if you have any information or requests for what you'd like to see here, be sure to e-mail me (see Figure 4-9). This site is more than just a resource for tips and tricks—it also includes information on updated drivers. The resources on this site have breathed new life into tons of PCs that were drowning under the strain of Windows 95 problems.

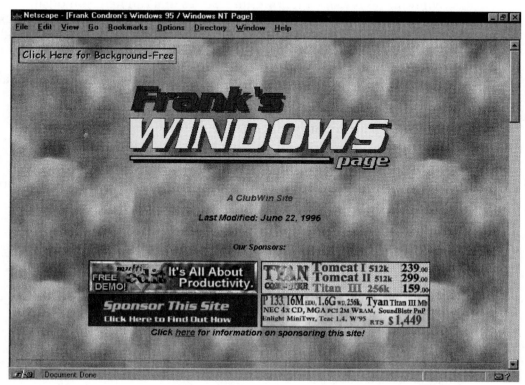

Figure 4-9

Windows 95 Unleashed

http://www.supernet.net/~edtiley/win95/win95unl.html

This page by the book's author, Ed Tiley, includes a link labeled, Some of my favorite tips and tricks. There's another link about ClubWin that might lead you to more help. Here's the inside stuff on ClubWin: We are a self-organized group of individual computer professionals and advanced users from the U.S., Canada, and Europe who among us have hundreds of thousands of hours experience with Microsoft Windows 95. Within the group are hardware, software, applications, networking and support professionals who have made a commitment to assist others and provide information and support for others using Windows 95.

Windows 95 home page

http://198.105.232.4/windows

This is Microsoft's home page for Windows 95. You can get to it from their main home page, but this is a short cut straight to the Windows 95 area. You'll find FAQs and Technical Support answers, tips, and news updates. You won't be surprised to discover that it's optimized for the Windows 95 Internet Explorer and *not* for Netscape, but it still is a good resource.

The (Unofficial) Windows 95 home page

http://www.southwind.net/~leeb/win95.html

Here's another Windows 95 resource that includes a walk-through of a sample setup of a PPP Internet connection and a sample SLIP connection. It's not designed to provide general Windows 95 help, but if you're having trouble getting Windows 95 connected to an Internet service provider, this site might get you launched into cyberspace.

The Microsoft Windows newsletter

You can stay abreast of the latest developments in Windows 95 from a weekly on-line Microsoft newsletter subscription. Here are the steps to subscribe:

◉ Send an Internet e-mail message to: *enews@microsoft.nwnet.com.*

◉ Leave the Subject line blank.

◉ In the body of the message, place only these words: *subscribe winnews.*

Once you've subscribed, you can discontinue your subscription at any time by using these steps:

◉ Send an Internet e-mail message to: *enews@microsoft.nwnet.com.*

◉ Leave the Subject line blank.

◉ In the body of the message, place only these words: *unsubscribe winnews.*

Netscape basics

FOR YOUR Hands-On World Wide Web exercises, I'll use the Netscape Navigator 3.0 Web browser for Windows (see Figure 5-1). The Netscape Navigator is the most widely used network browser in the world today. Even if you don't use Netscape, much of the chapter will be beneficial because you're going to get a lot of productivity concepts that apply to all Web browsers.

Why did I choose Netscape? Netscape has become the de facto Web standard, evidenced by the number of Web pages that have a statement similar to "This page was designed to look best with Netscape." If you don't have it . . . get it.

Independent statistics show that more than 75 percent of the Web browsers currently used on the Internet are Netscape Navigators. Today, millions of people are navigating the Internet with Netscape Navigator. The exercises in this chapter will transform you into an efficient, productive power-user of the most popular Web browser in use.

Netscape has serious competition from the Internet Explorer, which was introduced with Microsoft Windows 95. Within months of the release of Windows 95, the Internet Explorer was available for a variety of other operating systems, including earlier versions of Windows. Who knows if Microsoft will pull into the lead or Netscape will become the second software company to beat Microsoft? (Intuit's Quicken clobbered Microsoft Money in the financial software market.) Both Netscape and the Internet Explorer are easy to use, with each edging out the other in certain areas. Let's look briefly at each one.

Internet Explorer

The main problem (at least in spring 1996) with the Microsoft Internet Explorer is that it renders pages differently than Netscape (see Figure 5-2). Sites that look balanced and well-planned in Netscape might look somewhat askew in Explorer. Of course the reverse is true, but not to the same degree. And more importantly, very few sites are designed specifically for Explorer, although some are offering visitors a choice of selecting pages optimized for either Netscape or Explorer.

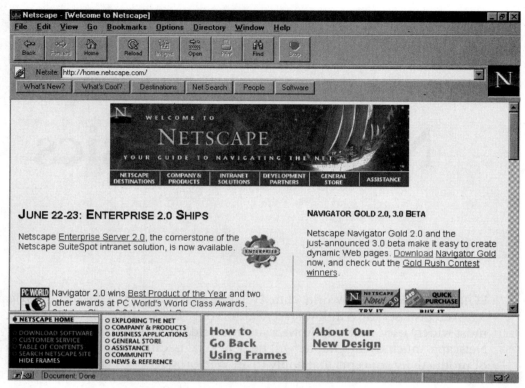

Figure 5-1

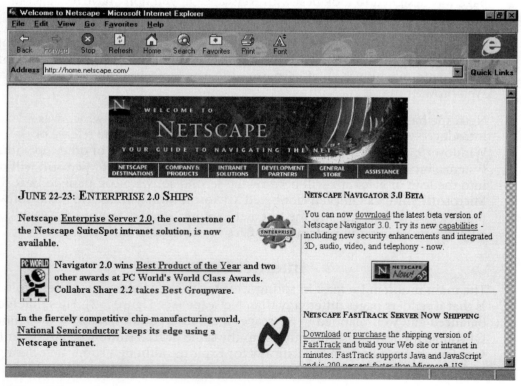

Figure 5-2

▶ *The basics*

One of the Explorer's chief strengths is that its user interface is a seamless extension of the Windows 95 interface. For example, the bookmark feature in Explorer uses the same folders as everything else in Windows 95, so there's nothing new to learn. The Explorer bookmark folder is more powerful and easier to use than Netscape's bookmark feature. Of course, Netscape probably will upgrade their bookmarks to use the Windows 95 folders, and might have done so by the time you read this.

Netscape Navigator

Netscape has more features than Explorer. Some are minor, but I miss them when I occasionally experiment with Explorer. For example, in Netscape you can more easily navigate without the mouse. Netscape's chief strength, however, is in its extension to the basic HTML standards. Web page designers can use these extensions to create a wider variety of designs and, blessedly, spare us from looking at an endless stream of look-alike sites.

Netscape has a strong, built-in e-mail feature, though it lacks the power of a dedicated Internet e-mail application such as Eudora. Netscape mail has other trade-offs. For example, Netscape mail uses its own proprietary address book. Windows 95 enables you to create a single address book that can be used across applications such as Internet Explorer, e-mail, and faxing. That spares you from making double entries, as you'd need to do if you used Netscape's e-mail.

The e-mail features in both Netscape and Explorer will leave you wanting a dedicated package such as Eudora. One day, most likely, both will be good enough to eliminate the need for a stand-alone e-mail application, but for now, consider them works in progress.

Okay, enough of that. I know your main interest in Netscape isn't for its e-mail features anyway, so let's get an updated copy of Netscape and move into the Hands-On training.

Getting the latest Netscape

If you don't have Netscape—or if you'd just like to get the latest version—you can download a free trial version from the Internet. You can purchase the commercial version of the Netscape Web browser directly from Netscape by calling them at 415/528-2555, faxing them at 415/528-4140, e-mailing them at *sales@netscape.com*, or by visiting their on-line store on the Web at *home.netscape.com.* Find the link that leads you to download the latest version of Netscape.

You can use the URL listed here as a starting point for discovering all of the Netscape products available today. Usually they have beta test versions of the next generation that you might be tempted to try. Perhaps one or two people in your organization could use the latest beta version, but mainstream users should stick with a registered copy of the latest official release. That's not because there ever have been any significant problems with the beta versions, but they can be annoying to use because they expire after only a few weeks. Using beta copies forces users into a routine of regular downloads and updates.

So, assuming you've got Netscape Navigator ready to go and you've got a TCP/IP connection to the Internet, let's begin the Hands-On exercises.

Creating some on-screen elbow-room

Most Web pages are too large to fit into the Netscape main screen all at once, but you'll want to see as much as possible. In this first Netscape exercise, I'll have you maximize Netscape using a Windows command, then eliminate some buttons that unnecessarily clutter the screen; then I'll give you keystroke equivalents to replace the buttons I've had you hide.

Hands On

Objective: **Maximize your Netscape viewing area.**

❏ Start Netscape with an Internet connection.

Netscape might automatically do this for you when you start it. There are so many ways to get an Internet connection that I must leave that part up to you and your computer professionals, or your Internet service provider.

❏ Press **CTRL+L**, type *home.netscape.com*, and press **ENTER**.

Notice how this document appears on screen; especially note how little of the document you can see at one time. Scroll through this document using your **UP ARROW** or **DOWN ARROW** keys or your mouse. Now let's improve your view.

❏ Double-click the title bar to maximize Netscape on-screen.

If your view already looks like the screen shown in Figure 5-3, you can skip the next two steps.

❏ Click **Options** then uncheck **Show Toolbar**.

❏ Click **Options** then uncheck **Show Directory Buttons**.

You don't need the two bars you just turned off. The buttons on both of them either have keystroke equivalents, right-mouse-button equivalents, or are used occasionally enough that they do not merit full-time screen space.

Once you've eliminated these two button bars (see Figure 5-3), you'll enjoy the increased viewing area. Of course, you also can eliminate the **Location** bar, but that's a crucial navigation tool that you most likely will prefer to keep. The next table lists simple keystroke and right mouse button replacements for the buttons you just hid.

Toolbar Button	Equivalent
Back	**ALT+LEFT ARROW** or right mouse, **Back**
Forward	**ALT+RIGHT ARROW** or right mouse, **Forward**
Home	Click **Go, Home**
Reload	**CTRL+R** or **View, Reload**
Open Location	**CTRL+L** or **File, Open Location . . .**
Open File	**CTRL+O** or **File, Open File . . .**
Print	**CTRL+P** or **File, Print . . .**
Find	**CTRL+F** or **Edit, Find . . .**
Save	**CTRL+S** or **File, Save As . . .**
Stop	**ESCAPE** or **Go, Stop Loading**

▶ *The basics*

Directory Button	Equivalent
What's New!	Click **Directory, What's New!**
What's Cool!	Click **Directory, What's Cool!**
Handbook	Click **Help, Handbook**
Net Search	Click **Directory, Internet Search**
Net Directory	Click **Directory, Internet Directory**
Software	Click **Help, Software**

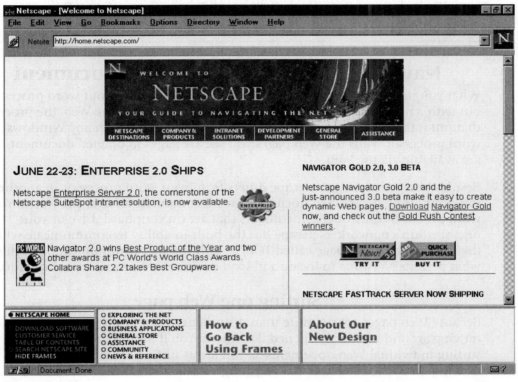

Figure 5-3

Surf the Net

Now it's time to surf the Net. If you skipped chapter 2 ("Breathing space for cyberspace"), please put a bookmark on this page and go back and read chapter 2 now. Nearly everyone is overwhelmed by the unfathomable depths and incomprehensible breadth of the resources that the World Wide Web can bring to a computer screen. You need to be ready for it. But if you are ready now . . . let's jump into cyberspace!

Hands On

Objective: **Start surfing the Net.**

❏ Start Netscape with an Internet connection.
❏ Double-click in the **Location** text entry box.
❏ Type *www.marketing-coach.com* and press **ENTER**.
❏ Click on **McGraw-Hill WWW Training Manual**.
❏ Click on **Glossary**.

> This is an on-line glossary for my series of McGraw-Hill Internet books. We'll use this document to learn some quick browsing methods.

Navigating a downloaded Web document

What you have seen so far is akin to viewing documents in your word processor, but with a read-only restriction. When you see a screen on the Web, the process that put it there is similar to when you open a document with any Windows word processor. Thus the Web pages you see are pages in opened documents that are available via the Web.

Besides being read-only, Netscape differs from your word processor in another important way: It can open documents from computers all over the world. Your word processor only opens documents that are on your hard drive or your organization's network. Netscape has the built-in ability to communicate with the Internet via a language called TCP/IP. This Internet communication ability is what permits Netscape to locate and load documents from all over the world.

Surfing one Web page

Because Web pages are no more than documents, let's review some shortcuts to moving around within an opened document. You'll need to be as efficient at surfing individual Web documents as you are at surfing the entire Web. The example you've loaded now is a very long Web document that defines the commonly used Internet terms. Later, I'll show you how to save this document and turn it into an accessible reference source.

Hands On

Objective: **Learn to surf one Web page.**

❏ Press **DOWN ARROW** to scroll down through this document.
❏ Press **UP ARROW** to scroll up through this document.
❏ Use your mouse on the scroll bar on the right of the screen.

> Use the arrows at the top or the bottom to scroll up or down. Grab the elevator button (square box) on the scroll bar and drag it up or down to more quickly scroll long distances.

❏ Press **CTRL+END** to jump to the bottom of this document.
❏ Press **CTRL+HOME** to jump to the top of this document.

- Press **PG DN** a couple of times.
- Press **PG UP** a couple of times.

   Remember these keystrokes throughout all your Web surfing. When your computer is pushing the limits, using the mouse places a strain on your Windows resources. If the mouse acts sluggish or skittery, try using these keystrokes instead.

Finding the information you need

All the power that's built into Netscape would be nearly useless if it weren't for the existence of a wide variety of Web search engines. In fact, Netscape has several features that have helped the search engine developers to make their services more user-friendly. Thus, search engine development has been a two-way street, with Netscape increasing the demand for more search engine power while at the same time contributing to the very power increases that it demands. The result has been to bring you an array of fast, powerful, and comprehensive search engines that will help you locate nearly any topic in cyberspace.

HYPERJUMP

Search engines

Software applications that help you find information within computer information files are called search engines. They have two basic functions. The first is to run through the information files word-by-word and build an index of the words it finds—much like the index in the back of this book. The second function is a user interface that accepts keyword input that the search engine uses to locate your search request.

You won't be able to keep track of all of the search engines that are available on the Web. I constantly see new services emerge. I'm going to profile two of them for you here because they both are highly popular, powerful, and representative of basic Web search techniques. Once you've used these two, learning the others will be a snap. There are two reasons to try alternative search engines: 1) The others might better suit you personally than the two profiled in these exercises; and 2) The ones used here might be too busy.

In the Continuing Education section at the end of this chapter you'll get URLs and summaries for several others. You most likely will add an array of search engine URLs to your bookmark list under the category Search Resources so you always will have them handy to answer your research demands.

Lycos

Lycos is a creation of Carnegie-Mellon University in Pittsburgh (see Figure 5-4). It's oriented toward keyword searches and offers several search options. This engine is fast and comprehensive, though at times, you might believe that it's slow. Just remember, you are sharing this service with millions of people around the world. Consider the wonder that it works at all!

Let's run through an exercise to demonstrate how to use Lycos to look up a specific topic.

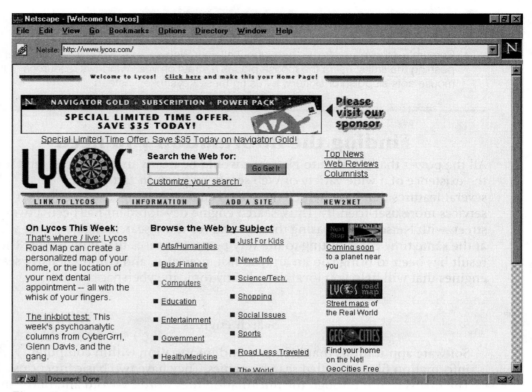

Figure 5-4

Hands On

Objective: Learn to search the Web with Lycos.

❏ Press **CTRL+L**, type *www.lycos.com*, and press **ENTER**.

Netscape no longer requires you to precede Web URLs with that cumbersome *http://*, so get in the habit of omitting it.

❏ Click **Enhance your search** to see search options.

❏ Click in **Query** and type *hot air balloon*.

❏ Double-click in **Min Terms** and type *3*.

This means that Lycos will give a higher score to documents that contain all three terms you entered. It also will show documents that contain any two terms or any single term, but the weighting will favor documents with all three terms.

❏ Double-click in **Max-hits** and type *25*.

❏ Click **Start search** and wait.

When I performed this search in April of 1996, Lycos reported "Found 37,660 documents matching at least one search term. Printing only the first 25 of 170 documents with at least scores of 0.010 and matching 3 search terms. Browse through the listing you received and see your results."

❏ Press **CTRL+END** to jump to the bottom of this lengthy page.

❏ Click the right mouse button and click **Back**.

You could click **back to the Lycos Home Page** but you didn't get here from the home page, so we only needed to go back one page. Note that you also could click on **Next 25 hits** to continue displaying more of the listings that matched all three terms.

❏ Try some searches on topics that interest you.

❏ Reset the **Min Terms** text entry box if necessary.

You can read more about using Lycos by clicking on some of the links on its home page. You can get details on the searching mechanism itself by clicking on **Search language help** on the search form page.

Yahoo!

Yahoo! is one of the earliest Web search engines (see Figure 5-5). Yahoo's primary search orientation is topic-based. Instead of looking for your information by a keyword search, you can scan broad categories to find things that catch your eye. Yahoo! also includes a keyword search, but it's so similar to Lycos that I'll just have you use its topic-based searches.

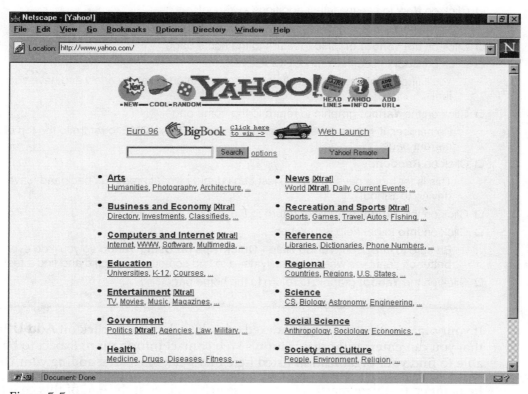

Figure 5-5

Hands On

Objective: **Learn to search the Web with Yahoo!**

❑ Press **CTRL+L**, type *www.yahoo.com*, and press **ENTER**.

This page offers more options than Lycos, but still includes a keyword search text entry box. You can click on **Options** to tailor your search more precisely. For now, though, we'll explore some of the other search methods that Yahoo! offers.

❑ Click on any major topic or subtopic and follow the thread.

For example, click on **Business and Economy**, then click on **Marketing**, then browse the list.

❑ Click on the **Yahoo!** graphic to return to the home page.

❑ Click on **Popular** to see the 50 most popular Yahoo sites.

Check out some of them if you want to.

❑ Click on the **Yahoo!** graphic to return to the home page.

❑ Click on **Headlines** to see news categories.

❑ Click on a news category to see related headlines. Check out some that interest you.

❑ Click on the **Yahoo!** graphic to return to the home page.

❑ Click on **New** to see the latest additions to Yahoo!

Note that Yahoo! is growing by hundreds of links per day.

❑ Click on the **Yahoo!** graphic to return to the home page.

❑ Click on **Cool** to see the Yahoo! COOL Links.

You'll find on this page a dazzling array of unrelated links. Try a few and have some fun!

❑ Click on the **Yahoo!** graphic to return to the home page.

Remember, if you can't see this graphic press **CTRL+HOME** to return to the top of the current page.

❑ Click on **Random**.

This is for those days when you just can't decide what to read. Sit back and leave the driving to Yahoo!

❑ Click on the **Yahoo!** graphic to return to the home page.

❑ Click on **Info** to get help with Yahoo.

Be sure to check out **Yahoo Help - Quick Tips on Using Yahoo** so you'll do even better on searches when you really need to find something specific and find it fast.

❑ Click on the **Yahoo!** graphic to return to the home page.

If your organization is not yet indexed on Yahoo, be sure to click on **Add URL** so that you can enter your organization's Web contact information. Expect to be able to find your organization listed here in a week or so after adding your URL.

Remember, there are many other good search engines at the end of this chapter in the Continuing Education section, as well as on the page we've been using for our Web exercises.

Marking your trails

With the power of such amazing search engines at your fingertips, it's easy to wander off into cyberspace and get yourself lost. You'll be jumping from one hypertext link to another, ever more deeply probing the depths of cyberspace, and then you'll decide you want to return to a screen you saw earlier. But you'll have no idea how to find it again because you never actually saw or typed the URL—it was just the result of choosing one of the dozens of hypertext jumps you've made. All you've got is a vague memory of how the screen looked, and now you want to see it again.

Fortunately, the Netscape folks experienced this lost feeling enough times that they created some tools that you can use to mark your trail through cyberspace. Let's see how Netscape can help you quickly return to screens you've seen before.

Back and forward

The simplest trail-marking features are Back and Forward. Netscape includes three methods to activate these two features, but I'll show you only two because one method uses the Toolbar buttons that I had you remove earlier—no need to waste screen space when you have these convenient alternatives.

Hands On

Objective: Activate the Back and Forward features.

❏ Click the right mouse button anywhere on the current Web page.
❏ Click **Back.**
❏ Click the right mouse button anywhere on the current Web page.
❏ Click **Forward**.
❏ Press **ALT+LEFT ARROW** three times.
❏ Press **ALT+RIGHT ARROW** three times.

View history

If the document to which you want to return is a long way back, these might become tedious navigation tools, although you can jump back very rapidly using the **ALT+LEFT ARROW** keystroke. Still, there are more direct routes back to pages you have previously viewed. Let's practice using them now.

Hands On

Objective: Use the Netscape History list to find previous pages.

❏ Press **CTRL+H** to view History.
❏ Use **UP ARROW** or **DOWN ARROW** to scroll to any document.
❏ Press **ENTER** to return to that document, then press **ESCAPE** to close History.
    Those steps used the keyboard; now let's try two different methods that use the mouse.
❏ Click **Go, View History . . .**

❏ Click on any other document, click **Go to**, then click **Close**.

❏ Click **Go** then click on the book's home page.

If you activated this menu with **ALT+G**, you might prefer to make your selection by pressing the underlined number of the document you want to see.

The **Location** text entry box in Netscape includes a history list. Use your mouse to click on the drop-arrow at the end of **Location** and then click on any link to which you want to return. With all of these techniques at your fingertips, you should never lose track of an interesting site or valuable information.

Netscape caching

When you use the commands you just learned, you might notice that the screens load more quickly than they did originally. That's because Netscape stores downloaded screens (called caching in computer talk) so that it doesn't have to download them from the Internet again if you decide to return. The larger the cache size, the more screens Netscape can hold and the faster your system will respond to Back and Forward. Netscape has two caches: one in RAM, and another on your hard drive or network that it uses once the RAM cache is full.

The default cache sizes that are set in Netscape are compromises to accommodate computers that have little free memory. Hard disk prices have dropped so dramatically that you might now have more free disk space *after* installing all of your applications than you used to have when your hard drive was empty. RAM memory remains relatively expensive, so it's not likely you have a lot of free RAM going to waste. You can increase both cache sizes to improve speed by following these steps:

Hands On

Objective: Increase Netscape's cache size.

❏ Click **Options, Network Preferences . . .**

❏ Click on the **Cache** tab (see Figure 5-6).

❏ Double-click in the **Memory Cache** text entry box.

If you've got 16 megabytes of RAM, you can try setting this to 4000 kilobytes (4 megabytes). If you run a lot of other applications at the same time, you might have to live with a smaller Netscape memory cache, perhaps 2 megabytes. Whatever your computer's memory cache, you'll have to balance this setting against other memory demands.

❏ Double-click in the **Disk Cache** text entry box.

❏ Type *32000* and click **OK**.

The version of Netscape used for this book accepted a maximum disk cache of 32 megabytes. You can try more on your system if you like—perhaps they've updated this feature—but when I set mine above 32000 kilobytes, Netscape changed the setting to zero (0). If you attempt to set your disk cache greater than 32000, be sure and return to see if Netscape accepted the higher setting.

❏ Click **Options, Save Options**.

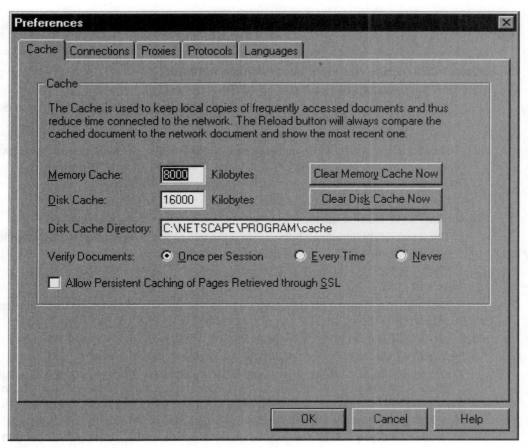

Figure 5-6

Switching applications

What if you need another application while you're surfing? Remember that Windows has multitasking ability. That means that it can perform more than one function at a time. Here are two techniques to keep in mind when you're surfing the Net.

You can switch to other open Windows applications by cycling through them with the **ALT+TAB** key or by clicking on the Taskbar to see your current applications. This is particularly valuable when you hit (during peak hours) a Web site that uses extensive graphics. You can **ALT+TAB** to another application and get a little work done while Netscape continues to download. For example, you could jump to Eudora and compose an e-mail message. It's not much, but at least you can save a little time instead of watching the hourglass.

Run multiple Netscape sessions

You can open multiple Netscape Windows, although this certainly is not a solution to long download times. But it does permit you to see two Web pages at once—or three Web pages, or more! When you create multiple Netscape sessions, each occurrence is a separate Windows task that will appear on the Taskbar and to which you can switch using **ALT+TAB**. Follow these steps to open an additional Netscape window (see Figure 5-7).

Hands On

Objective: **Learn to open multiple Netscape windows.**

❏ Click **File, New Web Browser** or press **CTRL+N**.

This opens a new Netscape window that loads your default home page. You might be able to see the first session in the background. You can navigate in either one now, setting them both to different URLs. If you can see both of them, you can use your mouse to switch back and forth. It's probably best , however, to run them both maximized, so let's do that now and learn how to switch between them when they're maximized.

❏ Double-click in the title bar of the new Netscape window.

Do this *only* if the current Netscape window is not already maximized.

❏ Activate the Taskbar to see both of them.

The icons will be identical, but you'll see the title of the current page in each session in square brackets after Netscape.

❏ Click on the first Netscape session you had open.

❏ Press **ALT+TAB** once to return to the new Netscape window.

Note that this menu also lists in square brackets the name of each window's current document.

❏ Press **ALT+TAB** once again to return to the first window.

❏ Press **ALT+TAB** once to return to the new Netscape window.

Of course, you don't have to run these windows maximized. You might want to use the Restore command (the middle icon in the upper-right corner) and then size them so that you can see both Web pages at the same time, perhaps to compare two Web sites.

❏ Click **File, Close** to close the new Web browser.

Notice that **Close** closes only the current window, and that you still could select **Exit** to quit Netscape, but when you open multiple windows, you use this command to close just this window. Closing one will not terminate your Internet connection, because you still have the first Netscape window open. Be sure you still have the glossary document loaded.

Use the Netscape Find command

Many of the hypertext Web pages that you'll view include jumps to bookmarks within the same document. You'll be able to tell if you've jumped to another spot within the same document because the URL will not change except for the very end, onto which will be appended a pound sign (#) and the bookmark name.

But you won't always find the information you want by using hypertext jumps. Sometimes you'll need to search the full text of the current Web document. Netscape has a Find feature that we'll practice now. For this exercise, let's say you want to look up the definition of the acronym ISDN.

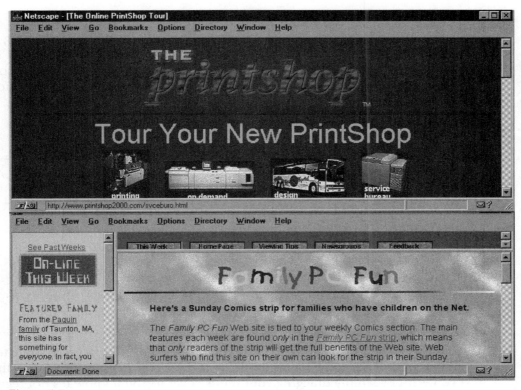

Figure 5-7

Hands On

Objective: **Learn to use the Netscape Find feature.**

❑ Press **CTRL+H** and go to the glossary.

❑ Press **CTRL+F** or click on **Edit, Find**.

❑ Type *ISDN* and press **ENTER** to jump to that phrase.

> This only finds text within this specific document. This is not searching the Web itself. It's not even searching other documents that are on the same Web site. This feature finds text only within your current Web document.

Using the information you find

Finding an important business lead, tip, or idea can bring value to your organization. Finding some research material you've been seeking can be a huge relief. Discovering exciting information on the Web that you never knew existed is exhilarating. But once you find something, you need to know how to transfer it into your system in a useful format. There are numerous options and you probably will use them all, depending on the information you've found and on how you plan to use it later.

Copying and pasting Web pages

Probably the quickest, simplest, and most overlooked option for transferring Web text is with the Windows clipboard and the Copy and Paste commands. If you can see the information, you usually can paste it into your word processor. After the transfer, you can reshape and reformat the text, embellish it with nice fonts, and print it as part of a larger document.

Hands On

Objective: Learn to transfer Web text into your word processor.

❑ Find your word processor icon and start the program.
❑ Use **ALT+TAB** to cycle back to Netscape.
❑ Drag your mouse to highlight the ISDN listing.
❑ Press **CTRL+C** to Copy it to the Windows clipboard.
❑ Use **ALT+TAB** to cycle to your word processor.
❑ Press **CTRL+V** to Paste the copied text into a blank document.
   You now could go back to Netscape and grab more text from my glossary or get more from any Web document in the world!

You won't be able to grab all of the text you read on the Web, because some text actually is part of a graphic image. In those cases, you won't be able to grab the text you want by simply dragging your mouse over it. You'll know it's not regular text because, as you drag your mouse, the text will not highlight.

 NET TIP Netscape has a command that will automatically select all of the text on a Web page. You can press **CTRL+A** or click **Edit, Select All**. Then use the normal Windows command to copy the selected text to the clipboard.

Printing in Netscape

If you only need to read the document and don't need to use it in your word processor, you can print the document directly in Netscape. This is a quick way to get a hard copy of Internet information, but it is, of course, completely inflexible; you can't reformat it.

When you print the document directly, you'll get all of the graphics as you see them on the screen. Netscape offers optional embellishments for printed Web pages that include headers and footers with name, date, and URL. I'll show you these printing setup options later.

Printing a Web document is perfect for information such as airline schedules and data tables, when all you need is a quick printout or when you need to see the graphics images as well as the text.

Hands On

Objective: Learn to print a Web document.

❑ Click **File, Print Preview** then use **Zoom In** and **Zoom Out**.
   Zoom in to better see the header and footer on each page. Use **Two Page** and **One Page** to change views and use **Next Page** and **Prev Page** to turn document pages. You can print from the preview screen by clicking on the **Print . . .** button, but instead let's return to the regular browsing screen and choose some page setup options.

▶ *The basics*

❏ Click **Close**.

❏ Click **File, Page Setup . . .** (see Figure 5-8).

The best settings for **Page Options**, at the top-left, will depend upon the printer you're using, so we'll let you experiment with those. The same applies to the **Margins** settings. Uncheck **Document Title** if you want to remove the title from the header of each page. Uncheck **Document Location (URL)** if you want to remove the URL from the header of each page.

❏ Click **Page Number, Page Total** and **Date Printed** as desired for the information you want included in the footer of each page.

❏ Click **File, Print . . .** then select options as desired.

❏ Click **OK** to print our URL Summary.

If you don't have a printer ready right now, you can click **Cancel** to end this exercise without printing.

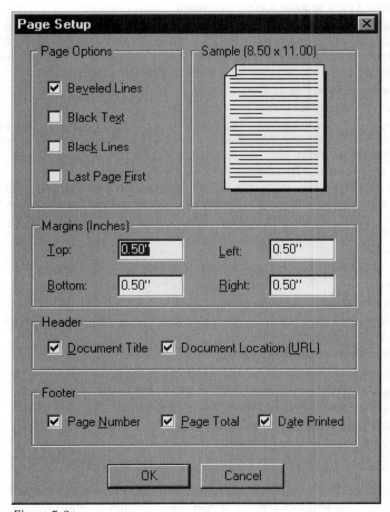

Figure 5-8

Saving Web documents

You can use Netscape to save a Web document, but if you're not careful the document will be saved with all of the hypertext markup language (HTML) codes. If that happens, you'll need to clean out the extraneous codes to get down to only the text you need. Check out the sidebar on how to get and use a WordPerfect for Windows macro that will strip a WordPerfect document of all HTML codes. Also, there is a Netscape option that cleans the HTML codes from the document as it saves.

Hands On

Objective: Learn to save a Web document.

❑ Click **File, Save as . . .** or press **CTRL+S**.

Netscape creates a name for you that's extracted from the title of the Web document, then it appends the extension htm, which is DOS syntax for hypertext markup language (HTML). You can, of course, change the name as desired.

❑ Click on the **Save File as Type** drop list.

❑ Change to **Plain Text (*.txt)** (see Figure 5-9).

You don't have to actually use the *txt* extension—the document will be saved as plain text even if you keep the *htm* extension as long as the file type has been set correctly with this drop list.

❑ Use the **Drives** and **Directories** windows to set the desired path.

If you're on a network, you can click the **Network** button to access your available network drives. Put this document in a directory that you commonly use for word processing because you'll open it later in this exercise. Please write down or remember the directory.

❑ Click **OK** to save the document.

❑ Use **ALT+TAB** to switch to your word processor.

If your word processor is not running, start it now.

❑ Click **File, Open . . .** or press **CTRL+O**.

Navigate to the saved Web document and double-click on it to open it and display the conversion dialog box.

WordPerfect for Windows only: (see Figure 5-10)

❑ Click the drop-list arrow to get a list of formats.

❑ Select **ANSI (Windows) Text CR/LF to SRt** and click **OK**.

❑ Click **File, Save** or press **CTRL+S** then click **OK**.

Microsoft Word for Windows:

❑ Click **File, Save** or press **CTRL+S**.

At this point, the document you had in Netscape now has been saved in the format of your word processor. If you didn't switch to plain text, you'll see a lot of HTML codes. You can use the macro to remove them (see next sidebar), or you can return to Netscape and save it again in the plain-text format.

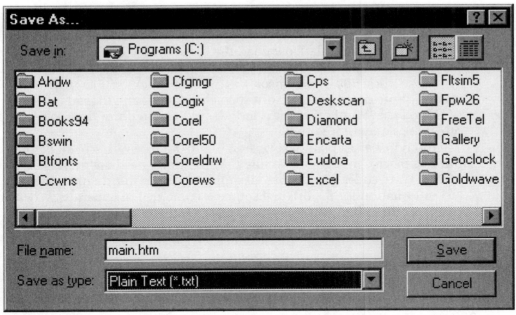

Figure 5-9

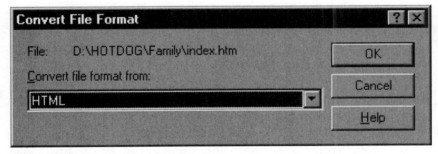

Figure 5-10

Cleaning HTML codes from saved Web documents

If you don't switch Netscape into the right saving mode, or if someone sends you an HTML document, cleaning out the HTML codes will be an agonizing task. But if you don't clean out the HTML codes, you won't have easy access to the plain text. So, to make your HTML documents more useful, I've written a macro for WordPerfect for Windows 6.0/6.1 that automates this tedious task and will clean an HTML document in seconds.

Of course, before you use such a document, consider carefully the document's copyright. Documents placed on the Web do not lose their copyright. Read Appendix A on copyrights if you aren't sure what rights you have to use this document. Your best bet, however, is to be up-front about using it and e-mail the copyright holder for reprint permission. People often are glad to grant permission, especially if you cite their URL in the document in which you use their text.

You can get my HTML cleaning macro (*htmclean.wcm*) by visiting this book's home page at *www.marketing-coach.com/mh-web* then jumping to the WordPerfect Macro link. Download the macro and copy it into your Word-Perfect default macro directory. (To find this directory, start WordPerfect for Windows, click **Edit, Preferences . . .** , double-click on **File**, then click on **Macros**. Write down the directory, then click **Cancel** and **Close**.)

If you use WordPerfect for Windows, you can perform this next exercise; otherwise skip past it for now.

You now have a plain-text version of the original Web screen. Before you run this macro, though, make sure that you don't need anything inside any of the HTML codes. Sometimes all of the copyright information or the contact information for the original source is contained in hypertext. When you clean out the codes, you will lose everything that's between a pair of angle-brackets (<sample HTML code>).

Hands On

Objective: **Run the WordPerfect for Windows Hyper-Clean macro.**

❑ Open a document that contains HTML codes.

❑ Press **ALT+F10**, type *htmclean*, and press **ENTER**.

   This will take from a few seconds to a minute or more, depending on the document's size. You can click on **Cancel** or press **ESC** to abort early.

❑ Click **File, Save** or press **CTRL+S**.

❑ Click **OK** to save the document in WordPerfect format.

Saving images

The last method you have for extracting Internet information into useable formats is to save graphics files. Netscape makes this very easy. All you have to do is click your right mouse button on any Web page graphic and choose the correct save option.

Hands On

Objective: **Learn to save a Web page graphic image.**

❑ Press **CTRL+H** and return to this book's home page.

   As a reminder, it's at *www.marketing-coach.com/mh-web*.

❑ Click the right mouse button over the cover image (see Figure 5-11).

❑ Click **Save this Image as . . .**

❑ Select a directory in which to save it.

❑ Click **OK**.

   The image has been saved in the Graphics Interchange Format (compressed graphic images). At the time this book was written, Microsoft Word could not handle GIF or JPEG files directly. Corel WordPerfect 7 will handle both file types for importing and exporting.

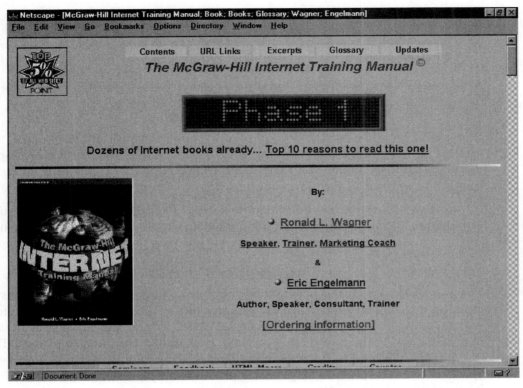

Figure 5-11

Right mouse button bonuses

If you used the right mouse button in the last exercise when you saved a graphic, then you might have noticed that the menu had several other shortcuts. I'll run through one of them with you now in case you missed them or didn't save a graphic. To see these commands actually function, you'll need a Web page that has a graphic image. Continue to use the book's home page.

Copy a link location

Netscape also uses the right mouse button to give you an easy method to copy the URL of a hypertext link into your Windows clipboard. You then might use **ALT+TAB** to cycle to your word processor or to your reserved URL storage file (see chapter 4, Windows Wide Open) and paste in the URL. As you've seen, some URLs are a real mess to retype, so this method might save you a lot of time, aggravation, and mistakes.

Hands On

Objective: **Save a link location to the Windows clipboard.**

Start with the McGraw-Hill glossary page.

❏ Place the mouse over the **Book Home** link, but don't click.

Read the link's URL on the status line at the bottom of the screen. You don't want to type that, do you? Remember, Web addresses are case-sensitive; you will have to get every character exactly right if you attempt to retype them.

❑ Click the right mouse button and click **Copy this Link Location**.
> The URL is now in the Windows clipboard. If you wanted to paste it into another Windows application you now would use **ALT+TAB** to switch applications, then press **CTRL+V** to paste it.

Bookmarks

Bookmarks are the next step beyond marking an electronic trail. Bookmarks create a permanent file that saves the URL of any Internet document and assigns it a plain-language name. You can pop up your bookmark list any time and quickly jump to all of your favorite sites.

I'll show you four different bookmark features: 1) adding bookmarks, 2) editing bookmarks, 3) modifying and arranging the bookmark list itself, and 4) turning the bookmark list into your own personal home page.

Adding bookmarks

There are two ways to add personal bookmarks in Netscape. The first is so easy you don't even need a hands-on exercise to learn it. Whenever you see a site for which you want easy access, simply press **CTRL+D** for the Add Bookmark command. Using the mouse, the steps are: click **Bookmarks, Add Bookmark**. The current URL is added to the bookmark list under the main folder unless you've specified another folder to be your default. I'll show you later how to move bookmarks to any category.

You also can add bookmarks directly to the list (see Figure 5-12). This has the advantage of enabling you to enter bookmarks for sites you've yet to visit or to add bookmarks to a selected category. Let's try it now.

Hands On

Objective: Add a bookmark directly to the listing.
❑ Press **CTRL+B** or click **Window, Bookmarks . . .**
❑ Click on the top folder on the list.
❑ Click **Item, Insert Folder . . .**
❑ Type *Practice* and click **OK**.
> This creates a new folder under the main folder.
❑ Click on the folder Practice.
❑ Click **Item, Insert Bookmark . . .**
❑ Type *Internet Glossary* and press **TAB** to jump to **Location (URL)**.
❑ Type *http://www.marketing-coach.com/mh-guide/glossary.htm* and click **OK**.
❑ Click on the folder Practice.
❑ Click **Item, Insert Bookmark . . .**
❑ Type *Lycos* and press **TAB** to jump to **Location (URL)**.
❑ Type *http://www.lycos.com* and click **OK**.
❑ Click **Item, Insert Bookmark . . .**
❑ Type *Yellow Pages* and press **TAB** to jump to **Location (URL)**.
❑ Type *http://www.yellow.com* and click **OK**.
❑ Click on the top folder on the list.
❑ Click **Item, Insert Folder . . .**
❑ Type *Internet Resources* and click **OK**.
> This creates another new folder.

▶ *The basics*

❏ Click on the top folder on the list.
❏ Click **Item, Insert Header . . .**
❏ Type *Directories* and click **OK**.
> You can continue the lesson now by adding folders for your own categories. Here are a few more suggested headings that you could create now:

❏ Search Resources
❏ Reference Resources
❏ Corporations
❏ Universities
❏ Miscellaneous

Now that you've set up all of these folders, I'll give you two exercises that will let you check out your bookmarks and sort your bookmarks for quicker reference.

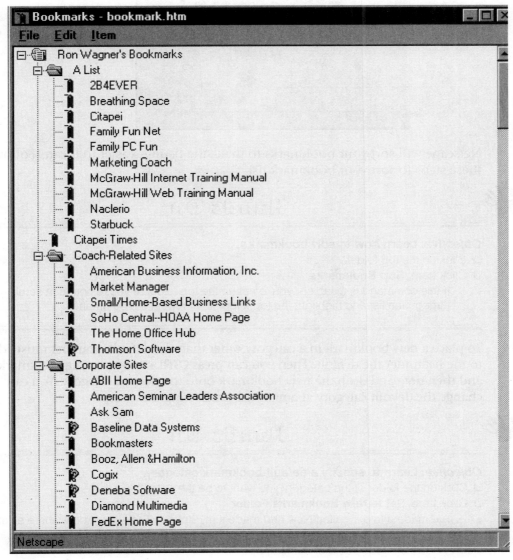

Figure 5-12

Hands On

Objective: Check bookmark URLs.

❏ Click **Bookmarks, Go to Bookmarks**.

❏ Click **File, What's New?** (see Figure 5-13)

❏ Click **Start Checking** to have Netscape verify your bookmarks.

> If you only want to check out some of your bookmarks, select the ones you want to check before starting the check. To do that, hold down either **CTRL** key as you click so you can select multiple links.

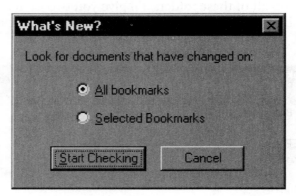

Figure 5-13

Netscape will sort your bookmarks to make the listings easier to locate. Follow these steps to sort your bookmark list.

Hands On

Objective: Learn how to sort bookmarks.

❏ Click on the top folder.

❏ Click **Item, Sort Bookmarks**.

> If this command is disabled, you're not on the top folder. If you're not, then scroll through the list and highlight the top folder, then repeat the command.

To place a new bookmark in a category other than the default, you first must add it to the list under the default. Then you can press **CTRL+B** to open the bookmark list and then drag and drop the new bookmark onto the desired category. You can change the default category at any time by following these steps.

Hands On

Objective: Learn to specify a default bookmark category.

❏ Click on the folder of the category you want to be the default.

❏ Click **Item, Set to New Bookmarks Folder**.

> I've made a folder called New and made it my default. That way I know where all of my new bookmarks are so I can easily move them later to their proper folder.

❏ Press **ALT+F4** to return to Netscape.

> From now on, all of the bookmarks you add with **CTRL+D** will go to this category.

The basics

Editing existing bookmarks

Sometimes a URL for which you've created a bookmark will change, or you'll get some new information about a bookmark site that you'd like to add to the description. Netscape makes bookmark editing a snap.

There's a bonus associated with this procedure. When editing a bookmark, you also will see the date it was added and the last date it was visited. Sometimes, therefore, you might want to start this process just to see that information even if you do not need to edit the link information.

Hands On

Objective: Learn to edit a bookmark.

❏ Click on any existing bookmark.

❏ Click the right mouse button, click **Properties**.

❏ Make any necessary changes, then click **OK**.

❏ Note the two dates near the bottom of the dialog box.

Modifying bookmarks

The order of the folders and the document references under each folder can be rearranged at any time simply by dragging any entry either to a new folder or to a new location under the same folder.

Hands On

Objective: Modify the bookmark listing.

❏ Drag and drop Internet Glossary onto the Internet Resources folder.

❏ Click on Internet Resources.

❏ Click **Item, Insert Bookmark**.

❏ Type *Yahoo*, then press **TAB**.

❏ Type *http://www.yahoo.com*, then press **ENTER**.

❏ Drag and drop Yellow Pages onto the Directories folder.

❏ Click on the folder Practice and delete it by pressing **DELETE** or by clicking on **Edit, Delete**.

    Now that you've rearranged everything, let's sort your bookmarks.

❏ Click on the top folder.

❏ Click **Item, Sort Bookmarks**.

❏ Click the exit button or press **ALT+F4** to exit the Netscape bookmarks window.

There are several ways to use your bookmark list to surf the Internet. Here's a summary:

◉ Press **CTRL+B** and double-click the item on the list.

◉ Click **Bookmarks, Go to Bookmarks . . .** and double-click the item on the list.

- Click **Bookmarks** and click on the drop-down menu or submenu of bookmarks.
- Press **ALT+B**, then use **DOWN ARROW** to highlight the link you want, then press **ENTER**.

Selecting the menu folder

While you were editing your bookmarks, you might have found a feature that lets you control which folder Netscape uses to build the drop-down menu mentioned in the last bullet above. I'll give you a Hands-On exercise that will illustrate how to use this feature.

Hands On

Objective: Learn to set the drop-menu folder.

❏ Press **ALT+B** and stop.

   This keystroke has activated the bookmarks drop-menu. Note that, by default, this menu begins with your main folder. The only folders you see here are the ones directly off this main folder. If an entry here has links under it, you'll see a triangle next to its name and you can see the links by highlighting their parent folder. Let's do that.

❏ Press **DOWN ARROW** until you highlight Internet Resources.

   You now can see the links under this folder.

❏ Press **G** to **Go to Bookmarks**.

❏ Click on the Internet Resources folder.

❏ Click **Item, Set to Bookmark Menu Folder**.

❏ Press **ALT+F4** to close the bookmark window.

❏ Press **ALT+B** to see the bookmark drop-menu.

   Now the only items you see on this menu are the ones under the Internet Resources folder. This feature might not make a lot of sense right now, with so few links and folders, but when you've got hundreds of links you might want to change the menu folder for a while to more easily activate links in a focused category. But you eventually will want to restore your main folder as the menu folder. Let's do that now to finish this exercise.

❏ Press **G** to **Go to Bookmarks**.

❏ Click on the main folder at the top of the list.

❏ Click **Item, Set to Bookmark Menu Folder**.

❏ Press **ALT+F4** to close the bookmark window.

❏ Press **ALT+B** to see the bookmark drop-menu.

   Note that right now, the first two items on this list are the only ones that have underlined letters. That means that you can activate these items with keystrokes. You could press **A** for **Add Bookmark** or **G** for **Go to Bookmarks**. Now I'll show you how to set up your own underlined letters so you can activate your actual links with keystrokes.

❏ Press **G** for **Go to Bookmarks**.

   Stop here and go on to the next exercise.

Setting up ALT letters

We'll use the opened bookmark window now to edit your bookmarks so that you'll be able to activate some of them with keystrokes. You most likely will have far more bookmarks than just the 26 letters of the alphabet, but you can single out your most frequently used bookmarks.

Hands On

Objective: Learn to set ALT letters on your bookmark menu.

❑ Click on Internet Resources.

❑ Click the right mouse button, click **Properties**.

❑ Press **HOME** to move to the beginning of the entry.

❑ Type & and press **ENTER**.

> When you place an ampersand in front of a letter on a link's name, that letter will be underlined on the bookmark menu. You do not have to use the first letter. Let's continue.

❑ Click on Internet Glossary.

❑ Click the right mouse button, click **Properties**.

❑ Press **CTRL+LEFT ARROW** to move to the beginning of Glossary.

❑ Type & and press **ENTER**.

❑ Click on Yahoo.

❑ Click the right mouse button, click **Properties**.

❑ Press **HOME** to move to the beginning of the entry.

❑ Type & and press **ENTER**.

❑ Press **ALT+F4** to close the bookmark window.

❑ Press **ALT+B** to activate the bookmark menu.

❑ Press **ALT+I** to activate Internet Resources.

❑ Press **ALT+G** to go to Internet Glossary.

Saving your bookmarks

Your bookmark file might become one of your most valuable business assets. It might contain links to crucial business partners from around the world. Netscape keeps this valuable resource in its program directory. Many people do not regularly run a backup of their program directories. If your Netscape program directory isn't backed up frequently, then you could lose valuable contacts.

Periodically copy your bookmark file to a floppy or to a directory on your PC or your network that is included in regular backup sessions. Don't trust this to chance—your Netscape bookmark file might be one of your most treasured business resources. Protect your bookmark file.

Bookmark summary

Bookmarks are an important feature of Netscape, because they will speed your work by enabling you to save any URL you find on the Internet. Please note that the bookmarks are not limited to saving URLs of Web documents. You can use a bookmark to save the URL of anything on the Internet: FTP sites, Gopher sites, and newsgroups. You even can create links to local HTML documents on your organization's own network server and create an Intranet effect even if your organization doesn't have an Intranet.

HYPERJUMP

Intranet
An internal Web that runs on your organization's own network. The documents on an Intranet usually are kept private and are not accessible on the World Wide Web, although they could be. An Intranet is a powerful productivity-enhancing tool that is sweeping through organizations of all sizes. In fact, I've written an entire book on Intranets, *Implementing and Managing Intranets* (McGraw-Hill 1996).

Creating your own home page

When you start Netscape, it automatically loads your default home page. Your home page can be any site on the Internet or any hypertext document on your own system, even if you are using a stand-alone PC.

If you haven't modified Netscape since you installed it, you probably have their Web page set to be your home page. They're nice folks and they have a good Web site, but you can turn your bookmark file into a tailored home page that can boost your productivity.

Hands On

Objective: **Turn the bookmark file into your home page.**

❏ Click **Options, Preferences . . .**
❏ Click on the **Styles** tab.
❏ Click **Start With:, Home Page Location:**
❏ Click in the text entry box immediately below this button.
❏ Type *file:///bookmark.htm* and click **OK**.

   Note there are *three* slashes after the colon (see Figure 5-14).

   Now every time you start Netscape it will load your bookmark list in hypertext. The folders will show up as bolded headings and each entry will show up as a hypertext jump. If you place your mouse—without clicking it—over a highlighted jump, you can read the URL in the status bar at the bottom of the screen. Any descriptions you manually entered on your bookmark list will show up as regular text under its associated hypertext jump entry.

The McGraw-Hill WWW Training Guide home page

Now that you know how to change Netscape's default home page, you might have better ideas than using your bookmark file as I showed you in the last exercise. For example, you might find a really terrific hypertext document somewhere that contains a treasure trove of fabulous Web sites. Wouldn't that be nice? I thought so; that's why I've created a URL Summary document.

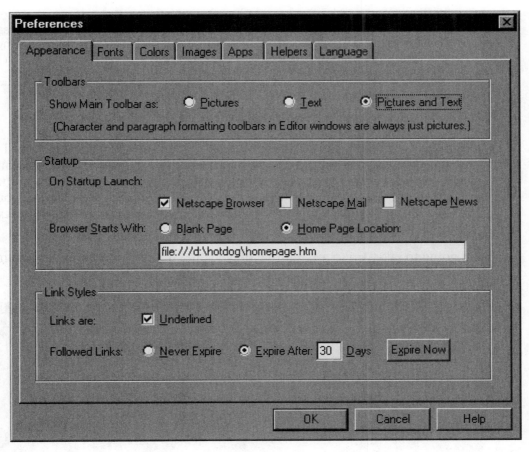

Figure 5-14

Hands On

Objective: **Use my URL Summary as your default home page.**

❑ Press **CTRL+H** for History.

❑ Go to the book's home page.

❑ Click on **URL Summary**.

    Wait for the page to load fully; it's fairly large.

❑ Click **File, Save As . . .** or press **CTRL+S** for the save dialog box.

❑ Change to your Netscape directory.

❑ Click **OK** to save *mh_links.htm*.

❑ Click **Options, Preferences . . .**

❑ Click on the **Styles** tab.

❑ Click **Start With:, Home Page Location:**

❑ Click in the text entry box immediately below this button.

❑ Type *file:///mh_links.htm* and click **OK**.

    Now every time you start Netscape it will load *The McGraw-Hill World Wide Web Training Guide* URL Summary as your home page.

You later might modify this file to add your own links and remove some that you don't find useful, or you can return regularly to the book's Web site and download and save updated versions. Feel free to copy and distribute this list to anyone—you have my permission, provided you leave the title and copyright information intact.

Advanced Netscape features

Now that I've covered the technical aspects of using Netscape to navigate us around in cyberspace, you've seen all the basic Internet tools that you'll need. I've postponed any discussion of using Java and Netscape Plug-Ins until the advanced chapter, which follows this one. You don't need to use Plug-Ins. You always have the option of bypassing the feature. But there is one advanced feature that you might encounter without having the option to circumvent it: Netscape frames (see Figure 5-15).

I'm going to take you to an example of Netscape frames and demonstrate some of the quirks. Follow this Hands-On exercise.

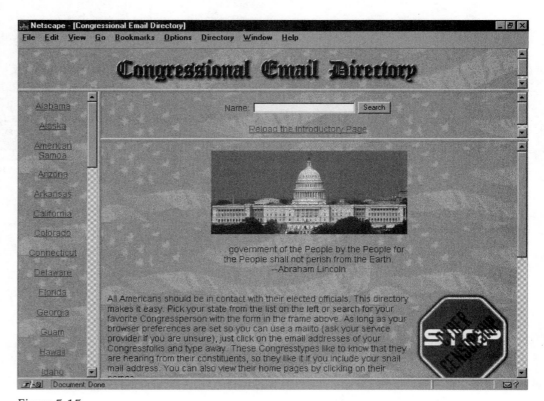

Figure 5-15

 ## Hands On

***Objective:* Learn how to use Netscape frames.**

❏ Press **CTRL+L** for location.

❏ Type *http://www.webslingerz.com/~jhoffman/congress-email.html* and press **ENTER**.

▶ *The basics*

Here's the Congressional E-Mail site that's referenced in the chapter on government sites.

❑ Click on your state's link in the left frame.

You've now jumped to the listed site.

❑ Click the right mouse button in your state's frame.

❑ Click **Back in Frame.**

❑ Place mouse over your state link again, but don't click.

❑ Click the right mouse button while over this link.

❑ Click **New Window with this Link**.

This opens the same site, but in its own Netscape window. You now have two Netscape sessions running simultaneously. You could use this one as long as you'd like to thoroughly check out this site, but let's get back to learning about frames.

❑ Press **ALT+TAB** to cycle back to the frames session.

Note, as you do this, that there are two Netscape icons on the panel.

❑ Press **ALT+TAB** to return to the new session.

❑ Press **CTRL+W** or click **File, Close** to close this session.

You're now back in the frames session. You need to learn how to navigate sites if you want to work in one of the frames windows. One of the keystrokes you normally use will not work in frames as you might expect.

❑ Press **ALT+LEFT ARROW** to go Back.

You might have expected that the frame would go back to this site's original frame, but instead Netscape went back to the previous document. Continue on now to learn how to go back and forth within a frame.

❑ Press **ALT+RIGHT ARROW** to return to the frames site.

❑ Click again on your state's link in the left frame.

❑ Click the right mouse button in your state's frame.

❑ Click **Back in Frame**.

❑ Click the right mouse button in the left frame.

❑ Click **Forward in Frame**.

Check out the listings under Continuing Education for more frames-based sites. That's the end of the exercises for this chapter, so let's close Netscape for now.

❑ Press **ALT+F4** or click **File, Exit**.

If your main interest is basic Web surfing, then you're ready to begin using Netscape now. You can launch yourself straight into cyberspace in Phase 2 and save the next chapter for later.

If you want to use Netscape's advanced features, then don't miss the next chapter. It's optional, but it covers these valuable topics:

⦿ Internet e-mail using Netscape
⦿ Mailing lists using Netscape
⦿ Newsgroups using Netscape
⦿ Advanced Netscape applications

Continuing Education

WWW FAQ

http://www.boutell.com/faq

With so much cyberspace to surf, where do you start? Start here. This on-line Frequently Asked Questions site is an excellent site for new Web users. Most of the other sites listed here are information-searching resources, so you might want to try this site first to get a better overview of what's out there waiting for you in cyberspace.

Truly awesome Web stuff

http://www.clark.net/pub/journalism/awesome.html

The URL listed above is not the same as the URL listed in the Hands-On exercise earlier in this chapter. This is a generic address that gets you into the site. From this URL you'll branch off depending on whether you're using Netscape or Internet Explorer.

"The glory and the grandeur of the Internet all on one site" is their claim to fame. They've got the Truly Awesome list (last count: 30 sites) and the merely Awesome list (last count: 101 sites). Be sure and check out the latest update at this address. From here, you can spend your entire life surfing the Web—of course you still will be farther behind that you are today, but at least you will have a fun trip.

Point Communications Top 5

http://www.pointcom.com

These folks scour the Web searching for the most valuable sites. They award their logo badge to the winners, then list them by category so you can find the best sites quickly and easily. In addition to listing top Web sites, they have Internet news, general news, hot topics, and even politics. Be sure to put this site on your bookmark and check it often to help you stay abreast of the latest Web developments.

All-In-One Internet search

http://www.albany.net/allinone

Awesome! That word applies to this site as well. It's the most comprehensive research tool on the Internet today—of course, by the time you read this, who knows! It's a compilation of various forms-based search tools found on the Internet that have been combined to form a consistent interface and create a convenient all-in-one search engine. If you can't find it through this site, it isn't worth finding.

Open Text Web index

http://www.opentext.com

An excellent search site that provides both simple and compound search strings (see Figure 5-16). Click on Open Text Web Index to get to their Simple search engine. This site also enables you to search the Web in several languages besides

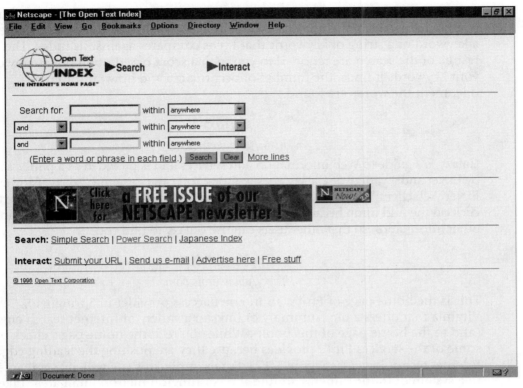

Figure 5-16

English: Deutsche, Francais, Italiano, Nihongo. Check the options you want, enter a keyword or phrase, and click on **Search**. You also can select more detailed searches using the optional hypertext links to **Power Search** and **Weighted Search**. Like other search engines, Open Text is growing rapidly. They index tens of thousands of Web pages per day.

Yahoo directory

http://www.yahoo.com

This is a staple Web search engine. It's got just about everything you could want. The search mode is based upon your browsing through hypertext-linked tables of contents to find topics that appear to match your area of interest. It's getting plenty of competition now, but it was among the pioneers and deserves a look simply because of the huge number of people who learned from the early work that Yahoo did.

Lycos

http://www.lycos.com

This Internet search tool was created by Carnegie-Mellon University in Pittsburgh, and is one of the most popular sites on the Internet. It's based upon a vast index of keywords that it has pulled from HTTP, Gopher, and FTP files all over the Internet. At the beginning of July, 1996, Lycos had indexed 47.8 million documents. Go see how many pages it's indexed today.

The Lycos index searches document title, headings, links, and keywords to build a reference against which you can search the Internet. You find topics by entering a keyword or a string of keywords that Lycos compares against its index. The results of the search are reported to you with a score based upon how many of your keywords it finds, the number of occurrences and how far into the document the words are found.

Galaxy

http://www.einet.net

Galaxy is a guide to Web information and services and is provided as a public service by EINet and a variety of Galaxy guest editors. You can cruise the Galaxy using either EINet Web client: WinWeb for Windows or MacWeb for the Macintosh. Be sure to click on the Add jump because it will let you enter your own home page URL and other information so that other users can use Galaxy to find you.

Erol's hot list

http://www.erols.com

This is the home page of Erol's, an Internet access provider in Springfield, Virginia that offers a nice summary of links to a variety of Internet search engines (and to the home page of this book). While you're at the home page, check out some of the services Erol's provides because they are pushing the leading edge of Internet technology (see Figure 5-17). For example, this site will give you access to a system of traffic cameras around the Washington metropolitan area. Take a look and see what you're missing—the traffic here is so much fun!

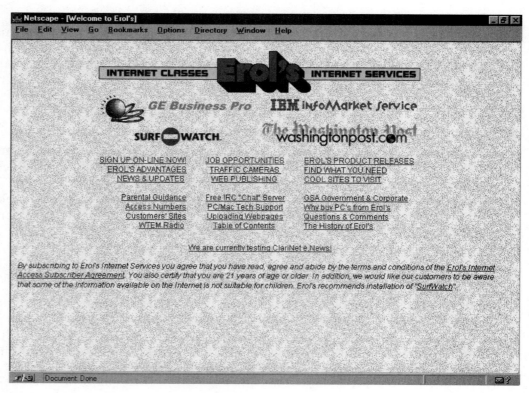

Figure 5-17

Whole Internet catalog

http://gnn.com/gnn/GNNhome.html

Here's a rich source of additional Web material. Click on The Whole Internet Catalog link on their graphic. You also will discover Virtual Places and tips on building your own Web pages.

UIUC weather world

http://www.atmos.uiuc.edu/wxworld/html/top.html

Here's a top candidate for your bookmark list. It's the Web version of the popular University of Illinois Weather Machine Gopher service. Here you'll find a comprehensive collection of current weather information. The main menu presents a convenient one-page summary with links to popular, weather-related items. Everything else is on lower-level menus.

Once you've found the URLs to specific city information, you can put those direct links on your bookmarks. For example, I'm living in the Northern Virginia region of the Washington, DC metro area, but Tulsa, Oklahoma is my hometown. I still feel connected because my bookmark menu has links to all kinds of Tulsa weather information as well as to local weather.

InfoSeek

http://www.infoseek.com

InfoSeek is a newer full text search service that makes finding information easy. It has a user-friendly interface (see Figure 5-18) that enables you to search Web pages, Usenet News, more than 50 computer magazines, newspaper newswires and press releases, company profiles, medical and health information, movie reviews, technical support databases, and much more. *Internet* magazine called InfoSeek the best search tool on the Internet. It functions much like Lycos. This is a commercial service, but the costs are reasonable. Check out their Web page for current pricing structure.

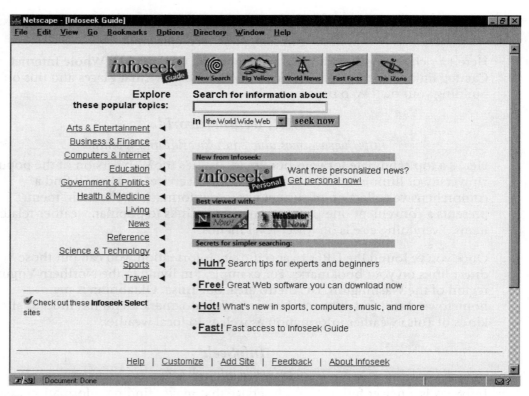

Figure 5-18

Advanced Netscape

THIS CHAPTER has three separate phases that will cover advanced Netscape features: Netscape mail, Netscape newsgroups, and Netscape Plug-Ins. The Netscape mail application might provide all the e-mail power you need. The Netscape newsgroup reader simplifies and streamlines your access to the Usenet by integrating the function into the Web browser. Netscape Plug-Ins will enable your copy of Netscape to bring you live-action Web pages and interactive Web sites.

Today, most Internet users have a stand-alone application to handle their e-mail. Netscape, however, is trying hard to give you one-stop-shopping. It includes both a good e-mail application and a good newsgroup reader. Neither are the most powerful available, but they both can serve the needs of many users. And they have the advantage of being included at no extra cost and they don't require any additional disk space or installation. If those advantages appeal to you, then complete this Hands-On chapter to learn how to make Netscape handle almost all of your cyberspace tasks.

E-mail

E-mail is the most commonly used aspect of the Internet and its usage is growing daily. You'll find a confusing array of e-mail applications on the market, but I suggest you evaluate all of them based on *your needs* rather than based on *advertising hype*. To simplify your selection, I'll narrow down the list of possibilities to three options and point out the pros and cons of each:

- Microsoft Exchange
- Eudora Pro
- Netscape Mail

Microsoft Exchange

Microsoft Exchange has two main advantages: It's free with Windows 95, and it integrates smoothly with Windows 95. It also permits you to use different font faces, sizes, and colors, and to include advanced text formatting; however, only other Microsoft Exchange users will see those special effects, because other e-mail applications will ignore the formatting information.

The first release of Exchange did not even provide for using an automatic signature file—a glaring omission that says Microsoft is not yet serious about having this application be used as a professional e-mail tool. Count on improvements in future releases, but until then this is the least useful e-mail option of the three.

Eudora Pro

As of the spring of 1996, Eudora Pro by Qualcomm is the best Internet e-mail application available. Eudora Pro can easily fulfill all of your Internet communication needs, because it's rich with advanced features and it will fully support the most demanding professional user. For example, Eudora Pro can filter your incoming messages according to rules you specify, and then transfer them to designated folders. Both Microsoft Exchange and Netscape Mail permit you to drag-and-drop messages into different folders, but neither has Eudora Pro's rules-based automatic sorting that can eliminate the need to drag-and-drop.

The only disadvantage with Eudora Pro is that it's not free, though it is reasonably priced. You can download a shareware version of Eudora, but its features are limited; you might as well stick with Netscape mail. Eudora Pro, however, is worth the investment to any user who plans to conduct extensive business communication via e-mail. Eudora's advanced features can be a boon to your business that easily justify its added cost.

More on Eudora Pro

I'm not covering Eudora Pro in this book, but you can find Hands-On Eudora Pro lessons in another book I authored: *The McGraw-Hill Internet Training Manual* (*www.marketing-coach.com/mh-guide*). This book dedicates an entire chapter to Eudora Pro and will teach you how to set up Eudora's advanced features, such as filters and multiple signature files. Here's a quick summary of Eudora's advantages over Netscape 2.0 Mail:

- Eudora Pro's support for LAN connectivity makes it scalable from individual users to corporate networks.
- Eudora Pro supports the three major industry standard attachment formats, a necessity for cross-platform communications.
- Eudora Pro provides support for a wide variety of platforms, allowing Eudora Pro to exist in heterogeneous platforms and to bridge the gap between all PC computing environments.
- Netscape's message management functionality is also minimal; there is no filtering or ability to save a message to a text file. The Netscape product is an add-on to the WWW browser, designed for browser users with casual e-mail needs.

You can purchase Eudora Pro at its retail price directly from its manufacturer, Qualcomm, by calling them at 800-2-EUDORA, or by e-mailing them at *quest-rep@qualcomm.com*. If you call, however, even they will suggest that you buy Eudora Pro at a local store because the store can offer a large price discount—Qualcomm doesn't want you to pay retail.

> You can subscribe to Qualcomm's newsletter to stay abreast of the latest changes to Eudora Pro. Send an e-mail message to *majordomo@qualcomm .com*, leave the subject line blank, and enter only the text *subscribe quest_news* in the body.
>
> They also have an unmoderated newsgroup that discusses Eudora as well as general tips and ideas on using Internet e-mail. Send an e-mail message to *majordomo@qualcomm.com*, leave the subject line blank, and enter only the text *windows-eudora-forum* in the body.

Why you might not need another mail package

Positioned between Microsoft Exchange and Eudora Pro is the Netscape e-mail application. It's free; it includes a signature file and enough features to satisfy most basic e-mail needs. Aggressive power-users, however, will want Eudora Pro until Netscape makes some serious upgrades.

Netscape mail has the unique advantage of seamless integration with the Netscape Web browser. This integration means that while you're surfing the Net, you can check your e-mail by clicking on an icon (see Figure 6-1). Netscape mail, therefore, is an excellent choice for many users.

Netscape mail has another edge on its competition because, if you send HTML documents to your recipients, they will see the pages in Netscape's familiar graphical format. So let's learn how to use the free e-mail application that's included with your Netscape Web browser.

Figure 6-1

Setting up Netscape e-mail

Another Netscape advantage over stand-alone mail applications is that you might already have done some of the setup work when you first installed Netscape. Those tasks won't be duplicated, and the parameters you need to change will use a familiar set of dialog boxes.

The next Hands-On exercise will guide you through Netscape mail setup. Before you begin, be sure you have on hand all the necessary technical mail information. Check with your network administrator or with your Internet service provider if you don't already have the information. This is the hardest part, but it actually is quite simple if you have the required information.

Hands On

Objective: Learn to set up Netscape mail.

❑ Start Netscape.
❑ Click **Options, Mail and News Preferences . . .**
❑ Click on the **Servers** tab (see Figure 6-2).
❑ Click in **Outgoing Mail (SMTP) Server**.
❑ Enter your SMTP Mail Server information.
   Part of this will contain your domain name. For example, mail.yourdomain.com is typical.

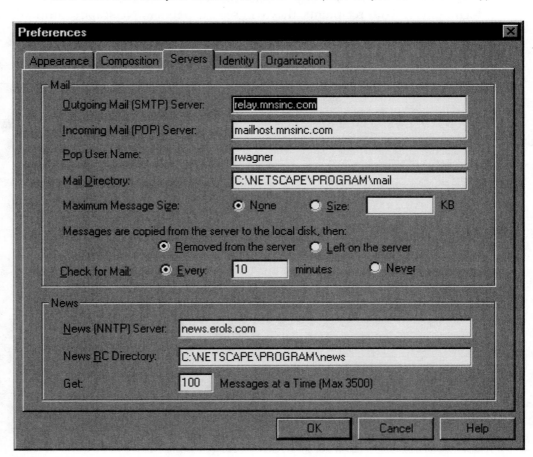

Figure 6-2

❑ Click in **Incoming Mail (POP) Server**.

❑ Enter your POP Mail Server name.

❑ Click in **POP User Name**.

❑ Enter your basic e-mail name.

> This will be the part of your e-mail address that precedes the @ symbol.

❑ Click in **Mail Directory**.

❑ Enter the drive and path for your mail folders.

> Be sure that you select a drive and path that gets backed-up regularly. Your e-mail folders might soon contain some of your most important business information and contacts. Most users leave this under their default Netscape directory and forget to ever back up the files. That could be a costly oversight.

❑ Check None after **Maximum Message Size**.

> Don't specify a maximum message size unless you know of some limitation that will prevent you from receiving large messages.

❑ Click on **Removed from the server**.

> This will delete your e-mail messages from your mail server after they are downloaded. Don't select the option to leave them on your mail server without checking your mail administrator's opinion.

❑ Click on a **Check for Mail** option.

> If you check **Never**, then you will have to check manually for e-mail. Checking **Every** and specifying a time will alert Netscape to automatically check mail for you while you're browsing.

❑ Click on the **Appearance** tab.

❑ Check a **When sending and receiving electronic mail** option.

> If you're using Windows 95, you can tell Netscape to use the Exchange client for your mail and news. If you select the Exchange option, then you won't need to complete any of the Hands-On exercises after we've finished this setup exercise. The default is to let Netscape handle your mail and news.

❑ Select the remaining appearance options as desired.

❑ Click the **Composition** tab.

❑ Check the **MIME Compliant** option.

> If your recipients get scrambled messages, then come back here and check the 8-bit option. These days, however, you can pretty much count on people having MIME-compliant e-mail.

❑ Select an option for your outgoing messages.

> You can set your software to log outgoing e-mail messages on disk. Most people will store them on disk. You should use the same directory here that you specified earlier for your mail files.

❑ Check **Automatically quote original message when replying**.

> This will include the entire original message in your reply messages. It will place a bracket symbol (>) in front of each of the original lines. This is a valuable option, because it will greatly speed the accuracy and increase the recipients' degree of understanding of your replies.

❑ Click the **Identity** tab.

❑ Click in **Your Name** and enter your real name.

❑ Click in **Your Email** and enter your e-mail address.

❑ Click in **Reply-to-Address.**

> Enter either the same e-mail address you entered in the box above or another e-mail address, if desired.

❑ Click in **Your Organization**.

> This is optional. Enter the real name of your organization.

❑ Click in **Signature File** (see Figure 6-3).

Enter a path and filename for your signature file. For example, your path might be *C:\NETSCAPE*. For the file name, use *MAIL-SIG.TXT*. We'll use this name when we create your signature file after we complete this setup exercise.

❑ Click **OK**.
❑ Click **Options, Save Options**.

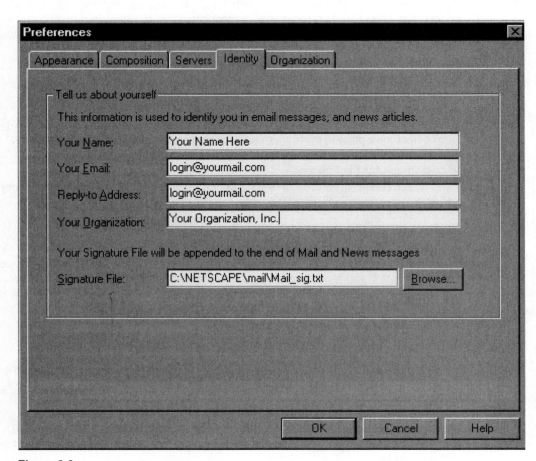

Figure 6-3

Creating your signature file

Now that you've specified a signature file in the setup phase, you need to create the file you told Netscape to use. I've included a sample that will help you design your own (see Figure 6-4). It's just a simple text file, so we'll create it using the Windows 95 Notepad. Follow these Hands-On steps.

Hands On

Objective: **Learn how to create a Netscape mail signature file.**

❑ Activate the **Start** button.
❑ Click **Programs, Accessories, Notepad**.

▶   *The basics*

❏ Create your signature.

> Be kind to your readers. Remember that everyone to whom you send e-mail will see these lines at the end of *every* one of your messages. Keep your signature file short.

❏ Press **ALT+F4** or click **File, Exit**.

❏ Press **ENTER** or click **Yes** to save the file.

❏ Select the directory you specified in setup.

❏ Enter the filename *mail-sig.txt* and press **ENTER** or click **OK**.

Eudora Pro lets you save two different signature files. Then on each message you can select either signature or None. Netscape mail simply uses this one signature file on every outgoing message.

Figure 6-4

E-mail messages

The next set of Hands-On exercises will show you how to create and send e-mail messages using Netscape mail. It covers the basics that you'll need to send inquiries to Web sites when you need to ask them for more information. More detailed help on Netscape e-mail is available from the Netscape home page.

Creating new e-mail messages

Now that you've completed the Netscape mail setup, sending e-mail messages is a simple procedure. Netscape stores the messages you send in a folder called "Sent." I'll cover Netscape mail folder management at the end of this e-mail lesson. Before you learn to use Netscape mail, you will want to setup the Netscape address book and enter some frequently used e-mail addresses, so let's begin there (see Figure 6-5).

Figure 6-5

Hands On

Objective: **Learn to use the Netscape address book.**
- ❏ Click **Window, Address book**.
- ❏ Click **Item, Add User**.
- ❏ Enter a Nickname using *lowercase* text only.
- ❏ Click in **Name** or press **TAB**.
- ❏ Enter the person's real name.
  Use the form of Lastname, First name.
- ❏ Click in **E-Mail Address** or press **TAB**.
- ❏ Enter the person's e-mail address.
- ❏ Click in **Description** or press **TAB**.
  This is a good place for other contact information such as phone number, fax number, company and snail mail address.
- ❏ Click **OK**.

Be sure to back up the directory in which your addresses are stored—this file could contain some crucial business information. If necessary, use the **File, Save As** command to copy the *address.htm* file to a directory that gets backed up.

Mailing documents

There are several ways that you can start an e-mail message within Netscape. From within Netscape, you can press **CTRL+M** or you can open the Netscape Mail window and click on the **To: Mail** button. Also, you often will see a link on a Web page that lets you send a message by clicking. When you click, you will get the same e-mail window that you'll use in the next exercise.

Hands On

Objective: **Learn to send a message with Netscape mail.**
- ❏ Click **File, New Mail Message** or press **CTRL+M**.
- ❏ Enter an e-mail address (use your own for practice).
  Or, click on the **Mail To** button to go to the Netscape address book. Highlight the recipient's name, click **To**, then click **OK**. The e-mail address information is entered for you.
- ❏ Click in **Subject** or press **TAB** twice.
- ❏ Enter text for a subject.
- ❏ Click in the message window or press **TAB**.
- ❏ Type your message.
- ❏ Click on the **Send** button, or click **File, Send Now** or press **CTRL+ENTER** to send the message.
  The message, the recipient, and the date and time will be saved in the Sent folder in your Netscape Mail window. You should be back in Netscape now, so let's verify that information.
- ❏ Click **Window, Netscape Mail**.
- ❏ Click on the **Sent** folder under the **Mail Folder** column on the left.
  By default, your messages will be arranged by date in descending order. The next few steps will show you how to change the sort order, which will be very helpful when

you've accumulated a long list of sent messages. Because you've only sent one message so far, these steps won't do much, but you'll learn the principle.

❑ Click **View, Sort**, then choose a sort option.

❑ Click **View, Sort, Ascending** to reverse the current sort option.

❑ To view your message, click on it in the right window.

By default, you will see a shortened form of the message header. This option gives you plenty of information for most messages. If you experience difficulty with a message, you might want to see more of its header information. The next step will change the header display option to help you troubleshoot.

❑ Click **Options, Show All Headers**.

The other menu items are optional in most cases, so you now have all the basics for sending e-mail messages. You can read the Netscape help for information on the more advanced features.

Attaching files

Often you'll want to send a file along with your e-mail message. You can send *any type* of file. That includes word processing documents, spreadsheets, graphics, programs, software drivers, and databases. Netscape will send files such as these without altering even a single byte. The recipient will get exactly the same file you have on your system and, if your recipients have the necessary application, they will be able to see files as you do on your system. The file attachment feature is a fabulous tool for long-distance collaboration.

Hands On

***Objective:* Learn to attach a file to an e-mail message.**

❑ Click **To: Mail** or press **CTRL+M** to start a new message now.

❑ Enter yourself as the recipient.

❑ Enter *Test Attachment 1* as the subject.

❑ Enter *Hands-On attachment test* in the message window.

❑ Click **Attachment**, then click **Attach File**.

Use the "Enter file to attach" dialog box to navigate to your Netscape bookmark file, but you should be in that directory now. If it's not, then you'll find it in your Netscape directory. It's named *bookmark.htm*.

❑ Highlight to file to send.

❑ Click **Open**, click **OK**.

The selected file is now attached to this message and will ride along with it across cyberspace. You can repeat the steps above and attach a list of files to one message.

❑ Click **Send** to send the message and the attachment.

You can attach large files to a message, but generally you can expect a limit on message size of two megabytes. This limitation varies and some systems have a much lower tolerance of large e-mail messages. Check with your mail administrator to find out any limitations that your system might impose.

Managing Netscape mail folders

Netscape lets you create a list of folders so that you can organize your messages, both incoming and outgoing. Once you've created the folders you need, you can drag-and-drop messages between folders.

This next exercise assumes you still have open your Netscape mail window that we used earlier. Here's our last Netscape e-mail exercise.

Hands On

Objective: **Learn to manage Netscape mail folders.**

❏ Click **File, New Folder.**

It doesn't matter where your cursor is located before you click on this command.

❏ Type *Personal* then click **OK** or press **ENTER.**

❏ Click **File, New Folder.**

❏ Type *Testing*, then click **OK** or press **ENTER.**

Now that you've got the hang of it, let's learn how to delete any folder you no longer need.

❏ Click on **Testing.**

Keep the mouse inside the left window.

❏ Click the right mouse button, click **Delete Folder.**

You cannot delete a folder that contains messages.

Newsgroups

Newsgroups on the Internet are experiencing an unprecedented explosion in growth. All newsgroups collectively are called the Usenet. Though you'll use Netscape to access Usenet newsgroups, that's about all that they have in common.

Newsgroups are electronic community bulletin boards that serve as info central for targeted topics. Messages are posted in the open and anyone who looks at the newsgroup will see all the messages that have been posted by all of the group's users. Your Internet service provider includes a news server that actually holds messages from all the newsgroups that they receive. Your provider might offer fewer than half the total number of public newsgroups.

How many newsgroups are there?

How many can you stand?

As I researched this book, I found there were more than 15,000 public newsgroups. But only a few months earlier I reported 11,000 in another Internet book. Today? Well, there's no way to tell. And that's just the public newsgroups—it literally would be impossible to count the private newsgroups because they can't be seen by outsiders.

Your Internet service might not make available all newsgroups. For example, I found one Internet service provider that offered 5450 newsgroups.

Another service provider might offer more or fewer newsgroups. My provider offers them all—a total of 15,600. Check with your Internet service provider (ISP) to find out how many newsgroups are available to your basic account and ask if you will get more by paying a premium above your basic fee.

Your ISP must pay a fee to provide some newsgroups so they might need to cover their increased costs by charging you a premium to receive these newsgroups. For example, the ClariNet news service charges your ISP one dollar a month for each Internet account. This is a bargain, but in the highly competitive world of Internet services, some providers cut costs by cutting out such premium services because few customers ask any more than how much per month when shopping for services.

So, if newsgroups are important to your work, be sure and ask about newsgroups when you shop for an ISP. You will need a service that can use a Network News Transfer Protocol (NNTP) server. If your organization is large, it might have an internal NNTP server—so check with your system administrator to discover if you can use your internal system to read newsgroups.

Because there are so many thousands of them, the Netscape newsreader enables you to select—from the master list of all the groups it finds on your news server—only the newsgroups you choose to see. This process is called subscribing, although your system maintains full access even to the newsgroups to which you are not subscribed. Subscribing and unsubscribing to newsgroups uses an internal process that is handled by Netscape.

At any time that you decide to see an additional group, you can subscribe and instantly see the group's postings. Similarly, if you unsubscribe to a group, your software merely stops displaying the postings, yet it remains available for resubscription. If you learn of a newsgroup that is not available to you, contact your Internet service provider and request that they add it. Subscribing simply means that Netscape automatically checks that group for new messages when you start its news reader. I'll cover subscribing later, because I'm first going to show you how to read newsgroup messages.

Reading

Before you can read newsgroups, you'll have to download the list of newsgroups that your news server provides. I'll give you a Hands-On exercise that will download the list and then another that helps you learn about reading the messages.

You'll find three windows in the Netscape news module. The first window lists the newsgroup names. If you've never opened your Netscape news reader, this list will be very short and only will contain the names of the lists that Netscape provides as a default. Don't worry; soon you'll have more than you could ever use.

To the right of the list window is a window that lists the headers of the messages within the newsgroup that's highlighted. The bottom window shows the text of each individual message after you've clicked on its header.

Popular Usenet newsgroups

Further complicating the newsgroup counting game: a lot of newsgroups that show up in the list in the left window are empty. During a trial run, while randomly browsing newsgroups to which I've never subscribed, about one newsgroup in three was empty. Nonetheless, there are thousands of active newsgroups. Here's a list of a few of the major categories:

TABLE 6-1. Usenet newsgroup categories

Category	Topics
alt	Alternative topics, many of which are just plain fun, so be ready for anything you can imagine, a lot that you never have and don't take anything you read here seriously. I'll use this in the Hands-On exercises.
bionet	Professional biologists.
biz	Business discussions, advertisements and postings of new products and services.
clari	ClariNet news services (requires a premium fee, though it may already be a part of your basic package).
comp	Computer-related topics.
k12	Kindergarten through 12th-grade teachers.
misc	Miscellaneous topics, but none as far out as alt.
news	The Usenet is so big it actually has its own group for news about itself.
rec	Recreational topics, you won't believe what some people consider to be recreation—here's something for everyone.
relcom	The former Soviet Union.
sci	Science topics.
soc	Social topics with an international flavor as well as covering religions.
talk	Not enough talk radio stations for you? At least you can get through to this one.

Some of these categories have thousands of subtopics. This is just a gentle orientation; the real thing is practically brutal. Read chapter 2, "Breathing Space for Cyberspace," before you get too deeply into newsgroups.

Each original article is listed against the left side of the right window (see Figure 6-6). Indented articles that appear under an article are related articles that are replies to the original. If someone replies to a reply, that article will be shown indented yet another level, etc. This hierarchical listing system creates a *thread*—sort of a focused, ongoing conversation. Threads help you easily track a focused conversation as if you were eavesdropping on it.

The first Hands-On newsgroups exercise will download the list of newsgroups that are on your news server. You should have the Netscape news reader open from the earlier exercises. If not, open it now.

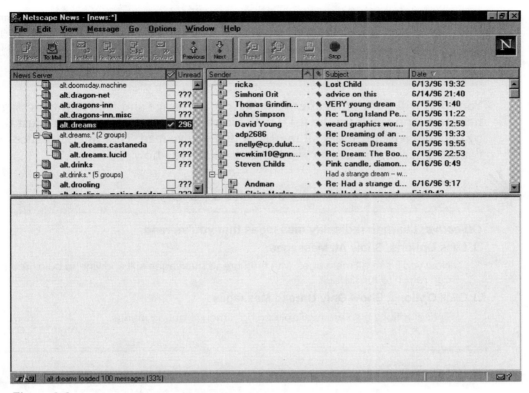

Figure 6-6

Hands On

Objective: **Learn to browse your newsgroups list.**

☐ Click on the **News** folder in the left window.

You'll see two folders in this window. One is **News** and the other represents your news server **(default news host)**.

☐ Click the right mouse button, click **Show All Newsgroups**.

The first time you do this might take several minutes. Netscape will alert you to wait while it downloads the newsgroups it finds on your default news server. Watch the progress bar in the lower-right part of the screen. The list you see will vary according to your news server.

☐ Click on **alt.***

Listings that end with an asterisk indicate that you are seeing a hierarchical header that leads to other topics beneath that level. Clicking on a topic will expand the listing to increasingly specific topic levels. Again, watch the progress bar because some headers, such as **alt.***, have a lot of subtopics and require some patience.

☐ Scroll down to **alt.quotations** and click on it.

The folder's message headers will be displayed in the right window. The number after the checkbox shows how many unread messages are in that newsgroup.

☐ Click on a message header in the right window.

The posted message will be displayed in the lower window.

☐ Touch the mouse arrow to the horizontal separator bar.

Drag the bar up or down to change the amount of the screen devoted to groups and headers or to the messages. You also can drag the vertical bar to change spacing between the windows. And you can complete your screen customization by adjusting the width of each of the header tags at the top of each window.

You soon will notice that after you click on a message and read it, the message's header disappears from the list. Don't worry, the message isn't lost, it's just that by default Netscape hides all messages that you've read. That often is a nice feature, but sometimes you want to go back. Here's how.

Hands On

Objective: **Learn to redisplay messages that you've read.**

❏ Click **Options, Show All Messages**.

Now you'll see all messages with the unread messages still showing in bold. You easily can return to the default.

❏ Click **Options, Show Only Unread Messages**.

These options also are available on right mouse button menus.

Start your own Usenet newsgroup

news.announce.newsgroups

Can't find a newsgroup for your favorite topic? Are you kidding? Well, if not, this newsgroup is for you! It contains posts of announcements of either the creation of new newsgroups or the consideration of proposed newsgroups. Newsgroups are created after a successful call for votes (CFV), which begins with a posting to this newsgroup. Also, calls for discussions, vote results, and creation notices of all hierarchies should be posted here as well. Post submissions for a CFV to *announce-newsgroups@uunet.uu.net*. Follow-ups will be redirected to *news.groups*.

Post only *after* reading about the process by checking out

- How to Create a New Usenet Newsgroup, found in *news.admin.misc, news.announce.newsgroups, news.announce.newusers, news.answers*, or in *news.groups*.
- Usenet Newsgroup Creation Companion, found in *news.announce.newusers, news.answers*, or *news.groups*.
- So You Want to Create an Alt Newsgroup? found in *alt.config, alt.answers*, or *news.answers*.

What if they reject me, but I don't want to give up?

There is a service that will bring you newsgroups that were deemed unnecessary or of too little use to store on corporate news servers. How many? Well, for $5 per month you can get 13,000 rejects. For details, e-mail to *ccaputo@alt.net*. Perhaps this service will bring you alternatives for creating your own newsgroup if the normal channels don't work.

You still will need to keep your main news service, but you can add this one—Netscape automatically handles multiple news servers if you use them.

Subscribing and unsubscribing

Because the list of newsgroups that you downloaded is ridiculously long, you'll appreciate the subscribe feature because it will limit your view to only those newsgroups you choose. It's a simple process, and you'll learn it in the next Hands-On exercise.

Hands On

Objective: Learn to subscribe or unsubscribe to newsgroups.

❏ Highlight the newsgroups to which you want to subscribe.

❏ Click the checkbox after the name.

> A checkmark will appear in the box when you've subscribed to its group. Browse through the list and check more groups. Be sure to check at least one that you don't want to keep so that later I can show you how to unsubscribe.

❏ Scroll to the **News** folder and open it if it's closed.

> This folder shows all of your subscribed newsgroups and their number of unread messages. The next time you return to Netscape newsgroups, you easily will be able to find new messages posted to the groups that interest you without being swamped under thousands of headings in the main newsgroup window.

❏ Click on any group to see its message headers.

❏ Click on a message to read it.

> Sometimes, after seeing a few day's worth of messages within a group, you'll decide to unsubscribe. Let's learn how to do that.

❏ Click on a subscribed newsgroup you wish to unsubscribe.

❏ Click the right mouse button.

❏ Click **Unsubscribe**.

> Of course, this newsgroup is still available to you at any time, and you can go to it manually by scrolling through your list of downloaded groups. Or you can directly add it back to the list by clicking the right mouse button on your subscribed newsgroups folder.

Replying

Often, reading an article will prompt you to make some snappy reply. Don't worry; everyone else gets the same urge when they read newsgroups. No one knows for sure exactly why this happens but that natural human urge to have the last word seems to be a fact of life and certainly is the foundation for the Usenet. There are two ways to reply:

◉ Post a follow-up article in the same newsgroup so that everyone in the world can see it. Of course, that's only if everyone in the world browses through this newsgroup, but it's there for anyone who wants it. Hint: be careful what you post!

◉ Mail a reply directly to the author of the article you're reading and keep it between the two of you. This is a good choice either when you have a narrowly focused reply that would not interest general readers in the group or when you prefer to keep the reply private—well, as private as e-mail can be, anyway.

NET TIP You can view detailed information about any message by highlighting the message and then clicking **View, Document Source**. This will move the message into a viewer window. In the setup, you can specify that you want Netscape to use the Windows Notepad as a viewer. If you do, then this function gives you a quick way to edit, copy, and save any newsgroup message.

The next exercise will show you both of the ways that you can reply to a newsgroup article. You should have an article on-screen from the last exercise. From there, we'll go to the reply function.

Hands On

Objective: Learn how to reply to newsgroup articles.

❑ Click on **Message, Post Reply** or click **Re: News** (see Figure 6-7).

The original message text will be included by default, but this is optional. It is, however, a good idea that will help other readers follow the thread. Please, though, **do not** use the entire text of the article. Generally, you can cut out most of it, leaving enough that your reply will make sense to other readers. Often, you can break up the article into chunks and insert immediately after each piece a reply that is tailored to that section of the original. Be sure to remove the original poster's signature file—we've all read enough of those without seeing them repeated.

If you need help on how to edit text in Windows, please be sure and complete the lessons in chapter 4, Windows Wide Open.

❑ Type your reply.

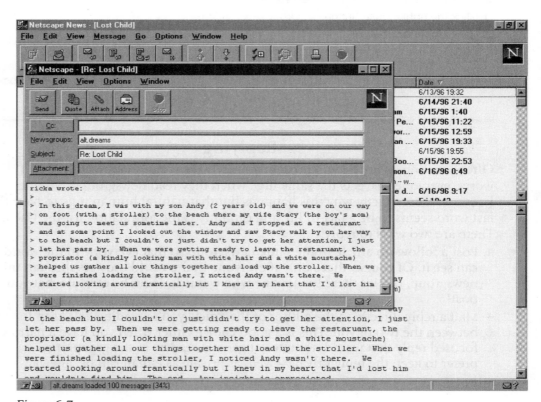

Figure 6-7

▶ *The basics*

❏ Click **Send** to actually post the article to this newsgroup or click **Cancel, OK** to return to the reader.

This posts a public message to the entire newsgroup. You can follow the next few steps to learn how to post a reply directly to the original poster so that no one else in the group will see your reply.

❏ Click **Message, Mail Reply** or click **Re: Mail**.

Often, this is the best reply method, but unfortunately, most people clog up the entire newsgroup with replies that would best have been sent directly.

❏ Type your reply.

❏ Click **Send** to mail the article to original poster or click **Cancel, OK** to return to the reader.

This posts a private message only to the original poster. Another option is to send a double reply, one to the group and one privately. Let's try that next.

❏ Click **Message, Post and Mail Reply** or click **Re: Both**.

❏ Type your reply.

❏ Click **Send** to actually post the article or click **Cancel, OK** to return to the reader.

This posts a private message to the original poster as well as a public message to the entire newsgroup. This might seem redundant, but keep in mind that the original poster might not check back into the group for days and might miss your reply message. A companion e-mail message directly to him or her will increase the chance that the original poster will read your reply.

Posting original Usenet newsgroup articles

Sometimes you'll have an original idea for a newsgroup. Or, perhaps, you might have a question that you believe someone in the group might be able to answer. In either case, you'll want to create and post an original article for the newsgroup. It's basically the same as posting a follow-up, with one major exception that we'll mention twice: the subject line will be blank unless you fill it in manually!

Hands On

Objective: **Learn how to post an original newsgroup article.**

❏ Click **File, New News Message** or click **To: News** to create an original message (see Figure 6-8).

❏ Type *your own subject*.

❏ Press **TAB** to move the insertion point into the message body.

❏ Type the body of your message.

This editing window is rudimentary, so you might prefer to use **ALT+TAB** to jump to your word processor, write the article there using the spell checker and thesaurus, use the Windows Copy command (**CTRL+C**), use **ALT+TAB** to return to Netscape and use the Windows Paste (**CTRL+V**) command.

❏ Click **Send** to actually post the article to this newsgroup or click **Cancel, OK** to return to the reader.

❏ Click **File, Exit** to close Netscape.

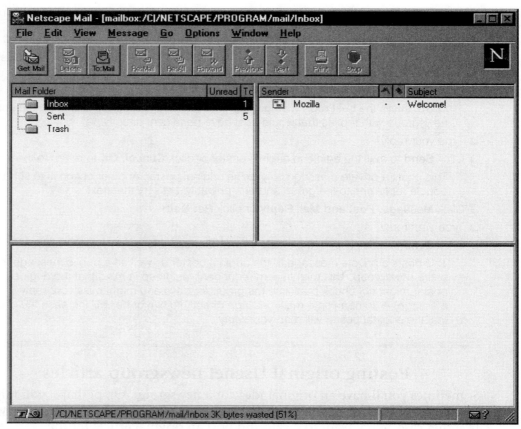

Figure 6-8

Nine keys to newsgroup netiquette

There's much more to newsgroups than knowing the technical steps that you've seen so far. When you use the newsgroups on the Usenet, you're jumping into a global realm that literally can reach anyone in the world. They are powerful communication tools that deserve a lot of respect, courtesy, discretion, and common sense. These nine keys will help you to improve our global cyberspace community and to boost their potential value to you and your organization.

1. Get the FAQs

Almost every newsgroup has a FAQ (Frequently Asked Questions) file. Look for it or ask for it. Most questions you'll ask as a newbie to a group already will have been asked repeatedly. The established users of the newsgroup are sick of browsing through posts that ask the same old questions. Get the FAQ and *read* the FAQ before you ask the group a dumb newbie question.

2. Lurk around first

Newsgroups can get quite personal and develop a timbre of their own. Each is slightly different. Until you've sampled that timbre, you don't know what might be considered offensive, rude or stupid. The proper term for sampling a newsgroup is lurking. You know the kind of people who don't lurk: the same ones who butt into your verbal conversations. If you post to a newsgroup where you've never lurked, don't be surprised if you quickly are flamed.

3. Remember the global community

Lurking will help you abide by this principle. Newsgroups likely will have members from all over the world. Keep this in mind when you post. For example, if you live in the United States don't refer to your country as America. Having done consulting and training work all over the world, we've seen how that reference is considered by people in other Americas to be inconsiderate. Also, ethnic and regional jokes will at best fall flat, could be misunderstood, and easily might offend thousands of your fellow Interneters.

4. Forgive and forget

If you read something annoying, offensive, misplaced, misguided, or just plain stupid, probably your best course of action is to forget it and move on. The Internet already has speed problems that are exacerbated by electronic tennis matches of flames and counter-flames. Every group seems to have one or two real idiots who seem to have never heard of netiquette and you'll come to know them quickly, so don't worry about the occasional accidental offender. Save your flames for the really bad guys. Or, consider e-mailing a chronic repeater's ISP— you might get his account canceled, which flaming will never do.

5. Follow the threads

Most interesting newsgroup posts evoke replies. Most up-to-date software links these posts together into threads that follow the same theme. Read the entire thread before posting a reply yourself. Several others might already have said the same thing. No one will appreciate reading your belated opinion. Reading the whole thread is somewhat of a corollary to the last key—forgive and forget. If a post really has you steamed, you can count on it annoying others as well and they probably already have done plenty of flaming for you.

6. Short and sweet

Remember an ancient adage on writing that says "I'm sorry this is so long . . . I didn't have time to make it short." You've got two ways to keep your posts short.

First, just keep them short. This truly does take longer than simply spewing forth every word on a topic that comes to mind. But the time you spend will be multiplied many times over by happy newsgroup members who in appreciation actually might read your post and actually might respond.

Second, don't make them long. This, too, can take more time than making them short. You soon will get sick of wading through replies in newsgroups in which the respondent copied the entire text from the original post, which you just read. (These people often tack on only the brilliant reply "I agree.") People can follow threads; you need not copy any more of a post than a brief contextual reminder. Sure, it takes time to delete chunks of a post that don't need to be repeated, but the time you spend will be rewarded.

7. Put it where it belongs

Stick to the subject. Usually you can tell by the title, but make sure you're in the right place by lurking and reading the FAQs file. Post only when you're certain you're writing to the right audience. Posting to the wrong newsgroup wastes a lot of resources. If you accidentally post to the wrong group, just forget about it. If you see an accidental post, ignore it. One of the most annoying events in newsgroups often begins when someone accidentally posts to the wrong group, then six people post to say how stupid this person is, then the person posts again to say to ignore the first post, which draws several more flames about brain size and family lineage, to which the original poster apologizes, then the apology draws a string of posts commenting on what a stupid waste of resources this whole event has been. Twenty messages can cascade out of a single errant post. Post correctly and remember to forgive and forget when others slip—hopefully, they'll do the same for you.

8. Remember you're invisible

No one can see you smile on the Internet. No one can hear you chuckle, either. If you joke, don't assume that everyone understands you're joking. Remember the global community. Jokes or twisted humor on newsgroups rarely come across as funny. If you must make a crack about something, at least use one of the emoticons we've listed in chapter 4, Netiquette, so that everyone will know that you *meant* it to be a joke. They still might not get the joke, but perhaps they won't get riled.

9. Use e-mail when appropriate

Newsgroups are an excellent place to get answers to tricky or obscure questions. If you've read the FAQs file, lurked in the background for a while, and followed all the threads, but still have a question—that's the time to post. But if the answer is not going to be of general use to the group, ask for replies by e-mail and make sure your e-mail address is included in your signature file at the end of your post. (It's supposed to be in the header, but a backup is a good idea.) Conversely, if you want to send a personal reply to a posted question, then use e-mail and spare everyone in the group the clutter of unnecessary messages.

Infomagnets

New newsgroups are appearing on the Usenet rapidly and existing groups are garnering new members faster than ever. One drawback to the newsgroup phenomenon, however, is that the wealth of information they offer can seem to be more of a burden than a blessing. With so many public newsgroups, you can't even read the subject lines for each day's new messages. And if you ever skipped a day's reading, you'd never catch up. You need a computerized news magnet to filter through the newsgroups and bring you the news you can use.

Generically, these computerized new magnets are called *infomagnets* because they can extract valuable needles from all the haystacks that choke most of the Usenet. There are two types:

- You can subscribe to a tailored news service that will send you articles after it finds the ones you want.
- You can write a program that scans the Usenet and pulls in the articles you specify.

I'll cover both methods. Let's begin by looking at one popular tailored news service as an example.

ClariNet news services

ClariNet e.News is an electronic newspaper that delivers professional news and information directly to your computer. It sends live news (including technology-related wire stories), timely computer industry news, syndicated columns and features, financial information, stock quotes and more.

You can receive, upon request, a free sample of selected articles that are posted to the Usenet newsgroup *biz.clarinet.sample*. If you want more information, contact ClariNet for a targeted sample of the news topics you want to track (see Figure 6-9). If that isn't enough, they will give you a free, two-week trial of the e.News with no obligation.

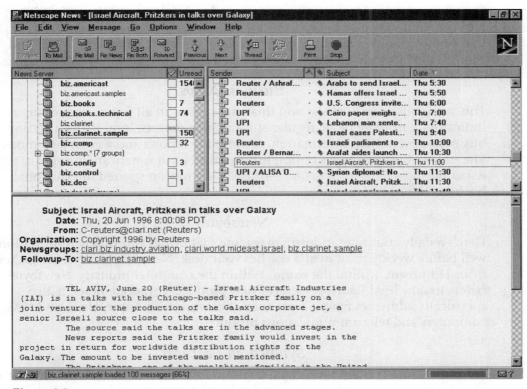

Figure 6-9

With the e.News, you can put the Internet to work for you to receive the news that directly impacts your life and your business. This is one answer to the Over-Information Age that can increase your Breathing Space, as I discussed in chapter 2. e.News combines the in-depth coverage of print media with the speed of broadcast media to give you the best of both worlds. Many U.S. media limit their international coverage for reasons of space and time, but e.News doesn't suffer from either of those limitations.

How e.News works

Many on-line services store the news on a computer at their site, but the e.News sends selected articles directly to you. When you want to read the news, it's available instantly because you won't have to wait while it's transferred via a modem—and you'll never again pay per-minute connect charges while you scan headlines trying to find news you need. Instead, everyone in your organization can read targeted e.News, anytime, for a fixed monthly fee—there are no per-user charges.

The e.News is delivered as a Usenet-style newsfeed. So, any standard Usenet reading capabilities will work and if your organization doesn't receive Usenet-style news, ClariNet will help you get connected for free, including free software. Hard disk space might become an issue, however, because a full e.News feed collects daily approximately four megabytes of data. Of course a carefully targeted feed will consume disk space at a slower rate. Let's look at the targeted e.News topics from which you can select.

Techwire

Specific categories for stories on science and technology and the industries around them: computers, electronics, health issues, space, aerospace, telecommunications, defense, biotechnology, research, education, AIDS, and more. It also includes a daily price report of computer industry stocks.

Business News

This service delivers business and financial stories on all topics: economic indicators, corporate news, regular stock market reports, legal issues affecting business, government information, commodity reports and a great deal more. The e.News Business News option features the North American, European, and Asian Business Reports of Reuters—the world's most respected international business information source.

Newsbytes

Here's a daily computer industry magazine that brings you timely information well before weekly print media reaches your desk. Newsbytes stories are gathered from 11 bureaus around the world. Within the computer industry, Newsbytes covers trends, legal issues, reviews of new products corporate news. It also specifically addresses news on products that work with Apple, Unix, and IBM computers and telecommunications products.

Syndicated Features

This service delivers top syndicated columns and features, such as etiquette from Miss Manners and movie reviews and cultural commentary from Joe Bob Briggs.

The Annals of Improbable Research

The e.News isn't entirely serious or stuffy. You can receive this journal of scientific funnies that includes Bizarro, an off-beat look at the world and Views of the World, which presents a series of daily editorial cartoons from newspapers around the globe.

Matrix News

Delivers a newsletter about cross-networking that covers the connections between all the computer networks worldwide that exchange electronic mail. Naturally that includes the Internet, but also covers UUCP-Net, BITNET, FidoNet and conferencing systems such as the Well and CompuServe.

Global and National News

This is a major news source that includes global and national news, sports, and features from the wire services of Reuters and The Associated Press (AP). It covers

U.S. and international news events, as well as regular coverage of sports (with detailed statistics).

As you'd expect from any newspaper, this service includes many standing features including editorials; columns on politics, entertainment and consumer products; reviews of books, movies, and videos; a daily almanac; and a daily news summary.

And something you can't get in a regular print newspaper: every two hours the e.News releases updated summaries of current events.

NewsClip news filtering language

Here's the second type of infomagnet. As mentioned earlier, this type enables you to filter your own information from newsgroups. ClariNet has developed a programming language that includes a high level of filtering control over Usenet newsgroup information and automatically sends you the filtered information. Earlier filtering programs only gave users control over the newsgroups they received and offered a kill feature that eliminated unwanted articles. For example, systems less sophisticated than NewsClip will let you kill articles that are posted by a user who consistently posts nothing but annoying trash. NewsClip, by contrast, puts at your disposal all the tools of a powerful programming language. NewsClip goes well beyond creating a kill file by giving you the ability to make positive selection choices as well as negative elimination choices.

Your only news-filtering limitations will be self-imposed and determined by how much time you decided to invest in writing the program. If you have a large organization, your organization almost certainly will enjoy a productivity payoff if someone invests in the programming time to write a targeted filtering system to get the news that you and your coworkers need.

NewsClip programs are compiled, so they not only filter newsgroups exactly the way you specify, but they work quickly. Your compiled NewsClip programs will accept, reject, or rate articles based on programming expressions that describe what you want to receive and what you don't want to see at all.

In chapter 2, Breathing Space for Cyberspace, I wrote about the use of kill files. Just a reminder here because you might want to reread that portion of chapter 2.

How you can use NewsClip

Compiled NewsClip programs can work interactively with you as you read articles in real time, usually with no noticeable delay. As you browse through your chosen newsgroups, you will see only the articles that you've specified.

The program can be run in the background while you perform other tasks or it can be run after business hours to filter your chosen newsgroups. To do this, you'll need a newsreader that maintains a newsrc (news subscription) file that contains a list of the newsgroups to which you subscribe. In unattended mode, your filter program will read your newsrc file, scan all unread articles and mark as already read any articles that fit your elimination criteria. Thus, you never will see those articles. Here's a list of usage examples:

- Screen out messages posted by a particular user, a group of users or even all users from a designated site. You even can screen out follow-up messages posted to articles by the users you've specified.

- Receive messages that contain specified keywords or that exclude specified keywords. For example, if you were a die-hard fan of the game of dominoes, you might select all articles that include the word domino but that exclude the word pizza.

- You'll see thousands of follow-up articles that copy the entire original message—perhaps duplicating thousands of words you already have read—and then close with I agree! You never will waste time on this kind of poor netiquette if you say to eliminate articles in which the amount of copied text greatly exceeds the amount of new text.

- Filter out all articles except for originals (so that your default is to not see any follow-up articles), and then have the program include follow-ups to articles as you specify.

- Specify priority handling of follow-ups to articles you have posted—or to articles posted by anyone within your organization as well as follow-ups to those articles.

- Make sure you get all the articles posted on any newsgroup by a known competitor. You can include either articles posted by anyone within an entire organization or posted by specific individuals within an organization.

- Ban the spam by filtering out cross-posted articles. For example, if an article is cross-posted 10 times, you can just about bet it's spam and your program will ignore it.

Unfortunately, ClariNet filtering requires that users be able to construct the filter and compile it with their own C programming-language compiler—not something mainstream users are likely to do.

That's the end of the newsgroup discussion and Hands-On lessons. Remember, for the Usenet to be a truly valuable business tool, you most likely will need to use one of the techniques we just discussed. Otherwise you'll spend so much time simply locating information that you might not get a net value from your work. And you don't want that to happen because you're going to be glued to your monitor in awe of all the other dazzling things that Netscape can bring to you. The rest of this chapter is devoted to outlining some of the spectacular developments on the World Wide Web.

Netscape Plug-Ins

The Internet changes too rapidly to pin it down in a book and among the fastest changing things about the Internet is Netscape itself. I won't even attempt to convince you that this book is the final word on any of the remaining topics in this chapter because there probably never will be any final word. As in music, television, and movies—there always will be new releases.

Nonetheless, there are some exciting developments that are hot for now and will remain hot for the next couple of years. So, I'll introduce you to them and help you understand them. You will, however, need to use the resources listed in the Continuing Education section at the end of this chapter to stay abreast of these rapidly changing technologies.

First, what in the world is a Netscape Plug-In? Plug-ins are small modules of programming code that let Internet developers create add-on applications for Netscape that extend Netscape's capabilities. Plug-ins appear to the user simply as specialized functions within Netscape and don't require a lot of technical knowledge on your part.

Second, how do Netscape plug-ins work? When Netscape Navigator starts up, it checks for installed plug-in modules in your Netscape folder or directory. Later, as you're navigating the Web, Netscape automatically loads the correct plug-in when you encounter a Web page that includes special coding (an embedded MIME type or custom file) that requires the additional programming code contained in a plug-in. The plug-in is discarded when the HTML page is closed.

This all is invisible to you once you've installed the plug-in. The first time, however, that you encounter a Web page that needs a plug-in, you'll be directed through the process of downloading the plug-in and installing it in your copy of Netscape. The times I've done this, it was a straightforward process with no glitches—I just followed simple, on-screen guidance.

With any plug-in, however, you'll have to decide whether or not it's worth your time and disk space in exchange for the added features. Often the plug-in just boosts the gee-whiz aspect of the site and contributes nothing to your finding the valuable information you might be seeking. A plug-in easily could be a megabyte in size. A file this size can take quite a while to download with a slow modem connection and then forever will consume space on your hard drive.

Third, what can Netscape plug-ins do? The limits are as large as cyberspace itself. No one can predict what's coming any more than Thomas Edison could have predicted that phone lines would one day carry the Internet.

Netscape Power Pack 2.0

The Netscape Power Pack 2.0 is a suite of companion utilities that helps you get the most out of Netscape Navigator 2.0 for Windows. As this is written, the product is available only in a downloadable beta version. The final release will be available on CD-ROM and will include an easy-to-use installation shell and 15 Netscape Navigator Plug-Ins. Currently, Power Pack 2.0 combines Netscape SmartMarks 2.0; Netscape Chat 2.0; Internet AntiVirus protection from Norton; CyberSpell, the spelling checker for Netscape Mail; and Netscape Navigator Plug-Ins from many leading third-party developers.

This single pack can be your one-stop answer for using advanced Netscape features, or it might be overkill if you don't plan to experiment. Of course you can just wait until you encounter a Web site that demands a plug-in and download only the plug-in you need.

To find sites for downloading add-on application software specific to your platform, start Netscape and click on **Help, Frequently Asked Questions**, then click **System Requirements**. You soon will have most of the popular plug-ins and helper applications. Once you've installed them, you'll be able to enjoy the enhanced capability of your Netscape browser. Many of the plug-ins are implemented through Java-based programming code that interfaces with the special features of the plug-in. Let's learn more about JavaScript.

Java and JavaScript

Netscape includes a built-in scripting language called JavaScript. JavaScript is based on the Java programming language developed by Sun Microsystems. Java gives dynamic programming capability to previously static Web documents. Java supports programming for the Internet in the form of platform-independent Java applets. Applets are mini-applications that function within a larger, parent application—Netscape, for example.

The home page of my last Internet book, *The McGraw-Hill Internet Training Manual*, features a Java applet (see Figure 6-10). It's an LED display screen that scrolls a continuous message that outlines the book's major features.

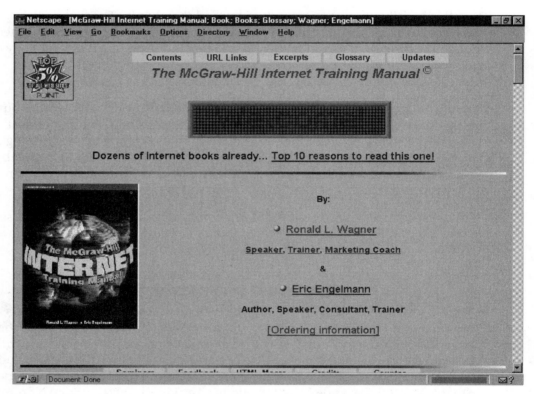

Figure 6-10

JavaScript supports most of the full power of Java, but reduces some of Java's strict programming demands. JavaScript is embedded in HTML documents and requires no special action from your PC to run the script. Thus, Netscape's JavaScript gives Web programmers the ability to create real-time action, animation, and interactivity for users.

Unlike a plug-in, you don't have to download anything before a JavaScript will run, because the capability is programmed into Netscape Navigator 2.0 and later versions. Let's take a look at some popular Netscape plug-ins.

Shockwave

Shockwave for Director delivers high-impact, interactive multimedia productions to the World Wide Web by bringing optimized Director productions—with interactive graphics, sounds, and animation—to the Internet. With support for streaming and caching movies, Shockwave for Director sets a new level of interactive performance (see Figure 6-11).

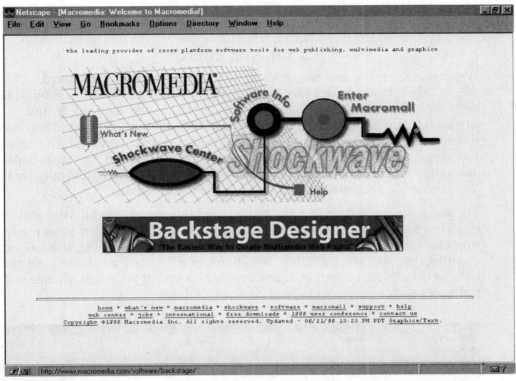

Figure 6-11

The Shockwave technology has been adopted by Netscape and many other companies for integration into their Internet browsers, authoring tools and related products. With Netscape Navigator 2.0 you can download Director multimedia movies as quickly as a simple digitized image. Because Director is embedded into Netscape, Director movies run seamlessly at full power on your PC.

Crescendo

We call the World Wide Web a multimedia environment, but in most cases that's a misused term because few Web sites include sound. They have stunning graphics, pretty colors, and even some feature animation. But click on almost any Web page out there and you will encounter stone cold silence. Can you imagine the feel and texture of a web site that had its own background music? Its own theme song? In the not too distant future, Web site background music will be expected just as much as it is in movies and television. Then we'll have true multimedia.

Crescendo is a Netscape plug-in that delivers the gift of background music. As you surf the Web, soon you'll have the ability to listen to background music on any site that includes it. And that might be most of them before long.

If you're responsible for creating your organization's Web site, you can use Crescendo yourself and give your visitors a treat. A theme song will help them remember your site and some well-chosen background music might keep them browsing longer. Of course, as with any plug-in, remember that first-time visitors who don't have Crescendo on their system will not hear your music unless they complete the necessary download and installation steps.

media.splash

Web pages are more interesting when they're interactive and animated. media.splash by Powersoft (see Figure 6-12) adds the advantage of motion to Web pages for developers, small business owners, course developers, and marketers. Anyone who wants to add visual special effects or interactivity to their websites can do so with no programming skills needed. media.splash includes pre-programmed smart.parts and point-and-click animation tools that make animation easy. Better yet, since media.splash was designed specifically for the Web, its files are remarkably small and quick to download.

The pre-programmed smart.parts can be used to increase productivity and quickly add fun effects to your Web application. Each smart.part has a predefined purpose, for example, to create an effect like wavetext, flying text, shadowtext, crashing text, zoomtext, fadetext, bar charts, or a flipbook animation. All you have to do is paste in your own text or graphics and, if you want, change some attributes such as color and speed, and you're done.

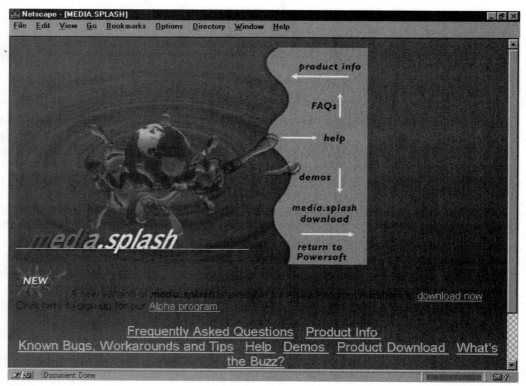

Figure 6-12

What's next?

The only safe prediction about Netscape plug-ins is that there will be more of them and you won't be able to keep up with them by reading Internet books. So how will you keep track? The answer depends on whether you're a Web consumer or a Web producer.

If you're a Web consumer, you don't have to worry much about new developments in Netscape plug-ins. Many will come and go without you ever hearing of them. When you encounter a Web site that requires a plug-in you don't have, you'll be alerted and directed to download and install the required plug-in. The procedure will be similar for all of them. But before you download any one of them, take a moment to consider whether or not your business will be advanced by the time and disk space you'll need to install it.

If you're a Web producer, you can't rely on learning about plug-ins by accidentally coming across them while you surf the Net. To keep up-to-date, you can regularly check the Netscape home page for new plug-ins. And you can regularly check the major Web search engines, such as Yahoo! and Lycos, by searching for the keywords Netscape plug-ins.

After two chapters on Netscape, you definitely are ready for Phase 2 in which I'll present a grand tour of some excellent Web resources. You should be able to handle anything you encounter on the sites covered in Phase 2. These Web sites will help you learn to use cyberspace to boost your productivity and profitability. I've focused on giving you general Web principles—because things change so fast—but you will get a valuable anthology of specific Web sites. In Phase 2 you will see:

- Business Web sites
- Web library resources
- Government Web sites
- Models of well-done Web sites

The Continuing Education section is next and it includes references that will help you track many of the topics discussed in this chapter.

 *Continuing Education*

Qualcomm
http://www.qualcomm.com

If you plan to use Internet e-mail as a serious business communications tool, you need the full power of Qualcomm's Eudora Pro (see Figure 6-13). You can start here, although you likely will be able to buy Eudora Pro in a local store or through a software mail order retailer. Either way, this site can be a source for news, tips and upgrades as Eudora improves. I've asked them specifically about the competition they're getting from Netscape mail and they outlined some exciting plans they have to make sure that Eudora remains the leading Internet e-mail application.

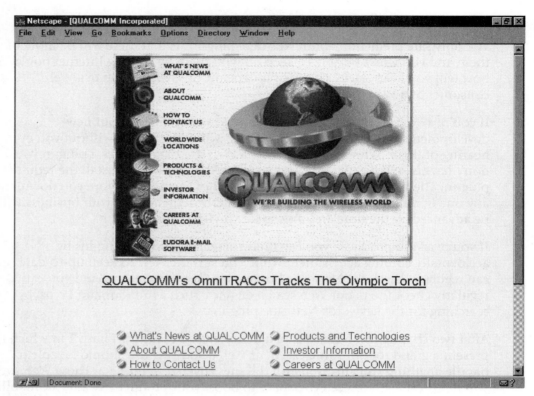

Figure 6-13

Netscape mail on-line help

http://home.netscape.com/eng/mozilla/2.0/handbook/docs/mnb.html

Netscape maintains an up-to-date on-line help system for their mail application. Don't worry about this enormously long URL. You can jump to it with a couple of mouse clicks. Just start Netscape and click **Help, Release Notes**, then follow the links to the on-line manual for Netscape mail.

Sun Microsystems

http://www.sun.com

Sun Microsystems developed the Java Internet programming language. You can be assured that Sun will remain a leader in Internet technology for a long time. As a Web consumer, you'll have little need for this site, but if you're responsible for developing your organization's Web presence, then you should consider adding this site to your bookmark list.

Macromedia

http://www.macromedia.com

Macromedia is the developer of Shockwave. From their home page you can visit the Shockwave Gallery and try some of the Shockwave movies there. This also is a good resource if you'd like to implement Shockwave on your site's Web pages because Macromedia's consulting team provides professional support for a wide range of development, technical and training needs.

Shockwave

http://www.shocker.com/shocker

Here's a Web site that links you to a vast array of other sites that use Shockwave (see Figure 6-14). There also is the Shocker mailing list to which you can subscribe using a form on this page. The mailing list will keep you up-to-date on developments and implementations of Shockwave sites.

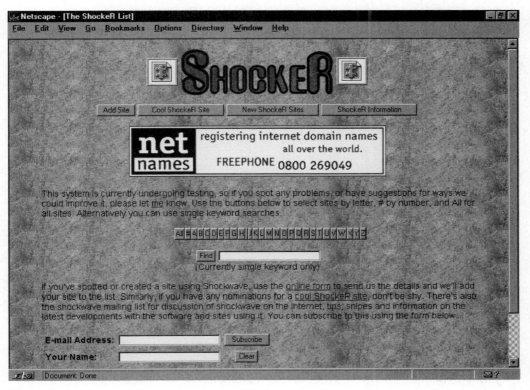

Figure 6-14

Unplugged!

http://www.neca.com/~vmis

This site has a link entitled—I'm not making this up, The Bare-Bones shebang about Netscape plug-ins. In one Web page, three guys from Vijay Mukhi's Computer Institute in Mumbai (formerly Bombay), India give you a glimpse of the weird world inhabited by those who understand and develop Netscape plug-ins. They also have an overview of Java and JavaScript.

PHASE 2
The world at your fingertips

THIS SECTION is for hands-on Web browsing. It begins by teaching the basic tools of Web searching and research—making sense out of the alphabet soup of Internet acronyms. The next three lessons will show you some of the most valuable Web resources so you can learn to quickly target the information you want to find. The last chapter analyzes some top-flight Web examples, pointing out the features that you will want to emulate. It includes a few how-not-to-do-it pointers as well.

- Chapter 7 focuses on one of the most important Web tools of all: the search engine. I'll show you some of the best examples, and I've included Hands-On exercises that will demonstrate some advanced features that will greatly enhance your ability to find even a needle in the cyberspace haystack.

- Chapter 8 presents some powerful business-related Web sites. These will include a wealth of corporate resources that can boost your productivity and keep you informed on the latest changes in the business world—both in cyberspace and in the real world.

- Chapter 9 gives you an extensive set of reference sources. You'll find out how to reach in a few seconds some of the world's major libraries. You also will learn how to exploit the vast caches of information you'll tap when you arrive at these sites.

- Chapter 10 is a collection of valuable government Web sites. You'll learn how to track down patents related to your latest invention or check demographics before expanding into new territory.

- Chapter 11 closes out your Hands-On training by showing you some client-centered Web examples. You'll want to check out these features to help you model some effective principles and techniques that will help make your own organization create a valuable site.

Web searching services

FOR A LONG TIME, I tried to think of a good metaphor to open this chapter. I wanted to say that the World Wide Web was growing like . . . but, what? Then it came to me: the Web *is* the metaphor. Someday, we might say that something is growing like the Web. But for now, *nothing* has ever grown like the Web since the Big Bang. Hey, that's it: The Web is the Big Bang of cyberspace.

Just as the Big Bang created too many stars to count, the Web has created too many documents to count. Fortunately, you're not going to need to count Web documents because a major part of the Web explosion has been Web searching services that can help you find the *stars* in cyberspace.

These Web searching services are called search engines, and before long we might not even be able to count their number. The reasons for their phenomenal growth is no surprise if you consider the main principle in my chapter on Client-centered Interneting: People are drawn to sites that deliver value, and Web search engines are the most valuable sites on the Web.

Without search engines, the Web would be like a phone system without phone books or directory assistance—you only would be able to use a site if someone gave you its location. Search engines locate Web documents based on your search criteria; these are either the topics you browse or keywords you specify.

Search engine principles

Web search engines are almost too powerful for their own good—or for your own good. You are unlikely to ever have a problem finding *something* on a given topic, but you might have a lot of trouble sifting through what you find to get *something you need*. There are tricks to using the search engines that will greatly enhance your success at locating targeted information.

We'll look first at how Web search engines work. Next, we'll move on to some searching tricks that will hone the accuracy of the searches you perform. Then I'll give you some tips on helping your clients, customers, and prospects find your site, and I'll close with an overview of some of the best search engines on the Web.

How they work

All search engines are based on computer-indexed information. Using a variety of methods, search-engine developers gather information from around the Web, then store it and index it. Web search engines use two different basic approaches that enable you to locate the information they have indexed.

One approach presents a list of categories. These categories are broken down first by major topic, and then each major topic is broken down into an increasingly detailed hierarchy of subtopics. The search service lets you browse through its topical index to see the Web documents it has stored. Of course, you have to guess the category under which your information might be located. Because there are no standards for dividing information into categories, you might have difficulty guessing the category under which the site's managers stored the information you want.

The second approach lets you perform a keyword search on the engine's indexed documents. This means that the search engine will give you a list of documents that contain a keyword, or keywords, that you specified. Because keyword searches don't rely on categories, they produce documents from a wide variety of topics—many of which might have nothing to do with the information you were seeking. Keyword searches are based on *boolean logic*.

Boolean logic

Boolean logic is a mathematical system consisting of a set of elements and operators that specify relationships between the individual elements. The system was devised in 1854 by the English mathematician George Boole. Internet search engines use three important Boolean operators: AND, OR, and NOT.

These operators are important tools for you in using search engines because they can be used to widen searches or narrow searches to get the results you need. I'll illustrate their use with the three words, *hot air balloon*.

Using AND

If you wanted to find hot air balloon sites on the Web, you actually need to search for documents that contain all three words: *hot*, *air*, and *balloon*. Otherwise, your search would produce a huge list of documents that contained any one of those words. The words could be entered as hot AND air AND balloon, but most sites assume the AND operator if you don't specify anything between words. In other words, a space is an AND operator. Some search engines use a symbol instead of the word AND.

Using OR

Because AND is the default for most sites, if you actually wanted to find pages that had any one of those words, you would have to enter hot OR air OR balloon. But stand back if you do this, because the list might melt down your PC. You'd be getting every indexed document that contained the word *hot*, or

The world at your fingertips

that contained the word *air*, or that contained the word *balloon*. Can you imagine the number?

Using NOT

The NOT operator can be used to eliminate pages that contain a certain word. For example, if you searched for hot AND air NOT balloon you would get just the hot air congressional sites in Washington, because all of the hot air sites that also contained the word balloon would be eliminated.

Read the directions

For the best search success, you need to know the default Boolean operator for the engine you're using. For example, if you enter *hot air balloon*, most sites use AND between the words, thus giving the highest priority to documents that contain all three words. However, some will treat each word separately unless you use *hot AND air AND balloon*. And others might require you to enter the words in quotation marks: *"hot" "air" "balloon."*

Improving your search success

In addition to using Boolean logic in your searches, some search engines let you specify wildcards similar to the wildcards you use in DOS filenames. For example, you could use hot air balloon* to find hot air balloon, hot air balloons, and hot air ballooning. That's a very simple example, and not really necessary, but wildcards can spell the difference between quick success and nagging frustration if you aren't sure how to spell a word.

Wildcards also can be valuable in searching for someone by name. For example, if you were trying to find Peter A. Russell, the author of the book *The Global Brain*, you could search for Pete* Russell to find strings that begin with Pete, have any number of character in between (including zero), and that end with Russell.

Another tool is the substring search. A substring is a portion of text that's contained within a longer string. Fortunately, most search engines automatically look for substrings. In the Peter Russell example, looking for Pete Russell would find pages with Peter and Russell because Pete is a substring of Peter.

NET TIP

Read the directions! Most sites have a button or link that will jump you to a set of detailed instructions. There's no substitute for reading these to be sure of the rules and the tricks. In fact, many of the engines, such as Lycos (see Figure 7-1), jump you to a user-friendly screen that can greatly increase your search accuracy with little extra effort. In Lycos, the link is titled *Enhance your search*.

A few sites allow natural-language searches. These are convenient and require the least thought, but then again, the results they produce might be less accurate. An example of a natural-language search could be "I want to find all of the sites that talk about hot air balloons." The search engine would use a preprogrammed set of rules to eliminate the words it found to be extraneous, and then search on the remaining words. You can't be sure, however, which words will be stripped and which will be included in the search.

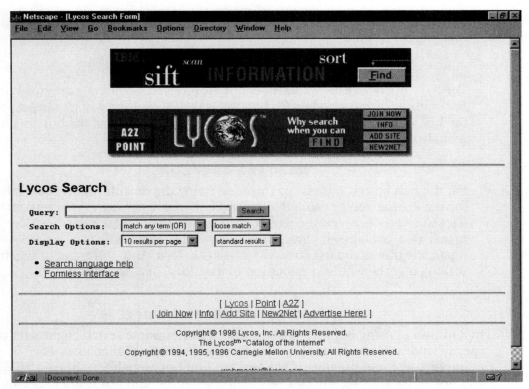

Figure 7-1

Helping others find your page

It's important to tailor your own Web pages so that others can more easily find your site when they're using a search engine. You can find lots of examples of what *not* to do. One lousy example is making the title of your Web page *Welcome to Our Home Page!* That's a perfect title, however, if you expect to attract visitors who've gone hunting for Welcome or Home Page.

Create an accurate title

The title of your Web page doesn't have to be pretty. It's only going to show up in the Windows title bar at the top of the Netscape screen. The title of my first book's home page is a good example: *McGraw-Hill Internet Training Manual; Book; Books; Guide; Glossary; Wagner; Engelmann.* You would find this page by searching for *Internet Glossary*, or *Internet Training*, or *Internet Book*, or *Internet Books*, or *Training Manual*, or *Training Books*, or *McGraw-Hill Books*, or *Wagner Books*, or *McGraw-Hill Internet*, or *Internet Training Engelmann.* Because of that title, this book was for many months one of only four Internet glossaries that could be found on Yahoo! by searching for Internet Glossary. There might be more today, but I wouldn't have had any hits at all if I'd made my title *Welcome!*

Submitting your own site

There are two ways to submit your own URLs to search engines so other people can find your site. First, you can physically go around to every search engine with which you want to be listed and look for their submission link. Second, you can visit a comprehensive submission Web site that handles multiple submissions to most of the Web's best-known search engines.

Each method has its advantages. The advantage of using a submission service is obvious: You use a one-stop, time-saving site that minimizes your workload. The advantage to doing it yourself is more subtle; you get to be more careful that your site is indexed in the best category, and that your listing is consistent with the pattern of other listings on that service.

I suggest that you try one or two manually to get the idea of how your listing looks after it has been indexed. You might be surprised at the keywords that are featured or at the title. You can't control the search engine, but you can control your pages. If you're not happy with the early results, delete the experimental listings, edit your Web pages, then resubmit and check the results after they have been indexed. After a few of these experiments, you'll have a better idea of whether to do the rest of them yourself or use a consolidated service. In either case, you'll have refined the indexing ability of your pages.

Submit It!

This is a completely free submission service, supported by paid advertising, that handles all of the major search engines. You can visit it at *www.submit-it.com* (see Figure 7-2). While you're there, you can test their Metasearch engine.

The PostMaster

Try the PostMaster at *www.netcreations.com/postmaster*. Before completing the lengthy submission form, be sure to read the FAQs file. This is intended to be a fee-based service, though they do allow some Try Before You Buy experimenting. If you don't follow their terms when you post your free submission, they say they'll bill you for the full fee.

Keywords

Make sure that your Web site has some appropriate keywords near the top of the home page. Some search engines score documents by the location of the keywords. If a keyword is found high in your home page, that word will generate a higher score than if the same word were buried deep within some linked sub-documents on your site.

Choose categories carefully

Finally, one important key to successfully being found can lie in going into each site individually to submit your page. By browsing the site thoroughly, you can learn the most appropriate heading under which to place your site's URL; and you can learn if the engine allows you to submit to multiple headings. Yahoo! is an excellent example. It allows you to list under multiple headings and it has so many headings that you have to be careful to choose the ones you expect your visitors to try.

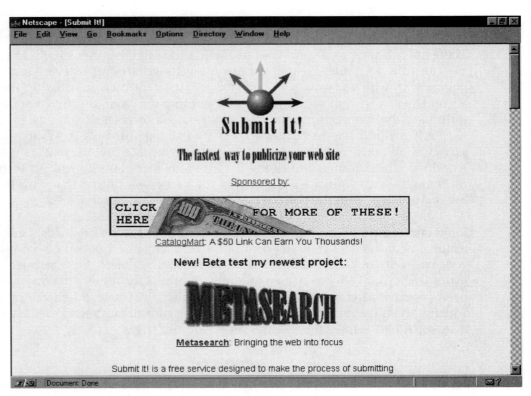

Figure 7-2

Web search engines

There are two categories of Web search services, free and commercial. Consider using both types when you're searching, as well as when you're submitting your own pages for indexing. While commercial services charge for performing searches, neither type usually charges you to submit your site for indexing.

The free services are much like broadcast television networks. Most of them include paid advertising (like NBC or Fox) and some of them are public services (like PBS stations) that are funded by corporations or universities. And, as with broadcast television, you can ignore the ads and use only the search tools. The commercial services are much like premium cable channels and come in two varieties, pay-per-search and monthly subscription.

Free search services

The Web's free search services come in two basic categories: search engines and metasearch services. The search engines are actual indexing computer systems that seek out data on the Web, index it, catalog it, and serve it up to users as requested. A metasearch search service taps into multiple search engines so your query will check a broader range of sources. I'll cover a few popular search engines and then profile one metasearch service.

Yahoo!

If you've read *Gulliver's Travels*, you've got to wonder why anyone would name themselves after the despicable Yahoos that Gulliver encountered, especially since this Yahoo! is so delightful (see Figure 7-3). Yahoo! offers two searching options on its home page. You can use a keyword search or you can browse through its listing by category.

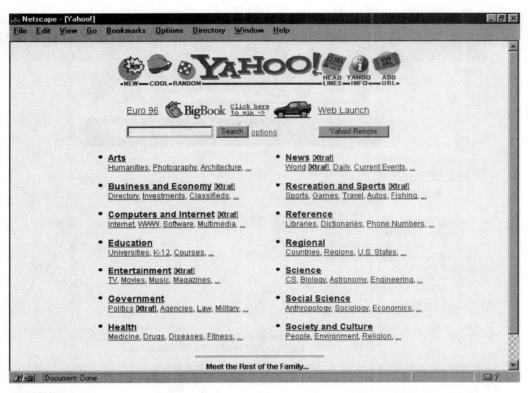

Figure 7-3

Keyword searches are the best choice when you've got some sites in mind, such as hot air balloon races; but those sites would be difficult to find if you browsed under headings. Under which heading would you expect to find hot air balloon races?

On the other hand, you might want to find pages that deal with a general topic, such as politics. If you performed a keyword search for *politics* you'd get every indexed page that contained that word. That would be grossly overwhelming. But worse, it's entirely possible for an important article about politics to *not* contain the word politics.

Fortunately, Yahoo! gives you both options right up front; but there's more. The top of the Yahoo! page has links to pages that give you New, Cool, and Headlines. These links will help you skip past the old stuff. And if you're just bored some night and want to read something about anything, you can spend the evening sipping Jolt Cola, eating Twinkies, and clicking on links under the Random link. Good luck!

Yahoo! also has a special page that lets you refine your search request (see Figure 7-4). Unfortunately, the path to this special page changes periodically. For a while there was a link called Options right next to the text entry box. As I wrote this book, that link had been replaced with another cool option, outlined below, but I couldn't find Options. I got to it by clicking on Search with the text entry box blank. That page, complaining about my lack of search talent, gave me a link titled *More . . .* that lead to a screen with the Options link next to the Search button.

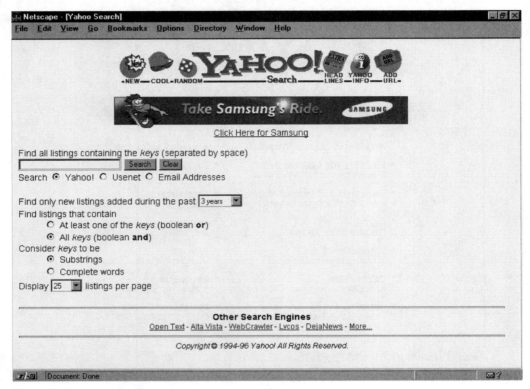

Figure 7-4

This page gives you the ability to choose between searching either the Web or Usenet for your keywords. You also can specify to use the OR operator and to force a search for whole words instead of substrings. The bottom of each Yahoo! page also has links to other popular Web search engines. If you click on those links, Yahoo! automatically enters your last search request and takes you to the new search engine's home page.

DejaNews

DejaNews is a search engine for Usenet newsgroups. It's become an extension of Yahoo! from which you can jump directly to DejaNews, or you can click on DejaNews after performing a normal Yahoo! search. The screen example shown here was the result of searching for the title of my last book, *The Mc-Graw-Hill Internet Training Manual* (see Figure 7-5). DejaNews builds a list of all the articles it can find among the Usenet newsgroups that contain the keywords you're seeking.

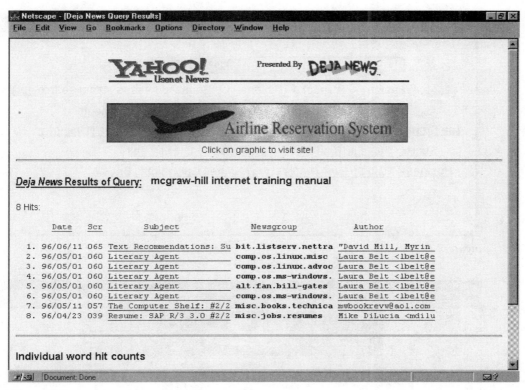

Figure 7-5

Yahoo! Remote

Yahoo! offers a special feature that, so far, is unique. It's called Yahoo! Remote and it's a miniature version of Netscape that contains only the Yahoo! search engine (see Figure 7-6). Once you launch the Remote, it's a separate Netscape window that can float around on top of the screen of any application. For example, you could place it on top of WordPerfect for Windows so that you could see a document and Yahoo! Remote at the same time. This might make it easier for you to search for keywords in the document you're writing. With Yahoo! Remote active, you can switch between Remote and any other application using **ALT+TAB**.

Finally, don't overlook the Add URL button at the top of the Yahoo! main screen. The key to using this is first to navigate to a category that is a logical choice for your own home page before you click on the link. When you're in the right place, clicking on it will start the Yahoo! procedure to add your page to that Yahoo! category. But be patient, because you can expect a delay of one to three weeks before your links appear under the category.

Lycos

What is it with these search engine names? After Yahoo!, you get to see another service named after a rather unpleasant creature, Lycos, named for some wild jungle spider. The tie-in to the Web probably made sense at some late night session over Jolt Cola and a bunch of Twinkies. Oh well, a Lycos by any other name will still search as fast (see Figure 7-7).

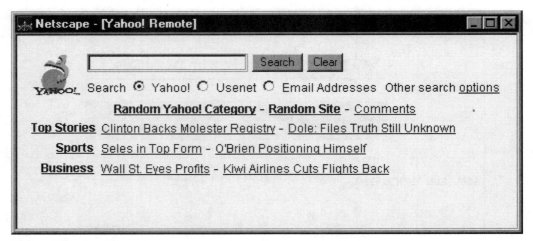

Figure 7-6

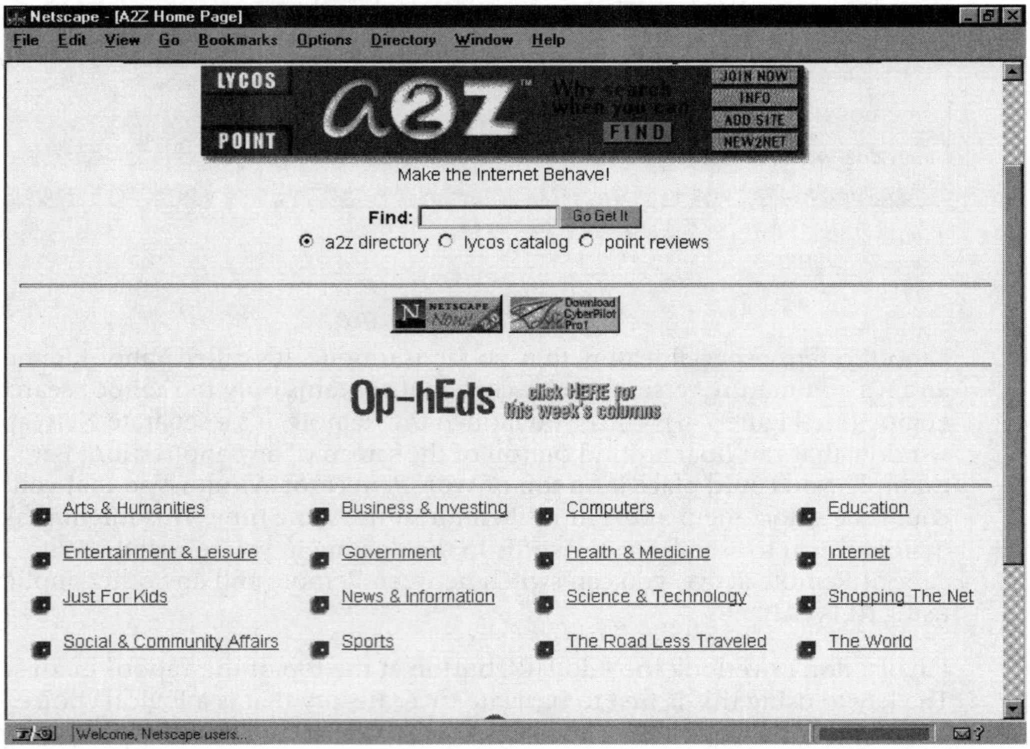

Figure 7-7

Lycos has a limited set of categories on its home page as well as the keyword search entry box. Lycos displays search results quite differently than Yahoo!. It lists all documents that contain *any* or *all* of your keywords. In essence, it gives you both an AND search and an OR search.

The AND results are presented first and include a score that's derived from how and where those words appear within the listed page. The highest score would go to a document in which all three keywords were present near the top of the document. The score drops as the words get more separated and farther into the

▶ *The world at your fingertips*

document. Of course, the score also drops on documents that contain only *some* or *one* of your keywords.

Lycos A2Z search

Lycos has a special feature called the A2Z search that offers a slightly less intimidating approach to Web searching. It doesn't list scores for sites, and thus it displays results a little more quickly. Where the full Lycos search displays document abstracts that contain actual words pulled from the Web pages themselves, the A2Z search includes a short synopsis of each site and also lists the Lycos category under which the site is organized.

Sites are included on A2Z based on the number of other Web sites that link to them. The current breakpoint for qualifying for A2Z is in the hundreds. For example, if your Web site is referenced on a dozen other sites, your site wouldn't qualify; but if several hundred other sites have included a link to you on their site, then you'd make the cut.

Naturally, the A2Z option is not as comprehensive as the full Lycos search, though it will have an overall higher quality of sites for the topic you want. For example, searching A2Z for hot air balloon produced 146 pages (see Figure 7-8), although they were presented in reader-friendly capsules. In the Lycos catalog, the same string produced 75,725 documents containing at least one term.

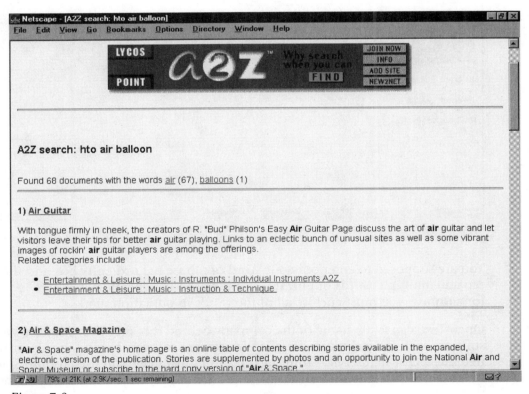

Figure 7-8

Open Text

Open Text has perhaps the most user-friendly main screen of any of the services. Its catalog is not as extensive as some of the larger services, but you nonetheless might achieve better overall results because of its interface (see Figure 7-9). For example, when I searched for my last book using *McGraw-Hill Internet Training Manual* as my query phrase, the only references it listed were five links to my site in the Yahoo! index. Still, it's a good service, so let's look at how those optional drop lists can help you:

- Search for your keywords anywhere in the document, or within the summary, the title, the first heading, or the URL.
- Narrow the search with AND, OR, BUT NOT, NEAR, or FOLLOWED BY.

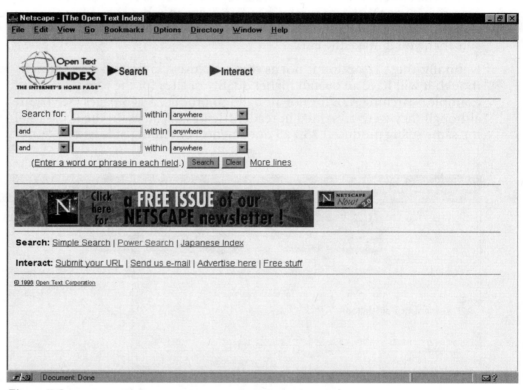

Figure 7-9

You are supposed to enter only one word or phrase per text entry box and then separate multiple words or phrases with the drop-list operators. If you're looking for a phrase, you must enclose all of the words in quotation marks.

Open Text also is the name of the company behind this site. They produce Web software such as Livelink Spider, the Web crawler software behind the Open Text free Internet search service. Your organization most likely can use Livelink Spider, because it also crawls sites on a private web (Intranet) and builds a unified index that anyone in your organization can use to search internal information just as the Open Text site searches Web information.

Alta Vista

At the beginning of this chapter, I said that nothing has ever grown like the World Wide Web—the Web is now a metaphor for other fast-growing things. I've included the Alta Vista search engine because its appearance so strongly confirms my statement about the Web's astonishing growth (see Figure 7-10).

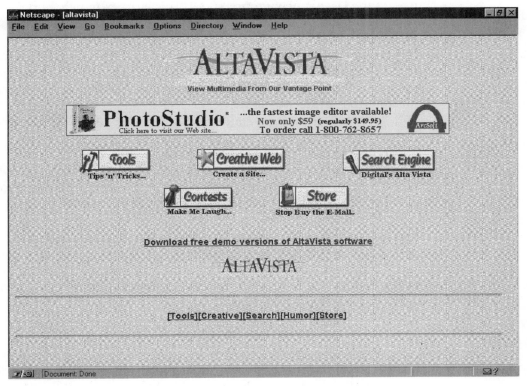

Figure 7-10

The Digital Research Laboratories in Palo Alto, California began the Alta Vista project in the summer of 1995. After two months of internal testing, they had produced an index consisting of the full text of more than 16 million pages. They made the site public on December 15, 1995. Within three weeks of launch, Alta Vista was servicing more than two million search requests per day. Within two months Alta Vista was receiving more than five million daily search requests on its index of more than 21 million pages—an incredible total of ten billion words!

Behind the scenes

Have you ever wondered what kind of computer system it takes to handle more than five million search requests per day and to store ten billion words in more than 21 million document pages? Here's a summary of the equipment that's working behind the scenes when you ask Alta Vista to help you out:

- AlphaStation 250 4/266, 256MB memory, 4GB disk. Two AlphaStations handle all external traffic to the site and run a custom, multithreaded Web server that sends queries to the Web indexer and News indexer.

- AlphaServer 8400 5/300, 10 processors, 6GB memory, 210GB RAID 5 disk. Two AlphaServers handle the Web indexing and the query engine. They are the most powerful computers ever built by Digital. The Alta Vista Web index is larger than 30 gigabytes, but most requests take less than a second.
- AlphaStation 250 4/266, 196MB memory, 13GB disk. This machine indexes the Usenet newsgroups spool. This is an extremely busy machine because of the furious pace at which new articles appear and old articles expire.
- AlphaStation 400 4/233, 160MB memory, 24GB RAID 5 disks. This machine maintains a news spool for the news indexer and serves the articles via http to users who don't want to know about news servers, but want to read Usenet news.
- DEC 3000/900 Alpha Workstation, 1GB memory, 30GB RAID 5 disk. The super-spider runs from this machine, fetching pages from the Web and sending them to the Web indexer.

Oh, don't be so impressed. In a few years, your kids will be using PCs bigger, better, and faster than these and they won't believe that back in the old days the entire Web could be indexed on one of these puny little things.

The Alta Vista engine has some powerful Boolean logic capability built in. And they even give you a sample of how to write it. For example they say, to find a bed-time story: "fairy tale" +frog –dragon. That means that you're looking for documents that contain the phrase *fairy tale* and that also contain the word *frog*, but that do not contain the word *dragon*.

All-In-One

All-In-One search is a metasearch service. It doesn't actually perform the search, but passes off your query to any one of a long list of actual search engines. This is a wonderful feature for checking the broadest possible set of resources. There are several on the Web, but I've chosen this one because it's highly rated, and the way they've broken down the categories gives it a user-friendly interface (see Figure 7-11). It's located at *www.albany.net/allinone*.

As you can see in this screen shot, All-In-One lists major search topics such as World Wide Web, General Interest, and Specialized Interest. Beyond this page lies options to search these categories: Software, People, News/Weather, Publications/Literature, Technical Reports, Documentation, Desk Reference, and Other Interesting Searches/Services.

All-In-One's ease of use lies in the plus signs that precede each heading. When you click on a plus sign, the heading's category expands and all of the related searching services under it are displayed (see Figure 7-12). In this example, I clicked on World Wide Web. On this screen, you can fill in your query and click the Search button. All-In-One will then submit your search to that service. Clicking on a minus sign will collapse the category back down to just a heading.

Let me close this section on free search services with a reminder to browse through the Continuing Education section at the end of this chapter. It can lead you to many more sites, including other metasearch sites such as C/Net's site at *www.search.com*, which is a treasure trove of Web searching services.

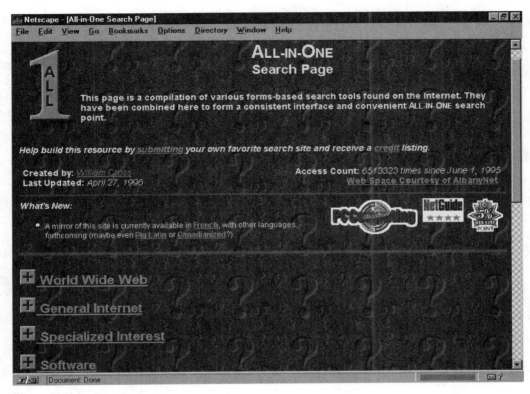

Figure 7-11

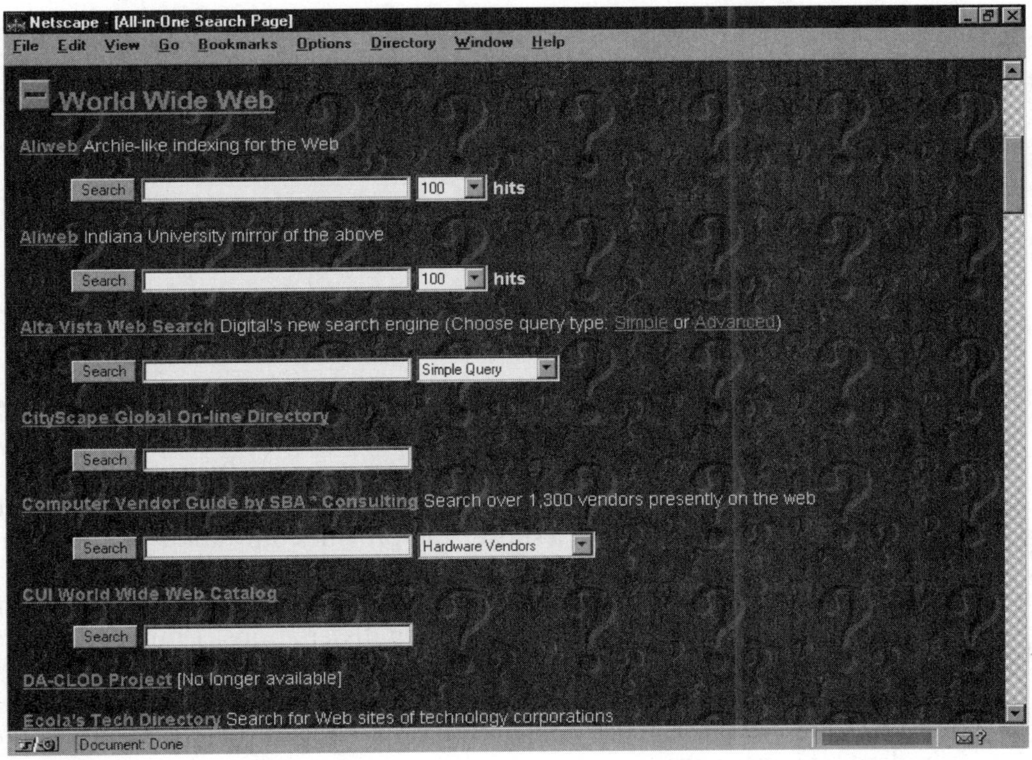

Figure 7-12

Web searching services ◀

Commercial search services

I've included two commercial services here because each offers a completely different approach to searching for information. The first, NLightN, is a superset indexer that dwarfs even the large search engines such as Lycos. The second is the famous Encyclopedia Britannica, but now in an on-line version. Both sites charge a usage fee, but Britannica sticks to its own internal information, while NLightN includes references from all over cyberspace.

NLightN

If you need in-depth research instead of hits on a free search list, then try the most comprehensive information on the Internet: NLightN at *www.nlightn.com* (see Figure 7-13). It's touted as "... the Web's largest library of meaningful information." It is the fast and easy way to find anything you want to know.

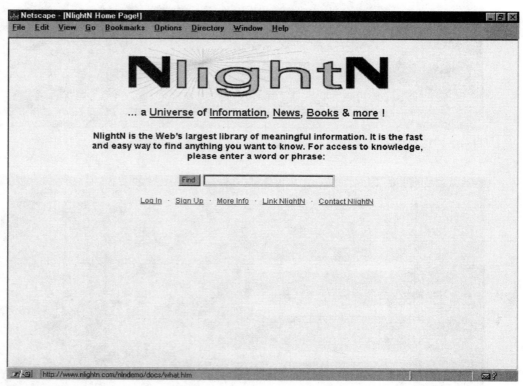

Figure 7-13

If you think Lycos is comprehensive, prepare to be dazzled—or overwhelmed. NLightN is so vast that Lycos is a subset and provides only about five percent of the information resources that NLightN has indexed. In other words, the NLightN index lets you search a universal index that's 20 times as large as that of Lycos! It includes 10 million books; 1 million dissertations; 1 million patents; hundreds of thousands of wire service records from more than 20 wire services; tens of millions of journal articles; book, movie, and audio-visual reviews; informal and formal searches of the full text of encyclopedias, dictionaries, and standard reference works.

NLightN is a fee-based service and you'll have to sign up for a membership. Take a trial run at this site and then brainstorm ways you can use it to put value-added services on your Web site—you're sure to find something here that your clients and customers will appreciate finding on your Web site.

Pricing is transaction-based rather than per-minute, and begins at ten cents. You'll pay only for the information you request when you click on a BUY or ORDER button. NLightN content providers set the price and that price is always shown, so you know the cost before you spend any money.

The resources listed represent the best reference sources in the world, such as: Library of Congress, National Library of Medicine, British Library, Cambridge Scientific Abstracts, ABI/INFORM, SPORT Database, Merriam-Webster, Film Literature Index, Magazine Articles Summary, Reader's Guide to Periodic Literature, U.S. Patents, Dissertation Abstracts, and many others. In addition to archived information, NLightN provides full-text indexing of newswire services, including Knight-Ridder, PR Newswire, Sports Wire, and Investment Wire.

Britannica Online

Britannica Online brings a venerable reference source out of the libraries and onto your computer screen (see Figure 7-14). It's priced a bit steep—actually, by today's Web standards, it's priced in the stratosphere; but this is an extensive, highly respected reference work that lets you cut and paste the articles you find and download the pictures. In addition, you won't have to pack a huge multivolume encyclopedia set when you move, and it will never go out of date.

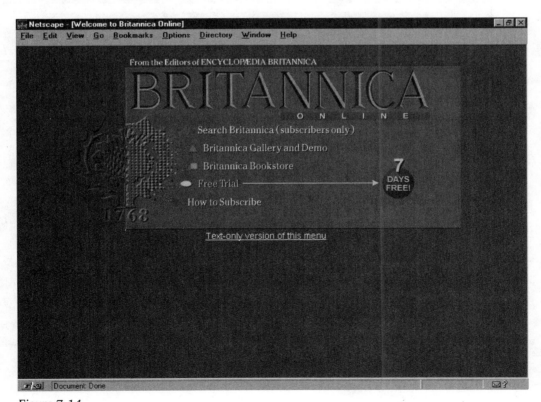

Figure 7-14

This service is offered for home, business, or academic use. The annual subscription price for home use is $150.00 U.S. per year, plus a one-time nonrefundable registration fee of $25.00 U.S. The annual subscription price for business use is $300.00 U.S. per year, plus a one-time nonrefundable registration fee of $50.00 U.S., for *each* single user. The single-user academic fee is $120.00 U.S. per year with no registration fee. Site licenses are available for multi-user corporate and academic environments, but you'll have to inquire via this site for rates.

Britannica Online offers a free seven-day trial period that will give you a temporary login ID and a password. Just visit the home page at *www.eb.com* and complete the instructions. Be careful that you don't accidentally sign up for the full service, because the registration fees are nonrefundable! Signing up is a two-step process that only takes a couple of minutes:

⦿ First, click on Step 1, complete the form, and submit it. They will e-mail you a validation code, but it will be in your mailbox in a minute or two.

⦿ Get the code from the e-mail message, then return to Netscape and complete Step 2. You only need the validation code once, but you *must* carefully record the user name they assign and remember your password.

Once completed, you'll have full access to the entire site (see Figure 7-15). You'll have to spend some time with it during this short trial period to see if it's worth the resources you can locate.

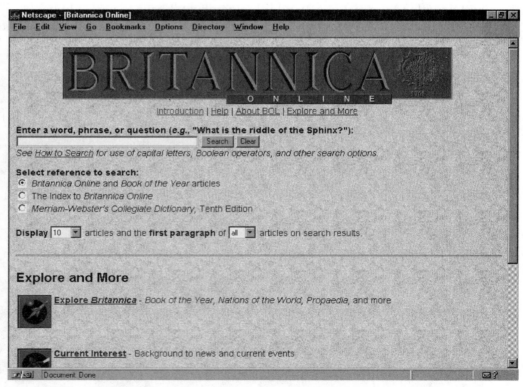

Figure 7-15

Commentary on Web searching

Browsing through the Britannica Online site gave me an interesting revelation. I realized how accustomed I have grown to the eclectic mishmash of information on the Web. It became clear when I searched both Britannica and Lycos for Carl Jung to compare the findings. Naturally Britannica Online found excellent references; ten of them, in fact. They were informative and well-written—I was favorably impressed.

But then I jumped over to Lycos and searched again for references to the most famous native of Switzerland. The differences were startling. Where Britannica had found ten nice, clean articles, Lycos pulled from cyberspace a dazzling array of Web pages that included all kinds of information about Jung. None were as clean as the Britannica listings, but does that necessarily make Britannica better? It's certainly a personal judgement, but personally, I sort of missed the wild variations in style, content, color, layout, and opinions.

Contrasted against the cleanliness of Britannica Online, the sight of all of those disparate, diverse, and untamed Web links reminded me of the line in My Fair Lady when Rex Harrison sings "I've grown accustomed to her face." I've grown accustomed to the face of the Web.

Okay, enough philosophy. Let's continue our exploration of Web resources by shifting gears in the next chapter to look at news and information-oriented Web sites.

 # Continuing Education

C/Net search

http://www.search.com

This is the nicest search site I've found. It's sort of a blend of a free service and a commercial service. Search.com actually blends its own commercial service in with other search engines. On the home page, for example, you'll see a link to search for shareware (see Figure 7-16) that looks like all the other links. That link, however, is owned by C/Net, the creators and sponsors of this site. This is an excellent example of Client-centered Interneting because it attracts visitors by providing value, and yet sells the sponsor's products. Nice job, but a little bit of a sneaky trick on unsuspecting newbies.

DejaNews

http://www.dejanews.com

This service was profiled earlier in this chapter as an extension of Yahoo!, but it's a stand-alone service that has its own domain name (see Figure 7-17). You can put this URL directly onto your bookmark list so you can get to it without going through Yahoo! or any other intermediate steps. DejaNews is extremely efficient and fast. Even searches that span huge quantities of data are finished on the server in a few seconds, even though it has the largest collection of archived, indexed Usenet newsgroup documents that can be found anywhere!

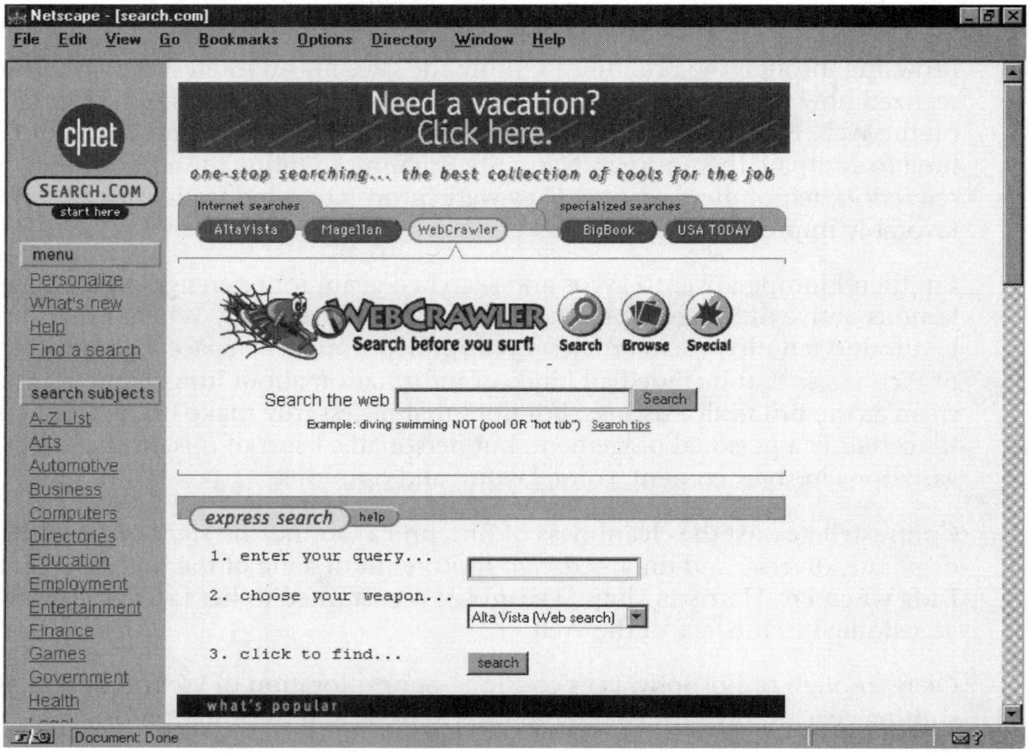

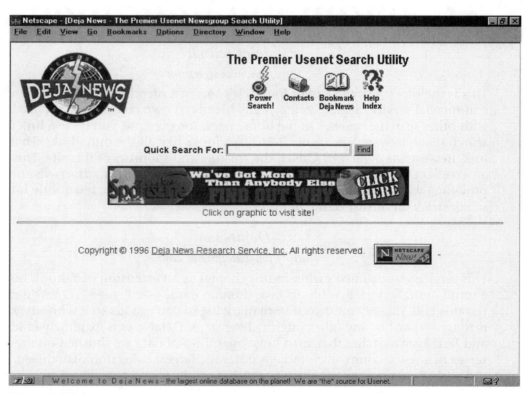

Figure 7-16

Figure 7-17

Netscape search

http://home.netscape.com/home/internet-search.html

This service is often overlooked—it's sort of a case of not seeing the forest for the trees. However, the Netscape Web site has a search browser that can be reached with a built-in menu link (see Figure 7-18). You don't need to type the URL above; just click **Directory, Internet Search**.

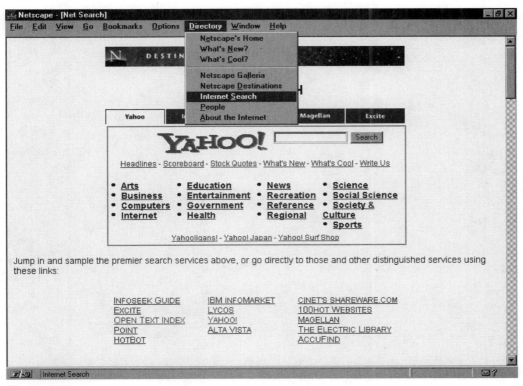

Figure 7-18

News and information Web sites

THIS CHAPTER FOCUSES on several types of Internet news and business information services. First I'll cover on-line news services, which can deliver more news than you ever wanted to know about any topic you can imagine. Blessedly, you also can use these services to filter out everything you *don't* need to know and get just the slice of news you truly need.

Major traditional newspapers, such as the *Washington Post* and *USA Today*, are going on-line. Additionally, there are many innovative forms of news delivery that bypass traditional news distribution systems. You'll see examples of both.

Next I'll give you some financial news links that can deliver stock quotes as well as track news that will affect corporate stock prices. These services can be used to track a personal portfolio, a major corporate investment plan, or even to track the ups and downs of your competitors. You'll also get some good resources for marketing tips and general business information and consulting services.

General news

The nation's newspapers and magazines are scrambling to go on-line. As this is being written, I've found 26 newspapers on-line just among full-service, primary newspapers that serve metropolitan areas with more than 1 million in population (see Figure 8-1). Most assuredly that number will be higher by the time you read this. And I didn't even try to count the smaller regions or smaller publications.

NewsLink

If you live in a large metropolitan area, you can find out if your area's newspaper is on-line by checking out the NewsLink page at *www.newslink.org* (see Figure 8-2). If you don't find it there, try searching Lycos or Yahoo for the paper's name. Of course you could call them, too, but that's not very high-tech—it wouldn't be right to use a phone to get a cyberspace address!

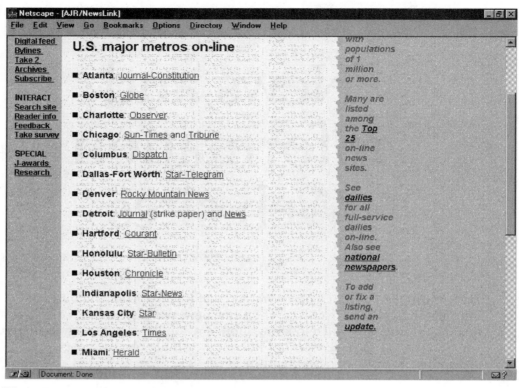

Figure 8-1

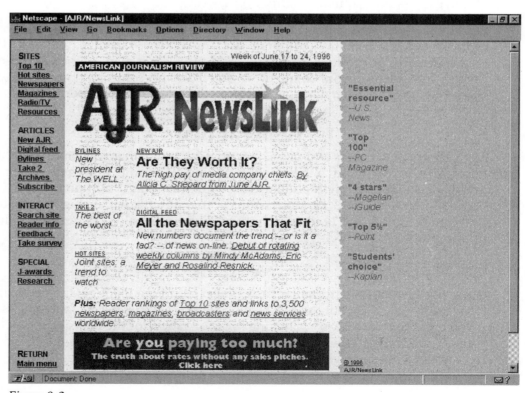

Figure 8-2

▶ *The world at your fingertips*

The NewsLink service is a must for your bookmark list. It's got listings and ratings for on-line versions of traditional newspapers, magazines, and broadcast news as well as links to Internet-oriented news services. You probably will find all the news you need by visiting their Top 10 list or their Best of the Year list. Each week NewsLink features one or more services that have made a particularly interesting addition to their list of on-line publications.

You might be interested in a commercial research report available via NewsLink. To learn more about the report, titled "Tomorrow's News Today," click on the Research link on their home page. Tomorrow's News Today taps hundreds of academic and professional resources to provide in-depth, up-to-date thinking on content, design, and marketing, with each source fully documented. This is not, however, merely facts, figures, and random opinions. You'll find well-reasoned analyses that are geared toward helping your organization focus its efforts on increasing profitability today and in the growing cyberspace world of tomorrow.

The "Tomorrow's News Today" report, now in its second printing, is a fact-filled, thought-provoking 45,500-word spiral-bound publication. It includes 178 pages of text, a 138-item research bibliography, 354 documented references, and more than 50 tables and illustrations. This report is a must for anyone currently on-line, contemplating a move on-line, or simply pondering the future of electronic publishing. It's a little pricey, but they have a wide range of discount programs available, including quantity purchases.

Broadcast news on-line

Both radio and television stations are creating cyberspace versions of their traditional formats. Perhaps one or more of your local television stations features its Internet site during newscasts. In the Washington area, for example, NBC's Channel 4 offers an on-line weather service (see Figure 8-3), which supplements their broadcast weather.

Washington's Channel 4 Web site offers in-depth weather reports, historical statistics, and updates on school closings that are affected by weather. They also sponsor special events; for example, when the Comet Hyakutake was passing near to the Earth, they offered viewing information and downloadable images of the comet that they collected from viewers around the Washington region. If you'd like to see the actual weather in your nation's capital, just click on the WeatherNet 4 News Cam link at *wxnet4.nbc4.com* (see Figure 8-4).

The NewsLink site at *www.newslink.org* is your best source of other broadcast news outlets that have established an Internet presence. The lists of available services are easy to find by using either hypertext links or buttons on the NewsLink home page—yet another reason why this site is a *must* for your browser's bookmark list.

The Washington Post

The *Washington Post* has created an on-line news service that offers a one-stop site for national, international, and Metro-Washington D.C. news and information at *www.washingtonpost.com* (see Figure 8-5). Their Web site makes available the information resources of The Washington Post—including background information, Post archives, photographs, news and classified ads. These

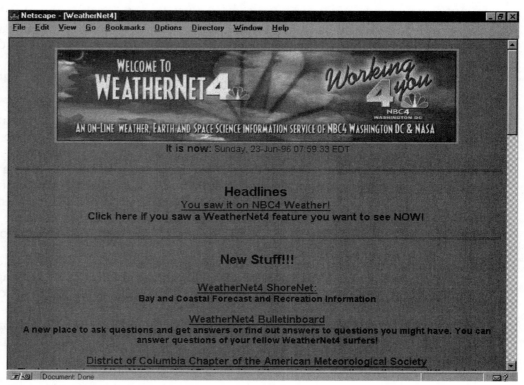

Figure 8-3

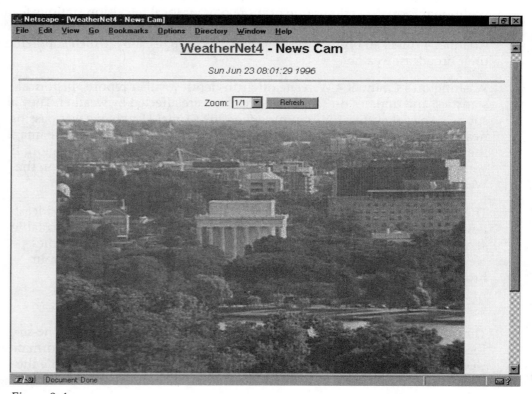

Figure 8-4

The world at your fingertips

Figure 8-5

resources, from news bureaus throughout the world, are available to anyone no matter where he or she lives, works or travels.

Local users will enjoy The Post's detailed metropolitan and neighborhood news and its comprehensive guide to entertainment in the Washington D.C. metropolitan area and surrounding suburbs. And even if you're not a local, you might find it interesting to see what's going on in the U.S. capitol. Or you can try searching the past week's classified ads and maybe you'll find a chance to buy a used car from a Congressman.

This site gives you the opportunity to participate in national—no, make that global—debates on the hottest political news topics in Washington. Check out the interactive section in which you can post a response to a selected Post article and read other responses from around the world.

Another valuable service is the Post's free, easy-to-use "Personal Portfolio" service that lets you build a targeted stock and financial news report from its Business section. Even if you don't build a personal portfolio, you can obtain current stock quotes, detailed financial news and check out the latest economic calendar. The financial section also has a global currency exchange report that would be an excellent Netscape bookmark for any world traveler or international investor.

If you're planning to visit the U.S. capitol, bookmark the Post's home page and read it regularly for a few weeks before your trip. Not only will you get a feel for upcoming special events, you'll find virtual tours of interesting local spots. Save these reports and then take the tour in person when you're visiting. Even if you never come, this could be a fun way to learn more about the most historic area in the U.S.

Tailored news services

In cyberspace, you no longer have to seek the news. Lucky you. With Internet news services, the news will seek you. There is a disheartening number of these services available, and the list is growing all the time. Worse, I can't tell you the right service to choose any more than I can tell you the right pillow to choose. The good news is that these services are inexpensive, they offer free samples, they are easy to find, and subscribing and unsubscribing is simple. Hence, the best strategy for choosing the right news service for you or your organization is to sample a lot of them and then decide.

The most obvious way to start your search for on-line news services is to check out the major search engines such as Yahoo and Lycos. Nearly all search engines have a news link. This most likely will point you to a mixture of news services, but you can browse through them to find the tailored services that filter the news for you.

Another way to find on-line news services is to visit the site at *potter.cc.keele.ac.uk/depts/li/eljourn.htm* (see Figure 8-6). The page is a lengthy collection of electronic newspapers, news services, and journals, as well as a link to the IDEAL World Wide Web service that delivers electronic access to academic press journals.

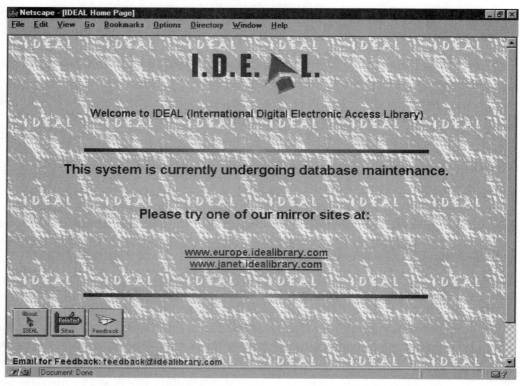

Figure 8-6

CRAYON

With so many services from which to choose, I knew I needed some very scientific criteria to select the one to feature here. So, after much browsing, I used the highly scientific method of picking one because it's got a cute name: CRAYON (CReAte Your Own Newspaper). The CRAYON news service is at *crayon.net* (see Figure 8-7). Though it made the cut because of its name, CRAYON turned out to be a marvel of Internet technology.

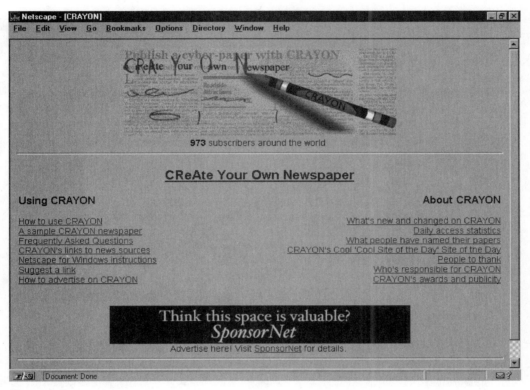

Figure 8-7

Creating your own newspaper with CRAYON is simple. Imagine going to your local paper office and telling them exactly what you want and do not want to read, and then the next day they deliver to your door a tailored version of their newspaper. Getting the information you need then would be faster and more efficient than ever before. This is how CRAYON works. You can even specify your own title, giving you a little taste of how it must feel to be Rupert Murdoch.

In addition to selecting the type of news you want, you can specify if the associated images are to be downloaded as part of your paper or included as on-line links. If you download them, be prepared for your daily paper to gobble more connect time.

You also can select the order in which you want your newspaper sections arranged. You can include multiple selections from any of the major headings: U.S. News, Regional and Local News, World News, Politics as Usual, Weather Conditions and Forecasts, Information and Technology Report, Arts and

Entertainment, SportsDay, The Funny Pages, The Tabloid Page, and New and Cool Web Sites.

CRAYON generates a Web page that will include links to the news features you select (see Figure 8-8). This generated Web page can be delivered one-section-at-a-time or in one big page. The one big page averages about 60K in size—which might cause problems with some computers and browsers—but gives you all of your selections in one continuous page.

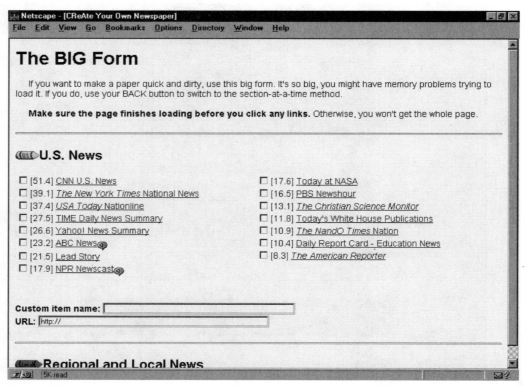

Figure 8-8

After CRAYON generates a Web page, you will have to save the page on your system. After it's saved, you can create a bookmark to it or make it your home page in Netscape.

 NET TIP If you specify a file as the URL in a bookmark or for your home page, you'll need to precede the file name with *file:///*. Note carefully: this syntax uses *three* forward slashes. For example, I created a bookmark to my CRAYON page with the URL entered as: *file:///c:\netscape\program\mypaper.htm*.

Also, remember that you can return to CRAYON any time and generate a new Web page, changing the links you select, the title, or the order of the sections you've chosen.

It hardly could be simpler and definitely can't be cheaper. Just watching this service work is an interesting experience. A word of caution, though: The page you generate with this service could be addictive. I can easily imagine starting from here and spending an entire day surfing through the ever-increasing cascade of links that all of your selected pages unveil. This is a must-get service.

Investment management

You'll find that the Internet offers just about as many financial services as it does news services. You'll be able to track stock portfolios, get real-time stock ticker tape, receive special alarm notices via e-mail if certain maximum or minimum stock prices are triggered, track financial headlines, and order tailored financial news reports.

You also will be able to access an incredible wealth of information on every company that trades stock publicly. This can be a boon when you're considering making an investment, or even if you're just curious about how your biggest competitor is faring.

NYU Edgar

New York University maintains a terrific site for investors or anyone who needs to research company histories or statistics at *edgar.stern.nyu.edu.* The EDGAR (Electronic Data Gathering and Retrieval) site was developed by the NYU Stern School of Business Information Systems Department (see Figure 8-9). Perhaps one of its most valuable features is the Profile Search that lets you search and view corporate profiles by entering keywords.

If you're investigating companies, you'll find plenty of uses for the links to the RR Donnelley Library of SEC Materials and Corporate SEC Filings. One of its richest resources is the link called Reciprocal Links, which will point you to a whole world of financial Web links. Be sure to check out their Interesting Links jump for such tidbits as the Economics of Networks.

I'll continue by showing you an excellent, full-powered stock reporting service that will give you automated, tailored financial reports, headlines, stock quotes, and complete portfolio tracking. My favorite stock service is Quote.Com (see Figure 8-10), which you can visit at *www.quote.com.*

NET TIP Remember, you don't have to own a stock to track it. You might sign up with one of these services simply to track the major players in your industry. I recommend setting up a portfolio with 100 shares of the target stocks so you can easily decipher the impact of stock price swings.

Tracking investment stocks

While I'll only profile one of the many different services available, you can see more by visiting the Web page at *edgar.stern.nyu.edu/reciprocal.html* and checking out its array of related links. I selected Quote.Com because it offers one-stop shopping for all types of the stock services and has a range of subscription levels that will allow you to tailor your service to your needs.

Quote.Com gave me a free demo account that I've used to set up a hypothetical stock portfolio. To retrieve your own portfolio, you'll have to enter a login and

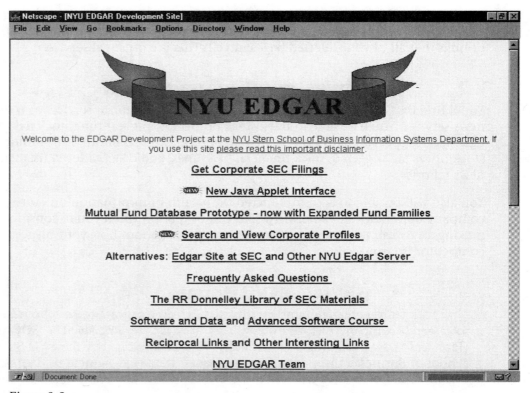

Figure 8-9

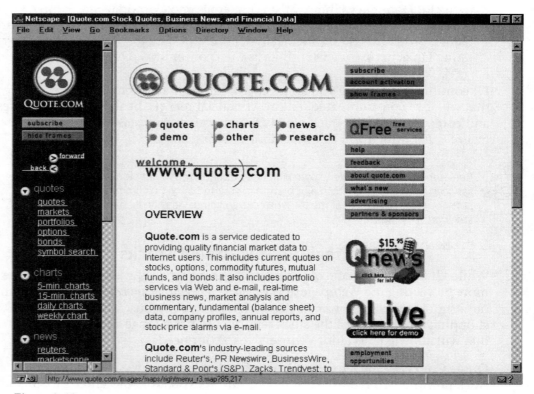

Figure 8-10

The world at your fingertips

password. You'll then be able to select from a list of multiple portfolios such as the sample portfolio displayed here (see Figure 8-11). From this page you can see that there are links to pick up Quick Quotes on other stocks, check financial news headlines, view a daily chart, consult an on-line stock guide, view a history file, or check your other portfolios. The buttons to Zack's Investment Research and to Trendvest are available at extra cost for basic subscribers, or free for higher-level subscribers.

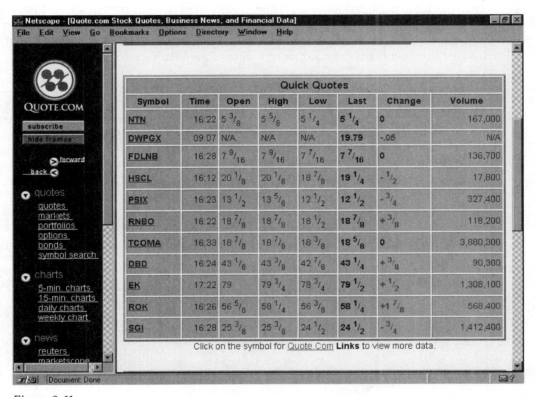

Figure 8-11

This portfolio is configured for viewing on-screen, but they offer several common formats that will permit you to easily enter this information in other applications. For example, they have ASCII comma-delimited, Quicken, and spreadsheet formats.

And here's the best part: You don't have to visit the Quote.Com Web site to track your portfolio. Quote.Com e-mails you a summary of your portfolios at the end of the business day so they'll be ready for you in the morning.

Financial news and reports

Quote.Com includes with each report it sends you, links to related stories on the stocks you've selected to track. If you've chosen a high-enough level of service, you'll be able to read the full text of these stories for free. If you have the basic service, you'll be charged one dollar per story that you select to read.

In addition to stories that affect your stock portfolio, you can enter the Quote.Com home page directly and search for stories on other companies. Perhaps if you find something interesting that pertains to your industry or business, you might add that stock to your portfolio, even if you have no plans to invest in that company.

AT&T Business Network

The AT&T Business Network service can keep you current on critical industry and business news. It lets you access its extensive reference sources, connect with a dynamic community of other business networkers, and take full advantage of a host of Internet business sources at *www.att.com/bnet* (see Figure 8-12).

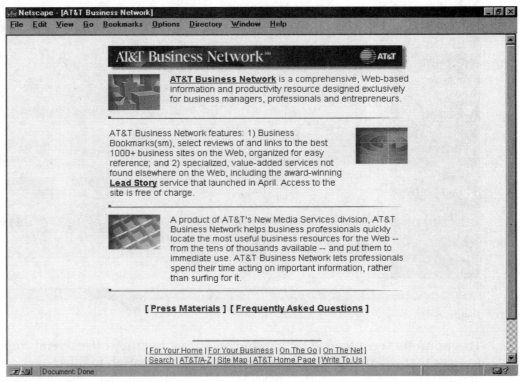

Figure 8-12

The AT&T Business Network features an incredible collection of on-line resources from leading publishers. I've assembled the current list in alphabetical order: Bunker Hill Consulting Group; BNA (Bureau of National Affairs); Business Travel News; CCH Incorporated; CNN Interactive; Cowles Business Media; Cowles New Media; Dow Jones Business Information Services; Dun & Bradstreet Information Services; Entrepreneurial Edge; Entrepreneur Magazine Group; Seth Godin Productions; Guerilla Marketing International; Individual, Inc.; Information Access Company; Inso Corporation; Investext Industry Reports; The Kiplinger Washington Editors; Nightly Business Report; Standard & Poor's; Thomas Register of American Manufacturers; Thomas Food Industry Register; TRW Business Information Services; TV HOST; Weather Services Corporation;

Weissmann Travel Reports; and Meg Whittemore of Whittemore & Associates. As amazing as that list is, it's growing steadily.

Let me guess: You never expected to find resources like that for free on the Internet, did you? Well, you haven't. The AT&T Business Network is a subscription service that costs, as this book is being written, $39.95 per month for 10 hours of access. Additional connect time is billed at $2.95 per hour. It's a real information bargain if you figure what access to all of that information would have cost a few years ago.

Now that you've seen so many Internet resources for business and financial news, I bet you quickly will learn to use it to improve your productivity and efficiency and to improve your products and services. With that in mind, let's turn to the next logical step: using the Internet to help you sell all you'll learn to do with on-line information resources.

Marketing sites

Internet marketing sites provide the full spectrum of marketing information. You can get help for selling your products and services and even for selling your business (see the sidebar below). You can find on-line ad agencies, marketing consultants, marketing software, and advertising forums. The Internet has brought us all a whole new world of marketing possibilities and channels. Fortunately, it also has brought us the tools to explore these new possibilities.

Often the key to finding the services or contacts you need will be to use the search engines profiled in the last chapter. To get you started, however, I've included some helpful sites here. As with most sites, you'll find links here to other, related Web sites.

Businesses for sale

Here's a Web site that was under construction as this book was being written, so you'll want to check it out today to see how it has evolved. AFC's Businesses For Sale is a meeting place for people who want to buy and sell businesses. If you're a seller, you can list your business here. If you're a buyer, you can search for businesses under a variety of categories—for example, geographic location, revenue size, and type of business. They also list links to several other business-for-sale Web sites. Visit their home page at *www.afc-inc.com* and check out the Continuing Education section for other similar services.

Marketing consultants

Marketing in cyberspace is a paradox: On the one hand it's completely different from any other marketing, and on the other hand it's the same as it's been for thousands of years. You might want to turn to some professional advisors to help your organization clear the hurdle of that paradox. Fortunately, some expert help is available on-line. Let's begin with one of the best: Poppe Tyson (pronounced poppy tyson), a venerable, well-established agency that has been at the forefront of the move into cyberspace.

Poppe Tyson

Poppe Tyson is an international advertising agency owned by Bozell, Jacobs, Kenyon & Eckhardt, the world's fourth-largest marketing communications company. There's more to them than size: They were selected as the 1995 Agency of the Year by *Marketing Computers* magazine (see Figure 8-13). Check them out at *www.poppe.com*.

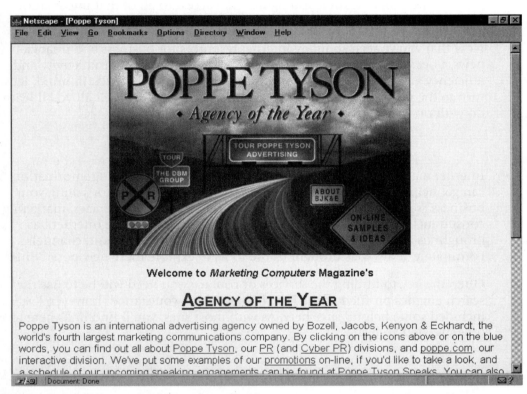

Figure 8-13

Some of Poppe Tyson's clients prove its ability to handle cyberspace marketing. For example, they are handling the marketing for one of the largest Internet service providers in the U.S., PSI Net of Herndon, Virginia. My favorite project of theirs has been their work in bringing the Indy 500 race into cyberspace. Beginning with the 1995 Memorial Day weekend, the Web site for the world's most famous race was introduced during commercial breaks by Valvoline Motor Oil, one of Poppe Tyson's clients. Poppe Tyson was able to coordinate both the marketing content and the technical expertise required to bring the Indy 500 and the Daytona 500 Web sites to life (see Figure 8-14).

NET TIP Poppe Tyson's Web site is a marvel of cyberspace value. Following their own version of my Client-centered Interneting principles, they provide a treasure trove of in-depth marketing expertise. And it's yours to read and print for free. Of course they hope to attract your business while you're surfing their site, but that's what well-done Web sites are all about.

Figure 8-14

GoSite

Perhaps your organization already has a successful marketing program that will translate to cyberspace. If you just need to launch an existing marketing program in cyberspace, then you need a service that can develop hypertext versions of your existing materials and transform your logo, graphics, and photos into Web formats that are ready to go worldwide.

Check out the GoSite service at *www.gosite.com* (see Figure 8-15) for details. Your costs for using a company like GoSite will be lower than with a full-service agency such as Poppe Tyson, but then you already will have paid for the development of your advertising program. GoSite can create Web graphics that fit your existing, traditional marketing programs and help you format your material into a valuable, user-friendly Web site. They also can handle creating your Web server, registering your domain name, uploading your Web files, and maintaining your entire site.

GoSite is a nice compromise between a full-service agency and a total do-it-yourself Web service provider. One tool they use to bridge the gap between the two is the GoGadget Administrator, an Internet site manager that makes simple work of some otherwise complicated tasks (see Figure 8-16). If you can click a mouse, you'll find that GoGadget makes maintaining a Web Site simple. You can automatically consolidate the files between your computer and your GoSite Server by clicking a button. Even Internet novices will quickly be able to set up and control e-mail POP accounts, forwarding files, and even auto-responding e-mail.

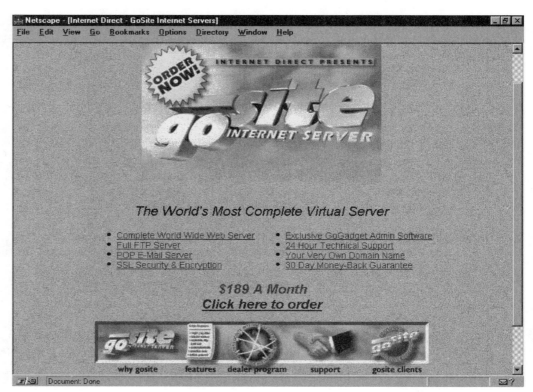

Figure 8-15

Figure 8-16

The world at your fingertips

Your Marketing Coach

If you need to market, but you wish marketing would go away, you need Your Marketing Coach. Designed for even smaller businesses than the previous two reviewed here, Your Marketing Coach is a do-it-yourself marketing program that's based on Client-centered Interneting (see Figure 8-17). Its home page is at *www.marketing-coach.com*, and also hosts the Web sites of this book and my first Internet book, *The McGraw-Hill Internet Training Manual.*

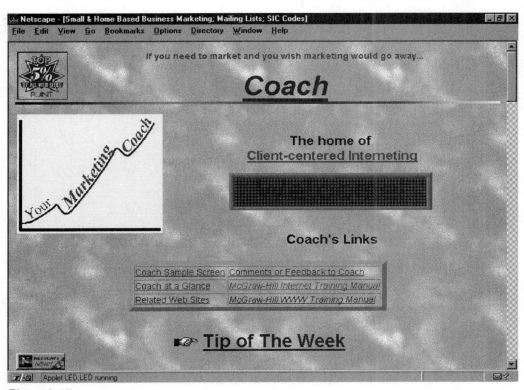

Figure 8-17

Coach works best for sole proprietorships and small businesses that market consulting and professional services. What type of person needs to market, but wishes marketing would go away? Accountants, engineers, architects, public relations consultants, writers, consultants, and computer programmers. These professions rarely are filled with good marketers, but they can't survive without marketing. Coach makes marketing easy with a software application called Market Keys that analyzes an existing practice and recommends ways to capitalize on its client list to bring in clones of its best clients.

The Coach Web site features regularly updated hot tips on marketing your consulting and professional services. It also has links to many other sites that provide valuable help for small and home-based businesses. Its best touch is the free marketing manuals that you will be sent if you complete the on-line questionnaire. Just fill in your mailing information and request the manual you want.

Department of Commerce economic data

This service offers up-to-date worldwide economic information on everything from copyright issues to international currency exchange rates. It's not technically on the Web, because it's a Gopher-search site maintained by the University of Michigan (see Figure 8-18). Most likely this site soon will find its way onto the Web, but its information is too valuable to exclude just because it hasn't yet made the transition.

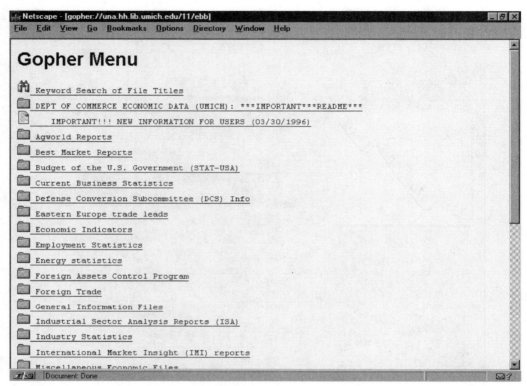

Figure 8-18

You can access the site within Netscape by entering the URL *gopher://una.hh .lib.umich.edu/11/ebb.* You'll see a long list of folders that contain documents on various business topics. Many of the folders produce lists of subfolders. Eventually you'll get down to a document you want, which can be retrieved by clicking on the document icon or the hypertext title. If browsing a long title list doesn't appeal to you, click on the link Keyword Search of File Titles at the top of the page. This link brings up a searchable Gopher index that lets you enter keywords.

NET TIP   The Gopher keyword searches performed on this Gopher site look for all terms separately. If you want to narrow a search by using more than one search term, you must manually insert the Boolean operators AND or NOT.

Better Business Bureau

The Better Business Bureau is a classic, traditional source for all kinds of business information. You can visit the Better Business Bureau site at *www.bbb.org* (see Figure 8-19).

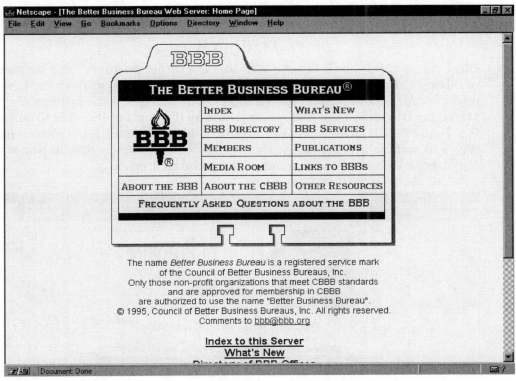

Figure 8-19

Like the rest of us, this venerable institution has moved into cyberspace to keep up with the times. For example, in February 1996, the Council of Better Business Bureau announced 15 companies as finalists for their first annual Better Business Bureau Torch Award for Marketplace Ethics. The award finalists were selected for demonstrating a commitment to exceptionally high standards of ethical business practices. Surely there's some inspiration for your own excellence lurking in the stories about such select companies.

I can recommend the Better Business Bureau Code Of Advertising as an excellent information source for use in reviewing your organization's marketing plan. For example, with all of the free things floating around on the Internet, you might want to read the Free topic in these guidelines before you apply that often-misleading word to your products or services. Another company-saving topic is their Scam Alert link that can keep you up-to-date on the latest con schemes. A good example is an exposé titled *Don't Get Scammed By Office Con Artists*; it reveals the explosion of fake offices that are being established to hide con artist activities. Expect to see these same principles mushroom on the Internet.

Business newsgroups

Newsgroups aren't a part of the Web, but they're such an integrated part of Netscape that you'll hardly know the difference. Start your Netscape newsgroup reader by clicking on **Window, Netscape News,** then browse through your list of newsgroup headings until you see the **biz.*** folder. Open this folder to reveal the topics inside, then click on any of them that interest you.

Mailing lists

Okay, this is a Web book, but the Web isn't the whole Internet. There are plenty of other good resources and mailing lists that often provide some of the best information you can find on special topics. One example is the Internet Marketing Discussion List that's maintained by the Point of Presence Company (see Figure 8-20). This service is beginning to blur the distinction between the Web and mailing lists because you can subscribe and unsubscribe on-line and also use the Web site to search and review archived articles.

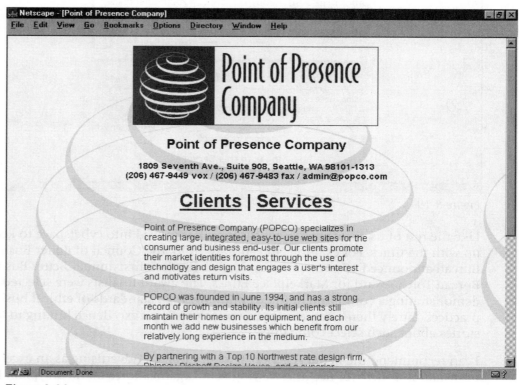

Figure 8-20

The Internet Marketing Discussion List is devoted to discussing appropriate Internet marketing practices and strategies. As this is written, it has more than 6250 subscribers and has been covered in many major Internet publications. From the mailing list's home Web page at *http://www.i-m.com* you can jump to a variety of links about Internet marketing (see Figure 8-21).

Subscribing and unsubcribing to the mailing list has been automated on the home page—just click the appropriate link. New subscribers will find useful the

The world at your fingertips

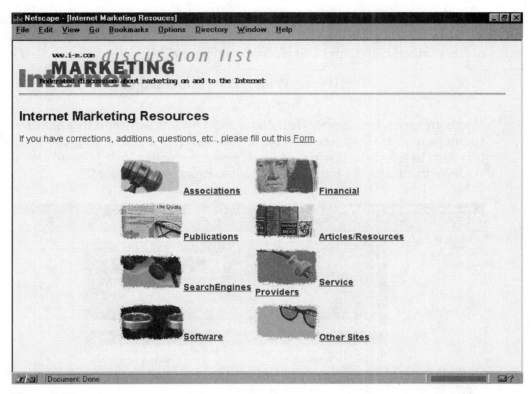

Figure 8-21

extensive archive of back issues that is searchable by keyword. Articles also are posted by date so you can go directly to the Point of Presence FTP site and browse through the entire listing of available files.

Perhaps one of the site's richest finds, however, is the Resources link on the home page. This page is a wonderful collection of Internet marketing articles assembled from all over the Web. For example, you can check out the Top Ten Internet Marketing Do's and Don'ts from Blackstone Marketing and Communications located at *www.IslandNet.com:80/~pb*. I also recommend *Slaves of a New Machine: Exploring the For-Free/For-Pay Conundrum*, Laura Fillmore's address to the *Making Money on the Internet* conference.

These sites merely are a starting point for finding business information on the Web. I've included more sites below in the Continuing Education section, and the next chapter focuses on libraries and research sites; but they, too, will give you even more business information.

 *Continuing Education*

Open Market commercial sites index
http://www.directory.net

Open Market Incorporated develops and markets software, services, and custom solutions that facilitate electronic commerce on the Web. Open Market applies both advanced technology and a business perspective to the expansion of business into an electronic marketplace. They offer solutions that address the needs of small companies and global businesses alike.

World Wide Web yellow pages

http://www.yellow.com

Here's an easy-to-remember URL that should find its way onto thousands (perhaps millions?) of Netscape Bookmark lists (see Figure 8-22). You can use this page to search for a wide range of businesses with a Web presence. World Wide Yellow Pages is a trademark of Home Pages, Incorporated.

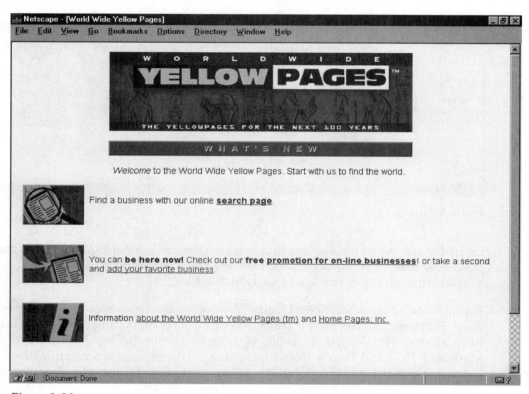

Figure 8-22

Certified business brokers

http://www.mgroup.com/cbb.html

Certified Business Brokers is a professional firm with a broad range of business skills and experience available to assist you in the sale or acquisition of a privately owned business. With over 60 years combined experience in business sales and acquisitions and a track record of over 1000 businesses sold, Certified Business Brokers can be an essential element in buying a business or selling your current business.

BizQuest

http://www.bizquest.com

BizQuest is a business service that maintains a database of international business transfer information (see Figure 8-23). They list both general businesses (up to

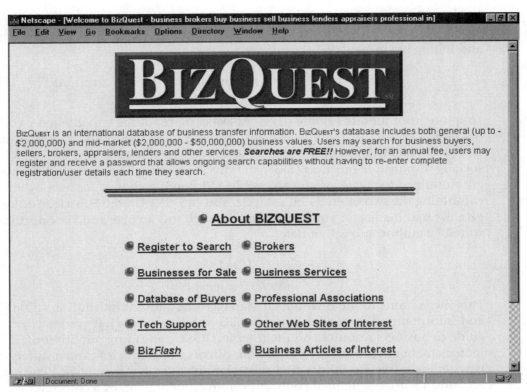

Figure 8-23

$2,000,000 in sales) and mid-market businesses ($2,000,000–$50,000,000) in sales. You might perform free searches for business buyers, sellers, brokers, appraisers, lenders, and other services, but you'll have to complete a registration form before each search. For an annual fee, they'll give you a password that allows you to search without having to register each time you return to the site.

M&A Marketplace

http://www.mktplc.com/cfnet

The M&A Marketplace Web site is designed for buyers and sellers of companies and for financial intermediaries who are involved in mergers and acquisitions (M&A), divestitures, and corporate finance. They've got links that let you explore companies for sale, buyers seeking sellers, joint ventures, financial sources, and a host of other related topics. Full searching and browsing capabilities are reserved for visitors with paid memberships (currently $9.95 per month). They even provide an area on the site for members to network directly with other members.

Business Exchange Network

http://www.biz-exchange.com

The Business Exchange Network is a clearinghouse of information for the buying and selling of small-sized to mid-sized businesses. Sales are handled through their Web site, as well as through several traditional avenues. They publish a monthly newspaper, Businesses for Sale, and two weekly publications, Business Buyers Weekly Report, and the Business Brokers, Agents, and Intermediaries Report. They offer another noncyberspace option for the information on their

Web site through a fax-on-demand system. If you're considering using such a service, you might want to read their articles dealing with all aspects of buying and selling businesses.

Socially responsible business mailing list archive

http://www.envirolink.org/archives/srb

To quote from the site's home page, "At last, a place for the enlightened discussion of Socially Responsible Business and Investing." This is THE forum for discussion and information exchange focused around aspects and topics of socially responsible business (SRB) and investing (SRI). The SRB and SRI topics are combined to create a more accessible and popular conference area by combining the two interrelated subjects. You can click on the Subscribe link to join the mailing list, or you can browse through this archive and view documents sorted by author, subject, or date.

IOMA

http://www.ioma.com

This site is home to the Institute Of Management and Administration (IOMA) and Information Services for Professionals (see Figure 8-24). It's an excellent guide to business resources on the Internet. IOMA, a leading publisher of management and business information, offers sample articles from a variety of newsletters, as well as 90-day trial subscriptions. Whether managing a law or accounting office, a defined contribution investment plan, or a computer network, professionals from virtually every industry can find invaluable career-enhancing information in these IOMA newsletters.

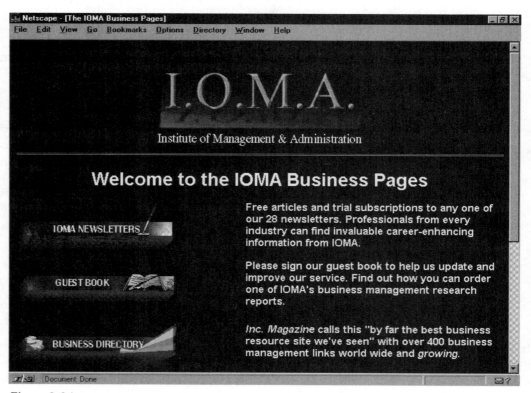

Figure 8-24

The world at your fingertips

Printshop 2000

http://www.printshop2000.com

It seems that everything is going on-line these days. The Internet revolution is hurting a lot of traditional mom-and-pop printing shops, but the major players have embraced cyberspace and are using it to increase their business. I've found that you might be able to handle all of your printshop needs on-line from the Printshop 2000 site (see Figure 8-25). They'll take your order over the Internet, let you e-mail in your files, and then they'll ship out the completed job. No more running out for your business needs, because you've now got a printshop on your PC.

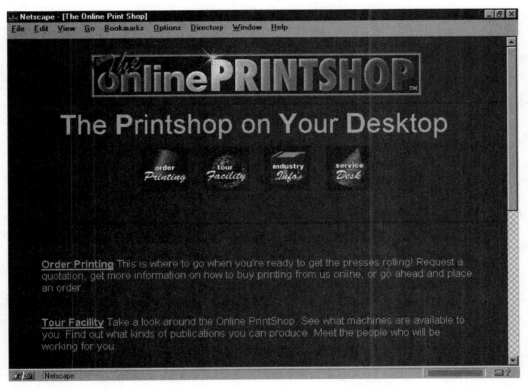

Figure 8-25

▶

Libraries, bookstores, and other research resources

ON-LINE bookstores and libraries come in two basic categories. One category is an electronic version of traditional bookstores. This means that when you enter them, you can browse through conventional printed books by author, title, or subject. Some of them improve upon the storefront bookstore by letting you search for books by keywords. However, their main business is selling you printed books. The second category is a truly cyberspace bookstore that lets you directly download entire books. Of course, some of these might also sell printed books, but their main business is electronically published material.

I'll first show you some on-line bookstores, then present some on-line libraries and finish with a collection of reference sources that either will help you find information or find links to other reference sources. I'll give you a sample and short analysis of some good bookstores, then follow with some good libraries. The Continuing Education section will help point you to some more resources, including general reference sources.

Bookstores

If you don't find enough through the sites featured here, you always can go to a search engine and find libraries and bookstores. If you do so, get comfortable with a snack and a drink nearby, because you'll be in for a shock at how rapidly the publishing world has transitioned to cyberspace.

Internet Book Shop

This site wins my gold star for the most titles I've ever seen on-line: 780,000! Every book they have listed has been classified into one of 2000 categories. Once you locate a book, ordering is simple and they list the shipping and handling charges. Jump to *www.bookshop.co.uk* (see Figure 9-1) and you'll be in for a literary treat.

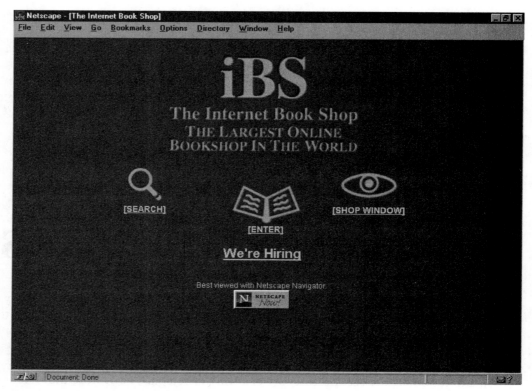

Figure 9-1

This site is a good example of Client-centered Interneting because its value extends well beyond being a convenient book source. They've achieved this with in-depth studies of various authors that includes cross-referencing more than 350 authors with more than 3500 titles in a Good Reading Guide. Each month they profile one new book as their Book of the Month; and they've created a powerful search engine that will locate books for you by title, author, ISBN number, publisher, or topic (see Figure 9-2).

You also will find special promotions, new developments, and a special section for new titles. And in case you don't find what you need here, they've included a section that lists links to other interesting sites. Here you'll find a rich variety of additional resources:

⊙ On-Line publications (literature, general, zines and alternate publications, Internet, and cyber-culture).
⊙ Authors' pages, publishers, and other on-line bookshops.
⊙ Archives and libraries.
⊙ Resources, art, and music.

While this is a commercial service, it's still worthy of your bookmark list because it offers so many client-centered value-adding features. You probably will find it useful for locating information on a variety of topics—it's definitely *not* limited to selling books.

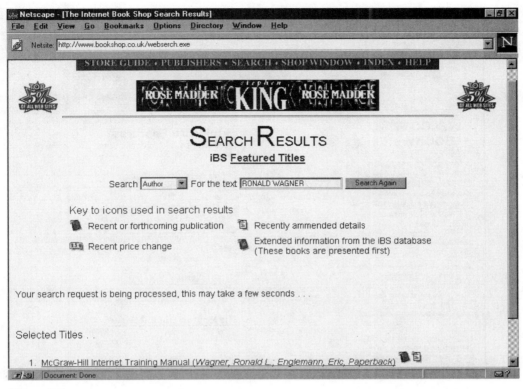

Figure 9-2

BookWire

Because the Internet Book Shop is in the UK, using them might cause you shipping delays or currency exchange problems; so I thought I'd put in a couple of local bookstores. Of course, these days local means in the same country. The first featured site is BookWire, located at *www.bookwire.com*, where you'll find an information-rich home page filled with links to book categories (see Figure 9-3). Starting from this page, you should be able to satisfy all of your book needs.

Just in case there isn't enough here, the folks at BookWire even include a link to other Web book resources. That's a nice example of one of the Client-centered Interneting principles I outlined in chapter 3: If you can't give your visitors what they need, graciously point them to sites that can. If you can't find the link, you can jump directly to this page at *www.bookwire.com/links/online_booksellers/ online_booksellers.html* and find other virtual bookstores and libraries.

This site is a good Client-centered Interneting example also because of its tables-based home page. They've created a modern, cool-looking home page without resorting to bandwidth-grabbing graphics. Even though it almost appears graphical, it's just simple HTML text in a table format. The result is a compact page that will download quickly even across a 14.4kbps modem.

From the home page, I suggest starting with the link BookWire Navigator that brings up all of their links by category on one easy-to-browse page.

Figure 9-3

How to get published

Does seeing all of these books stir up your own urge to get published, but you have no idea about how to begin? You won't be surprised that the Web can help you get your own book added to the lists you see here.

My literary agency is the Washington office of Adler & Robin Books, where I deal mostly with Bill Adler, Jr. and Lisa Swayne. The agency's claim to fame is being Number One in New York Times Bestsellers. They also are the second-largest computer book agency in the world. If you want to know how they achieved such success, visit their Web site at *www.adlerbooks.com*. Bill and Lisa know the publishing industry inside out and share some of their knowledge on-line. Your best bet is to jump to the link on how to get published.

Knowing Bill and Lisa has given me a fabulous advantage in my writing career, but I'm merely a small fish in a large and distinguished pond. Their client list reads like a Who's Who directory: Charles Osgood, Dan Rather, Dick Clark, Ed McMahon, Fran Tarkenton, Geraldo Rivera, Helen Hayes, Howard Cosell, Jeff Smith (The Frugal Gourmet), Joan Lunden, Larry King, Margaret Truman, Mickey Mantle, Mike Wallace, Nancy Reagan, Nolan Ryan, Phil Donahue, Robert MacNeil, Ronald Reagan, Sally Jessy Raphael, Senator Gary Hart, Senator George Mitchell, Senator William Cohen, Steve Allen, Tom Seaver, Tom Shales, Willard Scott, Jeff Davidson, and, of course, Ron Wagner.

The Web site includes postings of book ideas for which they are seeking writers, so check it out to see if you fit in, or post a note to them to propose your own idea.

The Bookstore

The Bookstore is a full-service on-line store at *intertain.com/store/welcome.html* that lets you browse by author or title and then order the book directly (see Figure 9-4). The Bookstore lets you create a profile so that you have to enter ordering information only one time because they'll keep it on file for your future visits. Once your profile is registered you can browse the site, read synopses of books that interest you, and click on the Buy button to add to your shopping list. They offer a variety of shipping methods, so you have options on the shipping costs.

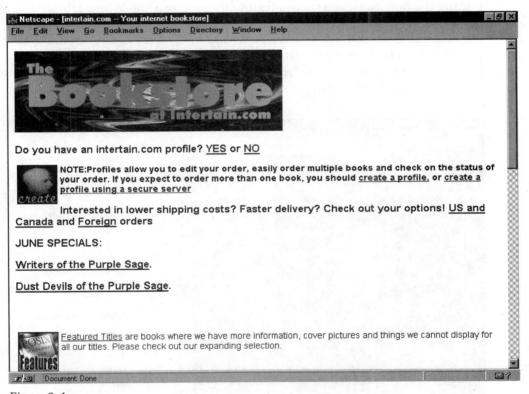

Figure 9-4

In addition to the author and title searches, you can search by keyword. For example, I searched for a book I wrote a couple of years ago with Bill Adler, Jr., entitled *The Weather Sourcebook* (Globe Pequot Press 1994). Naturally, I found it by searching for my name and for the title. When I tried the keyword search for weather, it appeared on a list of 84 other weather books. If you get a similar list, you'll be able to click a check box in front of each entry that interests you, then click a More button to see the full description of each selection you checked.

While you're visiting, be sure to hit the button for The Village. The Bookstore is just one shop in The Village at Intertain, a collection of stores available 24 hours a day, 7 days a week. The Village has many places to explore, exchange ideas with other people, and of course, shop.

Virtual libraries

First I'll present the newest form of library in the world: the virtual library. These usually are not affiliated with a traditional, physical library, but exist only in cyberspace. They all can point you to a treasure trove of information. Some actually store information on-site, but most are actually a collection of links to other Web resources. After showing you a few virtual libraries, I'll give you pointers to the Web sites of some traditional libraries that have gone on-line.

World Library

Putting the new Netscape frames feature to good use, the World Library presents a well-done, user-friendly front end that will speed your on-line information quests. Visit their home page at *www.scescape.com/WorldLibrary*, but make sure you've got a frames-capable Web browser such as Netscape 2.0 or later (see Figure 9-5). The right side of the screen gives you a separate scrolling window with links to different categories.

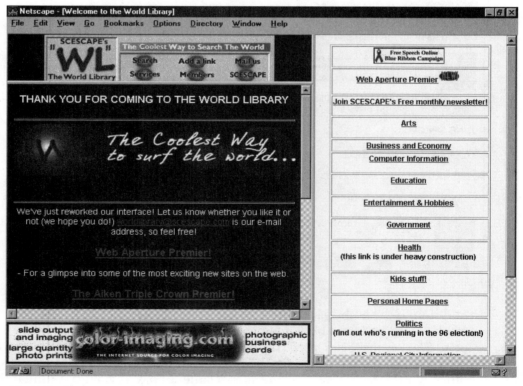

Figure 9-5

The left side of the screen is a list of publishers. You can scroll through this window to find links to the publishers' home pages. If you're new to using frames, you need a few tips on navigating through a site like this. Going forward is easy because you merely click on an interesting link as usual. But, if you try to go back to a previous page in a window clicking on the normal Netscape **Back** button or use **ALT+LEFT ARROW**, you'll jump back to the last *site* you were on and *not* the last page within the frames window. To return to a previous page within a frame window, click the right mouse button, then click **Back in Frame**.

In addition to the category links, you'll find a link to their on-line searching service. Realize, though, that this is not a Web search—it looks only at the resources they have cataloged. Through the category links, however, you'll be pointed to global resources on a rich variety of information.

WWW Virtual Library

The WWW Virtual Library uses a distributed subject catalog for topic organization. The home page, therefore, is a long listing of major topics for which they have references. The Web address is *www.w3.org/vl* (see Figure 9-6). I've included this because it's a nice contrast to the World Library featured earlier. This service uses the simplest possible Web page interface and is a good choice if you're using an older Web browser, a slow computer, or if you have a slow Internet connection. The pages here won't tax your computer resources, which is quite a switch from some of the virtual book sources I've seen.

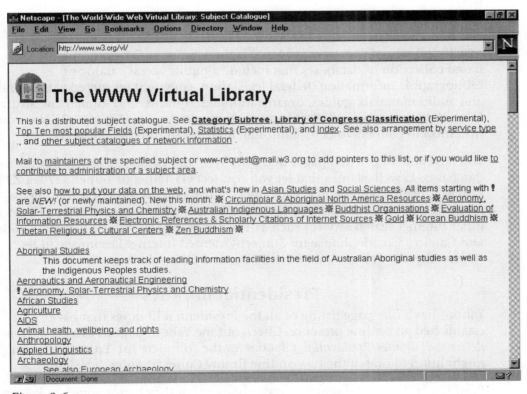

Figure 9-6

The links at the top of the page give you a variety of display options for the topic listing. Catalog Subtree expands the listings shown here into subtrees that go as deep as three levels (two levels under the major topics). The Library of Congress Classification redisplays the screen with a much shorter list of standard topics. There's also a link that lists resources by Subject, which is so comprehensive I've included it in the Continuing Education section. Don't let the plain appearance distract you from the wealth of knowledge that you can tap through this site— the plain appearance is a resource-friendly gesture.

Real libraries

The sites featured here are on-line outlets of traditional physical libraries. Some have provisions for borrowing material via mail, but many only let you use their service to search their archives and catalogs.

You'll find the whole spectrum from the massive Library of Congress to Presidential libraries, university libraries, and all the way down to small community libraries. This is a rapidly growing area on the Internet, and it's hard to predict what's on-line and what's not.

There are countless libraries in cyberspace, so I'll give you a representative overview and some resources that will point you to more. From those resources you'll find links you can follow to find everything that's available on-line in libraries.

Library of Congress

LOCIS (Library of Congress On Line) is the Library of Congress' mainframe-based collection of databases that include a public access catalog of bibliographic information, federal legislation, copyright registered works, braille and audio materials, guides, organization descriptions, and foreign law abstracts. From the home page, which is located at *www.loc.gov* (see Figure 9-7), you can find links to connect to LOCIS through a variety of Internet methods.

You'll be able to get Web pages that offer Web and Gopher searches of the databases, as well as links that let you connect via Telnet or Telnet 3270, a Z39.50 Gateway, or through the FTP. Even the U.S. federal government is joining us mainstream folks out here in cyberspace, because they even offer links here to other Internet search services such as The Awesome List, Whole Internet Guide and Catalog, Clearinghouse for Subject-Oriented Internet Resource Guides (University of Michigan), and the Categorical Catapult.

Presidential libraries

Yahoo! has a one-page listing of all the Presidential libraries that have established an on-line presence. Check out the Yahoo! page at *www.yahoo.com/ Reference/Libraries/Presidential_Libraries* for the complete list. From there, you might jump to one of the two on-line Jimmy Carter libraries.

Presidential libraries might be small libraries, but they have enough to keep you busy for the rest of your life if you did nothing else. Here's an example of what's available at the Jimmy Carter Library: Over 26 million pages of material from the

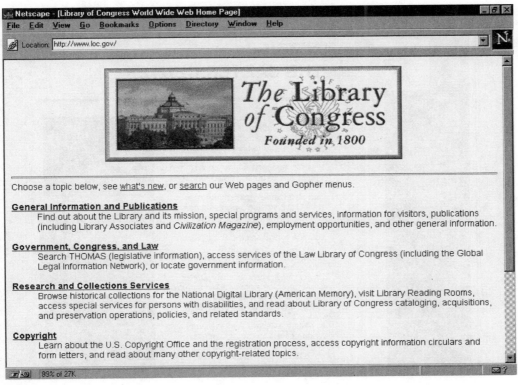

Figure 9-7

Carter White House are housed there, along with more than a million photographs, motion picture film, videotape, audiotape, and gifts to the President. The documents range from exchanges between President Carter and heads of state and diplomatic treaties to records of what was served for dinner and how many paper clips were used by the White House staff. The audio and videotapes and photographs document a wide variety of activities, ranging from the visit of world dignitaries to a footrace between the President and his daughter. Yikes!

If you live near any of the Presidential libraries, you can check their home pages for information on scheduled events and special programs held at the libraries, such as events at the Carter Center (see Figure 9-8).

University libraries

Jump into Yahoo! and click on the home page link **Reference, Libraries**, then click on **University Libraries**. When I tried that, Yahoo! displayed a list of 204 choices! Is that enough for you? The first nine at the top were marked New, which means that this list is going to be much larger by the time you click on the same links.

There is a **Special Collections** link at the top of the list that only had eight selections—at least something here is manageable. (You did read chapter 2 on *Breathing Space*, didn't you? If not, then you'd better read it and heed it before jumping into this bedlam.) The Special Collections link is a good thing to

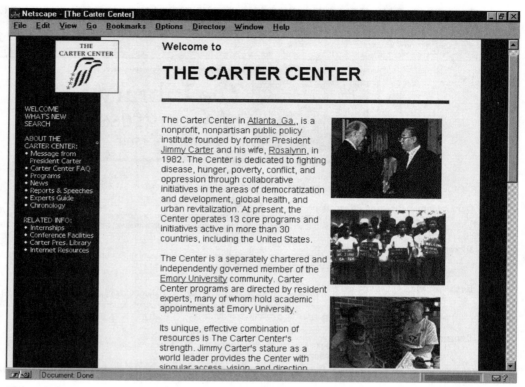

Figure 9-8

remember if you're having difficulty finding obscure information or rare books or images. These links truly have some unique research materials.

When you start clicking on the university library links, you need to be ready for anything. Most of them use hypertext Web pages, but you'll find Gopher and Telnet links. Gopher pages will hardly look much different than Web pages, except for appearing very plain. For more information on Telnet, read the accompanying sidebar.

Telnet

Many libraries let you tap into their main computer via a Telnet connection. Telnet is an Internet protocol that lets your PC become a remote terminal to a larger computer. Telnet allows you to establish a connection and log in so that all of your keystrokes are sent to the remote server. In this mode, you will see the screen output of the server as if you were operating a terminal directly connected to that machine. With a Telnet application you can establish a Telnet session using a dial-in modem and have access to the character-based Internet services available on the machine to which you have connected.

Windows Telnet applications are a snap to use and making the connection is easy, but you're on your own once you're connected.

Try it now if you have a Telnet application. Enter the host as *lib.dartmouth.edu*, and press **ENTER** (see Figure 9-9 on next page). Once you're in, you can search for books by author, title, or topic, but you'll be out of Netscape and you'll be using Dartmouth Library computer commands. To end the Telnet session, just click to close the window or press **ALT+F4**, then confirm **OK** to terminate the connection.

If you want a good Telnet client, visit the Web page at *www.state.ky.us/software/windows.html*, download the latest version, install it, and configure it. You might want to bookmark this page to get upgrades and for all the other links it contains to various Windows TCP/IP client applications, such as WS_FTP, Eudora e-mail, Archie, Finger, and Ping.

Whichever Telnet client you choose, be sure to add it as a helper application to your copy of Netscape. Detailed steps for adding Netscape helper applications are included in a Hands-On exercise in chapter 6, "Advanced Netscape."

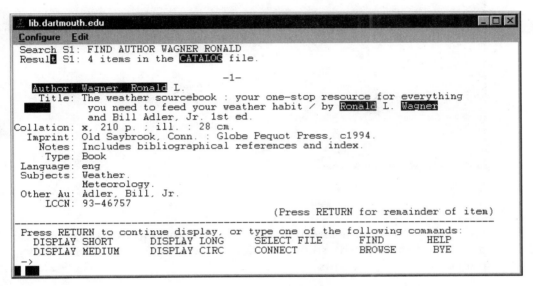

Figure 9-9

Local libraries

There's no pattern to the libraries that have established Web sites. For example, you'll find many small communities with an active on-line library presence, and yet some major communities that are not yet on-line. For example, Fairfax County, Virginia has the highest average education and income level in the U.S., so you'd expect it to have been among the leaders in cyberspace libraries. However, I discovered that there is a dilemma; it consists of huge information resources versus a budget crunch. If Fairfax County were smaller, they'd be able to get on-line quickly, but putting such a huge collection on-line in today's tight budget environment isn't easy.

Clearwater Public Library

I browsed through a few local libraries and selected one that I found to be an excellent model of what can be done by community libraries. The Clearwater, Florida Public Library (see Figure 9-10) has done an outstanding job of

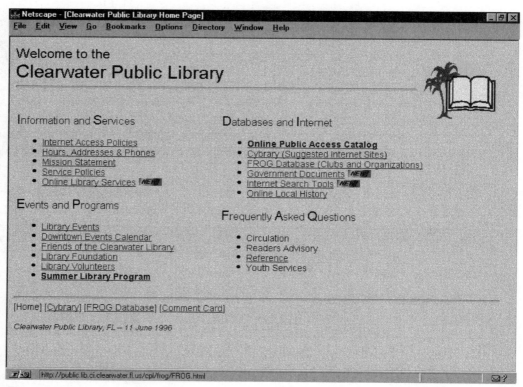

Figure 9-10

presenting their on-line research and resource services as well as giving local patrons a comprehensive source of information on hours, locations, library policies, and special events.

I liked the Cybrary link to Internet Resources that I found on the Clearwater home page (see Figure 9-11). The Cybrary link jumps to a whole menu of valuable features available in this cyber-library: the Card Catalog (Telnet to access their catalog file); the Reading Room (divided into Bibliographies, Literature, Nonfiction, and Periodicals); the Reference Desk; the Youth Room; and FROG (Florida Resource and Opportunity Guide). FROG is a wonderful resource that area residents can use to track activities, organizations, events, and programs that meet the daily information needs of citizens, businesses, and community organizations in the Tampa Bay Area. I realize that this won't do most of you much good, but if your local library's Web system isn't this advanced, perhaps you can use this to lobby for better service—it's an exceptionally well-done site for a local organization.

I would have put this site on my bookmark list just for the Reference Desk link—thank goodness there's so much more. The Reference Desk has everything from an e-mail link to Ask a librarian for something, to international currency rates, to Bartlett's Quotations, to nationwide Lottery Numbers, to Vital Records offices in every state. Finally, you can locate the right address to order a copy of your birth certificate!

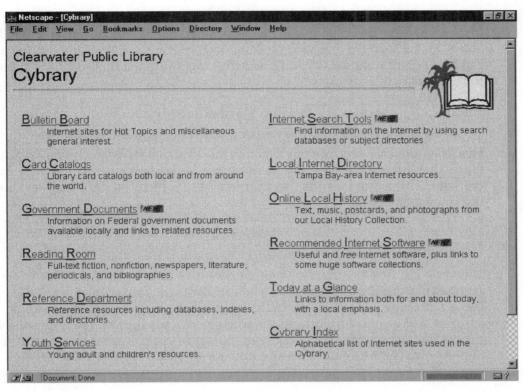

Figure 9-11

Local library summary

There are several ways to find out if your local library system is on-line. First, of course, you can call a local phone number and ask, or you can stop at a local branch for information about the system's on-line status. Or, without leaving home, you can use standard Web search tools—after all, it's not mandatory that you use the Web only to find far-away places. A Yahoo! or Lycos search for your city or county might be all you need, or you can jump directly to the page on community libraries at *www.yahoo.com/Reference/Libraries/Public_Libraries*. If your area library system isn't yet on-line, you might be able to help them, using some of the existing sites (such as Clearwater) as examples. If you're thinking of developing your HTML and Web publishing skills, volunteering to help a local library could give you excellent experience as well as a very public showcase for your talents.

 *Continuing Education*

BookWire library index

http://www.bookwire.com/links/libraries/librarymenu.html

Here's a powerful listing of Web-accessible libraries from around the globe. This is an excellent model of what the Internet does best. In fact, if you haven't read chapter 2, Breathing Space for Cyberspace, this site might make you run screaming from your computer. You literally could spend the rest of your life exploring just the links on this page and still tap into but a fraction of all that it offers.

You can use this Web page to tap into almost any information you want from libraries in these basic groups: Asian, Australian, Canadian, European, United States, and others. For example, tracking down the European option on this page can lead you to hundreds of worldwide resources through the Bodleian Library at the University of Oxford.

WWW Virtual Library

http://www.w3.org/hypertext/DataSources/bySubject/Overview.html

Here's a topic-oriented Internet reference site. Instead of keywords, you look for topics that interest you—or ones that intrigue you—there's something here for everyone. This is not like other topic-oriented sites like Yahoo!; it really is an on-line, hypertext library.

WebMuseum

http://sunsite.unc.edu/wm

This truly is a treasure trove of Internet resources (see Figure 9-12). It's a free art museum created by Nicolas Pioch, a student studying economics at the Ecole Nationale Superieure des Telecommunications in Paris. It's a personal creation that has no support, no funding, and no manpower. The WebMuseum is a collaborative work that encourages its visitors to contribute to expand and improve the WebMuseum. This site won a Best of the Web Award in 1994.

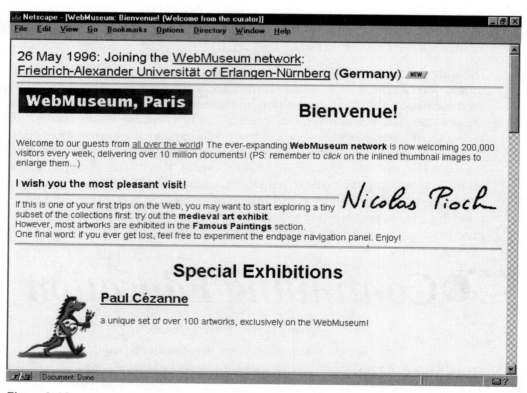

Figure 9-12

Britannica Online

http://www.eb.com

This is a commercial site. Its only free services are demonstrations and accounts for educational institutions. Full searches require a fee payment, but you get the full resources of *Britannica Book of the Year*, *Nations of the World*, *Merriam Webster's Collegiate Dictionary*, and the *Propaedia*. They have different fee structures for home use, business use, and for use by a college student. All levels of service require a nonrefundable registration fee and then an annual subscription fee, but they offer a 7-day free trial.

Reference Shelf

http://www.nova.edu/Inter-Links/reference.html

The Reference Shelf is a potpourri of reference sources collected from around the Web (see Figure 9-13). It's just a one-page site, but it's a top candidate for your bookmark list because you could stay busy for days exploring its links. A few valuable examples are City/Zip Code Lookup (with geography info), plus facts and maps for nearly every country in the world. The Perpetual Calendar link alone is worth bookmarking the list—where else can you instantly find a suitable-for-printing calendar for any month of any year?

Whole Internet Guide and Catalog

http://nearnet.gnn.com/wic

Sponsored by O'Reilly and Associates, the Whole Internet Guide and Catalog (see Figure 9-14) guides you through more than 2500 of the best sites the Web has to offer, organized into easy-to-surf subject categories. It's the home of GNN Select, your tour guide on this site to the World Wide Web.

Yale library listing

gopher://libgopher.yale.edu

Here's a Gopher URL that will give you pointers to all of the libraries in the world. You can perform a keyword search, or jump to listings by world geographic region. If you go the geographic route, you'll enter a hierarchical set of folders that will narrow down to the library you're seeking. There is a lot of resources here, so make like the Energizer bunny and just keep on going.

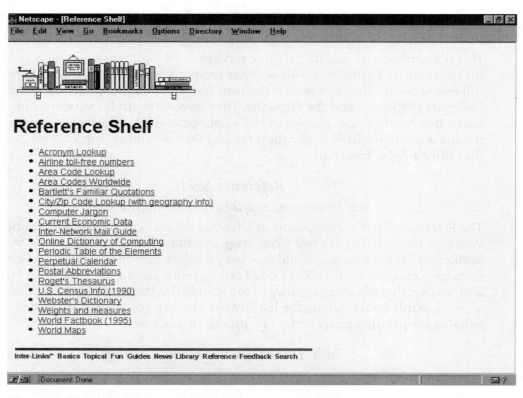

Figure 9-13

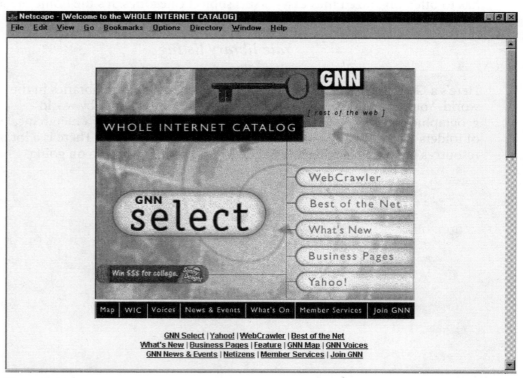

Figure 9-14

▶ *The world at your fingertips*

Government Web sites

WE'VE HAD A STRING of government shutdowns. Governments everywhere are struggling under budget crunches. They're running massive deficits. We're piling up record government debt. Government employees are suffering under unprecedented downsizing and layoffs. Trust and faith in the government is reported to be at an all-time low; we've got government-hating guys holed up in cabins in Montana. But through it all, somehow, your tax dollars have been hard at work in cyberspace. Nothing can stop the Internet, not even the problems currently facing government.

It's amazing, actually, that the government isn't the main focus of the Internet. We're lucky. Somebody back in the early 1960s was wise enough to realize that the Internet would be more robust if government stayed out of it. They were right. Fortunately, the government still doesn't control the Internet, although a few government leaders would love to find ways to do that.

Now that 30 years of freedom for the Internet have created a powerful, universal Web that connects us all, government is slipping back into the party—but mostly as an equal guest. Instead of controlling the Internet, the government sites you'll see here are very much like their civilian counterparts: They try to bring value to Web visitors.

The Web is an excellent resource for government information because we all need it and it's always hard to find. Before the Web, a search for government information often was a frustrating game of passing the buck. I think that when President Truman said "The buck stops here," a lot of government agencies took that to heart and began to try to pass everything on up to the Oval Office. With the Internet, finally, the buck stops wherever you want it to stop.

You can find on the Web just about everything you'd want to know about the government:

- Congressional records, laws, and regulations.
- Supreme Court rulings.
- Executive decisions.

- Indexes to agencies with phone numbers and addresses, and current information on-line.
- Copies of birth certificates, marriage licenses, business licenses, applications for forms, and sources for forms.
- Business hours, phone numbers, and directions.

I'll give you some samples of sites from all levels of government. Of course, you'll only see a few here, but they'll help you know what you can expect to find. Finally, the Continuing Education section will give you some good resources to track down Web sites from which you can obtain the government information you want.

Federal Government

The last chapter included a taste of government Web sites through its descriptions of a local library in Clearwater, Florida and the Library of Congress. Even though I've already covered the Library of Congress, I'll mention it here because it is an excellent resource for a large amount of federal government information. The Library of Congress includes information on:

- Federal Government: General Resources, Executive Branch and Independent Agencies, Legislative Branch (includes Congress), Judicial Branch, the Military, and the FOIA (Freedom of Information Act).
- State and Local Government: Indexes for state and local information, state maps, the Council of State Governments, and the National Center for State Courts.
- Foreign and International Government: General information by country, CIA Factbook, State Department information, world constitutions, foreign relations, NAFTA, GATT, the United Nations, and much, much more.

Certainly the Library of Congress site will give you lots of valuable information that can help you in your work and in your personal life. I'll profile a few services that I believe almost everyone can use.

Civilizing Cyberspace

If you work for a government organization or even if you work closely with them, there's a book that you might find helpful; it discusses many government-related issues in cyberspace.

The book is titled *Civilizing Cyberspace*, and is the product of Steven E. Miller (Addison-Wesley 1996). This quote from its preface will help you understand if this book is for you:

> Chapter two begins to describe the current policy debate, noting the implications of the currently dominant arguments favoring deregulation and free markets. Chapter three describes some of the reasons why U.S. leaders are for the creation of a National Information Infrastructure (NII) and gives a quick history of the Internet (see Figure 10-1). Chapter four tries to provide a context for some of the national debates by describing the major political camps, from libertarian to socialist in the telecommunications context. Of course, people rarely fit into neatly delineated categories, but understanding these general

philosophical approaches facilitates an understanding of the real motivations behind public statements. These general policy frameworks have specific meaning for the government, which is the most important focus for the creation of policy. Chapter five presents a menu of public sector policy options for the development of infrastructure and describes how the public interest was protected during previous projects ranging from railroads to cable TV. Chapter six analyzes many of the leading and rapidly evolving policy proposals now progressing through all three branches of the government.

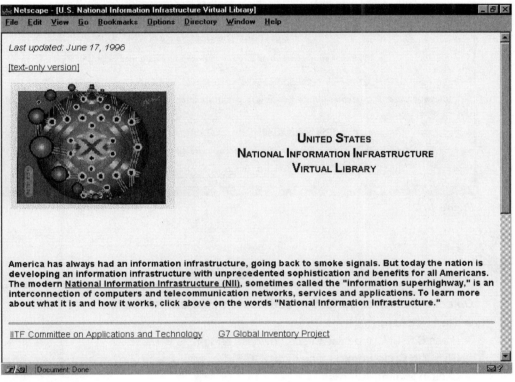

Figure 10-1

United States Postal Service

If you've got an address but no zip code, you can use the USPS Web page at *www.usps.gov/ncsc* (see Figure 10-2). The Zip Code Lookup link on this site can deliver a complete, 9-digit, USPS-regulation address; or you can use it to check an address or find out the city that goes with a zip code.

I'll give you a Hands-On exercise that will demonstrate how to use the USPS Zip Code Lookup.

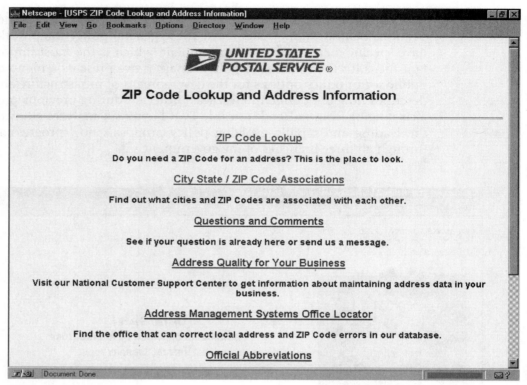

Figure 10-2

Hands On

Objective: **Learn to correct an address with the USPS Web site.**

❏ Start Netscape.

❏ Press **CTRL+L**, type *www.usps.gov/ncsc* and press **ENTER**.

❏ Click **Zip Code Lookup** (see Figure 10-3).

❏ Click in **Mailing Address**.

❏ Type *3000 timberwood* and press **TAB**.

❏ Type *herndon, va.*

❏ Click on **Process Address**.

Note that the address has been corrected (it's actually three words now) and the full 9-digit Zip Code has been added.

❏ Press **ALT+LEFT ARROW** to return to the previous screen.

❏ Click **Clear the Form**.

Enter your own address, but make a couple of errors. For example, if your address ends with Drive then reverse the abbreviation and use rd. Leave off your zip code or reverse a digit when you type it. If you make too many errors, the database can't figure out what you meant, but it will handle quite a few problems.

❏ Press **ALT+LEFT ARROW** until you return to the first USPS page.

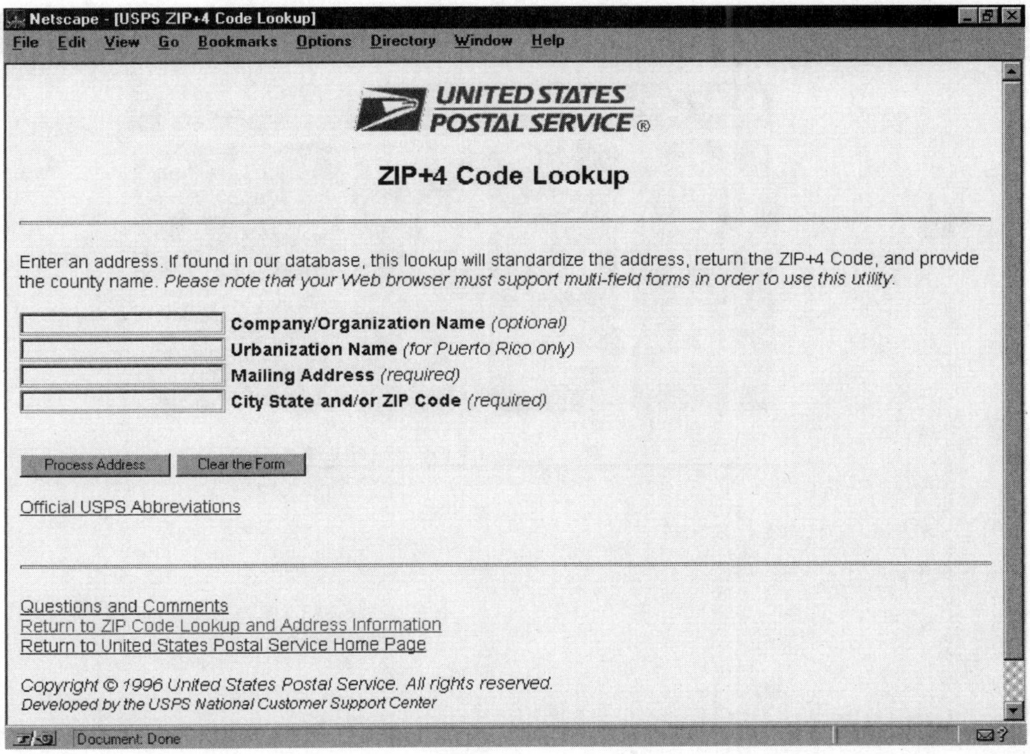

Figure 10-3

The USPS Web site can give you much more than this, including complete, current postal rate tables for every form of mail. You even can find out how to buy mail-order stamps. I'll bet that this Web site has made a lot of bookmark lists.

Census Bureau

You pay for the federal census, but how could you have used the collected census information before the Web? It hasn't been easy, but the Web changes that. Maybe a better question is "Now that you can get it, what do you do with it?" There is such a rich source of information available at the Census Bureau's site at *www.census.gov* (see Figure 10-4) that almost anyone in business can find something here to use. For example, before planning an expansion, a new product, or a marketing program, you can check the Census Bureau's Internet demographic information to help you make the decision.

Try the Market Place link to learn how to order Census Bureau information in hard copy or on CD-ROM, or you can try Data Access Tools to get a lot of the information on-line. The Economy and Geography links can be fabulous resources for developing business plans and proposals; and if you're not sure how or where to find what you want, click on Ask The Experts to send an e-mail question. This is a wonderful site that makes public a lot of valuable, yet previously obscure, information.

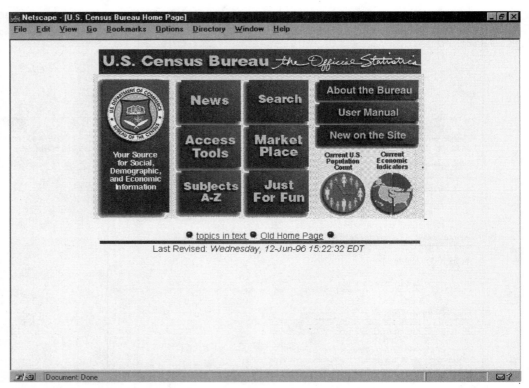

Figure 10-4

Small Business Administration

The Internet has revolutionized almost every existing business, but it also has spawned countless new business ideas. A massive wave of corporate and government cutbacks, downsizing, and layoffs has pushed a lot of employed workers to form small or home-based businesses. If you need to form your own business or if you work for a small business, then the Small Business Administration (SBA) Web site at *www.sba.gov* (see Figure 10-5) should be on your bookmark list.

You'll find links to the SBA's Program Offices, Special Interests, and Great Business Hot-Links. They also have an extensive shareware collection of more than 538 titles for applications that can help you run a small business. The shareware listing can be arranged either by an index, in one long listing, or by searching.

The new business links are Starting Your Business, Financing Your Business (see Figure 10-6), and Expanding Your Business. These links lead to pages that have compiled information from all over the Web and from other government agencies that offer information or assistance.

Congressional E-Mail Directory

There was a time when you could take pride in just finding out the phone number or address of your Congressional Representative and Senators. Now you can get complete contact information on them (phone, fax, snail mail, e-mail)

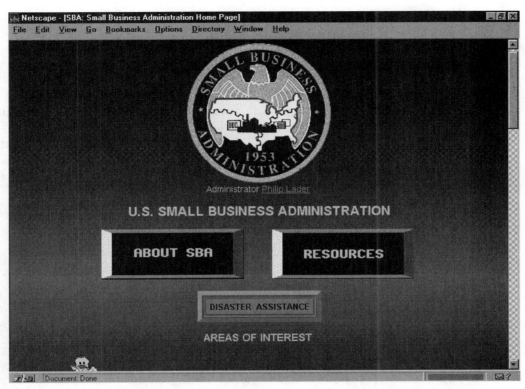

Figure 10-5

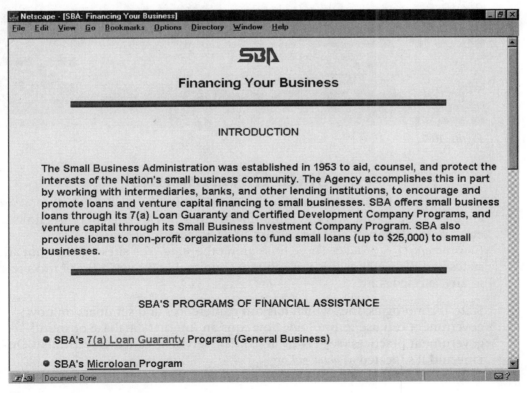

Figure 10-6

and jump to their Web sites. The Congressional E-Mail Directory went on my bookmark list the instant I saw it (see Figure 10-7). When you get to the individual state pages, you'll be able to click on a link for the Web page, and another to e-mail directly from within Netscape.

This site is a wonderful example of Client-centered Interneting because it achieves a very high-quality look and a user-friendly interface without resorting to bandwidth-hogging graphics. Bookmark this for two reasons: It is an outstanding information source, and it is a model of Client-centered Interneting.

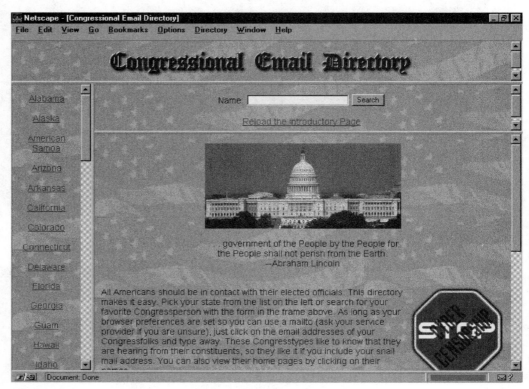

Figure 10-7

State Governments

Your first stop for state government information can be one of the major search engines. To save time you can jump directly to a Yahoo! page that lists links to every state, alphabetically (see Figure 10-8) by entering *www.yahoo.com/Government/U_S__States*. These links aren't the state Web sites—in fact not all states had Web sites as this was written—but it will give you a list of links related to any selected state.

State Technologies, Inc., which has run conferences and seminars on how government can use technology, now runs an Internet database of sound government practices (see Figure 10-9). The service is called Government On-Line and it's located at *www.gol.org*.

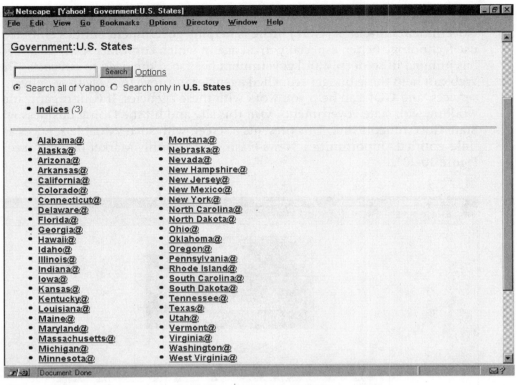

Figure 10-8

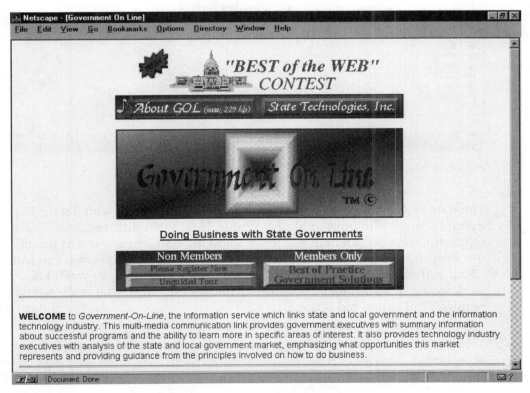

Figure 10-9

Government On-Line

Government On-Line's (GOL) niche is helping government entities embrace and use technology better, especially in an age in which corporate America already has jumped in so deeply and government has faced the need to cut costs. The Web can help these budget-crunched agencies improve the way they deliver services, and GOL can help you work with these agencies. If your organization is working with state governments, visit this site and hit the Doing Business with State Governments link. This presents a screen with such valuable services as links entitled Opportunities, News Flash, and Monthly Market Bulletin (see Figure 10-10).

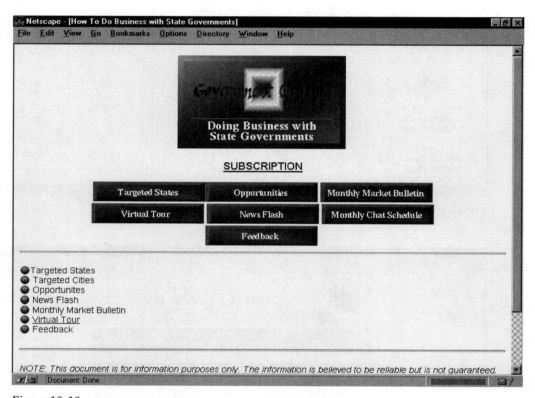

Figure 10-10

The state-specific links are rich resources on doing business with a state. For example, you'll find links to Market Profile, How to do Business, and New Opportunities that can help you understand the state's needs and to locate instantly the contacts you need (see Figure 10-11). For example, you can learn about authorization procedures by contract value threshold, so you'll know what work would qualify under discretionary budget rules and what levels would require a full sealed-bid process.

NET TIP   Remember to check the Library of Congress for resources for state and local government information. The Web page at *lcweb.loc.gov/global/state/stategov.html* gives you a meta-index of state and local information, state maps, links to individual state home pages, and some organizations that pertain to state and local government issues.

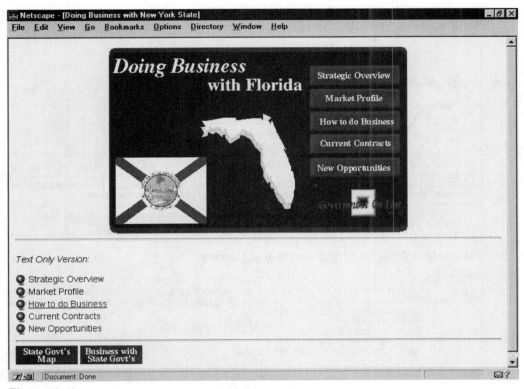

Figure 10-11

Local governments

I have begun the next chapter with an in-depth analysis of an excellent local government Web site: that of Fairfax County, Virginia. I chose it for its client-centered interneting properties, but it also follows nicely after all of these government sites. Fairfax County has attracted with its Web site numerous companies that either have moved to or done business in the county.

The challenge (as always on the Internet) is finding the site you want. Of course, you can turn to Yahoo! or Lycos and search the state name; but if you're looking for a good bookmark site that can be a ready reference to information pertaining to local governments, try visiting *www.civic.net:2401/lgnet* (see Figure 10-12). This site is maintained by the Local Government Network (LGNet), a service of The Innovation Groups and The Center for Civic Networking.

Information available here includes training, workshops, conferences, on-line help, publications, and an on-line resource directory. If your organization does business with local governments, be sure to list your products and services with the Vendor Directory and Information. This is a central location for state vendors to publicize contacts, on-line catalogs, purchase schedules, and special offers. This link leads to a forms-based database that will accept your information directly from this page.

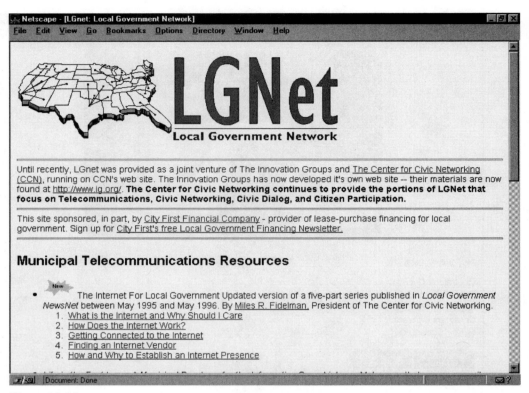

Figure 10-12

Cities

There are too many cities to count, right? Well, not too many for the Internet. I've found a Web site that lists on-line information on 2,039 cities and 745 other destinations! City.Net, located at *www.city.net*, is the Internet's most comprehensive guide to communities around the world (see Figure 10-13). City.Net is updated every day to provide easy and timely access to information on travel, entertainment, and local business, plus government and community services.

Once you locate the city you want, you'll learn things about the city that even the mayor doesn't know. Radio stations, television stations, newspapers, city directory, transportation, maps, sports teams, universities, magazines and zines, virtual tours, schedules of events, parks, and tourism information are all covered. If you travel a lot, this is another must-have bookmark site; if you check here before you go, you'll feel like a native when you arrive. Naturally, not every city is represented, but the most popular travel destinations have extensive coverage.

If your ties to your hometown have fallen victim to our high-tech, high-mobility society, use this site to savor a taste of home. No, no, I'm only kidding— Netscape's taste-and-smell plug-in isn't out of beta test yet.

Airports

Picture this: You're late catching a flight. You've jammed your clothes into your suitcase, rushed out the door without eating, and driven like a NASCAR racer to

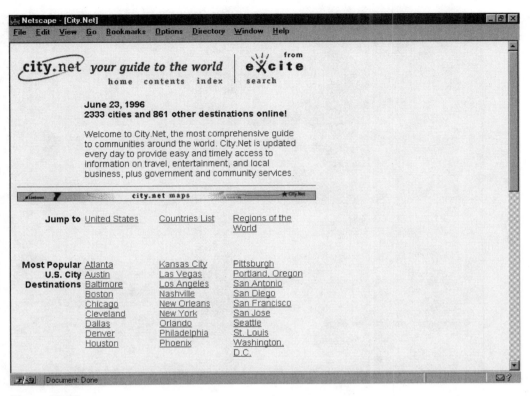

Figure 10-13

make it on time. You burst through the doors and knock down three people getting to a scheduling monitor to check your gate. Then you see it: it's delayed an hour, or worse, canceled. What would you have given to have seen that monitor at home? Commercial airline information is a valuable commodity, and it's perfectly suited to the Internet. You can't yet get it in real-time, but major airports are regularly going on-line (see Figure 10-14), and before long you'll be able to check departure and arrival screens at home.

Only a few airports are on-line as this is written, but I've learned that many are working on their Web sites. Most of the ones that are on-line have major upgrade plans. That's good, because there's much to be done; but the Oklahoma City Will Rogers World Airport is an example that shows what a good airport Web site eventually will do for us. It's located at *www.flyokc.com*, where the home page has links to several on-line services. The Airline Schedule link (see Figure 10-15) held promise, but turned out to only show what will be. At present, it's just a static, monthly schedule of flights with no real-time information.

As I browsed airports, I saw a graphic illustration of the one-world, global community that we're building with the Internet: Moscow's Sheremetyevo-2 Air Gateway (see Figure 10-16). When the Internet was first conceived in the early 1960s, can you imagine what the founders would have thought if they had known that one day anyone in the U.S. could pull up a map of the gates at the Moscow airport? That actually would have been a terrifying thought. Now, it's only slightly amazing—we accept it quickly and start wondering when they'll offer real-time flight schedules.

Government Web sites ◀

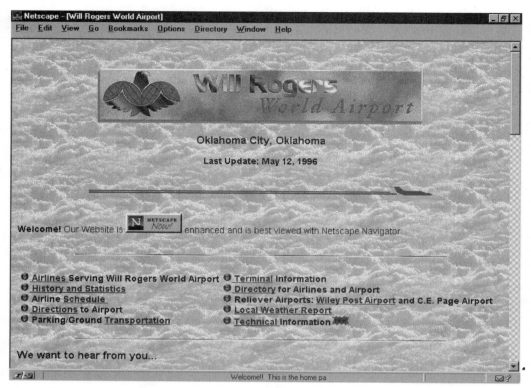

Figure 10-14

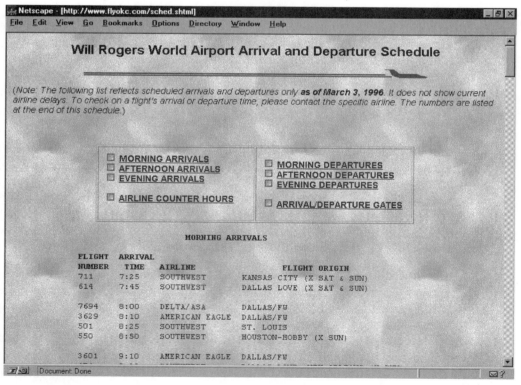

Figure 10-15

The world at your fingertips

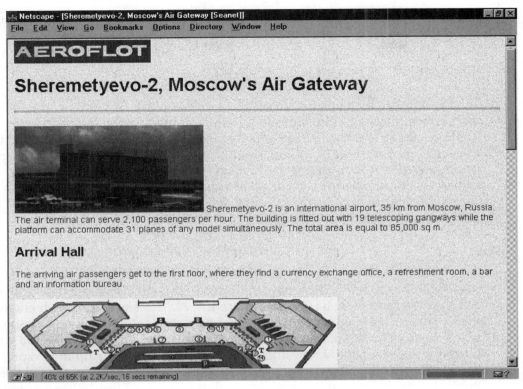

Figure 10-16

Shortcomings aside, current airport Web sites illustrate how the Internet is changing our lives by conveniently bringing us valuable, hard-to-find information—no matter where in the world it's located. If you think about it in absolute terms, it's almost barbaric that we've had to go to airports without seeing the schedule monitors until *after* we're there. It's too late then! The Internet is growing rapidly to bring airport screens—and countless other such timely information services—into our homes in real time.

The next chapter starts with another example of important, yet obscure, information being made readily available in a searchable format for easy retrieval. Take notes in this chapter and track the ease-of-use features you might be able to model on your own Web site.

 **Continuing Education**

Federal Government
http://www.fedworld.gov

FedWorld is a hypertext menu of various federal government computer resources. The National Technical Information Service (NTIS) introduced FedWorld in November 1992 to help with the challenge of accessing U.S. government information on-line. Most of the links are to other Web sites, but it also includes Telnet links to several federal computer systems. You'll find most links under the

Index of Subject Categories, but you will find direct links to some popular sites, including Web, FTP, Gopher, and Telnet sites.

Yahoo!

http://www.yahoo.com/Government

The Yahoo! search engine has an excellent one-stop page for government information. This page lists links to government by category, so it offers a different slant from some of the other listings. You could use this if you had but a vague idea of the type of information you wanted, but had no idea what agency could help you. A key to using this site well is to click on the **Sub Category Listing** link to expand the categories into a myriad of subcategories. You also can click on **Indices** to get a listing of other Web sites that can help you find government information.

Federal Government Web Locator

http://www.law.vill.edu/Fed-Agency/fedwebloc.html

Sponsored by Villanova University Law School, this site lists more than 200 Federal Government Web sites (see Figure 10-17). This site has a search engine that is an excellent tool if you've got a question about a topic but don't know which agency could handle your request. For example, what agency would you contact if you wanted to know about the progress on cleaning up the Exxon Alaska oil spill? A search on the words oil spill produced a link to the Oil Spill Public Information Center. I don't know about you, but I would have started with the EPA and probably surfed a long time to find that site.

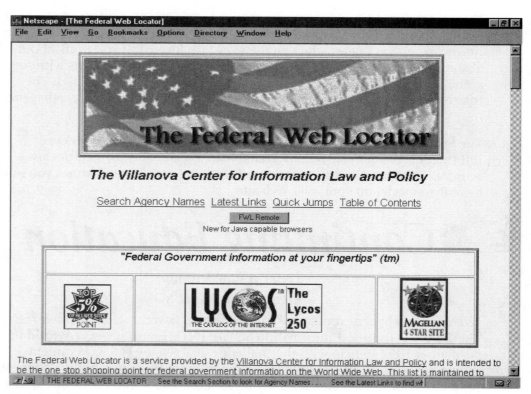

Figure 10-17

U.S. government Web site

http://sunsite.unc.edu/govdocs.html

This site enables you to search for U.S. government documents on the Web, such as press releases, speeches (including some audio and video clips) and the National Trade Data Bank. Take careful notes, because many of the references you find here may be good value-added links for your clients and customers for which you can provide links on your Web site.

USA CityLink

http://banzai.neosoft.com/citylink

You can use this site to find information on cities around the U.S., and you can submit links to your own city. The USA CityLink Project (see Figure 10-18) lists cities, states, and freenets. Here's what they say on their home page: "The USA CityLink Project is a city's interface to the world. It is the Internet's most comprehensive listing of World Wide Web pages featuring U.S. states and cities."

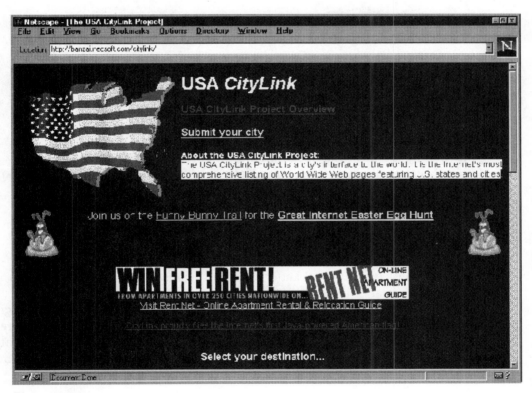

Figure 10-18

Public Technology, Inc.

http://pti.nw.dc.us

PTI creates and develops technology innovations in the public sector (see Figure 10-19). The organization conducts its work with participating cities and counties, some of the most change-oriented jurisdictions in the country. The work, involving elected officials, general managers, and technical specialists, progresses through a cycle of research, development, and commercialization. PTI is

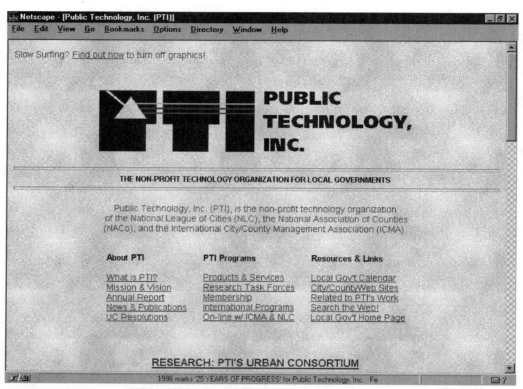

Figure 10-19

sponsored by the three major national local government associations: the National League of Cities (NLC), the National Association of Counties (NACo), and the International City/County Management Association (ICMA), representing more than 20,000 local government entities.

State and local government on the Net

http://www.webcom.com/~piper/state/states.html

This is the home of the PIPER Letter, which provides original, practical, and policy-level assistance to government agency managers, policy makers, and technical staff in dealing with questions regarding public information in a digital age. Cut from their FAQs file is a description of their mission: "These pages are intended to provide convenient access to a wide variety of links to government information. The Glimpse search engine provides easy access to the links on our sub-pages."

Regional Economic Information System

http://www.lib.virginia.edu/socsci/reis/reis1.html

The Regional Economic Information System (REIS) data base provides local area economic data for states, counties, and metropolitan areas for 1969 through 1993. Statistics in the database include personal income by source, per-capita personal income, earnings by two-digit SIC code, full- and part-time employment by industry, and regional economic profiles. The REIS database is produced by the Bureau of Economic Analysis.

StateSearch

http://www.state.ky.us/nasire/NASIREhome.html

StateSearch is a service of the National Association of State Information Resource Executives (NASIRE), and is a topical clearinghouse to state government information on the Internet (see Figure 10-20). In addition to listing links to some featured special-interest Web sites, StateSearch provides links to information on commerce, state governments, state home pages, energy, tourism, state treasures, licensing and regulations, records, education, and employment.

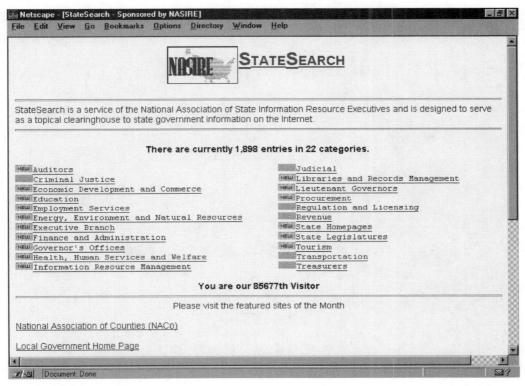

Figure 10-20

Client-centered Web sites

I'LL CLOSE Phase 2 of your Internet training with examples of well-done Web sites that will spark the fires of your imagination and set the stage for Phase 3, in which you'll begin to learn how to implement your own Web presence. I'll analyze one site fully, then give you a Top 10 list of good uses for a Web site. The Continuing Education section will point you to several other Web sites that employ techniques your organization might adopt.

One of the most important factors in Web site design is to focus on the needs of your visitors. In other words, one of the most important factors in Web site design is client-centered interneting, which I presented in chapter 3. In this chapter you'll begin to see client-centered interneting in action.

The Web enables you to make available massive amounts of information in a nonlinear format. This book, in contrast, is in a linear format—you only can access its information one page at a time. A footnoted, indexed encyclopedia gives you an improvement over a pure linear format, but you still must flip pages and drag out multiple volumes to obtain nonlinear information access. The Web changes all that.

Breaking old restrictions

The hypertext markup language upon which the Web is built frees you from presenting your information in a linear format. The first site I'll profile, the Fairfax County Economic Development Authority, presents, in an easily accessible format, volumes of text that otherwise would be an avalanche of linear information. The nonlinear structure of hypertext documents means that each reader gets a tailored version of your information, structured according to the links that each chooses to follow rather than structured according to the way you decided to present the information.

The Web enables us to get to know each other on our own terms by bringing a new perspective to the old adage "You never get a second chance to make a good first impression." Hypertext documents will present different first impressions of your organization to different people because each will see what they want to see rather than what you believed would appeal to the majority of a mass audience. Thus, hypertext enables your organization to present a good first impression to a wide variety of visitors.

As you surf through cyberspace, always look for features that you can employ in the design of your own Web site. The rest of this chapter will give you examples and show you how to save them for future reference.

Fairfax County
Economic Development Authority

The Internet can provide a tremendous boon to governments and to government agencies. We're going to analyze a site that combines both (see Figure 11-1), an agency of the government of Fairfax County, Virginia, near Washington, D.C. It's run by the Fairfax County Economic Development Authority (FCEDA).

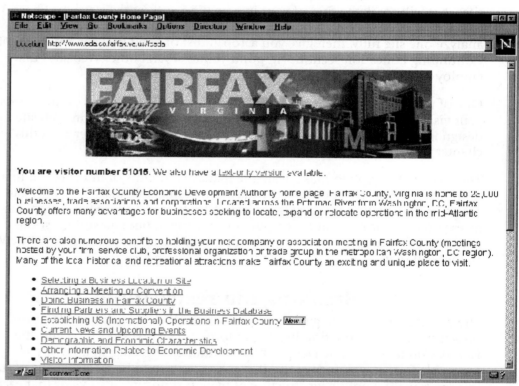

Figure 11-1

This site definitely will give different first impressions to a variety of visitors. For example, if you visited this site because you wanted to hold a business conference in Fairfax County, you'd see a different site than if you visited this site because you wanted to know how to obtain a business license and open a branch office.

▶ *The world at your fingertips*

Why Fairfax County? Five good reasons.

- This is a well-done Web site.
- Fairfax County is extremely prosperous; it is the top county in the U.S. for average education levels, and usually places in the top two or three counties in the U.S. for per capita income.
- Fairfax County has generated business from this Web site.
- I want to profile a noncommercial site.
- I live in Fairfax County (that's a very good reason)!

Hands On

Objective: Analyze a client-centered Web site example.

❑ Start Netscape with an Internet connection.
❑ Double-click in the **Location:** text entry box.
❑ Type *http://www.eda.co.fairfax.va.us/fceda* and press **ENTER**.

Text-only version

You can't assume that every visitor will appreciate your graphic images. Graphic images require far more bandwidth than text, and can make your site annoyingly slow. Until you know that all your visitors have cable modems, you should offer a text-only option at the top of your home page. FCEDA has done that. Click on **text-only version** to see how this page is simplified (see Figure 11-2).

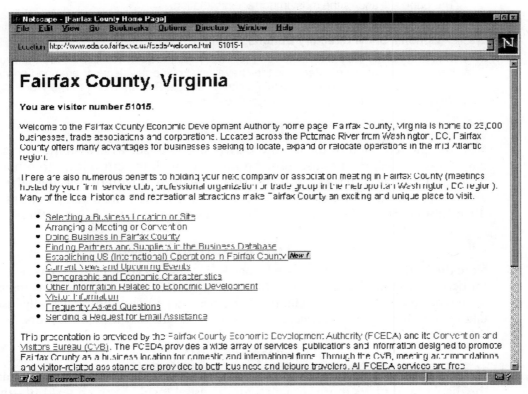

Figure 11-2

This option requires little extra work, and it might generate repeat business from a valuable client with a slower connection. Even if most users in the U.S. had high-speed modems, a text-only version still would make sense for the FCEDA because they are attracting international businesses to Fairfax County. Overseas connections are going to be slower, and often the phone systems are not on par with the U.S. phone systems.

Click the right mouse button, then click **Back** to return to the original, graphics-based page.

Check out different views

A well-done Web home page will look good in Netscape with a variety of different viewing options selected. You cannot predict how your users will have their browser configured, so assume they have turned on every option and thus have reduced their screen space to the minimum. Let's view this page at both extremes.

Hands On

Objective: **Learn to test a Web page in different views.**

❏ Click **Options**. Make sure that all three of these options are checked:

> Show Toolbar
>
> Show Location
>
> Show Directory Buttons
>
> The page still shows the most important information.

❏ Click **Options, Show Toolbar**.

❏ Click **Options, Show Directory Buttons**.

> This probably is the best way to run your Netscape browser. You don't need the two bars you just turned off, because they have keystroke equivalents or are used only occasionally and do not merit full-time screen space. See chapter 11 "The World Wide Web" for a table of Netscape's shortcut keystrokes.

Now use the scroll bar or the **UP** and **DOWN** arrows to see what's on the home page. Most well-done sites use a brief home page with hypertext links to other pages and to other Internet resources. This page fits that pattern. Scroll all the way to the bottom and note the row of hot buttons. There are several features at the bottom of this page that are good examples to model. Let's discuss them.

Home button

Note the Fairfax Home button (see Figure 11-3). That's a good item to have, even though you technically haven't left the home page. (Note the URL has not changed from what you entered in the Hands-On exercise steps.) This button actually just takes you to the top of this page. Be sure and make this easy for your visitors.

Configure button

Here's a rarely seen feature. This Configure button enables the user to customize the display and offers more choices than the usual toggle between text-only and full graphics options. Let's see how it works.

▶ *The world at your fingertips*

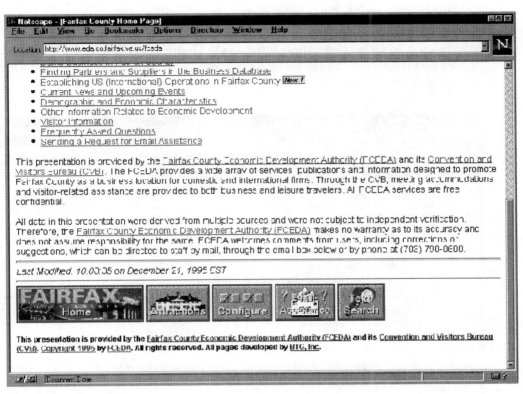

Figure 11-3

Hands On

***Objective:* Test the Configure button**

❏ Click **Configure**.

❏ Under the Icons option, click **Text** then click **Make Changes**.

❏ Press **CTRL+END** to jump to the bottom of the page.

   Note that the buttons have been replaced by normal hypertext jumps.

❏ Click **Configure** again.

❏ Click **Default Values** to restore the original settings.

❏ Click **Make Changes**.

❏ Press **CTRL+END** to jump to the bottom of the page.

Configure is a nice bonus feature, but it's something you can't expect to be able to implement on your own without training that's beyond the scope of this book. Check with your Internet service provider, a consultant, other Internet books, or some of the sites we list in this chapter's Continuing Education section.

E-Mail button

Every Web home page you create should have an e-mail link so users can contact you easily. Don't ever make them work hard to reach you for more information. After all, you started this whole Internet adventure to increase contacts.

There are several ways to implement an e-mail request. Click on this button to see the FCEDA solution. It is not actually e-mail; it's a form that will transfer information from you into their system (see Figure 11-4). You'll find true e-mail replies by visiting other sites we've listed, which is a simple solution that nearly anyone can implement.

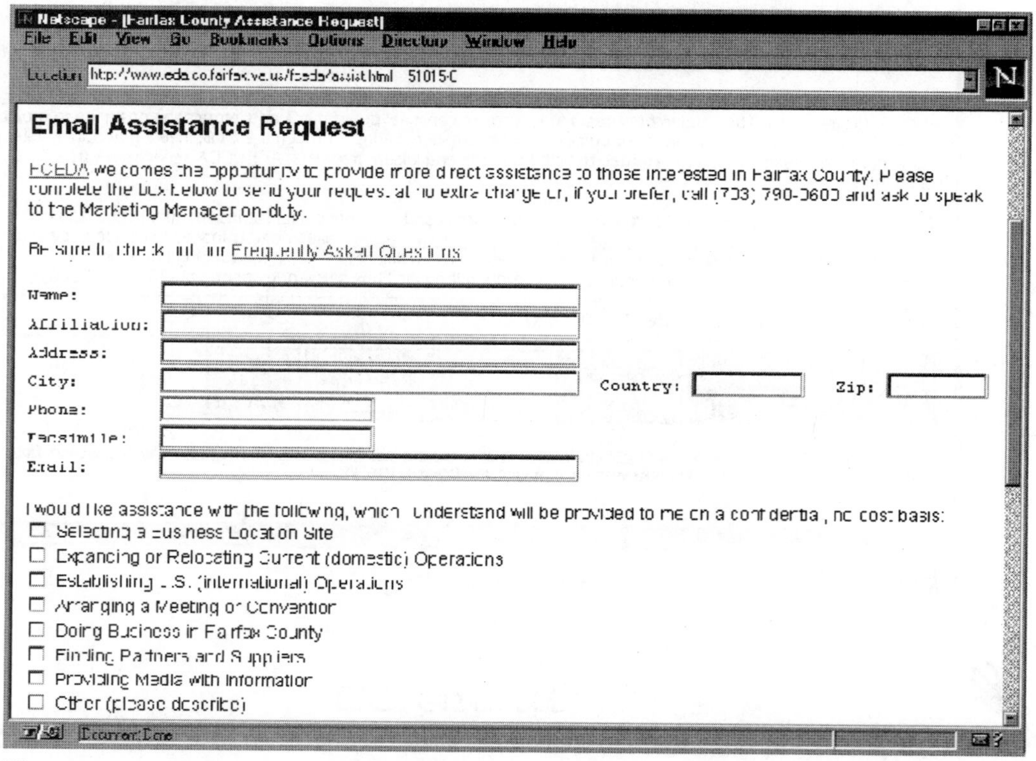

Figure 11-4

Hands On

Objective: Examine a form that accepts user information.

❏ Click **E-Mail Assistance**.

Note the URL change. You're in the same fceda directory, but Netscape has loaded a different page.

❏ Scroll through the screen and check it out.

Since it's a single page, you can use your **UP** or **DOWN** arrows to scroll, and you can use **CTRL+END** and **CTRL+HOME**.

❏ Click the right mouse button and click **Back**.

❏ Press **CTRL+END**.

The method the FCEDA uses here is more technical than using a regular e-mail reply, because it provides a customized reply form. Completing this form places the information in a database on the FCEDA server. While more difficult than e-mail to implement, it improves user-friendliness by providing a list of check

The world at your fingertips

boxes that can save users some time by making information requests require only a mouse click. You also can ensure you get the information from each visitor that you want.

Text search button

On some sites, text searches are optional, but on an elaborate Web site such as this one, it's a necessary example of client-centered interneting. If you were considering doing business in Fairfax County, you might want to locate information that would help you establish your business. Getting this information by phone might waste a lot of time and long-distance charges while you're getting switched to the right person, but the FCEDA transferred the burden to themselves by creating a Web page that lets you quickly look up whatever you want and print it once you've found it. That's client-centered.

Let's try it. If you were going to start doing business in Fairfax County, you might want information about obtaining a business license. We'll find out if the Internet has made that easy for us.

Hands On

Objective: **Demonstrate a Web site text search feature.**

❏ Press **CTRL+END** to drop to the bottom of the current page.

❏ Click on the **Text Search** button.

❏ Click in the **Search Keyword(s)** text entry box.

❏ Type *license* and press **ENTER**.

   The first item on the list is a hypertext link to a Frequently Asked Questions (FAQ) file that will help us.

❏ Click on **Frequently Asked Questions**.

❏ Click on **What do I need for my firm?**

❏ Click on **Doing Business in Fairfax County**.

❏ Click on **Licenses, Permits and Regulations**.

❏ Click on **Business, Professional and Occupational Licenses (BPOL)**.

   Read about how you could obtain the forms necessary to apply for a business license in Fairfax County. As you can see, you could click on a hypertext link and also read information about Fairfax County business taxes.

This is a terrific example of the power the Internet is bringing to us all (see Figure 11-5). How would you otherwise even begin to locate information like that about a county? Someday, perhaps all progressive local governments will make economic development information available via the Internet. When that day comes, we all will be able to find speedy answers to obscure questions.

Within two months of this site going on-line it had attracted at least four companies that were interested in doing business within Fairfax County. One prospect (who never before had heard of Fairfax County) was planning to relocate there based upon what it discovered from this Web site.

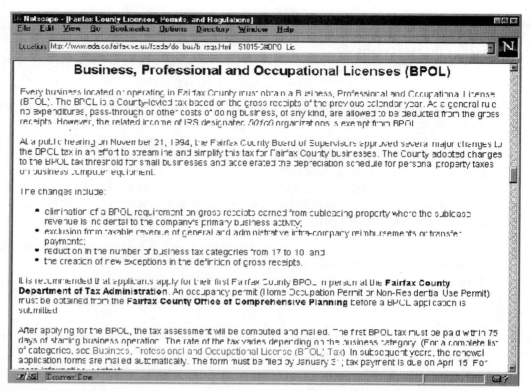

Figure 11-5

The Web site not only attracted the interest of the relocation prospect, but the Web site itself was a factor in that company's decision because the Business Directory at this site would direct other businesses to services that the new company planned to provide.

What if you're in a small organization?

So your organization is not as large as Fairfax County, and you want to know how you can put up such an elaborate site without maintaining your own Web servers? No problem. Fairfax County doesn't have its own Web servers, either. The FCEDA site is maintained on servers at the BTG Corporation, the company that developed the FCEDA site.

You'll have no trouble finding service providers who will maintain your Web site. You can establish your own domain name and get a Web service provider to set up your site as *www.yourname.com*. For example, Jeff Davidson, who contributed much of the material for chapter 2 (Breathing Space for Cyberspace), is the founder of The Breathing Space Institute. Jeff got a Web service provider to register his domain name and place his Web site at *www.brespace.com*.

If you don't need your own domain name, another option is to tag onto a larger Web site. All you need is a directory on someone else's server. You'll find far more providers who can handle this service and the cost will be surprisingly low—adding your page is very little trouble for someone who already has an established domain. For example, the Web site for this book is located under another domain name because I didn't want to establish a domain name just for this book. So I put this book's Web site at an existing site whose address is *www.marketing-coach.com*. The book's Web pages went into a new directory on that site so that the book's complete URL is *www.marketing-coach.com/mh-guide*. You can create any number of home pages on any domain, merely by creating new directories under the root directory and adding that new directory to the URL.

FTP to upload

Your service provider will give you a directory into which you can upload files for your Web site. You won't be able to do this with Netscape (at least with the version that was out when I finished this book). You'll need a stand-alone FTP application that gives you these crucial capabilities on the remote computer: upload files, create and remove directories, delete files, and rename files. Many sites won't let you upload directly into your web page. Direct access to your Web pages is required if you plan to create and frequently update your own documents. Many providers also restrict programming and image-map applications. Shop around.

Leased lines

Another option for a Web site is to lease a full-time, dedicated line and set up your own Web server software on one of your own computers. Until recently, that option has been prohibitively expensive for anyone but a major corporation, but it rapidly is evolving and might soon become a solution even for very small organizations. Check with ISPs today and ask about leased lines and Web server software. It might be quite affordable by now. Also, check in chapter 17 for help on creating your own Web server.

I'll close this site analysis with one more hands-on exercise that demonstrates another service you might want to provide for your clients, customers, and prospects. Fairfax County maintains a database of registered businesses that includes company information and a description of each registered business's services and products. Let's take a look.

Hands On

Objective: **Demonstrate a database search.**

❑ Click on **Finding Partners and Suppliers in the Business Database**.

❑ Click on **Perform a search**.

❑ Scroll down to and click in **Description keyword(s)**.

❑ Type *Internet*.

❑ Click on **Perform Query**.

   Now you can browse through a list of Fairfax-based companies that provide Internet consulting services (see Figure 11-6).

There are many uses for similar services within your Web site. For example, if your organization represented public speakers, you could maintain a database of

Figure 11-6

your clients and have a search engine similar to the one on the FCEDA site. When meeting planners contacted your site seeking information about public speakers, they could perform a keyword search on topics of interest to their own organization and get a list of candidates for speaking to their group. Let's consider some other Web site usage ideas.

Top 10 uses for a Web site

Here's that Top 10 list of Web site ideas that we promised earlier. Perhaps these Web ideas will help you add value to your organization's Internet presence.

10. Personal

Family newsletters; announcements; baby pictures; graduations; weddings; favorite Web links; friends on the Internet; favorite photos; on-line greeting cards; sound files; video clips; resumés.

9. Clubs and groups

Event schedules; membership information; membership rosters; links to related Web sites; alumni clubs; reunion schedules with directions and maps; volunteer coordination; by-laws; notices of rule changes; meeting minutes; club announcements; nomination of officers; elections; book reviews; recipes and cookbooks; trip directions and maps; travel suggestions; travel stories with photos and maps.

8. Local sports teams

League schedules; team standings; player and coach rosters; volunteer coordination; weather contingencies and postponements; links to sponsor home pages; directions and maps to playing fields, gymnasiums or sports arenas; carpooling information.

7. Politics and government

Campaign information, schedules, events; community news; party platforms; candidate standings; poll results; on-line candidate debates; on-line voter discussions; voter forums; candidate slates; constituent newsletters; pending legislation; representative's newsletters; FAQs pages; voting information, registration information, voting locations and times; election results.

6. Community information

Local laws and regulations; civic promotion; homeowner's associations; building codes; event schedules; school sports events, plays and schedules; school lunches; voting information, poll locations and maps; transportation information, schedules and maps; disability information and ADA compliance; community service; announcements.

5. Entertainment

Theater schedules; play schedules and review; restaurant takeout menus and ordering; concert schedules, ticket availability and ordering; restaurant suggestions, menus, prices, reservations and maps; restaurant reviews; movie reviews and movie schedules.

4. On-line publishing

Customer newsletters; industry newsletters; political commentary and campaign information; special-interest magazines; daily updates; consumer alerts.

3. Working together

Joint projects; sharing documents; on-line scheduling; on-line statistics; company calendars; company special events; employee-of-the-month awards; special recognition; conference information, schedules and maps; meeting minutes.

2. Customer support

Frequently Asked Questions (FAQs); on-line assembly instructions; on-line manuals; parts lists and ordering; sales; tips and ideas for using your products; other Internet sites that will help your clients and customers; reporting software bugs and distributing fixes; product release notes.

1. Business presence

General business information, hours of operation; phone and fax numbers, mailing address; directions and maps; on-line brochures; product brochures; order forms; surveys; forms; an internal, employees-only Web page.

Using the examples you find

As this chapter has demonstrated, you can learn a lot by seeing well-done Web examples; however, seeing them and using the techniques they employ are two different matters. You'll encounter many pages that use features of HTML that you've not yet mastered, especially as you're learning to create Web pages. Fortunately, Netscape has several commands that let you save or view the HTML source code behind the documents you see on the Web.

Viewing Web page source code sometimes will reveal HTML codes that you didn't know about (or in some cases, that aren't even in your documentation). Netscape constantly creates extensions to the basic HTML specification, and you might learn of them sooner by viewing examples than by waiting for them to appear in official documentation. So let's learn the techniques for saving and viewing Web pages in Netscape.

Saving Web documents

Netscape can directly save onto your hard disk or network any Web page you find. You then can read it to glean tips or use Copy and Paste to pull sections of code into your own pages. Naturally, you'll need to honor copyright laws, but most likely you're only copying a bit of code because it's faster than finding the reference in your documentation and typing it from scratch.

Hands On

Objective: **Learn to save a Web document.**

❑ Click **File, Save as . . .** or press **CTRL+S**.

 Netscape creates a name for you that's extracted from the title of the Web document, then it appends the extension htm, which is DOS-syntax for hypertext markup language (HTML). Change it if you desire.

❑ Use the **Drives** and **Directories** windows to set the desired path.

 If you're on a network, you can access your available network drives. Put this document in a directory that you commonly use for word processing because you'll open it later in this exercise. Please write down or remember the directory.

❑ Click **OK** to save the document.

The results of these steps are different from the Hands-On exercise in the Netscape chapter because that exercise stripped the HTML codes as you saved it; but in this case you retained all HTML codes (which you specifically wanted to do).

Viewing document information

If you just want a peek at the source code, remember to click **View, Document Source**. Netscape includes its own source-code viewer, but it doesn't let you edit, print, or save the codes you view. This can be very inconvenient if you'd like to use Copy and Paste to transfer a portion of a viewed page into a Web page that you're authoring. I recommend that you configure your copy of Netscape to use the Windows Notepad to view source documents. This will give you some basic editing and saving commands that can improve productivity.

Hands On

Objective: **Configure Netscape to view document source with the Windows Notepad.**

❏ Start Netscape.

❏ Click **Options, General Preferences**.

❏ Click the **Apps** tab.

❏ Click in the **View Source** text entry box.

❏ Type *c:\windows\notepad.exe* and click **OK**.

> If your notepad is in another directory, click **Browse**, then navigate to your notepad.exe file.

❏ Click **OK**.

❏ Click **Options, Save Options**.

Saving graphic images

Netscape doesn't need any special viewer to display or save Web graphics. It lets you save any graphic that you can see on the screen, and the right mouse button is the only tool you need.

Hands On

Objective: **Learn to save a Web page graphic image.**

❏ Start Netscape.

❏ Press **CTRL+L** and type *www.marketing-coach.com/mh-web*.

❏ Click the right mouse button over the cover image.

❏ Click **Save this Image as . . .**

> Select a directory in which to save it.

❏ Click **OK**.

> The image has been saved in its native format, either GIF or JPEG.

Once you've saved a graphic, you can view it again by loading it directly into Netscape from your hard drive, or you can load it into any graphics application that handles the format in which it was saved. Many of the graphics you encounter will be protected by copyright laws, but you can e-mail the page's webmaster for permission to use any of the graphic images on his or her page. I've found that most people are happy to grant permission, especially if you'll give them credit and cross-link your site to theirs.

NET TIP

The current version of Netscape won't let you save background graphics. If you've got Windows 95, you can save background images by opening the same page in the Microsoft Explorer, because its right mouse button menu includes an item that lets you save background images.

Copying and pasting text

If you only need a small portion of the text on a Web page, you can highlight it with your mouse and use the Windows Copy command, then Paste it into any Windows application. Usually text obtained this way won't work well when you paste it because it won't be in word-wrapped paragraphs. Instead, there will be large gaps and you'll have to manually delete the extra hard returns and spaces.

I've developed a macro for WordPerfect for Windows 6.1 that will strip out all of the blank spaces and extra hard returns from text Pasted after it was copied from a Web page. The macro is available on this book's home page under the link to macros. Just follow the links to download the ASCII macros. Once you find the right spot, you also will find detailed instructions for completing the download as well as for incorporating the macro into WordPerfect for Windows.

 NET TIP The ASCII macro was designed to clean up all ASCII files that have extraneous hard returns and spaces. The macro strips away the extraneous codes and puts two spaces between all sentences.

Another way to avoid getting extraneous codes is to load the page into the viewer via **View, Document Source**. Carefully highlight and Copy the desired sections, then Paste them into your word processor; or you could save the entire document, load it in your word processor, and then strip away everything except the section you want.

 # Continuing Education

Point's Top 5 Percent
http://www.pointcom.com

For a grand tour of some of the Web's best sites, visit the Top 5 percent club run by Point Communications. This service indexes all of its selected sites so that you can search for them by topic or by keyword. And don't forget this URL, because when you've mastered the art of Web page design you can submit your own home page for consideration. If you're selected, they'll send you an official notice and tell you how to secure a whole collection of their Top Five Percent logos that you can include on your site.

Best of the Net
http://gnn.com/wic/botn

GNN created this site to honor its selections for the annual Best of the Net awards. The awards recognize the best of the best—i.e., Internet sites that stand out among even the most useful and entertaining resources. Sites that are featured on Best of the Net are divided into ten categories. Each category has an Amateur and a Professional division. Be prepared to take good notes when you visit, because you'll find some outstanding examples of how to use the Internet to deliver value to your clients and customers.

Seven wonders of the Web

http://www.penncen.com/7wonders/7wonders.html

This site's claim to fame is Spotlighting New and Original Sites on the World Wide Web (see Figure 11-7). It's a good bookmark candidate if you want to track the latest hot Web sites because they place a new site at the top of the list each day. You'll see the whole range here, though, because they don't feature only business-related sites. You can at least count on them being in reasonably good taste—except maybe, perhaps, well, uh, an occasional interesting site. For example, the day I wrote this, one of the current Seven Wonders was the World Wide Belch Contest, in which participants recorded belches and e-mailed them in. Is this what Dr. Vinton Cerf had in mind when he developed TCP/IP? I'll bet.

Figure 11-7

Setting up shop on the Internet

http://www.netrex.com/business.html

This page is by Andrew Dinsdale (with Netrex) and features a list of hypertext jumps that will help you with numerous Web technology questions. Here are some of the topics you might use as you are preparing to launch your own Web site: Introduction to Electronic Commerce, Commercial Use Strategies, The Dos & Don'ts of Online Marketing, Get Connected, Security, Employees, and finally, Government Involvement. As you would expect, each of these topics not only offers its own information, but serves as a jumping-off point for a vast array of other sites around the Web. Starting with this one address alone, you could build a substantial library of Web technology documents.

BTG Incorporated

http://www.btg.com/

The Web site of the Fairfax County Economic Development Authority was created by BTG (see Figure 11-8). BTG was among the original builders of ARPANET, the predecessor of today's Internet. Their home page will connect you to some other excellent Web sites and tell you about BTG's professional services. If it can be done on the Web, BTG can handle it for you, including maintaining your Web site on BTG's secure servers.

Figure 11-8

PHASE 3
Creating your own Web site

THE REMAINING LESSONS are devoted to helping you get on the World Wide Web. You'll learn how to plan, design, and manage a good Web site, and how to leverage your Internet presence so that you get multiple, cascading benefits from your work. You also will learn the basics of Internet security issues, setting up customer ordering systems, and collecting money and information from customers.

Two chapters are devoted to some of the most exciting developments on the Web: graphics and live-action tools. If you're wondering how to use these features to enhance the value of your Web site, then don't miss these chapters. Finally, I'll close the book with an under-the-hood look at the engines that power the World Wide Web—Web servers.

- Chapter 12 covers security. Once your system is opened to the Internet, security becomes a critical issue. This primer will help you understand what's needed to safeguard your priceless internal data, your company secrets, and your customers and clients.

- Chapter 13 is a primer on cyberspace money issues. This is a fast-moving target (fast being the speed of light), so I won't even try to give you all the answers; you will get a solid overview and then a Continuing Education section that will show you how to keep up-to-date with changes.

- Chapter 14 covers developing and publishing Web pages. It features primers on add-on packages for WordPerfect and Word as well as powerful, stand-alone Web editors. You'll learn about an exciting new development: applications that convert existing WordPerfect and Word documents into HTML Web pages. Yes, you might be closer to going on-line than you thought.

- Chapter 15 gets you started creating, downloading, converting, and using Web graphics. You'll also learn about scanning images, photo scanning, photo retouching, and graphics conversion.

- Chapter 16 will help you learn to breathe some life into your Web site. This will include an introduction to audio, video, animation and virtual reality. Advanced Web features are rapidly increasing the standards for good Web sites, so this chapter includes an extensive Continuing Education section that is a gold mine of advanced Web topics.

◉ Chapter 17 closes with Web server basics. You need to know what you can expect to tackle on your own, what to pass on to your organization's experts, and when to hire outside consultants. Even if you won't be involved directly with a Web server, this will give you a good look behind the scenes of the Web.

Internet security

BECAUSE your hottest new project and ideas may now traverse the uncertain regions of cyberspace, every worker needs to know about computer thieves. Of course, you'll never see one creeping up your alley with a bag of burglar tools. Computer thieves use high-tech tools that let them break into corporate information systems all over the world in a single night—all while sipping a soda and listening to background music. Skilled computer thieves can earn a living without leaving the comforts of home (or their college dorm room).

Actually, it's not all that bad. A few simple precautions will deter all but the most diligent computer hacker. Besides, ever since the 1990s started, it seems the watchword of our society has been precaution. You take security precautions in almost everything you do. Now you need to extend those practices to your Internet adventures.

Don't take this personally—hackers aren't after you in particular. They're out surfing the Net very much as you do, but with a different purpose in mind. Like you, they usually get interested in whatever appears to be easy. If you encounter a complicated Web site that's hard to understand, you will quickly move on because there are plenty of user-friendly sites. It's the same with hackers—only for them, *user-friendly* takes a sinister twist.

So how can a site be user-friendly for a hacker?

Some hackers use special computers that sniff Internet traffic for keywords that are of interest to their clients. If your organization sends a lot of unencrypted messages with interesting keywords, then your system will be user-friendly to a hacker. Your messages are like a signal beacon across the Internet; sending encrypted messages will turn off that beacon.

Hackers also play a game called "door rattling." It's the equivalent of snooping through a neighborhood and rattling doorknobs to see if anyone forgot to lock up. So, another user-friendly system for hackers would be any computer system that pops open when the door is rattled. Door-rattling thieves aren't after your company in particular—unless it's your doorknob that's unlocked.

If you've got secret information, you have to make it secure. You may be surprised at how little you need to do—often simple encryption is sufficient—because most Internet bandits are in for the quick buck. There are plenty of easy targets and unprotected data floating around the Internet.

Still, not everyone snooping the Internet is a door-rattler or a sniffer. There is a chance that a hacker will target your system directly. Your competitors can hire bounty hunters to track down your trade secrets and pull it off the Internet. In other words, someone might pay a hacker to break your encryption or to work on your doorknob even if it *is* locked.

When electronic bloodhounds find their quarry, your most private information quickly can be transferred, and hackers can collect their bounty; but you can protect your priceless information and make the bounty hunters look for another target—or at least wish they had.

Don't be a softie

Browsing some of the Usenet newsgroups will give you some horror stories that illustrate how the Internet can expose company secrets. The Internet has spawned a whole industry that trades on inside information on *soft sites*—companies with lax computer security that are easy targets for spying or just plain mischief. Later on I'll tell you about firewalls and other security measures that ensure that you haven't left open the door to your cyberspace vault.

There's more—even if you implement the best security measures, *you* might end up doing yourself in. Remember the fable about the Trojan Horse: The victims brought in the gift that held the seeds of their own destruction. Computer viruses often are disguised within modern-day Trojan Horses—programs that are interesting or useful, but whose true purpose is to damage your system. A computer virus is a self-replicating program that damages computer operating systems or data files. The Internet will entice you to pull in lots of outside files. If your company doesn't have virus protection, you're running on the edge. If it does, make sure you don't short-circuit the safeguards to save a few minutes.

Fortunately, Netscape offers built-in antivirus protection that's based on the Norton Anti-Virus software (see Figure 12-1). This comes with the Netscape Power Pack, and can be added even to older versions of Netscape that don't have antivirus protection built in. For now, let's find out more about other security threats that today endanger your organization's computers.

Sniffers and snoopers

Have you ever wondered how hackers can break into your organization's system? The simplest technique is to obtain the login ID and password of a system administrator.

But that's secure information, isn't it? So how do they get it? You might be surprised how often they use inside sources who sell computer security information. The rampant wave of corporate downsizing that is sweeping the U.S. has bred a whole generation of employees who do not hold a high degree of loyalty to large corporations. Selling a key login ID and a password might bring a

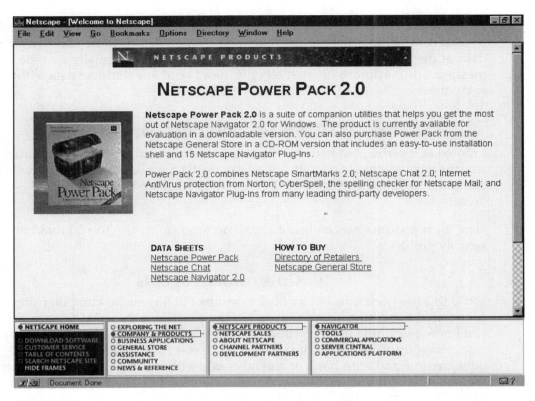

Figure 12-1

disgruntled employee the severance pay he or she believes is fair compensation for being dumped.

Alternatively, a hacker might use their snoopers and sniffers to find passwords that can gain them entrance onto a system where the system administrator's password might be found. A sniffer is an Internet program that monitors Internet traffic looking for data that it suspects might contain login IDs or passwords used to log onto its targeted systems.

When you login to a remote host using Telnet or FTP, your login ID and password travel across the Internet unencrypted. Most e-mail also can be monitored the same way. Any sniffer that has targeted your organization's Internet traffic can pick out login IDs from e-mail. If you e-mail a password to a colleague or business associate, you might also be inviting in a host of hackers.

Spoofing

Hackers can pretend to be a trusted user by changing their host login IP address to match a user's. They then force their data to take a particular path through the Internet using source routing, and having the last link in the route be the trusted user's system. Data sent back to the trusted user's host is then sent on to the hacker's system. Such masquerades, as well as the creation of bogus e-mail messages, are collectively called *spoofing*.

Thus, even if you receive a direct e-mailed request from someone you trust, you have to consider that the message could be a spoof. Before you e-mail sensitive data, at the very least be certain that the trusted individual actually sent the message. For maximum Internet security, never send any sensitive data without encryption.

Top 10 Internet security problems

I hinted at it earlier, but believe it or not, your organization's worst computer security enemy actually is itself. For all the media hype about hackers and computer theft, the criminals can't compare to what we all, collectively, do to ourselves.

Here, in approximate ascending order of occurrence, are the Top 10 Internet security problems.

10. Government agents

So far this has been rare, but in a few cases the FBI has raided computer sites and confiscated everything. Can't happen to your organization, right? Are you sure you know everything that everybody is doing on your system? If one of them posts secret information on the Internet, then you could hear a knock on the door anytime and see a band of federal agents with moving vans and warrants to remove your equipment. The telecommunications bill passed by Congress in early 1996 created a whole new class of criminals: just about everyone. Even moderately offensive language—stuff that you'll hear even in Disney films these days—can bring a jail sentence if used on the Internet.

9. Sniffers and snoopers

Unless your organization maintains a cache of sensitive information, you're not likely to be a target for sniffers and snoopers; but any research-oriented organization could attract eavesdroppers. Budget cuts have forced many companies to slash R&D spending, but a few bucks spent on hackers who monitor your data transmissions could replace a competitor's shut-down research laboratory. The good news is that a firewall will give your organization a relatively simple and highly effective preventative measure against the effects of criminals using sniffers and snoopers.

8. Credit card fraud

From what we've seen, most horror stories of credit card fraud are unfounded. First, people don't need the Internet to steal credit card numbers. Remember when you used to tear up all your credit card carbons? Today, trash bins behind strip shopping malls once again have plenty of credit card numbers and no one can backtrack to find out who got them. Besides, there simply are very, very few reports of credit card numbers being ripped off across the Internet.

7. Youthful hackers

Kids enjoy a challenge, and your system might be an inviting target. Kids, however, rarely are out to steal your data, and usually lack the fencing contacts for it if they did download something sensitive. They have, however, reformatted a lot of hard drives and deleted a lot of files. A simple tape backup system will protect you against most of them, of course, and firewall will keep them out in the first place.

6. Professional hackers

This is a computer security problem without borders. In 1995, a group of Russian computer hackers was accused of stealing more than $10 million from Citibank accounts in the U.S. Professional computer hackers not only enjoy their work, but they also enjoy the potential for enormous rewards. And if they're smart and are willing to work on the run, they're extremely hard to catch. We've been lucky so far because a lot of have relied too heavily on their genius-level brains and not enough on running—it's amazing how many times that law enforcement officials simply drive to the home of a suspect and pick him or her up while he or she's on-line.

5. Internal credit card fraud

This is a problem for any business and it probably will grow—but it didn't start with the Internet. The advent of the Internet and the expansion of credit card usage in lieu of bank checks has created a ripe environment for employees to obtain and sell the credit card numbers of your clients and customers. No firewall will prevent this, of course, just good internal corporate security and being alert to the possibility.

4. Inside jobs

Current employees easily can be tempted to upload to another computer some of your organization's sensitive data. With a few mouse clicks in a Windows FTP application, an employee can circumvent all your firewalls and do the work of legions of snoopers, sniffers, and hackers. Former employees, too, may have left with sensitive secrets or with passwords to come back in and get them later. In this era of rapid downsizing and outsourcing, you'll need to focus your security efforts on employees whose jobs might soon be eliminated—after all, they might consider the taking of sensitive corporate data merely to be a fair severance package—especially if they helped create it.

3. Viruses

This one is high on the list, but you might be surprised at the reason. It's not because of serious data corruption problems brought about by computer viruses. Viruses actually cause little data loss. Organizations of all sizes, however, have spent vast sums on virus prevention, monitoring, and cleaning. The cure usually is far more costly than the problem. Nonetheless, it is a necessary business expense, because if you don't spend the money to protect your computer systems from virus intrusion, you will one day lose data to a computer virus—it's almost guaranteed. However, good virus protection and tape backups will ensure that viruses won't destroy your business.

2. Hardware theft, fire, and failure

This problem far outstrips all the others I've listed so far. As a computer consultant, I've seen companies dropped to their corporate knees by theft, fire, and hardware failures. These security risks are not threats, nor are they theories—they are real and they happen every day. A regular routine of simple tape backups and off-site storage will give your organization a 100-percent insurance policy against these losses. Unfortunately, human nature and the laws of metaphysics have proven that the Friday when someone is too rushed to run a backup and take the tape off-site is the same weekend your computers will be stolen, or the office will burn to the ground. I am not kidding.

1. Computer users

And the number one cause of computer losses is—computer users. Bad password choices and compromised passwords. Accidental reformatting. Unintentional file deletions. Mistakes with software that publicly post sensitive data instead of sending it securely to a site. Flame wars by employees that generate negative attention or lawsuits. Failure to run regular backups (see Number 2). Intentionally circumventing firewalls or other security measures because someone is in a hurry—and that was just the opening that someone's sniffer or snooper was waiting to find.

Tape backup

Now that you're switching your business into the cyberspace mode, you are at a greater-than-ever risk of having your business destroyed by a computer data loss. For example, losing the mailbox files from your e-mail applications or losing your Netscape bookmark list could cost you a fortune in lost business.

I could tell you a slew of true horror stories that I've witnessed in my years as a computer consultant that all could have been prevented by tape backups. In fact, in most cases tape backup systems were in place, but using them had become a forgotten task.

If you're working on a network, you probably believe that your network administrator is handling all important backups. While that's true for normal data files, you'll find that by default most e-mail programs use the application's program directory or drive to store its mailbox files and address book. If these applications are installed on your local hard drive, then your mailbox files are not being backed up. If your local hard drive suffers a failure, you could lose all of your e-mail contact data.

If you don't work on a network, then partition your hard drive into C: and D:, keep all data files on D:, and backup D: at the end of each session. The Eudora Pro e-mail program lets you specify the location of mailbox and address book files, so keep these on D:, too, because they are, after all, *data files* and not *program files*.

Finally, buy extra backup tapes and keep a recent set of tapes *off-site*. Get into a pattern of rotating your latest backup with the off-site tapes. A backup tape that's left inserted in the drive slot won't do you any good if your computers are stolen or destroyed in a fire or a disaster.

Internet security measures

The hardest part of connecting to the Internet in a large organization might not be money issues or technical issues; it might be convincing management that corporate data will be safe. The only truly secure system is one that isn't connected to the Internet and that even trusted employees can't use. Of course, a truly secure system also is useless.

Network security measures try to create a compromise, balancing business needs against risks. Even modest security measures can keep out the bad guys, permit the good guys to use the Internet, and cool the fears of management. There are a lot of different solutions that depend on the size of your organization. Fortunately, the Internet itself has plenty of sources from which you can learn the latest in Internet security measures that will fit your organization. For example, you can bookmark the NIST Computer Security Web site at *csrc.ncsl.nist.gov /secalert* (see Figure 12-2).

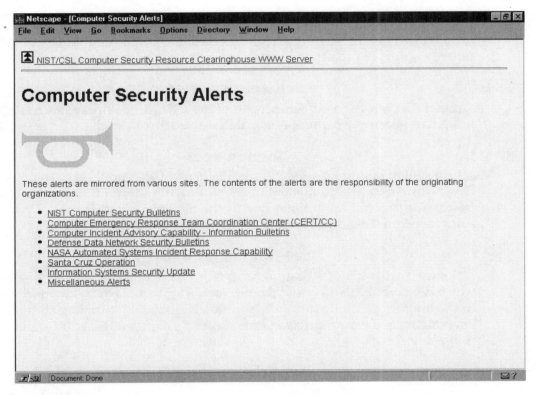

Figure 12-2

Small organizations can protect themselves from most security risks by contracting with outside providers to maintain a Web site on a remote system. No one can enter your system through a remote Web site, because it has no direct connection to your system. Large organizations, however, will need to employ one or more security measures.

Firewalls, restricted routers and proxy servers are devices used to control data traffic while allowing fairly free visits to external systems. Let's consider all three.

Firewalls

An Internet firewall performs the same functions as a firewall in a townhouse development or apartment complex—damage can be prevented from spreading.

Firewalls force all communications with the outside world through a single machine. The firewall creates a single entry point that monitors, and therefore can control, all external communications. Read the following sidebar for more details on firewall technology; or skip ahead, if you've had enough on firewalls.

Host-based firewall

A firewall is where Internet security is implemented in software running on a general-purpose computer designated for security protection. General Internet traffic flow (dirty) is outside the firewall. Internal network traffic flow (clean) is inside the firewall. Security in host-based firewalls (see Figure 12-3) is generally at the application level, rather than at a network level.

Router-based firewall

A firewall where the security is implemented using screening routers as the primary means of protecting the network.

Screening router

A router that is used to implement part of the security of a firewall by configuring it to selectively permit or deny traffic at a network level.

Bastion host

A host system that is a strong point in the network's security perimeter. Bastion hosts should be configured to be particularly resistant to attack. In a host-based firewall, the bastion host is the platform on which the firewall software is run. Bastion hosts are also referred to as *gateway hosts*.

Dual-Homed gateway

A firewall consisting of a bastion host with two network interfaces, one of which is connected to the protected network, the other of which is connected to the Internet. IP traffic forwarding is usually disabled, restricting all traffic between the two networks to whatever passes through some kind of application proxy.

Application proxy

An application that forwards application traffic through a firewall. Proxies tend to be specific to the protocol they are designed to forward, and may provide increased access control or audit.

Screened subnet

A firewall architecture in which a sand box or demilitarized zone network is set up between the protected network and the Internet, with traffic between the protected network and the Internet blocked. Conceptually, this is similar to a dual-homed gateway, except that an entire network, rather than a single host is reachable from the outside.

Terms Glossary from *USENET FAQ*, Copyright 1995
Trusted Information Systems, Inc. Reprinted with permission.

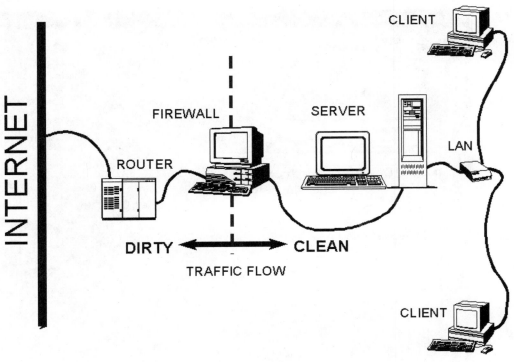

Figure 12-3

Restricted routers

Restricted routers block the function of certain protocols that hackers frequently use to break into computer systems. Limiting the kinds and sources of data traffic allowed on your system makes the hacker's job more difficult. When you try to install the latest videoconferencing, telephone, or other software on your PC and discover you can't get it to work, it might be that your Internet experts have restricted this type of data traffic for security reasons.

Proxy servers

Proxy servers are applications that act as a proxy between your secure network and the external Internet (see Figure 12-4). When you want to FTP a file, for example, your request goes to the proxy server, which sits outside of your system's firewall. The proxy gets the file for you and then sends it to you. This is safer than a direct Internet connection, but also slower and more expensive to install.

Viruses

Even the best firewalls can't protect users against viruses they find and bring home while surfing the net. That's because viruses enter a computer system disguised as normal information. The firewall will allow the information to pass, because a valid user has given authorization. Your only protection against computer viruses is to regularly check your entire system and to check all programs that you obtain from the Internet.

Internet security ◀

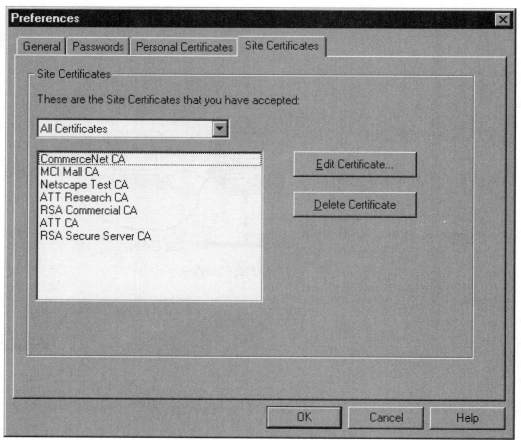

Figure 12-4

Passwords

Among the top security problems on the Internet are passwords that are easily broken. If hackers can get a foothold in your network—either by guessing a password or by using low-security public access—they can search for words that could be used as passwords by users with high-security access.

Passwords that are found in dictionaries, or that are used in documents, e-mail, or Web pages are ready prey for hackers. Passwords like TOPP$DOG (which can't be found in a dictionary, but is still easy to remember) are a safer choice.

Consider combining the case-sensitivity of Unix and the diversity of languages other than English to further enhance your password security. For example, your mail password could be as simple as coRReo, the Spanish word for mail. Even if you had a Spanish surname and a hacker used that as a clue to guess the word, he still would have to test thousands of uppercase and lowercase combinations.

Cyberspace vigilantes—tracking the hackers

If you believe that your organization might be a target for door-rattling hackers, your Internet service provider can help you protect your organization's data. At the same time, you can become a cyberspace vigilante, riding the superhighway 24-hours-a-day to stop hackers.

Rick Garvin, an Internet security expert at BTG Corporation, told me a story about how he helped a client become a cyberspace vigilante. A BTG client—a government defense contractor in the Washington area, with tons of secret, sensitive data— suspected that hackers were working at night to access their data. BTG set up an alarm mechanism on the client's system that would alert the system administrator at home. Sure enough, within a few days the alarm went off at 2 a.m. Knowing that the prospective thieves were on-line, the administrator was able to discover their location and report the incident to authorities.

Your data security needs might not warrant your being jarred out of bed at 2 a.m., but that is one possible solution and it has a ripple effect throughout the industry. Thanks to one system administrator's efforts,and BTG's technical assistance, one hacker paid a price for merely attempting his dirty work.

Perhaps BTG prevented that hacker from rattling your door next. I believe that's the way Internet security should be handled, because we all are in this together. The security problems I experience today could become your security problems tomorrow. We all, however, can discourage hackers by routinely and regularly following Internet security discipline. The success of your entire organization might depend on it.

For many organizations, their first need for Internet security arises when they want their Web site to accept cyberspace purchases by Web visitors. The issue of money and security on the Internet are closely intermingled. The next chapter continues with the security discussion, but moves in a different direction, focusing on how it will work with your Web site visitors; then it transitions from financial security to other cyberspace financial issues and concerns.

Continuing Education

Netscape security features

⦿ In Netscape, click **Help, On Security**

Netscape has contributed greatly to Internet security by including built-in security features. When you see at the beginning of the URL in the Location text entry box the string https:// instead of the usual http://, you know that Netscape is displaying a secure hypertext document. You also will notice a thin blue line underneath the Location text entry box. A third clue is that the small skeleton key in the lower-left corner of the screen no longer is broken—a complete, unbroken key means that you're reading a secure document (see Figure 12-5).

Computer security newsgroups

comp.security.announce

comp.security.misc

comp.security.unix

You can access the Usenet newsgroups on computer security information and read security solutions posted by the Computer Emergency Response Team (CERT).

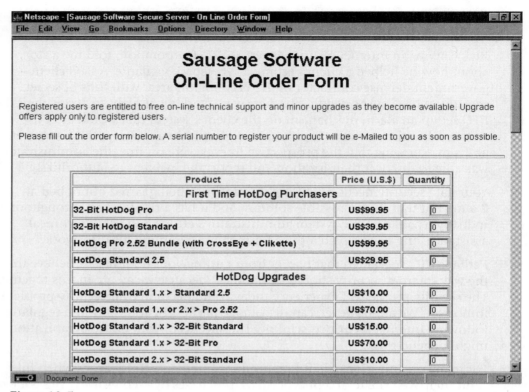

Figure 12-5

Computer security mailing list

cert-advisory-request@cert.org

You can get mailing list announcements on Internet security by sending a subscription request to this address. E-mail with a blank title and with subscribe in the body of the message.

Firewall product overview

http://www.access.digex.net/~bdboyle/firewall.vendor.html

This site could be considered to be a one-stop source for Internet security measures for your organization. Posted by Cathy Fulmer of Panasonic Corporation, it's a long list of hypertext links to sources of Internet security hardware, software, and consultants.

An introduction to firewalls

http://www.soscorp.com

Be sure and check out the link on this page (titled Introduction to Firewalls) that is produced by SOS Corporation, a New York City-based UNIX systems management company (see Figure 12-6). SOS can provide experts in computer security, systems programming, network administration, and systems management. They produce an Internet security application called Brimstone, a full-featured Internet firewall. I've singled them out here, however, because they also produce Freestone, a freeware firewall application that includes parts of Brimstone.

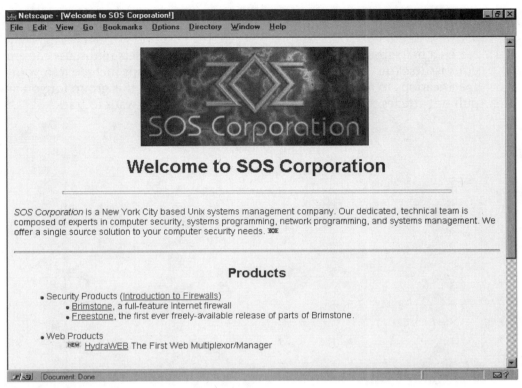

Figure 12-6

Site security handbook

ftp://ds.internic.net/rfc/rfc1244.txt

This is a huge document (253K in length) on Internet security that you can download via FTP. It's the product of the Site Security Policy Handbook Working Group (SSPHWG), a combined effort of the Security Area and User Services Area of the Internet Engineering Task Force (IETF). It also is available through the Web page of the Internet Society at www.isoc.org.

Computer security resource clearinghouse

http://www.first.org

This site is a Web page maintained by the National Institute of Standards and Technology in Gaithersburg, Maryland near Washington, DC. There's a jump on the home page called Training that brings up a page titled Training, Awareness, and Resource Publications; it is a directory of a variety of resource material for the computer security professional or trainer.

Site security handbook

http://www.ietf.cnri.reston.va.us/html.charters/ssh-charter.html

This Web page actually is titled Site Security Handbook (SSH) Charter, and it gives an overview of site security issues from the Internet Engineering Task Force (IETF). It has a hypertext link that will FTP the actual handbook, *Site Security Handbook for System and Network Administrators* (91,770 bytes).

Computer virus newsgroup

alt.comp.virus

Here's a newsgroup that provides an open forum for users to discuss computer virus issues. You can read this group regularly, or perhaps include it in your specifications to a news service company that will scan this group for you and pull out articles that contain only the information you want to track.

Cyberspace money issues

MONEY makes the cyber-world go round, just as it does in the real world. But why not? These days money is mostly just electronic energy zipping around between people and financial institutions, so the Internet is a natural tool for some of that zipping around. We all will need money in cyberspace, just as in the real world, especially as the distinctions between the two merge. Hence, I've devoted this chapter to cyberspace money issues. You'll find a mixture here, however, of security issues and financial issues, because on the Internet—as in real life—money and security are closely related.

Organizations of all sizes can use the Internet to conduct electronic commerce transactions anywhere in the world via the Web. Cyberspace retailers are selling everything from computer software to astrology reports to flowers. Financial merchants offer on-line banking, trade stocks on-line, and can accept credit card applications via wire. Internet travel services can let customers make their own reservations and buy airline tickets. Nonprofit organizations can accept membership applications on-line. Publishers can offer paid subscriptions to on-line versions of their publications.

However, don't let this focus on money issues distract you from seeing other uses for the secure technology that protects financial transactions.

The same security measures that protect your financial transactions can be used to circulate confidential marketing plans, product announcements, and private personnel information. Survey data and customer questionnaires can be collected because organizations can protect the privacy of its Web users by using secure documents. Geographically diverse organizations can exchange sensitive company financial data, market reports, research data, and new product ideas and designs. But that's enough digression—the main focus here is on money issues.

In business, we always consider two sides of the money equation: income and expenses. I'll start with income by giving you an overview of how money moves around in cyberspace; then I'll cover some expense issues that will help you plan and implement your organization's Web site.

The truth about credit card purchases

The security of making credit card purchases is a major topic of concern in every Internet class I teach. I find that most people are reluctant to use their credit card for Internet purchases. Most of these fears are unfounded and are based on some overblown anecdotes that people have read or heard about Internet credit-card security risks.

Most likely you, too, have read some bad news about Internet credit-card security. Credit-card transactions are but one aspect of exchanging funds on the Internet. There are many other options, but credit-card transactions are easy to understand, because they're related to something we all know; and they've been a hot topic in the press.

The problem with giving someone a credit card number on the Internet is that you can't be sure where your credit card information will travel and who might copy the information while it's en route. Because conventional data transfer on the Internet isn't encrypted, an experienced UNIX hacker might create a program that grabs and saves for later analysis any data that looks like #### #### #### #### ##/##. The hacker then could build a database of credit card numbers and (supposedly) use them to buy things for himself or fence the numbers to professional credit card thieves.

Unsafe at any speed

Unfortunately, the Internet is only one place where you can't be sure where your credit card information will travel and who might copy the information. Internet credit card number theft certainly is possible, and occurs occasionally, but it's no more of a threat than any other credit card transaction and is safer than most.

Consider other credit card transactions and you'll realize that there are plenty of easy ways for people to collect and sell credit card numbers without having the technical expertise, the tools, and the access required to hack the Internet. When you make a mail-order purchase or even hand your credit card to a waiter, you are risking theft by people who need far fewer skills than those of experienced computer professionals. It's far more likely that you'll be the victim of traditional credit card fraud than someone will intercept an Internet purchase you might make.

Internet technology actually makes credit card transactions safer than handing your card to a waiter. The basic technology is called public-key cryptography, the foundation of secure Web documents. Secure documents are encrypted, which means they are scrambled by the sender and unscrambled by the receiver. A secure document can't be read without a key that is used during the unscrambling process.

When you access a secure document with Netscape, you might see a warning before that document is transferred to your system. This might only occur on the first secure document you encounter, because the warning will include an option to stop such warnings in the future. If you mark the option as checked, you'll not see a warning on future secure documents. Whenever you accept a secure document with a public key, the site certificate is added to your Netscape preferences list (see Figure 13-1).

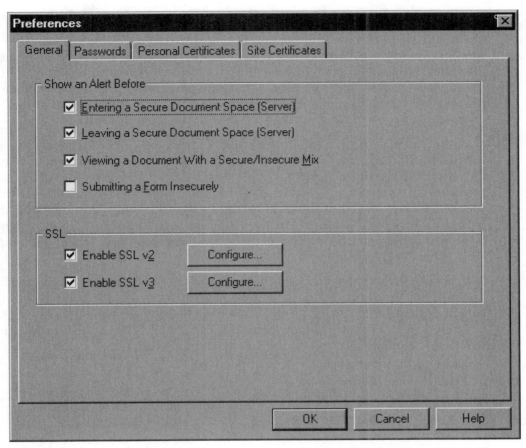

Figure 13-1

It might seem dangerous to deactivate the automatic secure document warning feature, but there are several other ways to recognize a secure document. With or without a warning, you will see a variety of other clues that tell you you're viewing a secure document:

- The skeleton-key in the lower-left corner of the screen—normally displayed as broken in the middle—will be intact.
- The thin, gray bar beneath the **Location** text entry box near the top of the screen will turn to blue.
- The document's URL will automatically change from *http://* to *https://* even if you entered it manually without adding the s on the end.

Public-key cryptography scrambles numbers and other personal or corporate data before it's sent, then enables the receiver to unscramble the original information. New technology being planned by credit card companies will let buyers pay by credit card without merchants ever knowing the buyer's card number.

If your site needs to accept credit card transactions, you'll have no trouble finding a Web developer who knows how to implement the technology. And whoever maintains your Web server almost certainly will know how as well. I'll have more on security in the chapter on Web servers.

Collecting tolls on the information highway

The real challenge to the Internet and the information age is how to get very small payments to creators of intellectual property without making everyone on the information superhighway run through countless electronic toll booths. It can be done, and we'll discuss later some emerging technology that will make possible very small payments (micropayments).

One toll-collecting method would be to employ advertising, as is done in other electronic media. This is a rapidly growing phenomenon. You'll see Web pages sprinkled with logos that advertise site sponsors who help the site owner cover the costs of maintaining a database, newsletter, or search engine. In exchange, the sponsors get to place a link on the site—usually a graphic of their logo—so that visitors quickly can get information on the sponsor's product. You might be able to help finance your Internet costs by selling space to sponsors. You also might be able to increase traffic at your site by sponsoring well-done, related sites that already have high traffic.

Another option is to dispense Internet cash that can be collected in very small amounts any time you get a piece of information. Internet cash also has the benefit of being able to keep all transactions private. When paying by Internet cash, even the merchant you pay might not know who bought their information. Some early companies that offer on-line payment plans are:

- First Virtual (*www.fv.com*)
- DigiCash (*www.digicash.com*)
- Cybercash (*www.cybercash.com*) (see Figure 13-2)
- ATS (*www.versanet.com*)

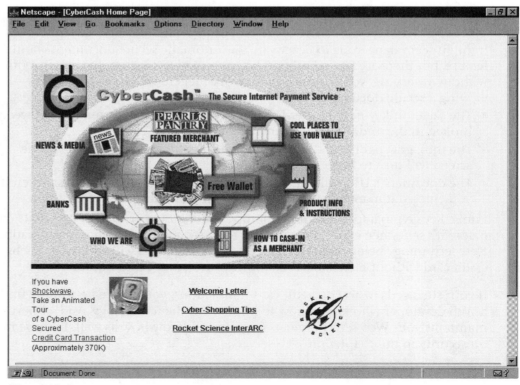

Figure 13-2

▶ *Creating your own Web site*

The other side of the privacy coin

Privacy cuts two ways, though. Criminals are eager to find new ways to hide and launder income from illegal activities. Terrorists want to eliminate money trails that can lead authorities to them or their sponsors. The U.S. government is exploring ways to monitor transactions, but Internet privacy systems—especially secure data-encryption and digital cash—would make their mission much more difficult. No one knows how this conflict will play out, or whether an acceptable compromise can be found between Big Brother and anarchy. Meanwhile, as the government is pondering options, the Internet is rapidly creating its own monetary system—let's learn more about this phenomenon.

Internet commerce systems

Many potential merchants are anxious to sell information, search services, software, and audio or video clips on the Internet—perhaps your organization is among this group. When these merchants do begin to sell in the Internet, they'll find an eager cadre of potential clients and customers; but that's going to take some consumer education, because today most things on the Internet are free. Thus, under the present system, owners of intellectual property have little incentive to make their valuable information goods accessible through the Web. This will improve as Internet collection systems become more secure, reliable, and inexpensive.

Free Internet products abound today because Internet commerce is only a small percentage of sales for most companies that distribute products via the Internet. As the balance shifts in favor of the Internet, companies will be less able to subsidize their Internet service sales with traditional sales.

For example, let's look at the costs of obtaining an upgraded software driver for a printer. For years we all expected to be charged a few dollars to cover the company's cost of producing and mailing a diskette that contained the updated files. Today, however, you can download updated files for free directly from a company's Web site. But this can't continue. Companies bear some distribution costs even when they use the Internet for file updates. The good news is that they will be able to cover their Internet distribution costs for far less than it costs to cover mail distribution of diskettes. Few of us would mind being charged fifty cents or a dollar for instant delivery of a file update; but for now, there is a gap in what buyers expect to pay and what sellers need to charge.

Countless entrepreneurial groups are developing Internet commerce mechanisms that will bridge this gap between sellers and buyers by creating a common and inexpensive Internet marketplace. Let's consider some of the features that these groups may employ in the commerce systems that are being developed.

Micropayments

The Internet marketplace will explode when it is able to support *micropayments*. Micropayments will enable merchants to profitably sell information for as little as 10 cents. But for these *micromerchants* to flourish, the Internet will need to exact extremely low accounting and billing costs, with transaction costs as little as one cent for a 10-cent item.

Internet commerce systems that support micropayments will enhance the quality and variety of information products sold and bought on the Web. Those selling the information—even micromerchants selling a single page of information—will receive fair compensation for their products and be able to remain in business.

To learn more about the implications of micropayments on both your business and your personal life, check out the Web site of Dr. Brad J. Cox, Ph.D. at *www.virtualschool.edu/mon/TTEF.html.* Brad is a professor at George Mason University in Fairfax, Virginia, and this site is the home page for his book *Superdistribution: Objects as Property on the Electronic Frontier* (Addison-Wesley, 1995).

Security!

Internet commerce systems have to provide secure transactions for both your organization and your customers. When you sell products via the Internet, you'll need assurance that hackers cannot sniff your traffic for passwords that will enable them to download products without paying; and your clients and customers will want assurance that their credit card information will remain a private matter between the two of you.

In client/server systems such as the Internet, transaction security is a two-way street. Both your system (the server) and the buyer's system (client) must use software that includes security features. The Netscape Web browser has built-in security features already, so most of your buyers will have the required software. This means that, in effect, Internet security is now a one-way street, with the responsibility falling to the merchant to create a secure service. The majority of your Internet buyers—those using Netscape—already have handled their end of the security loop.

Certified delivery

Another Internet commerce requirement is for certified delivery of on-line transactions. Certified delivery protects both sellers and buyers, especially when the product's value is time-sensitive. The seller needs to be able to prove that the buyer got the product on-time, while the product had the value for which the buyer paid. Sellers also need to know when they transmit their information that they will get paid.

The same system needs to give buyers the assurance that they will not be charged if there is some system problem that prevents delivery. Buyers do not want to be charged just because the seller's system transmitted the information. This will require an information exchange between seller and buyer that will verify that delivery can be accomplished and that payment can be made. The seller's system will transmit electronic products only after the availability of a valid payment is confirmed. At the same time, certified delivery also means that your clients and customers are charged only when the information actually is received. It's a tricky Catch-22 situation, but system developers have created programs that protect both sides of the seller-to-buyer partnership.

Automated flexible pricing

Few businesses charge the same price for the same product for all buyers. Because a lot of factors can affect your pricing, your organization's Internet commerce services need to offer discounts and be able to handle premium pricing. Here are some pricing factors that your Internet commerce system will need to consider:

- Prepaid, subscription-type sales that will track the buyer's balance of available funds, sending information without charge for buyers with balances and requiring additional payments for new subscribers or for those who've depleted their balance.
- Discounts—perhaps even free copies—for buyers who are a member of a site license group that has paid a flat rate.
- Volume discounts for buyers who are members of a preregistered consumer group, user group, or government agency.
- Volume discounts for a single buyer who is a frequent customer.
- Premium surcharges for purchases made during peak-hour access and discounts for off-peak access.
- Time-sensitive charges that could invoke a premium for information downloaded today, discount that same information tomorrow, and offer it next week to potential new customers as a free sample.
- Price quotations for buyers who are shopping, but not ready to buy. The system needs to record quotations with the database records of your prospective buyers so there won't be price confusion when the buyer returns to complete the sale.

A typical commerce group

Let's look in depth at a company that describes itself as a business model for a commerce server. The NetBill project (see Figure 13-3) has teamed with strategic business partners Visa International and Mellon Bank Corporation. NetBill research, however, is funded in part by a grant from the National Science

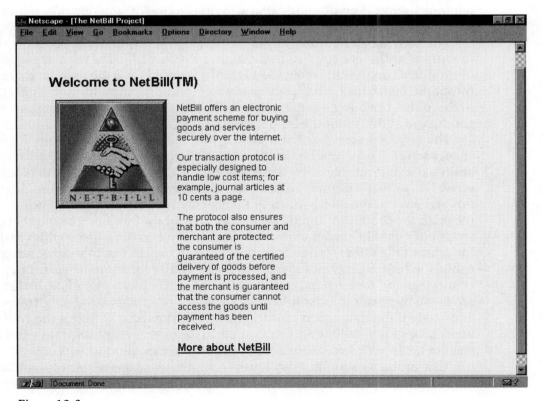

Figure 13-3

Foundation (NSF). While NetBill has a growing full-time and part-time staff—drawn mainly from the ranks of Carnegie Mellon University (CMU)—much of its development has been completed by students in project courses taken as part of CMU's graduate program in Information Networking.

A commerce server is a set of standards and the software that implements those standards so buyers can pay merchants on-line. A commerce group—such as NetBill—maintains commerce servers that link to financial institutions for both your organization and for your clients and customers. These links not only handle the actual financial transaction, but they certify the delivery of both product and payment. NetBill's project group handles both sides of certified delivery.

NetBill uses a financial transaction protocol that supports flexible pricing and can calculate customized quotes for individual buyers and handle pricing approvals. It uses digital signature technology to provide account security on both sides of the transaction. Buyers can sign orders digitally using a key that is never revealed to the merchant, so eavesdroppers cannot intercept credit card numbers and approval authorizations.

The ins and outs of a commerce server transaction

When a buyer requests an electronic product from a merchant, the buyer's client software sends a digitally verified purchase request to the merchant's server. The electronic product is transmitted to the buyer in an encrypted format. Encryption transforms data into a format that is unreadable by anyone without a secret decryption key that will unlock the information and restore it to a readable format.

The merchant's information server computes a cryptographic checksum (a series of arithmetic operations that detect whether a file has been damaged or modified) on the encrypted message. After transmitting the product to the buyer, the merchant's server then sends an electronic payment order (EPO). At this point, the buyer has the goods, but not the key, required to decrypt the goods; and at this point the buyer has not yet been charged.

The buyer's system calculates a checksum and sends a reply to the merchant's server. When the server receives the EPO reply, it compares its checksum against the one computed by the client library. If the checksums match, the server knows that the buyer received the encrypted goods without error. After this verification, the merchant creates a digitally verified invoice that includes the price, the checksum, and the decryption key for the product. The merchant sends both the EPO and the invoice to a commerce server, which verifies that the product identifiers, prices, and checksums all match. The commerce server debits the buyer's account (which was prefunded), credits the merchant's account, logs the transaction, and saves a copy of the decryption key. It then sends the merchant a digitally verified message with an approval code (or an error code if the transaction failed). Finally, the merchant forwards the commerce server's reply and the decryption key to the buyer's client software, which enables the buyer's software to decrypt the information product.

This probably sounds ridiculously complicated, but computers handle the whole process in a few seconds.

Multiple users and accounts

NetBill supports many-to-many relationships between consumers and accounts. This means that a single corporate or academic account might authorize many users to charge against it and obtain special pricing. Also, individual consumers might maintain multiple personal accounts. One user on every multiple-user account must be designated as the account owner, and someone must be designated as the account administrator. An authorized administrator can use a standard Web browser to open an account, view and change an account profile, authorize funds transfers into the account, and view current statements of account transactions and balances. Account information checks by administrators are handled as regular financial transactions to ensure authentication and security.

Account creation is one of the largest costs associated with traditional credit card and bank accounts. The automatic account creation features of commerce servers help to limit costs for both consumers and merchants. Low-cost account creation is going to be a key contributor toward developing widespread micropayment systems.

Account types

A commerce account currently comes in two basic flavors:
- Debit model (pre-paid)
- Credit model (post-paid)

In the debit model—used by DigiCash and Cybercash, for example—buyers must deposit into a commerce account sufficient funds to cover anticipated purchases. Buyers first would deposit real money (via check or credit card) with DigiCash or Cybercash, and then go surf the net with electronic money.

In the credit model—patterned after traditional credit card vendors—transactions are accumulated and billed to the buyer's commerce account at the end of a billing period. These accounts, again like credit cards, have a pre-established dollar limit for each buyer. Both models give both merchants and consumers instant on-line access to transaction status and statement activity.

Other uses for commerce servers

So far, I've focused only on the sale and purchase of electronic goods and information, but there are plenty of nonelectronic products to sell, and a good commerce model must support the purchase of traditional goods and services. Let's consider a few possibilities:
- Ticketing for entertainment events and for airline reservations. The airlines are setting the stage for this as they begin developing ticketless flights. Your ticket might be just a printed receipt with a code number that agents would match with their computer when you check in at the gate.
- Utility payments, such as for electric bills, phone service, gas bills, tax payments, and perhaps even lottery sales.
- Products that currently are sold via traditional mail-order catalogs.
- Contributions to charitable organizations or political campaigns.
- On-line video and audio, although at the present time this conflicts with the safeguards in certified delivery.

- Software application rental. Software could incorporate the client library in any application. Periodically the software would ask users to approve another purchase to get the next month's activity or issue of new software.

While most of the information exchanges on the Internet might continue to be provided by merchants for free, commerce systems will increase the incentive of creators and producers of information goods to supply more and better products. We all will benefit from the improved quality and increased quantity of new goods available via the Internet.

Costs of providing a commerce system

If you want to know more about how your organization can conduct financial transactions across the Internet, you'll need to refer to the URLs in the Continuing Education section at the end of this chapter. For now, let's switch to another angle on money issues: how much you might have to spend to get an Internet connection that will enable you to conduct Internet commerce. Again, you can't get all the answers from a single source, but this is a starting point that includes references to other sources.

Off-site commerce servers

If your organization's Web site is maintained off-site, then adding a commerce server will be inexpensive. For example, this book's Web pages are maintained by Digiweb (*www.digiweb.com*). Digiweb offers perhaps the best Web service value on the Internet, so if you are quoted a higher price ask your provider to outline the added services you're getting for the higher fee.

For only $20 per month, Digiweb provides a 25-megabyte Web site over a T-1 line with e-mail rerouting, domain name registration, and an FTP site. If you need to use their commerce server, they charge an extra $25 per month (see Figure 13-4). That's practically free commerce service, but there are a few limitations. Naturally, you can eliminate the limitations for more money, but it will be *a lot* more money. More on that in the next section, which covers on-site commerce servers. For now, let's cover the limitations that you face with a $25-per-month commerce server.

Do-it-yourself Web service

When you use a Web service provider such as Digiweb, they keep your normal Web pages on a normal Web server, with normal security. When you buy a commerce server option, they'll let you place your secure documents on their secure commerce server, but you can't place all of your pages there. This means that some of your pages will have a different URL from your normal Web pages. For example, if your normal Web pages were at www.yourdomain.com, your secure documents would be at www.starshine.digiweb.com/yourdomain.

Having a different URL won't make any difference in the steps your visitors must employ. Visitors will click on a link on one of your normal Web pages, and they'll be taken to the commerce server. Few will even notice that the URL is not located at your domain. When visitors have completed their transaction on your secure document, they will automatically be returned to your normal Web pages.

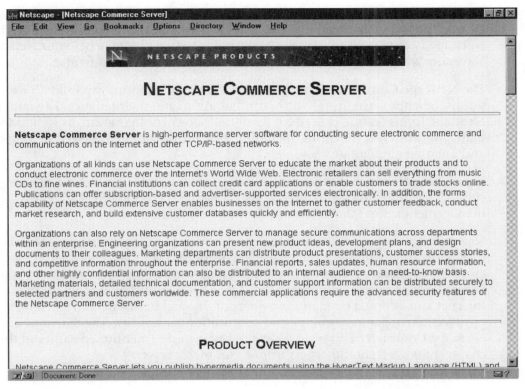

Figure 13-4

Only a few savvy users will even notice that they temporarily accessed a different server; it won't make any difference in the steps they would perform if you had your own on-site commerce server.

Why doesn't a Web service provider simply give you your own secure server? Cost. Remember the security keys I mentioned earlier in this chapter? Establishing one of those security keys costs a merchant about $700.

A bulk Web service reseller (such as Digiweb) divides up among many users the cost of establishing a security key. Thus, they only need to charge you an extra $25 per month. This simply means that if you're willing to pay more, you can indeed have it your way. For example, Digiweb offers a service under which they'll rent you a dedicated server for $250 per month. If you then paid to establish your own security key, everything would be kept on your own domain. Life is full of trade-offs, and this is one of them.

An off-site Web service and a rented commerce server are the best choices for small businesses or home-based businesses; but in a large organization with a full-time, professional computer staff, an on-site, dedicated server is going to make the most sense. So let's take a look at that option.

On-site commerce servers

If your organization has an on-site Web server, then its system administrator will handle the technical aspects of your commerce server. Your organization will run its own commerce server software on its Web server and will have its own key.

One of the best commerce servers available is made by the same folks who created the Netscape Navigator Web browser that you most likely are using. The Netscape Commerce Server uses a graphical interface that matches your Netscape Navigator to provide a uniform, easy-to-use operating environment.

The Netscape Commerce Server's user interface and its forms capability have point-and-click server installation, configuration, and maintenance. The familiar Netscape forms feature is used for the initial server configuration, as well as for managing all server functions, including user authorization, transaction logging, and ongoing configuration.

Because the Netscape Commerce Server accepts multiple IP addresses, it can support multiple domain names. It also adjusts to server load via a process-management system that allows dynamic configuration.

Naturally the Netscape Commerce Server provides topnotch security. After all, they're the ones who built the security features into your Web browser. It's an excellent commerce server example that offers advanced security features via the Secure Sockets Layer (SSL) protocol. SSL has been published openly on the Internet and adopted by major providers of Internet hardware and software products, financial institutions, and certification authorities. The SSL used in the Netscape Commerce Server provides the key features (mentioned earlier in this chapter) that you should expect from a commerce server:

- Data encryption, which ensures the privacy of Internet communications by encrypting the data while it's en route.
- Data integrity, which verifies that the information the buyer receives is exactly the same as what was sent.
- Server authentication, which allows any SSL-compatible client to verify the identity of the server using a certificate and a digital signature.

Netscape SSL incorporates public key cryptographic technology created by RSA Data Security. For more information, visit RSA's Web site at *www.rsa.com* (see Figure 13-5).

You might be surprised to find that the U.S. federal government could be interested in your Internet SSL security, and some security technology faces import restrictions. If you're concerned about international commerce transactions, Netscape can provide you with versions for export outside the United States and Canada. Check the listings in the Continuing Education section of this chapter so you can visit Netscape's own Web pages that will give you the latest information on its Internet commerce servers and security.

Summary of money issues

From both angles—expenses and income—Internet money issues are changing at hyperspeed; credit card transactions, digital cash, commerce servers, encryption, communications capabilities and communications charges are all changing and evolving. This book only can take a snapshot of one moment in cyberspace history; hence, you won't be able to rely upon any Internet book for the latest information on cyberspace money topics. If Internet security or Internet commerce becomes your responsibility, you'll need to track current technology and check with Internet professionals for the latest updates.

Figure 13-5

Never rely, however, on a single source for security or commerce information. Be sure to cross-check information you read on the Web and get second opinions from professionals you interview. I've seen incredible differences in price quotes for similar services—with the high quotes being on the order of ten times as high as the low quotes. You'll find plenty of Internet consulting companies out there who prey on the techno-fears of its clients by keeping security issues mysterious and charging very high fees.

The next chapter presents another Internet topic that is changing just as rapidly as the ones we've covered here: publishing on the Web. Publishing is closely tied with money issues for two reasons. First, creating the forms for money collection requires merging the money technology with Web publishing technology. Second, you might end up using the same source for solutions to both your money issues and publishing needs.

Continuing Education

Netscape commerce server software

http://home.mcom.com/comprod/netscape_commerce.html

All of your on-line credit-card sales can be kept absolutely secure by using the Netscape Commerce Server software. Netscape has RSA security built-in, using public-key encryption. This Web site probably always will be an excellent starting point for learning more about Internet security and for tracking technology updates and breakthroughs.

Network Money—The Future of Banking and Commerce on the Internet

http://nearnet.gnn.com/gnn/meta/finance/feat/emoney.home.html

This page is a feature of the GNN Personal Finance Center and features a splendid list of links to Web sites that deal with Internet money issues. A few choice examples are "An Introduction to Electronic Commerce" by Jason Solinsky. An article by Arnold Kling titled "Banking on the Internet" suggests that there is tremendous potential for micropayments to reduce unwanted junk mail and newsgroup pollution.

Network Money Sites on the Internet

http://nearnet.gnn.com/gnn/meta/finance/feat/links.html

The sites here will help you learn more about the development of Internet commerce systems. It's an annotated collection of links to the most interesting electronic commerce sites on the Net. In addition to some of the services mentioned in this chapter, you'll find links to experimental money-related sites and discussion of Internet cryptography in general.

Digiweb

http://www.digiweb.com

These folks provide the server for this book's Web site. On their home page you'll find a link to about their commerce servers. Because their main business is low-cost Web service, they have a few security limitations compared to a service that gives you a dedicated Web server. They do offer a dedicated server that will give you maximum Internet security; but even if you use their virtual server system, it very well could provide all of your security needs. Their home page also has a FAQs file that will tell you more about security.

GoSite

http://www.direct.net

GoSite is a full-service Web service provider. They will walk you step by step through the entire process of establishing, building, and maintaining a Web site. All of their service is SSL-encrypted. Where Digiweb offers a FAQs file, GoSite has 24-hour-a-day telephone support; but then, Digiweb is $20 per month and GoSite is $189 per month. GoSite, however, offers a lot of other services that are options at the lower-cost providers, and you could spend a lot on hiring consultants to do the work for you that GoSite includes with its basic service. If you need cgi scripts on your Web site, GoSite will handle the entire process after you tell them what you want.

Monumental Network Services

http://www.mnsinc.com

Monumental designs, installs, and manages World Wide Web servers that convert documents into home pages (Dynamic Page Generation), supports relational databases, and links Web pages to your network's information systems, thus allowing on-line transactions to be automatically entered into order processing, accounting, and inventory systems 24 hours a day with a high degree of fault tolerance (Distributed Transactions Processing).

Contact NetBill

http://www.ini.cmu.edu/netbill

Here's the Web site for Carnegie-Mellon's NetBill commerce server project that we profiled earlier in this chapter. NetBill's research is funded in part by a grant from the National Science Foundation (NSF), one of the founders of the Internet.

Digital Cash

http://www.digicash.com

Digital Cash (DigiCash) is pioneering a new system for transferring money via the Internet that effectively creates a new monetary system. DigiCash vendors accept payments from customers in the form of ecash money. For your customers to use this service, they first have to transfer some actual cash from their bank into ecash at DigiCash. With this account established, buyers then can shop Internet vendors who accept ecash. This system has more advantages for the vendor than for the client; but if your business is suffering collection problems, check out DigiCash (see Figure 13-6), because when a customer makes a buy, their ecash goes straight into your bank—you don't have to worry about credit card verification.

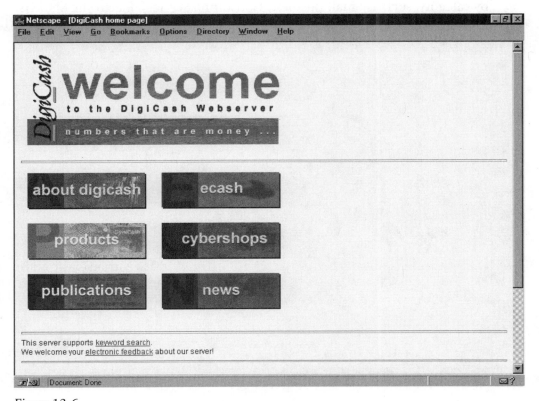

Figure 13-6

CyberCash

http://www.cybercash.com

CyberCash offers banks, merchants, and consumers the Secure Internet Payment Service (SIPS). SIPS protects consumer credit card numbers used for shopping on the Web and enables merchants to safely process credit card transactions over the Internet. By 1996, SIPS will enable consumers to use their own money for Internet payments. Check out this Web site for details on how your organization can use their system. CyberCash encryption software has been approved for worldwide export by the U.S. government.

Open Market commercial sites index

http://www.directory.net

Open Market Incorporated develops and markets software, services, and custom solutions that facilitate electronic commerce on the Web. Open Market applies both advanced technology and a business perspective to the expansion of business into an electronic marketplace. They offer solutions that address the needs of small companies and global businesses alike (see Figure 13-7).

Miscellaneous Web business sites

http://www.owi.com/netvalue

Here's a list of miscellaneous interesting Internet business sites that you can visit to see how they handle money transactions. This site is the home of Net.Value, The Web Strategy Forum. Instead of searching for specific businesses, you'll select by category, such as Small Business, Consulting Services, Electronic Markets, Virtual Catalogs, etc. There definitely is some inspiration lurking around on this site to fire up your creative engine.

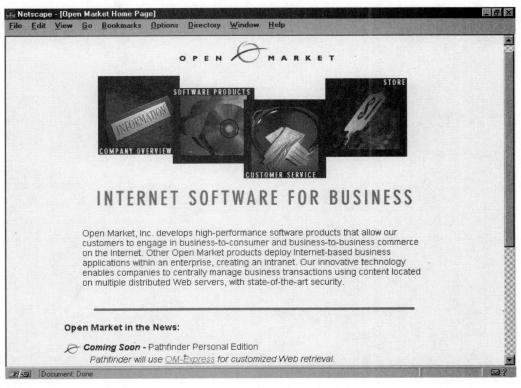

Figure 13-7

Publishing on the World Wide Web

WHEN THE Web debuted, writing hypertext, HTML-language pages required high levels of computer expertise, diligence and patience; but today, creating HTML can actually be enjoyable and as simple as using a word processor.

Producing World Wide Web documents has become so common that you can create them with WordPerfect for Windows and Word for Windows. Both applications offer free add-ons that greatly simplify the once-arduous challenge of creating simple hypertext documents. Now you can use an old friend as you become part of the Web. I'll highlight both their strengths and weaknesses so you'll know if you need something more advanced, and then we'll discuss those advanced Web editors.

However, there's more to writing for the World Wide Web than the technical side of producing hypertext documents. Knowing how to use tools doesn't make you a skilled craftsman. Because your Web site instantly will broadcast worldwide your organization's image, you'll want to get it right the first time.

I've included some home page tips that are tailored to organizational size that will help you know what *your* company can do in-house and when you need a consultant. When you've finished this chapter, you'll be fully prepared to become a player in the electronic world of the Web business scene.

Tools, tools, and more tools

There are more available tools for publishing Web hypertext documents than I can count. New ones are released almost daily. Before the recent dramatic expansion of Web tools, only programmers and computer specialists had the skills to create Web pages. The Web's popularity explosion has prompted major software developers to create tools that enable mainstream users to create Web pages.

It's become so easy, in fact, that you might already have created Web pages without knowing it. That's because some applications can convert existing documents—including graphics and tables—into perfectly-formatted Web documents.

Creating the very best Web pages still requires a technical expert because the leading edge of technology always stays ahead of the mainstream user. Someone always will be pushing existing technical limits, and if you want to play on the frontier, you'll need the skills of a full-time professional; however, most users today can create attractive, professional Web pages.

I'll cover basic Web-development tools in several categories:

- Word processor add-ons
- Conversion programs
- Stand-alone HTML editors
- Graphics software
- CGI tools
- Java

Each category will be covered in subsequent sections of this chapter. Some of the topics, however, will be covered here only briefly because they have a dedicated chapter later in the book.

Word processor add-ons

Corel WordPerfect for Windows includes a built-in HTML editor as well as automatic conversion of files to and from HTML, GIF and JPEG (see Figure 14-1). WordPerfect for Windows 6.1 and Microsoft Word for Windows each have add-onpackages that enable them to handle HTML files. The WordPerfect version is called the Internet Publisher and the Word version is called the Internet Assistant. These word-processor based HTML editors are ideal for casual Web publishers and for documents that are mostly text..

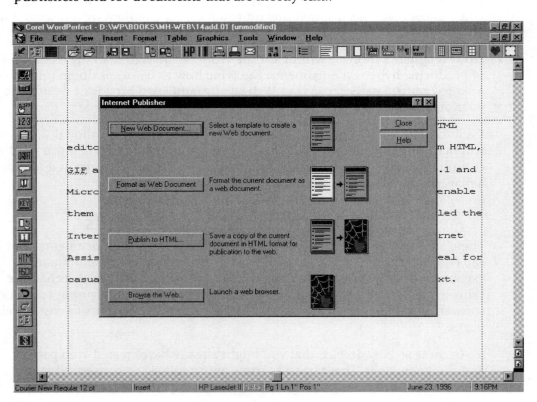

Figure 14-1

For example, I've helped the IRS use WordPerfect for Windows to rewrite 16,000 pages of tax code in hypertext. They don't need graphics or sound files, so WordPerfect is an excellent choice for the IRS assignment; nearly everyone involved in rewriting the tax code is an experienced WordPerfect user.

In fact, it's possible that most of the rewriting on the IRS project will be done in WordPerfect 5.1 for DOS! The powerful Styles feature in the trusty old 5.1 version (dating back to that ancient year 1989) enables its documents to automatically be turned into hypertext by WordPerfect for Windows. Such backward compatility also might be an important factor in your organization, because so many writers can't be dragged away from WordPerfect 5.1 even by the steamroller of Windows. The WordPerfect for Windows Internet Publisher, therefore, enables you to allow almost anyone to be involved in writing text for your Web site—even those users who refuse to give up DOS, or who still don't have a PC that can handle the demands of Windows.

You say it's easy, but how do I get started?

Programmers long have learned their craft by analyzing the source code of existing programs. It's much easier to learn to program by example than it is to start from scratch. Often programmers modify an existing program to fit their own needs. Using the same technique will help you learn to write HTML-encoded Web pages—study and modify existing Web pages.

When you encounter a Web page that has a feature you would like to implement, click **View, Source** to see its HTML source code. Netscape's default is to display the code in its internal source viewer; but if you want to edit the page or display documents that are too long for the internal viewer, you can designate any editor as your Netscape source viewer. The Windows Notepad application is a good choice (see Figure 14-2). To change Netscape's default HTML viewer, follow the steps in the next Hands-On exercise.

Hands On

Objective: **Learn to set Netscape's HTML source code viewer.**

❏ Start Netscape with an Internet connection.

❏ Click **Options, General Preferences . . .**

❏ Click the **Apps** tab.

❏ Click in the **View Source** text entry box.

❏ Type *c:\windows\notepad.exe* and click **OK**.

    You can enter any Windows editing application instead. If you don't know the application's full path and filename, click on **Browse**, select an editor from your system, then click **OK**.

❏ Click **Options, Save Options** to save the change.

Of course, if you want to save the entire source code, you can click File, **Save As . . .** and use the dialog box with the **Save File as Type** set to **Source (*.htm)**. Often this is overkill, because you might only want to save a small piece of a document's HTML code. With the Notepad as your viewer, you'll be able to cut out the chunks you don't need before you save the file.

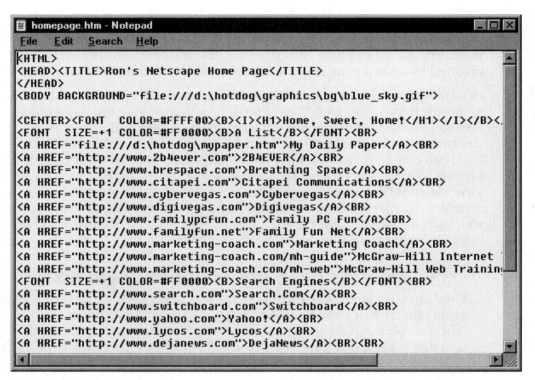

```
homepage.htm - Notepad
File   Edit   Search   Help
<HTML>
<HEAD><TITLE>Ron's Netscape Home Page</TITLE>
</HEAD>
<BODY BACKGROUND="file:///d:\hotdog\graphics\bg\blue_sky.gif">

<CENTER><FONT  COLOR=#FFFF00><B><I><H1>Home, Sweet, Home!</H1></I></B><
<FONT  SIZE=+1 COLOR=#FF0000><B>A List</B></FONT><BR>
<A HREF="file:///d:\hotdog\mypaper.htm">My Daily Paper</A><BR>
<A HREF="http://www.2b4ever.com">2B4EVER</A><BR>
<A HREF="http://www.brespace.com">Breathing Space</A><BR>
<A HREF="http://www.citapei.com">Citapei Communications</A><BR>
<A HREF="http://www.cybervegas.com">Cybervegas</A><BR>
<A HREF="http://www.digivegas.com">Digivegas</A><BR>
<A HREF="http://www.familypcfun.com">Family PC Fun</A><BR>
<A HREF="http://www.familyfun.net">Family Fun Net</A><BR>
<A HREF="http://www.marketing-coach.com">Marketing Coach</A><BR>
<A HREF="http://www.marketing-coach.com/mh-guide">McGraw-Hill Internet
<A HREF="http://www.marketing-coach.com/mh-web">McGraw-Hill Web Trainin
<FONT  SIZE=+1 COLOR=#FF0000><B>Search Engines</B></FONT><BR>
<A HREF="http://www.search.com">Search.Com</A><BR>
<A HREF="http://www.switchboard.com">Switchboard</A><BR>
<A HREF="http://www.yahoo.com">Yahoo!</A><BR>
<A HREF="http://www.lycos.com">Lycos</A><BR>
<A HREF="http://www.dejanews.com">DejaNews</A><BR><BR>
```

Figure 14-2

As this was written, neither WordPerfect nor Word included their HTML functions on their original distribution disks. Before you can create Web pages with either of them, you'll need to download the application's Internet add-on and then install it.

Downloading an HTML add-on

Here's the information you'll need to download the two add-ons outlined above.

WordPerfect Internet Publisher

- Start at WordPerfect's Web site at *www.wordperfect.com*.
- Click on the generic **Internet Publishing** link
- Click on the **Internet Publisher** link
- Click on the download link). This will transfer the file *wpipzip.exe* to your hard disk.

You'll need to put this file in its own directory, then execute it. It will install itself into your copy of WordPerfect for Windows. After that, you'll enjoy the freedom to create Web documents right inside your faithful, familiar friend. Or you can upgrade to Corel WordPerfect 7 and the Internet Publisher will be built-in.

Word Internet Assistant

Start at the Microsoft Web site at *www.microsoft.com*. You might have to scroll down to see it, but look for a drop list that says Select a Product. Click on the drop-list and select Internet Products. You'll find a link for the Internet Assistant on this page, under the heading Authoring Tools. This page has links for Word 6, Word 95, and Word for the Macintosh. Download the file *wordia.exe* into a newly created directory on your hard disk. Do not place *wordia.exe* in your Word system directory. Execute the file from its new directory and it will complete the installation and enable you to create HTML documents within Word. The download page for this file was created with the Internet Assistant (see Figure 14-3).

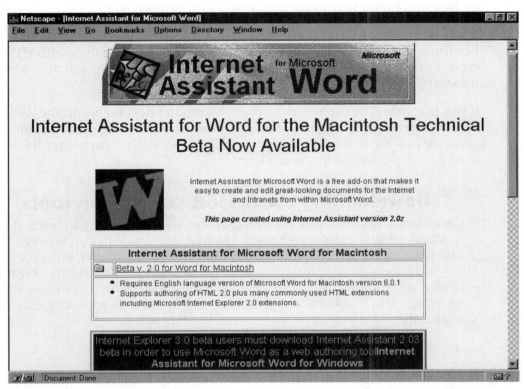

Figure 14-3

HTML conversion applications

HTML conversion applications will convert existing documents, databases and other file types to HTML format. They often do a better job than the word processor add-ons. Conversion applications can be especially valuable for productivity if you need to publish a large number of existing documents. I'll introduce you to two popular applications from Skisoft: Web Publisher and Web Presentation Service.

Skisoft Web Publisher

This application can be a major efficiency tool for organizations converting reams of documents. One of its biggest selling points is that its batch conversion mode can convert hundreds of documents in a single pass. It's not perfect, but it's a big leap up from using the Internet Assistant add-on for Microsoft Word and manually working through each document.

The Skisoft Web Publisher automatically converts files from Word, WordPerfect, AmiPro, and Excel, but it doesn't convert the native format of any of these applications. Instead, it accepts documents in the Rich Text Format (.RTF) that all of these packages include as an export option. So, Web Publisher won't directly convert your archives of ancient WordPerfect 5.1 text without first converting all of them into RTF; but even that process can be automated.

Tables are converted directly into Netscape-compatible HTML tables. The application converts normal word-processor images into GIF files. In addition, it builds a cross-linked table of contents and an index of key terms, with each item in the index linked to the appropriate text in your documents.

If you've spruced up your documents with numbered lists, bullets, and style headings, you'll be thrilled to know that it will convert all of these into HTML. It even converts bullets nested within numbered lists. Your styles can be converted into standard HTML heading codes.

If you're responsible for putting your organization's documents on the Web, the Skisoft Web Publisher might permit you to let writers in your organization continue to write in WordPerfect or Word. You can teach them to save final drafts in RTF, or you can convert the text later.

Downloading the Skisoft conversion tools

Go to *www.skisoft.com* (see Figure 14-4) and you'll find links to both of the products reviewed here (Web Publisher and Web Presentation Service). Before you download, read their FAQs file, which might answer any questions you have about the products. You only are licensed for free use of the downloaded applications for 30 days, then you'll need to register them to comply with copyright requirements. This site includes samples of documents and images that have been converted using Skisoft products.

Web Presentation Service

Skisoft also offers the *Web Presentation Service*, which publishes your PowerPoint presentations on the World Wide Web. Web Presentation Service converts a presentation of up to 20 slides into a linked collection of HTML text files and GIF graphics files that are ready to post on your Web Server. Each presentation slide becomes a full-color Web page. It automatically creates buttons beneath each slide that let site visitors jump forward or backward as they view your presentation. It also creates an Outline page that has a hyperlinked heading to its related slide.

Skisoft gives you several user-friendly methods to create great-looking Web pages without needing to become a technowizard. Actually, you soon will find that even the stand-alone HTML editors don't require a technical genius. Let's graduate now to the next step up the HTML development ladder.

How did HTML originate?

Have you ever wondered how HTML originated? HTML is based on SGML (Standard Generalized Markup Language). The development of SGML began in the 1980s. SGML became a formal standard in 1988. HTML used part of the SGML, added URLs (Uniform Resource Locators) plus the HTTP (Hypertext Transfer Protocol) and created the Web. This is making a long story very, very short, but you can read all about it at *www.brainlink.com/~ben/sgml*.

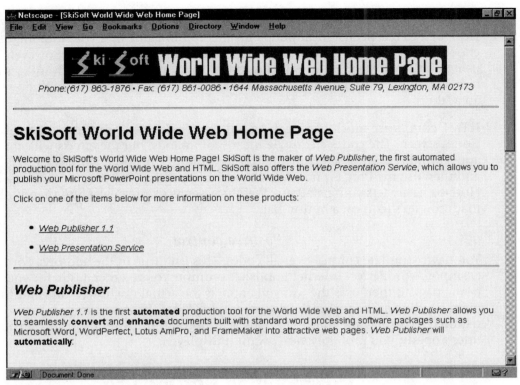

Figure 14-4

Stand-alone HTML editors

Stand-alone HTML editors are dedicated Windows applications designed specifically for creating HTML files. They offer more hypertext features, better control, and more flexibility than word-processor add-ons or conversion applications. As a trade-off, however, they require a greater learning curve and they lack some of the advanced word-processing features you've come to expect in Windows applications.

Here's a method you might use to ease your transition into Web publishing. Create your first Web pages in WordPerfect or Word, or convert some existing documents. After these HTML files are saved on your hard disk, open them in a stand-alone HTML editor. Seeing your own pages in HTML format is a good learning experience. Most likely you'll fine-tune some things that didn't convert as you expected. You might be surprised how quickly you pick up HTML using this method and learn to create Web pages directly in an HTML editor.

I've chosen four editors to profile here, because they each have distinctively different features, strengths, and weaknesses. The editors I've chosen are:
- HotDog Prox
- Netscape Navigator Gold
- HoTMetaL Pro
- HTML Assistant Pro

HotDog Pro

HotDog Pro has been a loyal puppy for me, so I imagine that you, too, might choose it as your own HTML editor. There are some disadvantages, however, in using HotDog instead of an HTML add-on. Then again, there are advantages in terms of control and flexibility, and it does things that you simply can't do with an add-on.

HTML editors are much like working full-time inside the WordPerfect Reveal Codes screen. The codes clearly delineate commands, but the effects will not appear on the editing screen while you're working. So, you'll work for a while, and then use the Preview mode to check the appearance of your work. Blessedly, HotDog easily lets you install any Web browser as its previewer and then it places that browser's icon on a button bar.

Positive control

You have complete control over all codes. This isn't true in the add-ons. For example, WordPerfect Internet Publisher prompts you to enter a title for your home page. It then uses the text you enter as the actual document title and as the main heading at the top of the document. In HTML, however, you are not required to display the title at all. This is important, because if you create your title properly, you probably won't want it displayed.

Downloading HotDog Pro

You can download a free trial version of HotDog so you can test it before you buy it. HotDog is a product of Sausage Software, located at *www.sausage.com* (see Figure 14-5). The Sausage home page offers two HTML versions: HotDog and HotDog Pro.

The Pro version has many additional features—including an HTML spell checker—but most importantly it has no file size limit, while files in the regular version are limited to 32K in size. Both versions give you a free trial period, after which you should register and pay the registration fee.

HotDog lets you create a true HTML title that doesn't display on your Web page. This frees you to optimize the document title so that people can find your site easily with Web search engines. For example, with an add-on you could be forced to have both the main heading and the title say "Welcome to the Acme Company Home Page!" That's fine if someone searches for *Welcome* or *Acme Company*. But what about people who are searching for the products or services you offer?

A more productive choice would be to keep "Welcome to the Acme Company Home Page!" as your first heading, but make your title—which won't be displayed on your Web page—say something like, Power Tools, Socket Wrenches, Oil Field Supplies. Any search on those key words will place your Web page high on the list of search results. That's much more effective than hoping a Web surfer out there already knows your company's name.

Overall, there are many similar control improvements that you'll enjoy with a stand-alone HTML editor. I've found that many people start out with an add-on, then switch to a stand-alone after they get frustrated with the limitations of the add-on application.

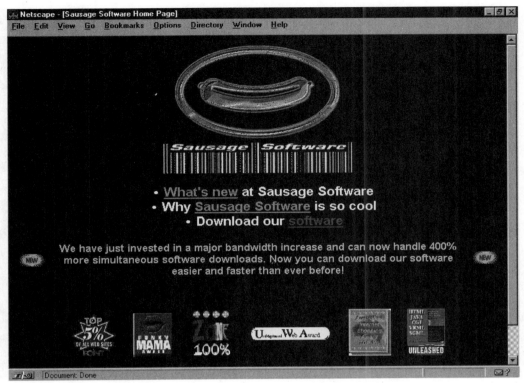

Figure 14-5

HotDog Snaglets

The folks at Sausage are trying hard to make life easy for Web authors. They offer a set of tools that embellish HotDog, help you create special effects, and enable you to implement advanced HTML features. They call these tools snaglets, which is derived from the Australian name for a hot dog: *snag*.

They've got one tool called FrameGang (see Figure 14-6) that will help you automatically create a Web page with frames. With some basic knowledge of HTML frames and your trusty mouse, you can point and click your way through frame generation for your Web pages. Using frames allows you to display multiple HTML documents on one Web page, and allow hyperlinks in one frame to interact with another frame.

Another great tool is CrossEye, an image-map editing utility that enables you to create clickable hotspots on graphic images without having to use the CGI script that is normally required to perform this task (see Figure 14-7). These hotspots might be linked to URL addresses, providing your Web visitors with a graphical jump to any Web link you choose. This a wonderful tool, because few people who build Web pages are able to use CGI scripts, either through lack of programming skills or because their Web service provider doesn't permit them. CrossEye allows nearly any HTML author to create client-side clickable image maps that don't require CGI scripts or special skills.

These are only two of the snaglets Sausage offers. Be sure to check their Web site often for updates on these as well as for releases of new snaglets.

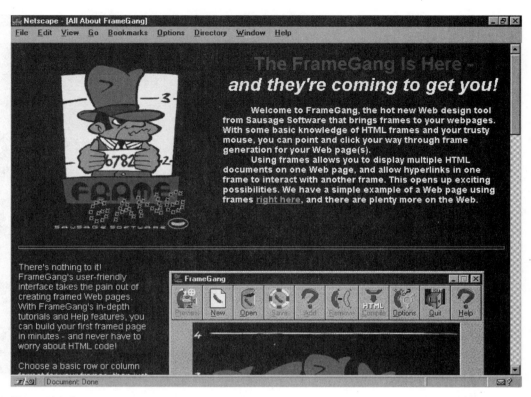

Figure 14-6

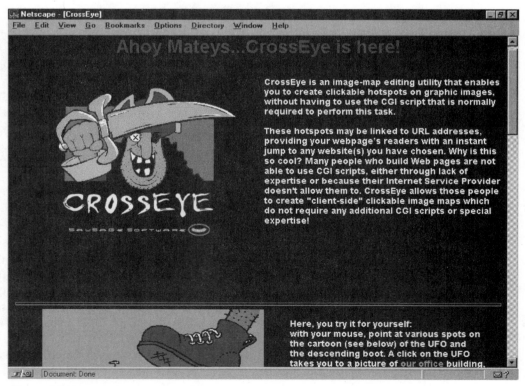

Figure 14-7

Netscape Navigator Gold

Netscape Navigator Gold is a glimpse of how all HTML editors soon will look. It gives you perfect WYSIWYG, because you actually work directly in Netscape! There's no question about how your pages will look in Netscape once they're on the Web. That's the good news.

The bad news is that this application is not ready for prime-time players. It's quirky and you can't get the level of control you can achieve in HotDog. I tried it first by opening some of my existing HTML documents. Naturally, they looked perfect. As I began to edit them, however, it quickly became the Humpty-Dumpty of HTML editors. My documents fell apart as all kinds of unexpected changes occurred, and all the kings horses couldn't put them back together again. I exited without saving!

I can't imagine that this is a permanent situation. Before long, Netscape will drive out the bugs and the quirks, and then you'll have the ability to draw Web pages directly into Netscape. This seems to me to be the ultimate in Web page design. But you'll have to try it yourself as upgrades come out, and decide when you're happy with its performance.

Downloading Netscape Navigator Gold

When used as a Web browser, Netscape Navigator Gold works exactly like the plain Netscape. The Gold version has a few added items on its File menu that let you create and save original HTML documents. It's easy to get, too. Simply go to the Netscape site at *home.netscape.com* and follow the links to download the Gold version installation file into an empty directory. You will then install it exactly as you did with your regular Netscape. I suggest that you put the Gold version in a separate directory from your regular version so you can have both. You're likely to need to download and install the Gold version often as Netscape publishes upgrades. Meanwhile, your regular version won't be affected, and you can count on reliable surfing.

HoTMetaL

While I didn't profile HoTMetaL by SoftQuad, it's nonetheless been the choice for thousands of HTML authors. Since you can get a free trial version, why not check it out for yourself and see if it suits your needs?

You can download a free copy of HoTMetaL Free. If you decide to use it, you can download the commercial version called HoTMetaL PRO. SoftQuad also has an advanced SGML browser and editor especially suitable for large organizations with extremely large document collections. Their Web site is *www.sq.com*. You can also use FTP to the directory *ftp://ftp.ncsa.uiuc.edu/Web/html/hotmetal/Windows* and then download the *hotm1new.exe* file. This is a self-extracting compressed file that will expand to about six megabytes. This version requires Windows 3.1 or later, and at least eight megabytes of RAM. Be sure and also get *install.txt* for setup instructions.

HTML Assistant Pro 2

HTML Assistant Pro 2, a product of Brooklyn North Software Works in Bedford, Nova Scotia, is much like HotDog Pro: It's a point-and-click editor for making Web pages. Running under Windows 3.1 and Windows 95, HTML Assistant Pro simplifies Web page authoring by using pushbutton tools so you don't have to remember complicated codes. Adding hypertext links involves simply copying and pasting the URL for the page to which you want to point. It uses child windows with their own menus, which will improve your editing speed.

It has a special feature called the Automatic Page Creator, which lets you create a Web page by filling in blanks. This feature simplifies the creation of forms and tables to simply clicking a button. Also similar to HotDog, it lets you designate any Web browser for previews so you'll be sure you're creating the look you want your visitors to see.

HTML Assistant Pro handles any size file, so your only size limitation will be in what you believe your visitors will be willing to wait for. As a bonus, Brooklyn North Software offers instant help via e-mail, a step-by-step tutorial that guides you through the creation of your Web page, a complete HTML Tag Reference, and a beginner's guide to understanding the HTML.

Getting your copy of HTML Assistant Pro 2

You'll have to order HTML Assistant Pro 2 with a credit card via e-mail, fax, or telephone. Current price is US $99.95 or Canadian $139.95, plus $10 shipping within the US, Canada, or Mexico, and $15 to other destinations. Canadian residents must include $10.50 GST and Nova Scotia residents must add $17.65 PST. Federal Express shipping to the US is available for $25.

Mail orders:

Brooklyn North Software Works, Inc.

25 Doyle Street

Bedford, Nova Scotia

Canada B4A 1K4

E-Mail orders: sales@brooknorth.bedford.ns.ca

Phone orders: 800-349-1422

Fax orders: 902-835-2600

HTML Assistant Pro has excellent aids for building tables and forms into Web pages. The syntax on both of those structures can be tricky, but after you select the basic format, this application lays out a sample for you with a user-friendly dialog box. All you need to do is substitute your own text into the sample.

Choosing between HotDog Pro and HTML Assistant is going to come down to personal choice. They both are excellent products, though I favor HotDog Pro. I suggest you bookmark the Web pages of both sites and follow the changes yourself. A good HTML editor can save you hours of work, so tracking updates will be time well spent.

Graphics software

Once you begin writing HTML pages, you won't get far without wanting to add some graphics. The popularity of color printers and the color graphics that now adorn millions of Web pages has encouraged development of a slew of advanced graphics programs. Corel Draw and Adobe Acrobat are popular commercial products, while PaintShop Pro and LViewPro are popular shareware products for graphic image manipulation. So many different applications are available, in fact, that I've devoted the entire next chapter to Web graphics.

Graphics tools let you make Web pages attractive and interesting. With these tools you can create image maps so that users can click on images and buttons for hyperlinks, instead of being limited to using text-only links. Netscape includes support for client side image maps that can be implemented without programming skills. I'll present more on this, including an example, in the next chapter. For now, let's get a quick overview of Common Gateway Interface (CGI).

Common Gateway Interface tools

Common Gateway Interface (CGI) is a programming specification for Web servers that makes it possible to have HTML pages tell the Web server to run programs that make your Web pages interactive.

CGI is called server side because it uses the server's processor to run the program. Input for the program is transmitted from the client to the server-based program. After the program runs, its results are transmitted back to the client.

User-friendly CGI tools include a wealth of valuable canned programming scripts that can be referenced (called by the Web server) in existing hypertext documents. In other words, you won't have to start from scratch for every specialized function you want your Web site to perform. Advanced tools such as Cold Fusion enable Web authors to create sophisticated database applications without doing any actual programming.

Two of the most common uses on the Web for CGI programs have been clickable image maps and e-mail forms. The use of CGI for clickable image maps is certain to drop now that Netscape enables client-side image maps that do not rely on the server's processor. However, for now at least, CGI formmail routines can interface with HTML forms on your Web page to create a user-friendly feedback form.

Getting e-mail feedback

You can see an example of a CGI e-mail form on this book's home page. Visit the Web site *www.marketing-coach.com/mh-web* and click on the Feedback link (see Figure 14-8).

You can save this page if you'd like to have an example of a mail feedback form, but you cannot simply copy the code into your own Web page. This form relies upon a CGI program on my site's Web server that actually handles the mail transaction. Your Web service provider probably has a standard CGI mail program that you can use. Once the formmail function has been made available to you, you can add it to your site by modifying the form on this book's home page and pasting it into one of your own Web pages.

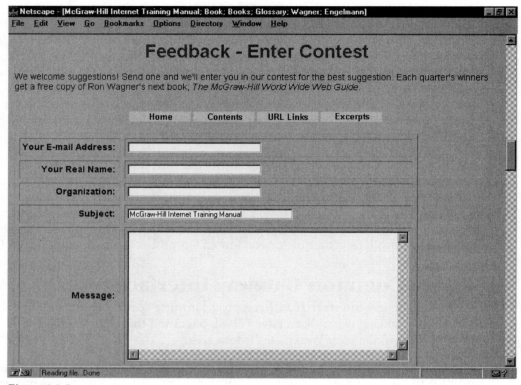

Figure 14-8

Java and JavaScript

Java and competitive variants enable a Web browser to download programming code from a Web server. The downloaded code extends the functionality of a browser so that it can perform elaborate tricks that are not built-in. Leading Web sites might use Java to nearly eliminate all Web browser limitations. The programming language required to implement Java applications is not yet for mainstream users, but you can hire a Java programmer to write some code if you've got an application in mind.

As opposed to CGI, Java is a client-side program. Because Java code runs on the client computer after being downloaded by your Web browser, it transfers the computing demands from the Web server to client computers. This permits a server to handle more traffic, because Java is transferred to the client computer and uses the client's processor.

Many users have computers that will not be happy running Java applications. So, until your average Web visitor has a Pentium, before you implement an elaborate Java application consider the computing limitations your visitors might face.

In a later chapter, I'll present more on Java, including some sample Java code; but while we're on the subject of considering the computing limitations of your Web visitors, I'd like to present some pointers for testing your Web site.

Testing your Web site

If you are involved in authoring Web pages and creating a Web site, you most likely also will be involved in the testing process. To create a truly user-friendly Web site, you'll need to consider four basic factors:

- Modem speed
- Web browser
- Windows screen resolution
- PC processing power

Even if you're not involved with the testing, be sure that you find out if the tests included consideration of these factors.

Test with a slow modem

Most likely your Web site's tests will be conducted on a hard drive in your own PC or on a network. You might be quite satisfied with its performance, then be shocked to see how it looks to a visitor with a 14.4 KBps modem. People are accustomed to seeing fast-paced television graphics, so you had better offer something incredible in exchange for making them wait. Of course, you might not be concerned about appealing to visitors with slow modems.

As a minimum, you can offer a text-only option at the top of your home page so that visitors with slower computers can bypass any fancy graphics your site might include. On the other hand, ask yourself why you've chosen to include fancy graphics. Is it truly because the graphics make your site better for your visitors? Or perhaps is it because someone wants to impress people with his or her graphics mastery? These days, it's pretty tough to create a graphic that will earn a "Wow, that's cool" response; but it's real easy to create one that will earn a "Forget it, I'm not waiting that long."

Test with different browsers

The differences have narrowed between the appearance of the displays in the top Web browsers. At first every browser seemed to have its own unique interpretation of HTML, and you could hardly recognize the same page on two different browsers. Now the field has been narrowed to two dominant browsers that are reasonably similar in their displays. Whether you design your pages for Netscape or for the Microsoft Internet Explorer, be sure to test it with the other browser. Netscape remains the standard, but Microsoft is working hard to get its browser to emulate the look and feel of Netscape.

You don't have to worry about pleasing visitors with other browsers. Anyone these days who uses something other than Netscape or the Internet Explorer is someone who wants to be different from the majority. They've grown accustomed to weird displays, they relish the differences, and they've learned to ignore the messages that say, "Designed for Netscape, click here to download your copy now."

Test with different Windows screen resolutions

Here's a tricky factor to consider. What are the implications of different screen resolutions? You can create a Web site that looks great on your own monitor at 800×600, but that falls apart at 640×480. For example, a heading that fits neatly across a page in the higher resolution might wrap into two lines at the lower resolution. People who view your page at higher resolutions won't experience such problematic differences.

Changing screen resolutions in Windows is not a quick procedure, because you must restart Windows after every resolution change. Here's a Hands-On exercise that will show you how to adjust Windows screen resolution. If you've got at least a 15" monitor, I highly recommend using 800×600.

Hands On

Objective: Learn to adjust Windows screen resolution

❑ Right-click an empty spot on your desktop.

   If your desktop isn't visible, click the right mouse button on the Taskbar, click on **Minimize All Windows**, then right-click the desktop.

❑ Click **Properties**.

❑ Click the **Settings** tab.

❑ Move the **Desktop Area** marker to 800×600.

   The Windows 95 default is 640×480. If your system already has been changed to 800×600, then click **Cancel** now and skip the rest of this exercise.

❑ Click **OK**.

   Depending on your video driver, you'll have to restart your system for the resolution change to take effect. If so, follow the prompts to shut down and restart your system now. When it reboots, you might have to readjust your monitor's display controls to resize or reposition the screen image.

Some premium video cards include a special driver that permits on-the-fly resolution changes without restarting Windows after each adjustment. I can't give you a Hands-On lesson to change resolution with a special driver, because each one works differently. Investing in such a card might be wise if you plan to regularly test your Web site in different resolutions. Of course if you're testing over a network, you might be able to find PCs that are running other resolutions and you can use them to compare your site's appearance.

HTML width percentage commands

HTML lets you specify the width of graphic images it will display. The width is specified in pixels. For example, on this book's home page, I wanted the cover image to be one-quarter of the screen width. Because I run my Windows in 800×600 resolution, I could achieve that result on my screen with the command **WIDTH=200**. Unfortunately, that would make my cover span nearly one-third of a visitor's screen if they used a 640×480 resolution, and less than one-fifth of the width of a visitor's screen if they use a 1024×768 resolution.

Fortunately, HTML includes a percent option on width specifications that can help your Web site accommodate visitors with varying screen resolutions. In my cover's graphic image coding I used the command **WIDTH=25%** to make sure that the cover has a consistent size under all screen resolutions.

Visitor PC processing power

Eventually we'll see Web standards that are as universally implemented as those on television. Until that time, consider the needs of potential computer limitations that your visitors might face.

First, remember that a lot of visitors will be using 486 PCs that will be strained to run a complex Java application. This is changing rapidly, because it's difficult to buy a new 486. Thus, before long you can create your site to work best on a Pentium or better, and just not worry about 486 traffic.

Also, think about your visitors' video displays. If you suspect that a lot of your visitors will be running in low resolution mode (640×480), consider designing and testing your site with your resolution set to the lower standard. A page that's well-laid out in 800×600 mode might fall apart when crunched onto a 640×480 display.

Decisions, decisions . . . too many choices

Are you feeling stressed over all of this information? It's a lot to digest. To simplify your decision-making, I'll conclude with some tips that might help you quickly eliminate a lot of things you don't need to learn. This will be a guide to deciding what tools you might need to get your organization published on the Web.

First, consider your organization's existing technical and personnel resources:
- Do you expect 10 visitors or 10,000 visitors to your Web site each day?
- Do you have UNIX gurus in-house?
- Do you have artistic and advertising talent in-house?
- Will your Web site require frequent updates, or will your information be fairly static?
- Do you need database searches, or can you convey your organization's information with simple documents?

Depending on your organization's resources, you might decide to keep your Web project in-house, hire consultants, or outsource the entire project. Let's run through some factors to consider for organizations of varying sizes. You might benefit from reading them all because there *is* some cross-over.

Large global organization

Organizations of this size (10,000+ people) generally have lots of customers, with resources to match. They generally have advertising people who can help with focus (and control the Internet fever that might result in a slipshod Web site); editorial staff who can ensure that grammar and writing are crisp (as long as they don't impede progress); computer professionals who can build elaborate scripts and database functions (or stall the project by trying to be too technical); and cautious management (who might slow down the whole project out of prudence).

I've found that when large organizations eventually get themselves on-line, they have failed to achieve many of the benefits available by being on the Web. This happens because large organizations have huge investments in reputation and organizational infrastructure that require careful analysis before any action is taken on a Web site.

The Internet also offers tremendous opportunities for an Intranet, which lets staff use the power of the Web to access internal corporate information (see Figure 14-9). Because control is decentralized and customers won't see it, each department often is free to immediately set up a Web server to ease their information storage and reporting needs. Even where field offices don't have Internet access, CD-ROMs containing data dumps of corporate Web servers can be shipped to them so that they have a (somewhat out-of-date) copy of the corporate databank.

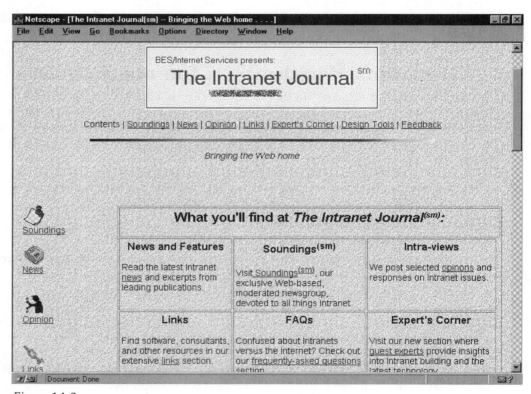

Figure 14-9

Tools

Tools that might be used by a large organization—one that handles the total Web project internally—include C compilers, multiple high-end PCs, multiprocessor PCs, and mini/mainframe Web server hardware; UNIX or Windows NT Web server software with on-staff technical support; advanced graphics editing tools like Corel Draw and Adobe Photoshop; document conversion tools; SGML (the parent of HTML), multiple browsers for testing; and database access tools such as Cold Fusion and Java programming.

Large domestic organization

Organizations in this size range (1,000 to 10,000 people) generally have enough of the internal resources found in giant organizations that they can expect to handle a Web project internally. Shipping out CD-ROMs to branch offices in organizations of this size probably wouldn't be cost-effective, but a private Intranet still is a powerful productivity tool and should be considered in conjunction with the organization's Web site.

Tools

Tools you might find used in this size range include C compilers, multiple high-end PCs, multiprocessor PCs, and minicomputer Web server hardware; UNIX or Windows NT Web server software with technical support contracts; advanced graphics editing tools like Corel Draw and Adobe Photoshop; document conversion tools; database access tools; and Java programming. A single fast server probably can handle all of such an organization's Web site needs.

Medium-sized domestic organization

Organizations in this size range (100 to 1000 people) probably will have one or more full-time computer specialists who can meet the technology challenges of the Internet. This person probably even will be able to handle installing an internal Web server. Expect your computer professional to be able to create Web pages with graphic images, simple Java scripts, and possibly even database applications.

Depending on types of customers, it might make sense to maintain a dedicated external Web server, but at this size an organization is in the crossover range and should consider renting space on an ISP's Web server. A tailored domain name still would be a must, however. Organizations in this size range probably will train additional staff to regularly produce simple Web documents and to rely on the computer professional to write or supervise production of database applications.

Tools

Typical tools used in this organization will be word processor add-ons; desktop publishing programs with HTML output support; a Windows NT server; a specialized HTML editor like HotDog; a commercial Web server like WebSite Netscape Communication Server, or Purveyor; and simple Java scripts.

What about UNIX?

UNIX experts usually do not abound in organizations in this size range or smaller; but if you have more than one UNIX guru in-house, you might want to take advantage of the wealth of UNIX support for Web servers and Internet applications.

Never, however, ever leave your company dependent on a lone UNIX professional. Replacing a lost UNIX guru is nearly impossible to do quickly. Information on your site might go stale before you can hire a replacement who can work through hundreds or even thousands of clever improvements that your former guru made to your system. Sticking with Windows-based products will give you an ever-increasing number of professionals on which to draw if you need a replacement.

Small organization

A small company (20 to 100 people) often will have a local area network (LAN) that easily can be adapted to an internal TCP/IP network and use an inexpensive Web server. Such an organization often will have a knowledgeable full-time computer specialist in-house, or a consultant who makes regular visits. This computer professional should be able to put up a simple Web site on an internal web—if your organization uses information intensely—and on an ISP's Web server for customer access.

Tools

Tools used in organizations of this size include word processor add-ons, desktop publishing software with HTML output and tools recommended by your ISP for image-mapped hyperlinks and database applications. Your ISP almost certainly will have an in-house staff with sufficient Web development skills to create a professional Web site.

Very small organization

Small companies (1 to 20 people), partnerships and sole proprietorships nearly always lack a computer professional, and thus will need to look for a Web service provider who can develop and maintain a Web presence. A turn-key Web site provider such as GoSite (featured in chapter 17) could be an excellent choice. Keep in mind that no one who uses your Web site knows its location, so your Web site can be maintained anywhere in the country—good to keep in mind if you find a real deal on Web server space on a server a thousand miles away.

Tools

Tools used in organizations of this size include word processor add-ons. (Nearly anyone skilled in Windows word processor usage can use them to put basic information on a Web page.) You'll want the Internet Publisher for WordPerfect for Windows, or the Internet Assistant for Microsoft Word for Windows. One of the Skisoft conversion programs could be a real time-saver.

After creating the basics, contract with a local Web-page designer to fill in your weak points. College campuses can be a good place to find HTML authors. You probably will find a suitable HTML author with a notice on a student union bulletin board or through an ad in the school paper.

You also might need an ad copywriter to help with the writing, and an advertising consultant and an artist to help with graphics and design. If you've used such marketing professionals before, you probably will find that they have expanded their services to include Web technology. In fact, I've discovered that students in many college marketing courses are developing Web pages in class exercises. So, perhaps a college student would be satisfactory in this aspect of your Web site development, too.

If information on your Web site needs frequent changes, you can update your Web site quickly if you use an ISP that permits you to FTP updates directly into the Web directory. You don't want the accuracy of the information seen by your clients and customers to depend on an ISP's schedule for updating your information. These services often are staffed by young people who might not understand the importance of responding to your schedule. But direct FTP capability will ensure that you have control over your Web site's content.

Summary

That's enough Web authoring material for now. Internet technology changes too fast to put any more details in a book. As with every chapter, this one includes a Continuing Education section that will give you valuable, ongoing sources of up-to-date changes. The next task is to help you learn about the graphics that have turned the Web into such a colorful landscape.

Continuing Education

The McGraw-Hill World Wide Web Training Manual

http://www.marketing-coach.com/mh-web

This site is maintained by the author of *The McGraw-Hill World Wide Web Training Manual*. The site includes the Continuing Education section from every chapter so you can visit any URL in this book without retyping it—except for this one, of course. More importantly, by the time this book is published many of the links will have changed, but the site is regularly updated and might include new, valuable URLs as I discover them.

O'Reilly Associates

http://website.ora.com

O'Reilly Associates has emerged as a powerhouse of technology on the Internet. They've published a library of more than 80 excellent technical reference guides that delve into details far more deeply than I have in this book. Actually, mainstream users might find the topics covered in this site to be too technical, but if you are performing or managing the hands-on work involved in publishing your organization's Web site, then you absolutely *must* place O'Reilly's URL on your Bookmark List.

Random tips and hints on constructing Web pages

http://www.nd.edu/PageCreation/TipsAndHints.html

Here's a Notre Dame University site that gives tips and hints on constructing HTML documents (see Figure 14-10). Be sure to check out the Clickable Graphics tutorial that gives you a clickable graphic map demonstration tutorial. This site is not an encyclopedic presentation on creating HTML documents—and it admits

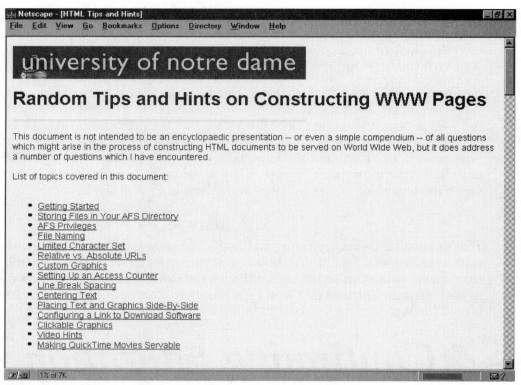

Figure 14-10

to being Mac-centric on some points—but it does address a number of issues that are encountered frequently. Bookmark this URL, because this Web site is also a good place to track HTML changes as well as other changes in Web technology.

Jeff Mallett's Web Authoring Page

http://www.cruzio.com/~tao/html.html

Here's an on-line guide to publishing on the Web by Internet guru Jeff Mallet. Click on any one of these headings to jump to fact-filled text that can help you get started with your Web publishing: Authoring HTML, Web Authoring, Authoring CGI Scripts, Java, and Authorization.

Self-taught Web publishing

http://www.lne.com/Web/Books/HTML

This is the home page for the books *Teach Yourself Web Publishing with HTML in a Week* and *Teach Yourself More Web Publishing with HTML in a Week*, both by Laura Lemight. These books describe how to write, design, and publish information on the World Wide Web. In addition to describing the HTML language itself, they provide extensive information on using images, sounds, video, interactivity, gateway programs (CGI), forms, and image maps. Through the use of dozens of real-life examples and actual HTML source code, the books help you not only learn the technical details of writing Web pages, but also teach you how to communicate information effectively through the Web.

The World Wide Web Handbook

http://www.ucc.ie/~pflynn/books/wwwbook.html

This is a Web site for *The World Wide Web Handbook: An HTML Guide for Users, Authors and Publishers* by Peter Flynn, published by International Thomson Computer Press. It profiles the book, including its Table of Contents and includes a downloadable version of the HTML Reference Card that is included with the printed edition of the book.

HTML specification 3.0

http://www.w3.org/hypertext/WWW/MarkUp/MarkUp.html

Here's a link to the table of contents for the complete HTML 3.0 specifications on-line manual. This is not a user-friendly guide to HTML, but it is a highly detailed reference source about all aspects of HTML, its development, and its specifications. HTML 3.0 has been designed to be created in a variety of different ways. It is simple enough to type manually and can be authored using WYSIWYG editors for HTML, or generated via export filters from common word-processing formats or other SGML applications.

Fill-out forms overview

http://www.ncsa.uiuc.edu/SDG/Software/Mosaic/Docs/fill-out-forms/overview.html

This site focuses on creating fill-out forms for your Web pages. One of its most valuable features is a listing of 13 forms done in HTML (at last count) that you can use as examples. They range in complexity from ludicrously simple to extremely advanced.

308

Web graphics

A PICTURE is worth—how much is it? A thousand words? Ten thousand? Whatever the number, the Web is a perfect illustration of that ancient adage. Remember that for nearly thirty years the Internet existed in text-only format, distributing technical and academic information between large institutions. In its text-only format, the Internet remained the enterprise of scientists and academics; but the creation of the Web permitted the Internet to go graphic, and the graphics are what made it go public.

Well-done graphics can make even static, boring technical information look appealing. Graphics also can create simple explanations for difficult concepts, and convey messages quickly and efficiently. Further, graphics can bypass language barriers by creating universal, pictorial labels and instructions—perfect for the World Wide Web.

Unfortunately, Web graphics have been a double-edged sword. While cutting easily through difficult concepts and making the Internet interesting to us everyday folks, graphics also cut severely into Internet bandwidth. The result is that the Internet—designed to carry efficient, text-only documents—is now clogged with millions of graphic images; but that's a price we're willing to pay, because without the graphics few people would ever venture into cyberspace.

There will be a happy ending to this, however, because technological advancements soon will alleviate Internet bandwidth problems. Until then, please go easy on the graphics if you are designing and creating an Internet site. Still, you should begin now to master Web graphics, because they are here to stay and your visitors will expect you to use graphics to improve your site's value.

Web graphics primer

You'll see two file formats in common use on the Web: GIF (Graphics Interchange Format) and JPEG (Joint Photographics Expert Group). GIF is the more common of the two, but JPEG is catching on fast. There are pros and cons to both, so you'll have to decide for yourself which to use.

I'll give you an overview of both major formats, tips on choosing the right one for a given application, overviews of graphics drawing, editing, and conversion software, and tips on graphics saving and editing. You'll find many excellent graphics resources from around the Web, including links to other Internet books that deal specifically with graphics and scanning.

GIF graphic files

The GIF format (Graphic Interchange Format) is good for all types of images and is compatible with a wide variety of graphics applications. GIF was developed in 1987 by CompuServe to be a device-independent method of storing pictures. GIF allows high-quality, high-resolution graphics to be displayed on a variety of graphics hardware and is intended as a common exchange and display mechanism for graphic images. A GIF picture file has an extension .GIF.

The 1987 GIF format was upgraded and released again in 1989, but used the same .GIF file extension. Some graphic applications distinguish the two GIF formats as GIF87 and GIF89. Even though the GIF 8-bits-per-pixel format only supports 256 colors and has relatively large file sizes, GIF remains one of the most popular choices for storing images. GIF format is best when used with images containing flat areas of color that have little or no shading. GIF is well-matched to inexpensive computer displays, because it can store only 8 bits/pixel (256 or fewer colors) and most PCs can't display more than 256 distinct colors at once.

Sizing Web graphics

The graphic images used on the Internet are sized by pixels. Pixels are dots on your screen. A typical Windows screen is made up of 640 pixels horizontally and 480 pixels vertically. For short, this is called a 640×480 screen resolution. However, Windows has other resolutions; another common Windows resolution is 800×600. Thus an image that is 240 pixels high would run 50 percent of the height of a 640×480 screen, but would occupy only 30 percent of the height of a 800×600 screen.

If your graphic displays in different sizes on different screens, you'll have difficulty planning the text so that it will fit around the graphic. Fortunately, HTML gives you two important (but little-used) tools to help control the relationship between text and graphics on your Web pages.

The clear break command

HTML has a code, <BR>, that causes a line break. You could use a series of consecutive <BR> commands to push your text down below the bottom of a graphic image. But if you put in just enough of them to push the text down past the graphic on a 640×480 screen, then the page will look different on a 800×600 screen. The solution is not to use multiple <BR> commands, but to use an option with the code that forces the next line break to occur *after* it clears the current graphic image. Use the code <BR CLEAR=LEFT> or <BR CLEAR=RIGHT>, depending on which side of the screen the image lies.

The percentage width command

HTML lets you control the width of graphic images with a WIDTH command that normally is expressed in pixels; but instead of using pixels, you can use a percent so that the size will be uniform across all screen resolutions. For example, if you used <IMG SRC=image.gif WIDTH=25%>, the image would be 160 pixels wide at a 640×480 resolution and 200 pixels wide at a 800×600 resolution.

NET TIP GIF Internet images are downloaded in 32 × 32-pixel blocks. Knowing this can help you increase your site's download efficiency. For example, if you size a graphic to be exactly 320×160 pixels it will download in 10 blocks by 5 blocks, or 50 blocks. But if you sized the same image at 330×165 it would require 11 blocks by 6 blocks, or 66 blocks. This would increase the download time, yet the on-screen size difference would barely be noticeable.

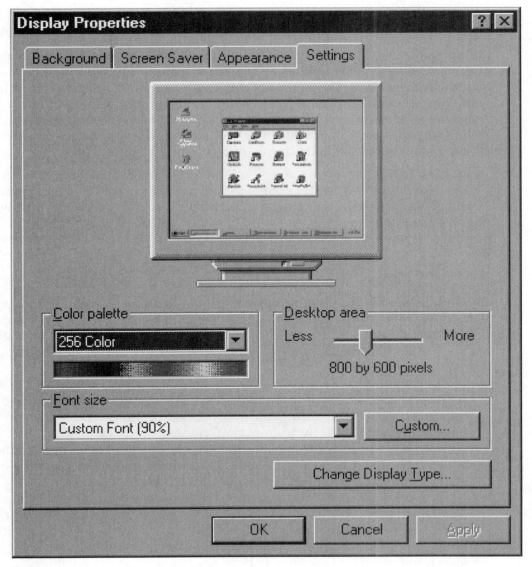

Figure 15-1

JPEG and JPG graphic files

JPEG (pronounced "jay-peg") is a standardized image-compression mechanism. The name JPEG is derived from the original name of the committee that wrote the standard, the Joint Photographic Experts Group.

JPEG is designed for compressing either full-color or grayscale images of natural, real-world scenes. It works well on photographs, naturalistic artwork, and similar material, but not well on lettering, simple cartoons, or line drawings. A JPEG picture file has the extension .JPG.

JPEG stores full-color information: 24 bits per pixel (up to 16.7 million colors). Therefore, with full-color hardware, JPEG images look much better than GIF files; and JPEG files can be much smaller than GIFs, so they usually are superior to GIFs in terms of disk space and transmission time.

I say "usually" because applications that save images in JPEG files or convert images to JPEG files permit adjustments to the image file that alter the image quality and file size. The compression method and/or percentage of compression is fully controllable, and directly corresponds to the quality of the compressed image.

It is possible to save a JPEG image in a file that is larger than its GIF counterpart. Of course, it also can be smaller. The trick is to learn to adjust the quality optimally, because there is a point of diminishing returns with every image. In other words, eventually you'll reach the point that increasing the quality adjustment doesn't improve quality, but does continue to increase the file size. That's why GIF can be a nice trade-off, because it creates a reasonable middle-of-the-road file in terms of balancing quality versus file size.

JPEG files often use a file extension of .JPG because of file naming limitations in MS-DOS and Windows 3.x. For example, if you use a Windows 3.x application to save a .JPEG graphic file, your system will convert the extension to .JPG. There will be no difference between the two files, and you can rename it with a .JPEG extension if you transfer it back to a UNIX, a Windows 95, or a Windows NT system.

Tips on selecting an image format

The best graphic format to use depends on the application and the desired effect. So, to make some sense out of all the possible choices, I'll share these tips from Kody Kline of *Extreme D.T.P.* in Tulsa, Oklahoma (see Figure 15-2). Kody is a master of computer graphics art, which you can see for yourself at *www.ionet.net/~kkline*.

All graphic images are rectangular in shape, even if they store pictures of irregularly shaped objects. If you want an irregularly shaped object not to have a rectangular image, you'll need to use GIF format. Only GIF lets you make a transparent background for your image. A transparent background creates the illusion of an irregularly shaped picture because the transparent background allows the colors behind the picture to show through the transparent color, even though the actual image outline remains rectangular.

If you want to reduce the download time of your large graphic images, you'll find that a moderately compressed JPEG image can cut the file size and download time by approximately 70 percent with only minor loss of quality. Much greater detail can be obtained in full-color photographic quality in a low-compression JPEG versus GIF because of the GIF color limitations.

Although the flashy 16.7-million color JPEG images might look excellent on your computer, remember that many people who access your Web site will not have adequate video hardware or the higher-speed modems to handle these images efficiently. GIF format supports an interlaced option that quickly displays a blurred full-size image of the GIF, then (during repeated passes) fills in and sharpens the image. This doesn't reduce overall download time, but at least it gives visitors a quick taste of the image that might entice them to wait.

Whichever graphic format you select, a compromise between a high-quality photographic image with millions of colors and concerns for long transmission times can result in a usable graphic that can deliver pizazz without visitors needing a nap during download.

Figure 15-2

Capturing images from Web sites you visit

You'll see a vast array of graphics as you surf the Internet, and Netscape makes it easy to save them to your hard drive. Of course you'll have to keep in mind that almost all Internet graphics are protected by normal copyrights, but you easily can e-mail the source site for reuse permission. If you want to include a graphic on your site because you're cross-linking to the source site, they'll be happy to grant permission to increase their site's exposure. Also, many times they'll tell you that the graphic is public domain and that you're free to use it anyway.

So, once the copyright considerations are handled, you can have a field day collecting graphics all over cyberspace. Here's a quick Hands-On exercise that shows you how to capture a graphic to your hard drive.

Hands On

Objective: **Learn to save an Internet graphic image.**
- ❑ Start Netscape.
- ❑ Press **CTRL+L**.
- ❑ Type *www.marketing-coach.com/mh-web*, then press **ENTER**.
- ❑ Place the mouse over the image of the book's cover.
- ❑ Click the right button.
- ❑ Click **Save this Image as . . .**

    Select an appropriate directory in which to save this image before you complete the next step.
- ❑ Click **Save.**

    You can open a saved graphic image in Netscape at any time, or you can reference it in one of your own HTML pages.

That was easy, but what about capturing the background image? So far, Netscape has not included that capability; but if you have Windows 95, you can download a background file with the Microsoft Internet Explorer. You can surf with Netscape for maximum compatibility, then quickly start Explorer if you encounter a background you'd like to save. Here's how:

Hands On

Objective: **Learn to save an Internet background graphic.**
- ❑ Double-click in the Netscape **Location** text entry box.

    This is where you see the URL at the top of the screen. It will now be highlighted.
- ❑ Press **CTRL+C** to copy the URL to the clipboard.
- ❑ Click the right mouse on a blank area on the **Taskbar**.
- ❑ Click **Minimize All Windows**.
- ❑ Double-click **The Internet** on your desktop.
- ❑ Press **CTRL+O** or double-click in the **Address** text entry box.
- ❑ Press **CTRL+V** to paste the URL, then press **ENTER** to load it.
- ❑ Click the right mouse button on a blank area of the background.
- ❑ Click **Save Background As**.
- ❑ Click **Save** to save the image on your hard drive.
- ❑ Select a directory and change the name as desired.
- ❑ Press **ALT+F4** to close Microsoft Internet Explorer.
- ❑ Use **ALT+TAB** to cycle back to Netscape.

Windows 95 lets you save an Internet background image to your clipboard so you can paste it into your favorite graphics application. The Internet Explorer also lets you designate an Internet background image as your desktop wallpaper.

Original graphics art

Creating a world-class site requires world-class graphics. Very few part-time graphics users can create the level of graphics that people expect to see today on the Web; and even if they do, they probably lack the expertise to optimize the balance between image quality and file size.

Nevertheless, perhaps your creative juices are stirring and you want to try your own hand at Internet graphics; or perhaps budget constraints won't allow you to hire a graphics artist or consultant right now. If so, then I'll give you do-it-yourselfers a quick introduction to creating Internet graphics.

Graphic drawing packages

A review of all the good graphics programs would be a book in itself, so I'll trim the list and show you some of the most popular—in other words, inexpensive—applications. In fact, some of them are *extremely* inexpensive—for example, free! These won't create the top-of-the-line, world-class graphics you read about in the last section, but then you'll save money. Everything involves trade-offs. Besides, if you're a novice, you most likely wouldn't be able to justify the time it would take to learn to use those highly specialized tools.

Client-side clickable maps

Until Netscape Navigator 2.0 was released, Web authors needed to use CGI programs running on the Web server to enable users to navigate via clickable image maps. The need for CGI programming skills put clickable maps out of reach of most Web authors. However, the new Netscape standard—called client-side clickable maps—is simple enough that most Web authors will be able to create clickable image maps.

Client-side clickable maps means that the coding is built into the Web page and all the action occurs on the client computer. Once the Web page is downloaded, the server won't need to be involved with handling the site's clickable maps. This helps alleviate some of the Internet bandwidth problems, as well as making it easier for authors.

In the last chapter, I outlined the HotDog Pro HTML editor that has an add-on application (CrossEye) that automates the tedious job of mapping coordinates on an image map. You can get CrossEye from the Sausage Software Web site at *www.sausage.com*.

With CrossEye, you won't have to write, test, compile, and upload a CGI script to handle the jumps. Instead, it generates simple HTML code and puts in the Windows clipboard. All you have to do is paste the code into an HTML page that you're editing in HotDog. Then, once your Web page is loaded into a visitor's browser, the image map code on your page handles all jumps.

CorelDraw

Since its acquisition of the complete line of WordPerfect products, Corel now has the most complete line of business software in the industry (see Figure 15-3). For years their CorelDraw graphics application has been an industry leader. The merging of the two product lines will help the WordPerfect word processor remain a leader in Web page development.

Another reason I included CorelDraw here is that it is available in many versions. Unlike most software vendors, when CorelDraw creates an upgrade it keeps its older versions on the shelf as well. This gives users a range of prices with a corresponding range of features. You can pay top dollar for the state-of-the-art latest version, or you can buy a deeply discounted, slightly older version that still might serve all of your graphics needs.

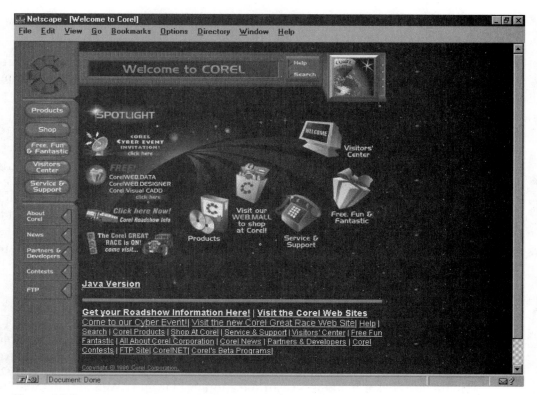

Figure 15-3

Corel also bundles its older versions with high-quality hardware products such as video display cards and scanners. If you're just getting into the Web and graphics and you've realized that your old video card is sapping your computer's performance, shop around for a card that includes a recent version of CorelDraw. These cards are no more costly than comparable video cards, and give you an excellent $150 to $350 drawing package for free.

I received CorelDraw 3.0 free with a Diamond Stealth video card and I received Corel Photo 5.0 Paint free with a Hewlett-Packard HP-4c scanner. The bundled products might be all you need, so test them before you buy upgrades.

Features for the Web

When you're selecting which version of CorelDraw you'll use, check if yours is recent enough to handle JPEG files. The older versions, Version 3.0 for example, do not; but even Version 3.0 handles GIF files, so you can use it for basic Web graphics jobs.

Even older versions of CorelDraw can create a wide array of special effects, including creating objects that appear as 3-D. You'll be able to control blending in shaded objects so you can adjust the appearance of their resolution. Corel imports and exports most of the major graphics formats. Considering the Internet's bandwidth limitations, which means that you should apply graphics sparingly, even older versions of CorelDraw might be all you'll need for a couple of years.

3-D Graphics

Even though CorelDraw and others have some 3-D capability, there are some stand-alone, top-end 3-D graphics packages available. 3-D graphics is a very hot topic as this book is being written. You'll need to check the latest versions on store shelves, read magazine reviews, or check out the Web sites of the various graphics application vendors. The bottom line: With moderate graphics experience you can expect to create some stunning 3-D graphics with the tools now available.

Paint Shop Pro

Paint Shop Pro is a shareware graphics application. This means that you can download a limited-license version and test it before you pay (see Figure 15-4). Paint Shop Pro is a user-friendly, powerful image viewing, editing, and converting program. With support for more than 30 image formats, and several drawing and painting tools, this might be the only graphics program you will ever need. It comes in both 16-bit and 32-bit versions. The 32-bit version runs under the Windows 95 and Windows NT operating systems, and takes full advantage of these 32-bit operating systems. The 16-bit version is an excellent choice for anyone using Windows 3.x.

This is an excellent graphics tool for Web-authoring beginners, and it will handle all of the graphics formats you'll need to get started. Check out its home page at *www.jasc.com/psp.html*, where you can read about it, check its lengthy feature list, and download a free trial copy. You won't beat this deal on a graphics program.

Figure 15-4

If you like it, you can register and pay the fee to get technical support and upgrades; and you've not invested any money if you find that you need a more powerful, professional-level graphics application.

Don't get the wrong idea; it has a lot of professional-level features, and can create some terrific graphics. For the money, this is the best value for Web graphics; but if you're not on a tight budget and you're ready to tackle the intricacies of some truly world-class graphics features, check out the next sidebar.

World-class graphics

Adobe Photoshop graphics software enables designers and photographers to create original artwork, correct color, retouch scanned images, and prepare professional-quality separations and output with complete flexibility. With a wealth of powerful painting and selection tools plus multiple layers, special effects filters, and lighting effects, Adobe Photoshop is a professional's dream application. You can learn more at the Adobe Web site at *www.adobe.com/Apps/Photoshop* (see Figure 15-5).

Photoshop includes more than 40 standard filters, including multiple choices for image sharpening, softening, stylizing, distortion, video, and removal of noise, dust, and scratches. Its powerful lighting effects let users apply multiple light sources to an image and choose from a range of colors, intensities, and angles.

You can use Photoshop to create an original image, or you can start with a scanned image. It lets you create effects in separate layers—like transparent sheets of acetate—upon which you can combine graphic elements, paint, and edit without changing the original background image. Photoshop's user-friendly interface permits you to drag-and-drop selections from different files or from different layers. You can save the finished image in a wide variety of different file formats, including GIF and JPEG. Its GIF support extends to the GIF89 format (which lets you create transparencies and interlacing).

LView Pro

Somewhere in between the full-featured graphic applications and the beginner's applications, you might find that you lose some graphics conversion abilities. Via the Web you can download an excellent shareware graphics conversion application called LView Pro. It was authored by Leonardo Haddad Loureiro of MMedia Research. You'll be free to distribute LView Pro to others for trial and leisure utilization. If you decide to use it in business, however, you'll need to register your copy with MMedia to comply with copyright regulations.

You'll find an amazing array of features considering that you can download this application free from the Internet. It lets you flip, rotate, resize, and crop images, and it gives you a full range of powerful image-enhancement tools. LView Pro can handle importing of BMP, GIF87, GIF89, JPEG, PCX, TIF, TGA, PPM, PGM, PBM, and DIB formats. Its GIF features include transparency that uses a simple dropper that lets you touch a background color that you want made transparent. A simple menu selection lets you tell LView Pro to automatically save all of your GIF files in interlaced format—an excellent choice if you expect your visitors to be using dial-up modems to browse your site.

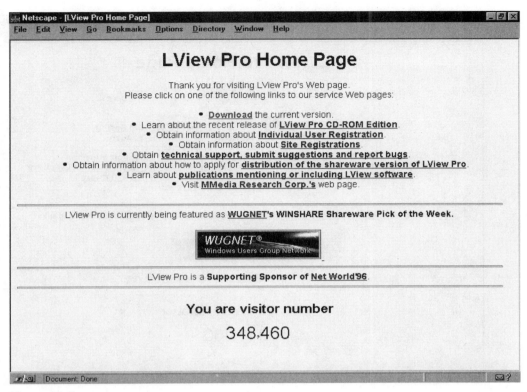

Figure 15-5

To get your copy of LView Pro, check out the MMedia Research Web page at *world.std.com/~mmedia/lviewp.html* (see Figure 15-6). You'll have a choice of either a Windows 3.x or a Windows 95 version. The last time I checked, the registration fee for commercial use was only $30, a true software bargain. While you're there to download the application, you might as well check out the link titled Transparent Color and save it, or print it so you can create transparent backgrounds for your GIF images.

Oh, no, there's more!

Just when you thought you had nailed down the facts on Internet graphics, things changed. There's a new graphics format emerging. It's all about lawsuits and patents and people fighting to collect money they're never going to be paid, but the result to you is a new format. After CompuServe had used the GIF format for seven years and after it had become a standard on the Web, some lawsuits were filed over alleged patent infringements. Someone thought they'd suddenly be able to collect royalties from everyone who uses GIF.

The real result? GIF had been showing its age in a number of ways even before the lawsuit, so the announcement only hurried the development of a new and much-improved replacement. Now we all have a new graphics format with the extension .PNG (pronounced *ping*). The PNG format (Portable Network Graphics) was developed as free software, and CompuServe intends it to be free of patent infringements.

For more information on PNG, check out its home page, which is maintained by Greg Roelofs at *quest.jpl.nasa.gov/PNG*.

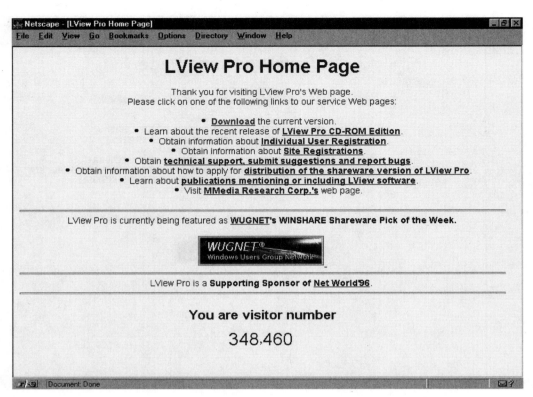

Figure 15-6

HiJaak graphics software

HiJaak 95 changes the way you work with graphics by integrating its graphics technology directly into Windows 95. Without ever having to run a separate application, you'll be able to view, organize, convert, and print graphics naturally and easily. HiJaak 95 also includes superb capture, conversion, and image-management tools, all with a choice working from the HiJaak application window or directly from Windows 95.

HiJaak 95 has extended Windows 95 with thumbnails of more than 75 graphics formats, and has added searching, viewing, printing, thumbnail updating, and converting to the Windows 95 shortcut menu. This unprecedented level of integration means that HiJaak 95 can help you perform your graphics tasks more efficiently than ever before. Its conversion handles almost every graphic format you can expect to encounter.

HiJaak performs all the usual graphics-enhancing tasks that you'll need, and includes a flexible and powerful screen capture application that enables you to capture and save any image you can see on your screen.

HiJaak Graphics Suite is an integrated set of graphics utilities that lets you easily add great graphics to your Web pages; and you don't have to be a professional to get excellent results with HiJaak Graphics Suite. HiJaak Graphics Suite includes HiJaak Browser, HiJaak Smuggler, HiJaak Paint, HiJaak Draw, and HiJaak Pro. With the suite you can browse, search, find, manage, create, draw, edit, paint, view, convert, trace, capture, scan, and print. As a bonus, it includes a clip-art library on CD-ROM that has thousands of images indexed by the HiJaak Browser so you get visual access to specific images without entering keywords.

Image scanning

Scanning is a computer function that transforms existing photos, graphic images, drawings, sketches, maps, illustrations, or even text into a digitized format. Once stored digitally, the captured image can be manipulated with computer graphics software. Scanned images can be retouched in the computer to optimize their on-screen appearance, or they can be printed or included in a word-processing document.

Your primary use of a scanner probably will be to capture images and save them in either GIF or JPEG formats that you can reference with HTML codes in your Web documents.

Because some quality always is lost during the scanning process, make sure that your original image is the best quality you can get. For best results, the images should have a high contrast and be perfectly sharp. Very much as with photocopiers, you might need to adjust the brightness and contrast to capture an acceptable image. You quickly will discover that there's a bit of an art to optimally scanning images, but I've included some excellent scanning resources in sidebars and in the Continuing Education section at the end of this chapter.

Scanner basics

For professional results, you should consider only flatbed scanners that are used on a desktop. A flatbed scanner is a scanning device that accepts flat art (photographs, drawings, clippings, or illustrations). Most flatbed scanners are designed to handle 8.5×11-inch originals in reflective media—images that reflect light. Some flatbed scanners will handle transparent media (such as Ektachrome transparencies, 35mm slides, etc.), but you might have to add a special transparency adapter to activate this function.

For increased flexibility in paper handling, you can find scanners that accept legal-size documents. If you need to scan a large number of existing documents, be sure you select a scanner that includes a document feeder option, because flatbed scanners normally accept only one document at a time.

Scanners will include scanning software, but the quality and features vary greatly. You're not likely to find a full-featured application bundled with any scanner, though all are adequate. If possible, stick to applications that give you the ability to scan and save in all the common file formats that you will want to use (especially GIF and JPEG). Good scanning software also should allow you to crop and rotate before or during saving. It's an absolute must that your scanner have a TWAIN (Technology Without An Interesting Name) module. TWAIN is a crucial feature, because it's supported by all major applications and allows you to scan directly into non-image-processing applications such as WordPerfect, PageMaker, CorelDraw, etc. It's amazing to watch WordPerfect insert a color photo directly into a document—what a way to spruce up a report or newsletter! (See Figure 15-7.)

Web graphics ◄

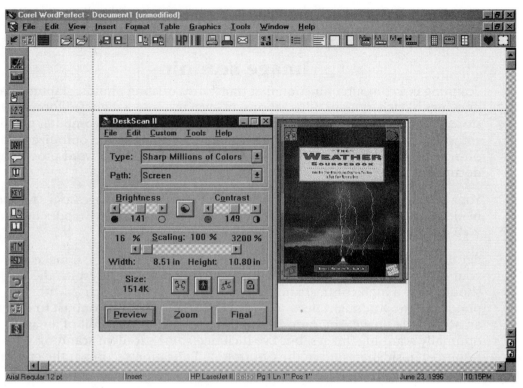

Figure 15-7

If you're interested in going beyond the basics of scanning, the next sidebar will take you about as far as you could want to go. A note of caution, though: This could become a full-time job.

Advanced scanning and graphics

You can access on-line graphics lessons that will teach you advanced scanning and other graphics techniques. You can learn everything from how to produce transparent backgrounds (a must for irregularly shaped images) to optimizing your graphics for size and download speed.

Advanced scanning

For some productivity-enhancing scanning tips, check out Michael J. Sullivan's Web site at *www.hsdesign.com/scanning* (see Figure 15-8). This is a fabulous scanning resource, but it's only the tip of the iceberg. For in-depth lessons and tips you can buy Michael's book, *Make Your Scanner a Great Design and Production Tool* (North Light Books 1995).

Michael is partner and artistic director of Haywood & Sullivan in Quincy, Massachusetts, an award-winning full-range design firm that excels at communication design using various media. He also is founding partner of Pilgrim New Media in Cambridge, Massachusetts, a multimedia titles publisher.

Advanced graphics

Jump to *www.warwick.ac.uk/~cudbh/I3course/graphics.html*, where you'll find a full set of graphics lessons from Bronwen Reid at the University of Hull, in the U.K. Lessons here include backgrounds, transparencies, and interlacing. Also, you can use this site as a jumping-off point for other sites with graphics tips.

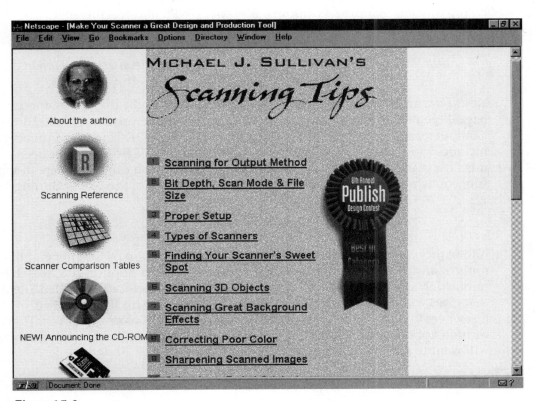

Figure 15-8

Continuing Education

Computer graphics virtual library

http://www.dataspace.com/WWW/vlib/comp-graphics.html

A dazzling array of sources for graphics that you can use in publishing your Web page. You could spend all day at this site alone. Unfortunately, this trip—with countless graphic images to download—can be annoying during off-peak hours, and impossibly slow during peak hours. Keep this URL, though, for the day that soon will come when you've got more bandwidth than you know what to do with.

Graphics viewers, editors, utilities and info
http://www.w3.org/pub/WWW/Graphics

This is the World Wide Web Consortium's collection of links to graphics shareware, demos, and information files available over the Internet. You'll find in-depth FAQs files for several major graphics formats, as well as recently posted messages on graphics formats and an on-line archive of past messages. They also include links that can guide you to Usenet newsgroups for different graphics formats and topics. Links to applications are accompanied by a designation for each particular platform: Windows, MS-DOS, UNIX, and Macintosh.

Yahoo GIF files
http://www.yahoo.com/Computers_and_Internet/Software/Data_Formats
4$& /GIF

Yahoo has an entire category for GIF graphics. Above is the direct URL for the page. If you're already in Yahoo, you can step manually through the categories: Computers and Internet, Software, Data Formats, and GIF. This page probably includes more on GIF than you'll ever need to know. GIF licensing has been a mess for years, but if you're a GIF graphics developer you can check here to make sure you're up to speed on the latest word on licensing of the GIF technology.

Adobe
http://www.adobe.com

Adobe probably offers the widest, most powerful selection of Internet graphic tools of any software vendor. In addition to the graphics applications, they have publishing applications, including a Web publishing application (called SiteMill) that gives you drag-and-drop Web authoring. Be sure to hit the link titled Elsewhere to discover a rich resource of other graphics links on the Web. These include not only other Web sites, but newsgroups and mailing lists to which you will want to subscribe.

Usenet graphic FAQs files
http://www.cis.ohio-state.edu/hypertext/faq/bngusenet/comp/graphics/top.html

Now that's a long URL, but it's equally long on content. This could be a primary contact point for graphics information, answers, and updates. If you've been elected to be your organization's computer graphics expert, you should put this URL on your bookmark list, because eventually you will need something listed on this page.

Scanning graphics
http://www.curtin.edu.au

This Web page is sponsored by the Curtin University of Technology, where they use Macintosh computers for the lessons (see Figure 15-9). The tips here, however, can be used for scanning files on any computer or format that you desire.

Web graphics sources
http://redtape.uchicago.edu/users/mdmendoz/art.html

This page says it best itself: "Have you ever needed a picture of an armadillo but didn't know just where to start looking for it? Well, hopefully this page will

▶ *Creating your own Web site*

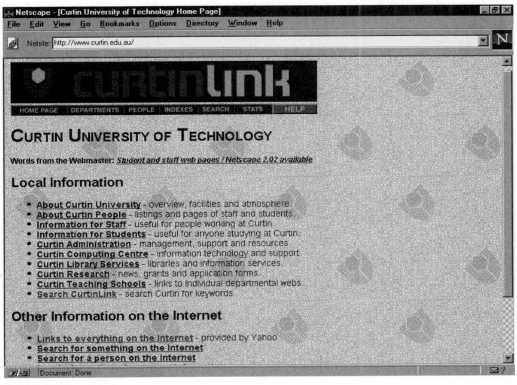

Figure 15-9

contain some help for you. From clip art to fonts to graphics, the links below will connect you to a wealth of art and graphics resources. Have fun!" I agree. This page is a perfect bookmark candidate for anyone who needs to locate graphic images for Web sites. At least start here, because many of the pages listed here will have other links, and you can always return for that armadillo.

Michael Sullivan's scanning tips

http://www.hsdesign.com/scanning

I've repeated this URL in case you missed it in the earlier sidebar, and so it will be included on the book's on-line version of the Continuing Education references. This outstanding site is a must see for anyone who will be scanning Web documents—bookmark it *now*.

Scanning FAQs

http://www.infomedia.net/scan

This page contains a wealth of scanning FAQs presented by Jeff Bone, formerly Electronic Media Coordinator at the University of Alabama at Birmingham School of Medicine, and more recently founder and president of Infomedia, Inc., a top-flight information systems integration and development company serving the southeast. To give you easy access, the topics on scanning artwork and photographs have been broken down into four primary categories: line art, halftones, grayscale, and color. In addition to these tips, you also can read about tricky (yet very important) resolution and copyright issues. If you don't yet own a scanner, be sure to check out the Scanner Roundup here before you buy.

326

16
Bringing the Web to life

THE HILLS might be alive with the *Sound of Music*, but the Web is alive with the sound of on-line music. And, because actions speak louder than words, you can forget about writer's block and begin expressing yourself through video clips, live-action video, or animated action on your Web site.

This is an exciting chapter that will show you how to configure your Netscape to play audio, video, and animation. All of these features are still pretty primitive, but the core technology is in place and it's advancing at the speed of light. Prepare to be thrilled at the sights and sounds you're going to pull in from all over the world.

Don't overdo it

The Web is getting overcrowded with gee whiz doo-dads that show off how talented their authors have become. Gee whiz technology certainly can draw in a Web surfer—after all, it *is* fun to watch. However, after the razzle-dazzle wears off, most Web visitors want to accomplish something.

Here's a survey done at Georgia Tech that will give you an idea of what Web visitors are seeking when they strap on their browsers and launch themselves into cyberspace: *www.cc.gatech.edu/gvu/user_surveys*. Start here and you'll learn what people like to do most on the Web (browsing) and what they like the least (shopping). Speed problems are the biggest complaint, so go easy on the graphics and other fancy stuff. In other words, make sure that the special effects truly make sense and improve the value of the information you're distributing.

For example, let's say you own a computer consulting firm. If one of your clients suffered a jammed laser printer late on a Saturday afternoon and didn't know how to open the case, she wouldn't mind the download time at all if your site offered a video that would help her. Taking a few minutes to download a file would be much better than waiting until Monday morning.

This chapter is an overview of the major Web special features that you'll see as you cruise the Net. Here's the menu for the delightful treats that await you:

- Java, the Web's own programming language
- Audio
- Video
- Virtual reality

Java

Java is an object-oriented programming language developed in the 1990s at Sun Microsystems, Inc. It was developed there by a team headed by James Gosling, and was intended for the microprocessors in small appliances. With this focus in mind, Java had to work on a wide variety of processors, and it needed excellent safeguards against locking up the processor. After all, you've become accustomed to your PC locking up occasionally, but how would you reboot your dishwasher?

While the Sun team developed Java, the World Wide Web grew up around them. Along the way, someone realized that the same characteristics that made Java perfect for appliance processors also made it perfect for the Web. The two technologies were married and introduced to the world in May 1995. Java will be a major factor in the Internet, changing the way we all work, play, and live.

What's in a name?

Contrary to rumors, Java does NOT stand for Just Another Vague Acronym. Java originally was named Oak in honor of a large tree outside James Gosling's window. Trademark considerations forced the team to come up with a new product name. That's a tough task in today's crowded markets, but *Java* hit the spot.

What's the difference between Java and HotJava? Java is the programming language. HotJava is Sun's Java-compatible Web browser. At first HotJava was the only Java browser available, but HotJava never really caught on because soon after Java became available, Netscape agreed to make its browser Java-compatible. Later, Microsoft added Java compatibility to its Internet Explorer, and that pretty much sealed Java's fate as *the* Internet programming language.

There are two other important factors in Java's incredible rise in fortune. First, Java is very much like the highly popular C and C++ programming languages used by the most serious programming professionals. This means that most programmers can learn it easily and adapt a lot of existing code. Second, it's much more forgiving than C or C++, so it's more fun to use and debugging is simplified. That means that novices can pick it up more quickly, and experienced C programmers will appreciate its relative ease of use. These factors combined will bring millions of Java applets onto the Web.

HYPERJUMP

Applet
Java programs are called *applets*, because they depend in part on code that's embedded into your Web browser. Without that code a Java program would be useless, so they're called applets instead of applications.

Sample Java input script

Many popular Java applets are written to receive input from a script file. This means that a lot of people will be able to add Java applets to their site without knowing anything about programming. They'll be able to write a script from scratch, or perhaps modify a sample script that the programmer included with the applet.

The Web site of an earlier Internet book I wrote has a good example of why the script feature is so significant. If you'll visit the book's home page at *www.marketing-coach.com/mh-guide*, and if you've got a Java-compatible browser, you'll see an LED display that carries a running message similar to the sign on the side of the Goodyear blimp (see the arrow in Figure 16-1).

This applet's programmer spent five days writing its code—and he is a highly-skilled and experienced programmer—but I was able to get the LED display working on my book's site in just an hour or so. All I had to do was study the syntax of the script and modify the sample that came with the applet. I then

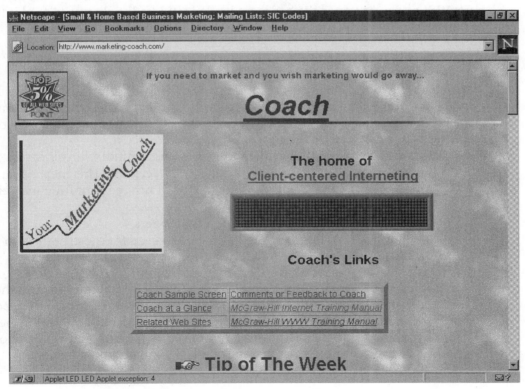

Figure 16-1

added the required HTML applet codes by copying and pasting from the sample file. Finally, I uploaded the new HTML page, the LED applet code, and my script file. That's all there was to it.

This small block of HTML codes tells a Java-compatible browser to run the Java code stored on my server's Web site. Note the second line of the code that specifies which script file to use. When a visitor loads my book's home Web page, their browser will run the LED applet and display the text as specified in this script (see Figure 16-2).

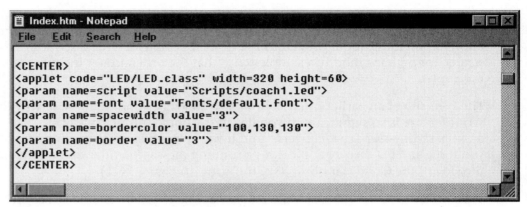

```
Index.htm - Notepad
File   Edit   Search   Help

<CENTER>
<applet code="LED/LED.class" width=320 height=60>
<param name=script value="Scripts/coach1.led">
<param name=font value="Fonts/default.font">
<param name=spacewidth value="3">
<param name=bordercolor value="100,130,130">
<param name=border value="3">
</applet>
</CENTER>
```

Figure 16-2

Of course, this script would be worthless without the Java code stored on my site's Web server; but once the code was loaded, all I had to do was to feed it the parameters in the script and watch it turn them into magic on the screen.

So what?

Think about your clients and customers when you're adding Java to your site and be realistic. Someday, Java will run easily on all systems, but today it can strain slower systems and annoy your visitors. People with 486-based or slower PCs might not see the cool show you planned.

There are several other considerations to keep in mind:

- Java is not enabled in the 16-bit version of Netscape. This means that most of your visitors with Windows 3.x will not see your little marvel anyway.
- Many visitors will have other non-Java browsers.
- The Java code takes extra time to download even for those users with Java-compatible browsers. Will your visitors agree that your Java application was worth the time they had to wait to get it?

Don't get me wrong, I think that Java is going to be a major factor in the Internet revolutionizing our lives; just not in the next year or two. I've added Java to this book's home page, but that's a client-centered application because I wanted you to be able to see an example. Make sure that your use of Java has a higher purpose than making you feel good about your site.

How your organization can use Java

There are practically no limits to what can be done with Java. You're going to see an explosion of Java applets on the market that will enable your organization to do almost anything you can imagine. The resources listed in the Continuing Education section of this chapter contain links to a lot of Java-powered sites. Start with these links and keep browsing for ideas of how your organization can use Java to deliver increased value to visiting members, clients, and customers.

Before Java, the only programming you were likely to encounter on the Web was CGI (Common Gateway Interface) programs that ran on the Web server. You might have seen CGI in action if you have filled in an information form and sent it to the parent company.

CGI works only on a two-way street. This means that user actions must interact with the Web server, which increases Internet bandwidth demands. Thus, CGI programs must go back and forth to verify user input. A busy site could cause user delays. Java, on the other hand, can perform data verification tests within the client's browser and will use the server only when the task is ready to send back. This will enable your site to provide better service to your visitors as well as allow your site to handle more traffic.

Banish programming forever

If you're sick of reading about all of this programming and you don't care which is easier (CGI or Java) because you have zero interest in learning either one, there are alternatives. You can create interactive brochures and databases on the Web without having to learn either CGI or Java, thanks to user-friendly applications that let you work in an intuitive environment. Then, when you're done, the applications handle the Web technical stuff.

Interactive brochures and catalogs

Made by AMT Learning Solutions, Interactive Brochure lets you easily create interactive multimedia presentations that can work over the Web. This application is perfect for presenting sales information for your products and services. A companion product, Interactive Catalog, lets you quickly set up an on-line sales catalog from which users can order directly. Combine this with a commerce server, and you've got an on-line sales outlet!

Now imagine being able to handle all of your corporate training over the Web! Interactive Brochure has an expanded version that creates interactive training sessions. It includes a testing, scoring, and reporting system that can handle all functions on-line, sending crucial scoring information to corporate headquarters from any office in the world. It's a perfect way to handle on-going training requirements at all of your offices and lets workers complete their requirements on their own time—or in their own *time zone*!

For more information, contact AMT Learning Solutions at *www.amtcorp .com*, or e-mail a request to *amtsales@amtcorp.com*.

askSam

askSam is the famous free-form database that lead Federal prosecutors to break open the Iran-Contra case. No human mind or ordinary database had been able to piece together the facts that prosecutors suspected could lead to filing charges. Once the information was entered into askSam, the big picture came into focus. A free-form database can deal with information that doesn't fit into traditional database fields.

Now, you can create an on-line askSam database that users can interact with from anywhere in the world. You can organize data that users input from the Web, or you can let users search through your database to retrieve information. This is a good Breathing Space tool, because it can help your organization make sense out of the flood of information that pours in every day over the Web. Sam doesn't care how much you dump in; he'll be able to index it and give you exactly what you want, when you want it. It's a perfect solution for archives of e-mail or Usenet newsgroup articles. Visit the askSam Web page at *www.asksam.com* for more information (see Figure 16-3).

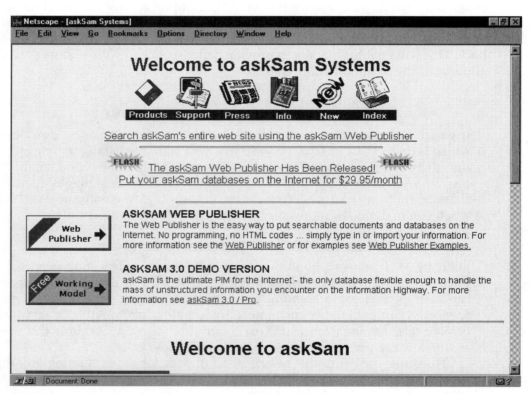

Figure 16-3

CGI isn't dead, and will probably be around for years; but Java will quickly replace many of its functions, especially for all the new people coming onto the Net who don't know—and don't want to know—anything about CGI.

Here is a list of some Java functions that already are in use on the Web:

- Clickable image maps
- User-friendly link buttons
- Active and interactive site navigation help
- Scrolling messages to present hot topics
- Sound and video players that activate automatically
- Automated visitor reply-and-response forms
- Calculators tailored for a specific use
- Spreadsheets that present tailored financial data

JavaScript

JavaScript is a simplified version of Java that you might want to investigate if all this talk of programming is giving you the jitters. You can find a lot of valuable JavaScript examples that you can use without programming knowledge. This isn't the same thing as the use of a script that I demonstrated in an earlier Java example. That was a script that fed parameters to a Java applet; JavaScript is another programming language.

JavaScript complements Java by bringing the useful properties of Java applets to less-experienced authors. JavaScript is a descendant of smaller dynamically typed languages such as dBASE. These scripting languages bring programming capability to a broader set of users because of their simpler syntax, specialized built-in functionality, and minimal requirements for object creation.

The next feature is something that works well with Java: on-line audio. Before Java, Web authors needed to create links on Web pages so that visitors could click and download an audio file; but Java enables Web authors to automatically play an audio file—a welcome message or a musical fanfare—when the page loads into a Java-compatible browser.

On-line Audio

On-line audio works by converting sound into digital information and storing that information in audio computer files. These files then can be transferred across the Internet and can be played on a wide variety of operating systems and computer platforms. You soon will see that sound files come in a lot of different formats, and that each of these formats uses a proprietary compression scheme to reduce the size of the saved sound files they produce. File compression is crucial to the spread of Internet audio, because sound files currently require very large file sizes in relation to the length of the sound clip. Don't be surprised to watch sound files grab 11K of disk space for every second of sound.

The use of on-line audio is increasing rapidly. Unfortunately there isn't a uniform standard for digital audio formats, though the field is narrowing. Here are the more common types you'll encounter in a Windows environment:

- WAV files (wave files, or common SoundBlaster-type audio files)
- AU files (common Internet audio files)
- RA files (Real Audio files, best for voice only)

Wave audio

Wave is the native sound format for Microsoft Windows systems. The short musical segments you hear sprucing up your Windows activities are wave files. The wave format is the least efficient of the three listed here, requiring approximately 50 percent larger files than AU sound files. Its main advantage lies in the huge number of wave files that are available—including lots of public domain clips. And, if you find a wave clip that you want to use, you can convert it to the more efficient Sun format, AU.

Sun Audio

One of the most popular Internet sound file formats is the AU format, also called the uLaw, NeXT, or Sun Audio format. This format can be used on most of the machines on the Internet that are equipped to play sound. It also produces reasonably small files that consume little bandwidth to transfer. It's a nice balance between audio quality and required transfer time. It definitely has sufficient audio quality for the typical sound clips you might offer, pretty much matching wave.

Real Audio

Real Audio is the commercial name of a company that developed the RA standard. It's rapidly gaining popularity on the Internet because of its extremely small bandwidth demands. In fact, with a good connection and a 28.8kbps modem, RA sound clips can play in real time. For example, I performed a download test while researching this book and, using a 28.8kbps modem, got a 5.71 second clip in less than five seconds.

Check out the Real Audio Web site at *www.realaudio.com* and download the latest version of their ra player (see Figure 16-4). While you're there, check out the links they have to other Web sites that use Real Audio so you can get some ideas on how to use it yourself.

When you've completed the download, you'll need to run the installation. After that, you'll be ready for an exercise later in the chapter when I'll have you install the default Windows audio player. In that exercise, you can substitute the Real Audio player instead, because the steps are almost exactly the same.

Netscape helper applications

Netscape cannot play sound files by itself. Instead, Netscape hands off the files to configurable helper applications, such as the Real Audio player. Netscape needs a helper application for each of the audio formats. There are many players available, and you can download them with Netscape. Some players are dedicated to playing only a single type, while others can play a variety of sound files. Whichever you choose, you'll have to install it as a Netscape helper application.

If you don't have an audio player configured, when Netscape encounters an audio file it will ask you what you want it to do with the file. Once the sound player is installed in Netscape for that type of file, it will handle future files of that type automatically.

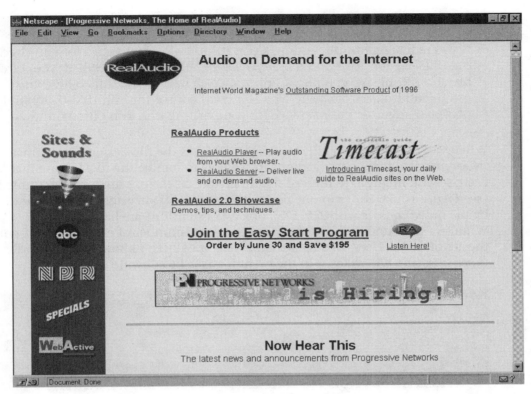

Figure 16-4

Differences in file formats

If you're going to offer audio on your site, before choosing a file format you should carefully consider your visitors and what you're delivering with the audio files. There are dramatic differences in file sizes and resulting download times. I ran a download comparison test to illustrate the real-life differences. I selected a clip from *Hollywood Online* (profiled later) that offers each of its sound clips in multiple formats.

Bandwidth comparisons

The clip I used was from a scene in the film American President, starring Michael Douglas and Charlie Sheen. The clip is 5.71 seconds long and goes like this:

Michael Douglas: She didn't say anything about me?

Charlie Sheen: Well, no sir, but I can pass her a note before study hall.

Here's a comparison chart of the test:

Format	Size	Download Time	Comments
ra	5K	5 sec.	Choppy, music barely audible, words not clear
au	44K	23 sec.	Music clear, voices excellent
wav	62K	32 sec.	Music clear, voices excellent

Your own results might differ. These were clocked on a 133-MHz Pentium with 24MB RAM, Windows 95, and a 28.8-Kbps U.S. Robotics Courier modem. The actual speeds are not the point, however; just look at the relative performance of the different formats.

Other formats

If you're having trouble finding a player for an Internet audio format, check out the site at *www.geocities.com/Hollywood/1158/sndutils.html*. If you offer sound on your site, you might link your Web page to this site to help visitors get a sound player. This site also is a good source for non-IBM-compatible players that you might reference for your visitors who don't use Windows.

When you download any file, Netscape compares the file's extension against its list of installed helper applications to see how to handle the file. During that last exercise, you might have noticed that many file extensions are preprogrammed (see Figure 16-5). For example, files with HTM or HTML extensions are handled by the browser. Files with ZIP, EXE, or COM extensions are handled by the Windows save function. You also noticed a large number of extensions for which the action is Ask User. This means that Netscape doesn't know how to handle those files, and will ask you in the event it's asked to download one.

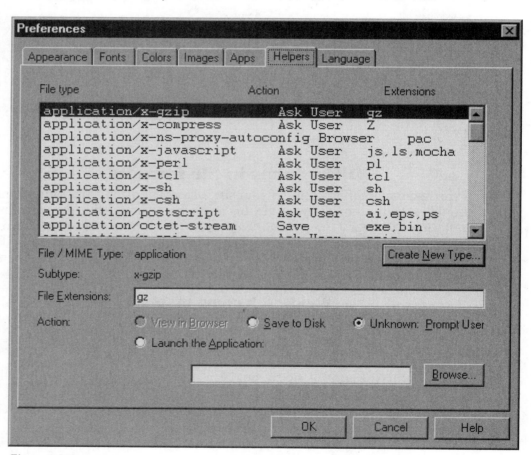

Figure 16-5

Configuring Netscape to play sound

In this next exercise, you'll learn how to install a helper application. I've selected the wave format for your exercise because you most likely already have the required sound player application on your hard drive, so I'll proceed with that assumption.

Hands On

Objective: **Learn to configure Netscape to play sound files.**

❑ Start Netscape.

❑ Click **Options, General Preferences**.

❑ Scroll down to **audio/x-wav**.

❑ Look on this line under **Action**.

> If this entry says Ask User, then finish the exercise, if it already lists a player application, then click **Cancel** now.

❑ Click the **Launch the Application** radio button near the bottom.

❑ Click in the text entry window immediately below this button.

❑ Type *c:\windows\mplayer.exe*.

> Your installation might be nonstandard and require that you click on **Browse** to search for the mplayer.exe application. Also, if you know you have another player on your system that you would rather use, then select it instead.

❑ Click **OK**.

❑ Click **Options, Save Options**.

You have just completed a basic helper application installation. We'll do another later, but you can use this dialog box to configure helpers for many other file formats. For example, if you exchange a lot of WordPerfect documents that use the standard WordPerfect file extension WPD, then you can use the same steps above to make Netscape automatically launch WordPerfect if you download a WPD file. The same could apply for Word DOC files, RTF files, or for Excel spreadsheet files.

Recorded audio

The use of recorded audio is increasing rapidly on the Internet. You can expect this growth to accelerate now that Java applets enable Web authors to embed automated sound into Web pages. Whether or not you automate their playing, sound files can be a nice addition to many types of Web sites.

You probably are only a few dollars away from having all the equipment you need to record a message and put it on your Web site. For example, Windows 95 includes an application with recording capability—just add a microphone and you've got a recording studio.

Your PC's sound card has a microphone input jack on it, next to the jack into which your speakers are plugged. Inexpensive microphones are now available at all large computer stores and electronics outlets such as Radio Shack. Make sure your microphone has the micro-plug and not a standard ¼" plug.

So, assuming you've got a sound card, speakers, and a microphone, here's how to record an audio file:

Hands On

Objective: **Learn to record using Windows 95.**

❑ Click the **Start** button.

❑ Click **Programs, Accessories, Multimedia, Sound Recorder**.

Get ready with your microphone before the next step.

❑ Click the red **Record** button.

❑ Say "One small step for multimedia . . . one giant leap for me."

❑ Click the square **Stop** button.

❑ Click the right-arrow **Play** button.

❑ Click **File, Save** to save the file to disk.

❑ Type *smalstep.wav* and click on **Save**.

❑ Press **ALT+F4** to close the sound recorder.

You now have recorded and saved a wave sound file that you can use on a Web site. If you'd like a more sophisticated recorder, be sure to visit the GoldWave site at *web.cs.mun.ca/~chris3/goldwave* and get its latest version (see Figure 16-6). GoldWave is a full-featured, professional-quality digital sound recorder. It supports many file formats (WAV, AU, IFF, VOC, SND, MAT, AIFF, and raw data) and can convert to or from these formats. It also has all kinds of editing and mixing controls, such as distortion, Doppler, echo, filter, mechanize, offset, pan, volume shaping, invert, resample, and transpose.

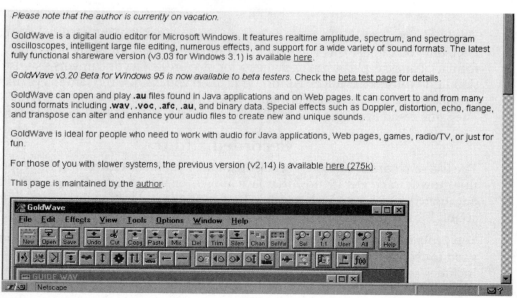

Figure 16-6

Downloading audio

Once you've recorded an audio clip, you might wonder how you get it on your Web site so that users can download it and play it. The user side is a cinch if their browser is configured to play audio files. Your side also is easy, too, because you reference the audio file with normal HTML codes as if it were a Web page or a graphic image. Here's a sample of HTML coding that would let visitors play the file you recorded in the last Hands On exercise:

```
<A HREF=sound/smalstep.wav>My First Clip</A>
```

In addition to modifying your Web page, you would need to make a new directory on your server for your sound files and transfer the smalstep.wav file to that directory. Future visitors to your site would see <u>My First Clip</u> as a normal, underlined hyperjump. If they click on it and their Netscape is configured to handle a wave file, the file would download and play automatically. If their Netscape was not configured for wave audio, Netscape would ask what to do with the file. At that point, the visitor either could save it to disk for later play, or point Netscape to an audio player.

To see more examples of on-line audio clips, visit *Hollywood Online Sound Bites* (see Figure 16-7) and have a ball. Careful, though! Don't try this at work—it's way too much fun! And—as if it's not enough fun by itself—this site has links to other Internet sound sources.

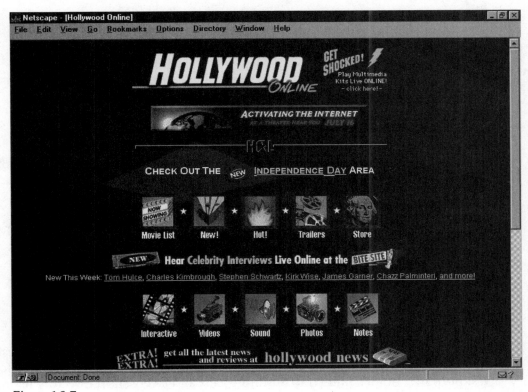

Figure 16-7

Real-time audio

How could I say so much about audio on the Internet without mentioning that you can use the Internet as a voice telephone? It doesn't exactly fit in here, but it's a related topic and an incredible Internet function.

Just in case you haven't heard already, you can use the Internet as a telephone to talk to anyone in the world without incurring any additional long-distance charges (see Figure 16-8). Most people simply don't comprehend it—or believe it—the first time they hear about Internet phone service, but it's true. After all, the Internet runs on phone lines, mostly maintained by MCI and Sprint (who started out in the long-distance business).

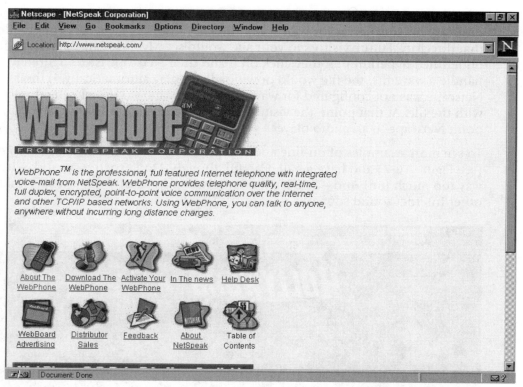

Figure 16-8

Internet phone service has a lot of room for improvement, but if you do any international business or if you've got friends in other countries, you probably won't care about the limitations. One problem with Internet phone service is that you can't just call someone, or ring them up. Both parties need the right software, the right hardware, Internet service, and both will have to be on-line at the same time. Another problem is poor audio quality, but it's not bad and quality will improve rapidly.

To learn how to use the Internet as a phone, check out the WebPhone site at: *www.netspeak.com*. This site includes Internet phone software and details on using the system (see Figure 16-9). You can download a free version of WebPhone for test purposes, but it's limited to 3-minute calls and a very short directory listing. The paid commercial version removes the limitations and lets you make unlimited calls anywhere in the world.

Finally, if you'll do a Yahoo search for the phrase *Internet phone*, you'll be inundated with listings. The last time I tried it I got 125 hits—see how many you get today!

On-line Video

Digital video standards have quickly been adopted by the Internet, and in particular by the World Wide Web. Because video fits so well with the expectations we all have developed for graphic displays on the Web, you'll see a rapid increase in Web video. Currently there are four common formats for video on the Web: MPEG, MOV files, AVI files, and HQX files. The HQX files are for

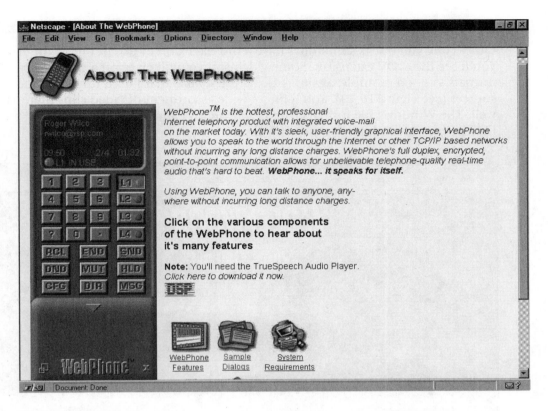

Figure 16-9

Macintosh computers, so I'll give you an overview and some resources for the other three formats.

MPEG

The MPEG (Moving Pictures Experts Group) is a group of people that meet under the ISO (International Standards Organization) to generate standards for the compression of digital video (time-sequenced digital images) and audio. The MPEG conducts approximately four one-week meetings each year. Between meetings, members work on topics discussed at the meetings.

Specifically, the MPEG defines a compression standard that reduces the storage space required for digital video. The compression standard ensures that, much like videocassette standards, we all can use each other's digital video files. The compression algorithms, however, are not defined. That's left to individual vendors, and that is where proprietary advantage is obtained even though MPEG is a publicly available standard.

The MPEG video files that are used on the Internet have a file extension of either .MPEG or .MPG. The MPEG core technology used in these files includes many different patents from different companies and individuals worldwide. Because the MPEG committee only sets the technical standards without dealing with patents and intellectual property issues, there are differences in the performance of video files from one vendor to the next, even though they use the same file extension.

QuickTime

QuickTime video files sometimes have a file extension of QT, but most often you'll see the MOV extension. Some video sources will give you a choice of formats. A good example, again, is *Hollywood Online* that I used for the sound sources (see Figure 16-10). You'll find a wide assortment of video clips there as well. The Windows file formats listed there are AVI and MOV, so you'll need a QuickTime video player for the MOV files.

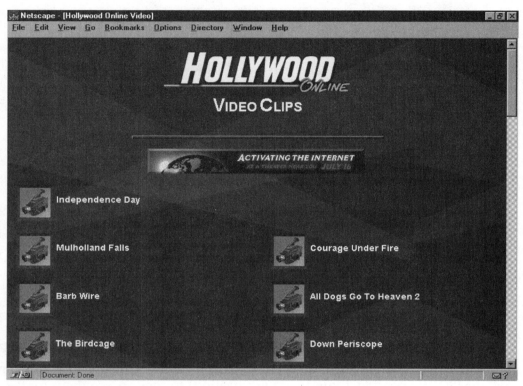

Figure 16-10

The QuickTime helper application installs in exactly the same way as the MPEG player that I use in the next exercise. So, all you need to play MOV files is a QuickTime (QTVR) player. To get one, visit the Sunvalley Software site at *www.kwanza.com/~embleton/service.html* (see Figure 16-11), click on the link for downloads to get the Apple QuickTime player, then download it and install it. Don't worry about the Apple in there, it also comes in a Windows variety.

After the QuickTime files are on your system, complete the Hands-On exercise listed under the MPEG heading below, but change it for QuickTime. The QuickTime helper application will be installed into Netscape under the *video/quicktime* listing.

If you're interested in more information about digital multimedia files, check out the following sidebar. From it you can learn more details, find more sources, and keep up with the latest industry changes such as player upgrades. If you've seen enough technical details for now, then skip ahead to learn how to configure Netscape to play video.

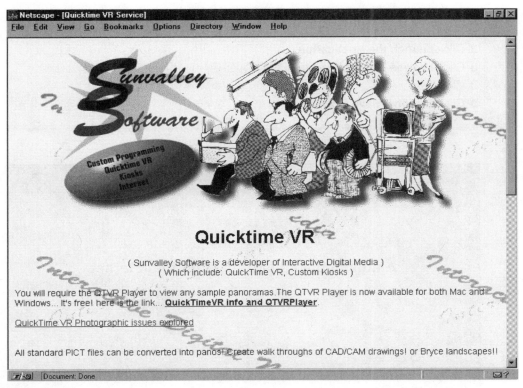

Figure 16-11

Multimedia file formats on the Web

For even more coverage on these topics, check out this Web site: *ac.dal.ca /~dong/contents.html*, maintained by Allison Zhang (see Figure 16-12). First I want to thank Allison for helping with some of the information in this chapter. Her home page is titled "Multimedia File Formats on the Internet: A Beginner's Guide for PC Users." Check out the Table of Contents to see all the topics offered. She also maintains a helpful FAQs file that can be a ready reference source as you learn Web multimedia.

Configuring Netscape to play video

If your installation of Netscape (before 3.0) does not include support for playing videos, you can use this Hands-On exercise to show you how to configure Netscape to use an MPEG player. If you don't already have one on your hard drive, check out the following sidebar for sites from which you can download a file that will install the latest version of an MPEG player application on your system. Once the application is installed, you can complete this exercise.

Hands On

Objective: Learn to configure Netscape to use an MPEG player.

❏ Start Netscape.

❏ Click **Options, General Preferences**.

❏ Click the **Helper** tab.

❏ Scroll down to **video/MPEG**.

❏ Click **Launch the Application**.

❏ Click **Browse** and locate your MPEG player.

❏ Click **OK**.

❏ Click **Options, Save Options.**

Figure 16-12

Point your visitors to a video source

If you include a video clip on your Web site, be sure to give obvious instructions to your visitors on how to obtain and install a video player. Here are two sources you can list for the MPEG player:

ftp.cic.net/pub/Software/pc/www/viewer/mpegw32h.zip

ftp.ncsa.uiuc.edu/Web/Mosaic/Windows/viewers/mpegw32h.zip

If you want to do the next Hands-On exercise you'll need an MPEG player on your hard disk, so you can use Netscape now to get it from one of these sources. The file is about 640K in size, so plan for some download time.

Videoconferencing

The Internet is exploding with real-time video technology. Already you can conduct videoconferencing and check weather and traffic. The 1980s brought us the great business revolutions of the fax machine, but the 1990s is the decade of videoconferencing. By the end of this decade, it will be a common business tool.

In fact, videoconferencing probably will be a common household appliance. Just imagine Thanksgiving Day dinner in front of a large, wall-mounted, flat-screen monitor. You'll be able to enjoy a family meal with relatives and friends from all over the country—all over the world, actually. You'll be able to do everything but pass the cranberry sauce. And I won't be surprised if the next decade brings us a technical solution for that limitation—3-D e-mail!

For a taste of videoconferencing, check out the Cornell University Cu-See-Me project (see Figure 16-13). They've done a lot of development work on Internet video and they're sharing their work on the Web site at *cu-seeme.cornell.edu*. What you'll see there will appear a little primitive by the standards of cable television. The key to using videoconferencing lies in seeing the possibilities that are demonstrated at this site.

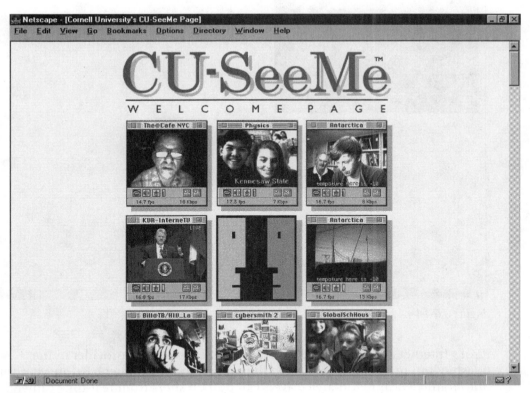

Figure 16-13

Real-time video

Many major cities around the world now have multiple live-action weather cameras linked to the Internet. There's something powerfully charismatic about being able to see a live-action shot of a city anywhere in the world. I believe you'll find it to be mind-broadening, graphic evidence that we all are one—everyone on the planet.

On-line camera images sap a lot of Internet bandwidth, and even then they only deliver some small, fuzzy pictures. They only update once every minute or two. However, remember the little black-and-white television sets of the 1950s, and consider the pace at which electronic advancements are racing into our future. Before long you'll be able to adorn your office wall with a real-time, wall-sized, stereo-sound shot of Niagara Falls (see Figure 16-14). For more scenic views from around the U.S., check out the Weather Cam site at *cirrus.sprl.umich.edu /wxnet/wxcam.html* and pick your favorite spot.

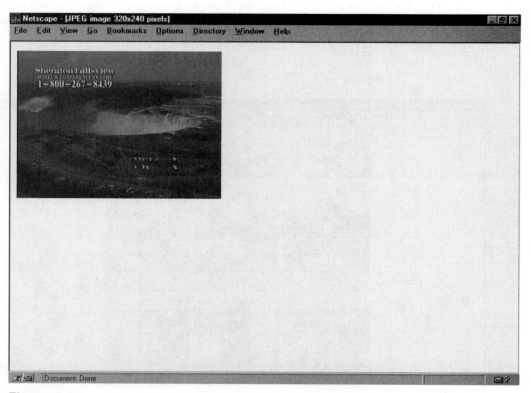

Figure 16-14

Erol's Internet and Computers, the largest Internet service provider in the Washington metro area, pioneered the on-line traffic cam here. Before venturing into traffic, Washington-area drivers can pull up shots from real-time cameras located all over the region (see Figure 16-15). Won't that be nice for when we all have Internet service in our cars? Of course that might *cause* more traffic jams than it alleviates, but at least you could flame that turkey in front of you!

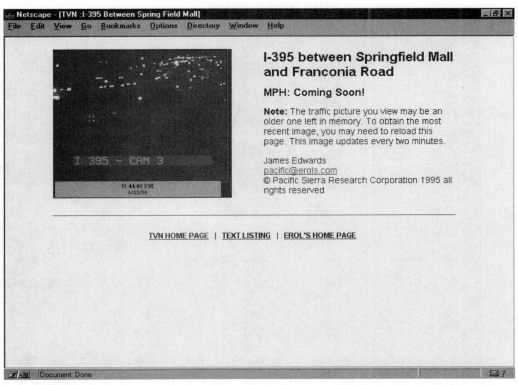

Figure 16-15

What's next after the traffic cam? Virtual reality, where you can stay at home and make yourself *think* you're out driving in rush-hour! (Or doing just about anything else you can imagine.)

Virtual reality

The next generation of Intel microprocessors, the Pentium Pro, includes built-in support for Web sites that use the Virtual Reality Markup Language (VRML). To learn more about it, visit the Web site at *www.intel.com/procs/ppro/intro/index.htm* (see Figure 16-16). This site features some VRML tours of Pentium Pro applications. You won't be able to view these tours in 3-D virtual reality without a Live3D player, which you can download at *www.netscape.com/comprod/products /navigator/live3d/index.html*. Take good notes when you get to this page, because it also lists the coolest VRML worlds on the Web.

Virtual reality definitely is *future* cyberspace reality. The Internet can't spare the required bandwidth, and few users have the required PC power. Furthermore, VRML programming is not going to be for the average office HTML author—so expect to see it only on sites where its use truly makes sense. If you think it might be for you, though, you can visit the Web site of a good book on VRML at *www.mcp.com/general/news7/vrml2.HTML*.

Of course, VRML will make enormous sense for some uses. For example, I asked Orhan Onaran of Erol's Internet and Computers about future uses for VRML. His organization has been discussing how it can help bring virtual reality shopping

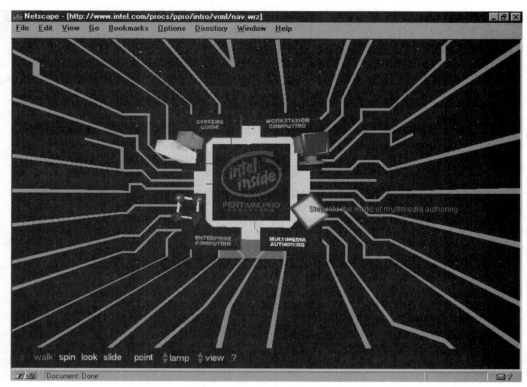

Figure 16-16

into the homes of its subscribers. Don't be surprised to soon be able to stroll through a grocery store on-screen, click on the items you want, and have them delivered to your door before you could have fought the traffic and waited in line to get them yourself.

However, at first you're going to see a lot of gee-whiz virtual reality gimmicks designed to show off the technology. That's normal, though. After all, there was a time when the Wright Brothers flew down city streets in Washington, D.C. just to show off their new technology. After the Wright Brother Effect wears off virtual reality, it's going to be the best thing that happened to our overcrowded, time-pressed society since the airplane.

# Continuing Education

Hooked on Java

http://java.sun.com/hooked

This is the home page for the book *Hooked on Java* (see Figure 16-17). You'll find supplements to the book, including bug reports, fixes, and new applets that are not included on the book's CD-ROM disk. If you don't already have the book, this site is an excellent source for Java samples; and even if you do have it, you can find other Java resources here as well as stay in touch with the latest developments with the Java team at Sun.

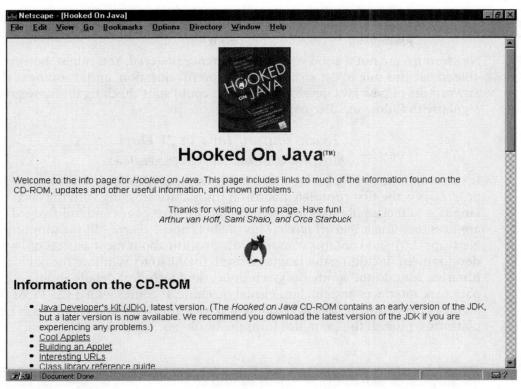

Figure 16-17

Gamelan Java applet collection
http://www.gamelan.com

Here's a vast array of Java examples, instruction, reference, sources, code, and applets. It's a very well-done site that gives you easy access to its resources by using the Netscape frames feature. It's a user-friendly site that's the best I've seen for Java applets. They also maintain a parallel site for JavaScript at *www.gamelan .com/Gamelan.javascript.html.*

Belle Systems Java resources
http://www.belle.dk

Here's Bjarne Jensen's Java home page in Denmark. Bjarne maintains a well-tested list of Java links that should be able to guide you to some sites that will give you a good start with Java. This site shows off a lot of the possibilities of the Net, such as: extensive use of the HTML language, Java Prestel emulator, Java Telnet emulator, and links (Java, magazines, graphics, HTML, and even OS/2 and ISDN). These features, plus his big joke collection, add up to several pages that you should see for yourself.

Netscape JavaScript
http://www.netscape.com/comprod/products/navigator/version_2.0/script/index.html

Netscape itself has a nifty Web site on JavaScript. It includes examples, JavaScript resources, sample programming code, an authoring guide, and some good technical overviews of both Java and JavaScript. Especially valuable is a section that directly compares the features of the two.

Java newsgroup

comp.lang.java

Newsgroups are not a good source for reference material. You might, however, be able to use this one to get an answer to a specific question; and if you hear about any rumors of new Java developments, you could start checking this newsgroup regularly to follow the discussions.

Teach Yourself Java in 21 Days.

http://www.lne.com:80/Web/Books/Java

If you're interested in learning more about working with Java, *Teach Yourself Java in 21 Days* is the first complete hands-on tutorial for working with the Java language and class libraries to create applets for Web pages and full-fledged applications. *Teach Yourself Java* covers the beta and 1.0 Java API (as supported by Netscape 2.0) and contains complete information about most aspects of Java development, including the language itself, the Abstract Window Toolkit class libraries, sounds and animation techniques, and technical details about packages, interfaces and the Java virtual machine. It comes with a CD-ROM that includes the complete Java development release for UNIX and Windows NT/95 platforms, plus all the examples from the book (see Figure 16-18).

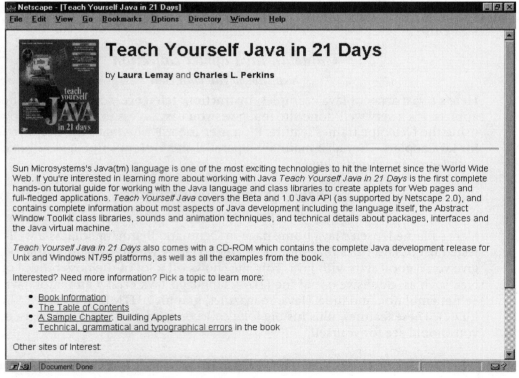

Figure 16-18

Hollywood Online

http://www.hollywood.com/movies/video.html

This site is fabulous! I could hardly stay focused on researching this book—it's a lot of fun. Its huge collection of photos, sound bites, and video clips come from the latest Hollywood hit movies, and you'll hardly find a richer source for photos, sound, and video. The photos are available in GIF and JPEG. Sound is available in four formats (AU, WAV, RA, and Macintosh). Videos are available in two formats (MOV and AVI). This site is a preview of what the Web one day will bring us, with full-length, on-line videos and instant access. It's a primitive preview, that's for sure, but the Web could move way past this in but a few years. Remember this URL, because one day it might replace your Blockbuster card.

Ear-Chives

http://www.geocities.com/Hollywood/1158/earchive.html

The audio clips on this site are taken from popular movies and television shows (see Figure 16-19). All files are in WAV format. Most were recorded at 11KHz mono, but all files have been run through digital reprocessing to enhance quality. Use these files to attach your favorite sounds or sayings to Windows events, objects, or dialog boxes, using sound utilities like Icon Hear-It or the Windows Sound System. Of course, you'll need to consider copyright issues before offering these on your Web site. The collection increases constantly, so check back often and enjoy!

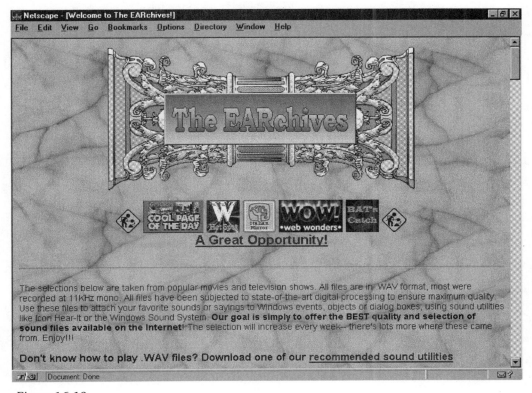

Figure 16-19

17
Web servers

ALL NETWORKS are based on *client-server* technology. Clients receive information from servers. Thus, during most of your time on the Internet you're working in the client mode. But you couldn't spend one second as a client without a server on the other end. My thanks go to everyone who establishes and maintains a Web server because without them our Web browsers would be worthless. So, thank you.

In this closing chapter I'll give you a look behind the scenes at the servers that form the underpinning of our World Wide Web. You can skip this chapter if you prefer, because you don't *need* to know about servers to surf the Web; but if you are involved in providing Web content, this chapter will give you some valuable insights into structuring your organization's Web server. Even if you're not responsible for Web content, this chapter will help you understand how Web material is made available for your Web browser.

Client-server basics

If you use a PC that's attached to a local area network (LAN), you might already have a feel for client-server technology. The basic idea is built around a central computer (server) that is powerful enough to transmit (serve) large amounts of electronic information. Once a server is available, other computers that can receive the transmitted data (clients) can be connected to the server. A server basically is a passive system. It doesn't do anything unless asked by a client to serve up some information. When asked, it serves the requested information, then returns to a passive mode until it receives another client request.

For example, on an office LAN a client computer can use WordPerfect to request that the server send a word processing file. The client computer then can edit the file and save it on the server. In chapter 1 I referred to Netscape as a read-only word processor that you use to read downloaded documents. So, the Web differs from an office LAN in that you cannot save documents on Web servers. Other than that, the Web really isn't much more complex at its core than a typical office LAN. (TCP/IP experts might groan at hearing such a huge simplification, but from a user's point of view, it's true.)

The main difference between the World Wide Web network and an office local area network is small, technically, but has enormous consequences. That difference is that the Web lets clients request information from servers anywhere in the world. That's one small step for computer technology, one giant leap for mankind.

You've seen throughout this book the giant leap. Now I'll close by looking at the small step that makes the World Wide Web possible.

On-site versus off-site

There are two basic divisions of Web servers: on-site servers maintained at facilities owned by your organization, and off-site servers maintained at the facilities of a Web service provider. With either option, your Web server will have a direct connection to the Internet that will enable anyone in the world to access your Web pages. Thus, your Web visitors will not be able to tell which of these server options your organization uses. Visitors simply enter into their Web browser your URL and your pages appear.

If you work in a small organization, especially a home-based business or a sole proprietorship, you're not likely to maintain your own Web servers and the required, dedicated Internet connection. The necessary capital equipment could represent a large portion of your organization's budget, and you simply can't afford to put your business on hold while you learn to set up a Web site that can handle financial transactions. Even after the initial setup, a Web server will require ongoing maintenance that will drain your resources. Hence, most small organizations—and an increasing number of medium-sized organizations—opt to rent server space from a Web provider.

Web Trends

While off-site Web servers reduce your headache potential if you're responsible for a Web site, on-site servers have several advantages. One of those advantages is the ability to track the visitor traffic on your server. A marketing department can learn a great deal about customer demographics by profiling a site's visitors.

There are several software packages on the market that will enable a Web server to log and report on a large variety of information about its visitor traffic:

- Which pages generate the most interest
- Which products/services are the most popular
- Advertising trends and effectiveness
- Geographic regions: local, national, international
- Top-level domain activity: commercial, education, military, and government
- Traffic patterns by time-of-day and day-of-week
- Type of Web browsers used by visitors
- Other sites that have cross-linked to your server

An application called *WebTrends* can create log files on your server and automatically produce reports that include statistical information that is enhanced with color graphs (see Figure 17-1). It can show you user activity by market, interest level, browser type, and whether the traffic is local, national, or international. Its report generation is flexible, and can be tailored extensively to filter the information it captures to suit your organization's needs.

WebTrends is a user-friendly Windows application that runs on Windows 3.x, 95, or NT. It's compatible with Netscape, NCSA, WebSite, Quarterdeck, Cbuilder, Microsoft, Oracle, Emwac, UNIX, Windows 3.x, Windows 95, Windows NT, and Macintosh servers. For more information, visit their Web site at *www.WebTrends.com*.

Organizations that are large enough to have a full-time computer staff might opt to have the staff set up and maintain an on-site Web server. I have, however, worked with very large organizations that have used off-site Web servers. There are no fixed rules, and your organization's solution will depend on many factors. The focus of the rest of this chapter is to help you find the best Web server solution for your organization.

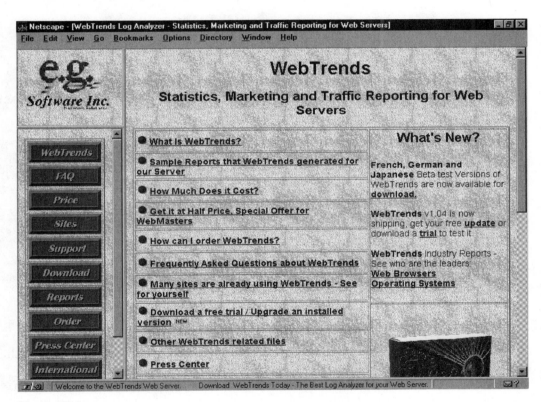

Figure 17-1

Off-site Web servers

In small organizations, you might choose to call in the experts and let them set up a Web site while you continue to generate revenue doing what you do best. A start-up fee, a base monthly fee, and transactions fees can quickly give your organization a turn-key Web site. Alternatively, you can get a provider to make available some server space and then you can create your Web site totally on your own. In between these two extremes you'll find services that assist you in creating your Web site. Hence, there are three distinct types of off-site Web service:

- Full-service Web providers that handle everything for you (see Figure 17-2)
- Consulting-service Web providers that provide the site as well as extensive design, authoring, and publishing services
- Do-it-yourself Web service providers that merely provide access to a Web server for pages you create.

Let's look at each of these three options.

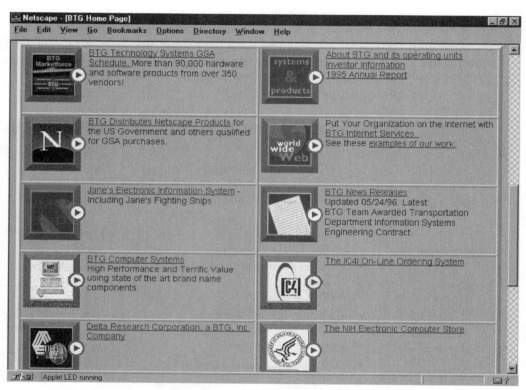

Figure 17-2

Full-service Web providers

Here are three typical solution options with approximate costs as quoted in the spring of 1996. Note that these costs are for complete *turn-key* systems, and assume that the provider does all of the work for you. You would give them a vision of your organization's Web site, and they would turn it into reality.

- Basic Web Presence—E-mail account via a PPP or an ISDN connection, up to five Web pages with one scanned graphic per page, a hyperlink on your Web page to your e-mail, and registration of your own domain name. This would not include any commerce server encoding. Setup price guideline: $500. You then would need to pay for your Web server space, which can be rented for as little as $20 per month.
- Enhanced Web Presence—All Basic features, up to 10 Web pages with 10 scanned images anywhere within those pages, one hyperlinked image map, an

autoresponder mail system for information inquiries, and one form page. Price guideline: $2,000 to $3,000. A site on this level still would easily work on a $20 per month rented server, but the autoresponder might add $5 to $10 per month per account.

- Virtual Store Front—All Enhanced features, up to 30 Web pages with 20 scanned images anywhere within those pages, two hyperlinked image maps, four form pages, a high-capacity server, and commerce server encryption. Price guideline: $6,000 to $10,000. A site this extensive still would fit on a $20 per month Web server rental, but might require renting a commerce server, which could add $25 per month.

NET TIP If you use an off-site service and have them register your domain name, be absolutely certain that they register it in your name. Without your knowing it, a Web service provider could register your domain in their name. If you ever decide to switch providers, they might demand a hefty fee to give up the domain name that you thought was yours all along. Don't leave this to chance—your business could hinge on it.

Consulting-service Web providers

A consulting-service provider also will register your domain name and set up your Web server without any effort on your part. They will interview your organization to establish its Web needs, and then they'll help you create and implement your Web site. Their responsibility will include guiding you through creating a user-friendly site. They will have automated software to streamline publishing your Web pages and performing updates as you need them. A service such as this can cost between $50 and $250 per month.

One of the best consulting-service providers, GoSite, charges $189 per month to maintain your Web site (see Figure 17-3). That might seem high, but they have on staff a team of talented graphic artists who will design and create your logo, hyperlink buttons, and clickable image maps. They'll create everything for you, publish it all on the Web, and maintain it. They'll implement forms that fulfill your needs, and you won't need to know anything at all about programming. A service such as GoSite would be an excellent choice for a small-to-medium company that wants to get on the Web without having to get technical.

Security considerations

What about site security when you use an off-site server? Off-site servers are no less secure than any other server, and they will require a password to gain access. Average users will not be able to get into your Web site, but a good hacker probably could break your password and gain access to your site. The good news is that they probably won't, because there's no profit.

If a hacker gained access to your off-site server, he or she could modify or wipe out any or all of your files. The question is "Why?" This simply isn't what hackers do, so your off-site Web site files are probably as safe as anything on the Internet.

There is no way a hacker can go through an off-site server to gain access to your on-site network, so your home office data is absolutely safe. Unless you keep sensitive, secret material on your off-site Web server, there's nothing of value for a hacker to hack. Even if someone did erase all of your Web site files, you would just change your password and upload the files again from your local computer.

Do-it-yourself Web service provider

A do-it-yourself provider will register your domain name and perform the server setup, but you'll need to understand enough about Web publishing to create and upload your own Web pages. If you want forms or clickable image maps, you'll need to learn how to implement those yourself. At this level, the provider is only responsible for storing your files and maintaining a reliable Internet connection for your site's access to the Web. This level of service is the least inexpensive: $25 for domain registration and server setup, then $20 per month.

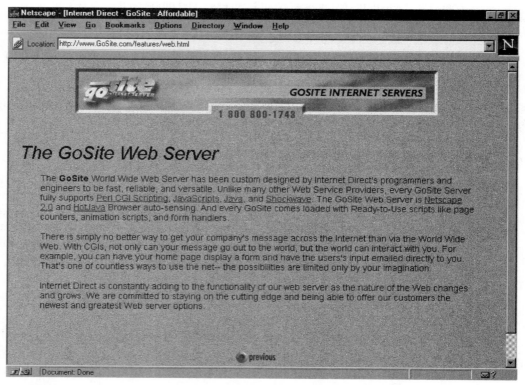

Figure 17-3

One excellent do-it-yourself Web provider, Digiweb, charges $20 per month for up to 25 megabytes of data, unlimited access, an anonymous FTP site so you can let your users download files, e-mail rerouting so you can use your own domain name for e-mail, and a private FTP site that you can use to exchange secure files within your organization. Digiweb (see Figure 17-4) is an excellent choice for a small company with people who know how to create a simple site, or that can contract with a Web consultant to create the site.

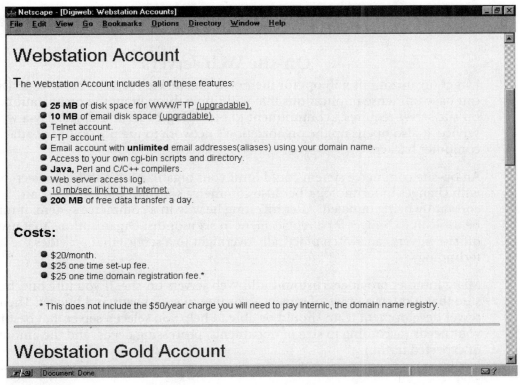

Figure 17-4

NET TIP

If you use a do-it-yourself service you'll need to give them a domain name to request on your behalf, but how do you know what's available? That's easy; just check directly with the InterNIC Whois server at *http://rs.internic.net/cgi-bin/whois*. This page will check any domain name you enter and report whether or not the domain name is in use, and will list the current owner if it is.

Off-site server summary

You can see that if you are able to create your own Web pages, Web server space can cost as little as $20 per month, and a commerce server option adds only $25 per month. You'll have to perform your own Web page editing work, or pay additional charges to have your Web pages created.

The consulting-service option is an excellent choice for the average small-to-medium-sized organization. The monthly costs are higher, but you won't need to locate and hire a consultant to create graphics or help with technical details. Be a careful shopper if you choose this option. Paying more might only mean paying more, or paying more could buy you some valuable expertise. I've seen services priced at $250 per month that provided no more value than Digiweb offers at $20 per month. On the other hand, a company such as GoSite provides a spectrum of valuable services for $189 per month.

The full-service option might require some deep pockets and a high probability that the site will produce measurable revenue returns. This level of service is a viable choice only for large organizations that are teetering on the edge of needing their own on-site Web servers. So, because we're close to the edge anyway, let's move on to the on-site server options.

On-site Web servers

Larger organizations will opt for their own on-site Web servers; but this decision can have immense implications that will ripple throughout the organization. An on-site server requires a commitment to providing 24-hour-a-day, 7-day-a-week service. It also opens up the organization's network to the possibility of attack by computer hackers.

An on-site commerce system could limit your organization's ability to keep pace with changes in technology, because commerce software and hardware are constantly being updated. After investing heavily in a commerce system, it might be difficult to budget for a replacement in six months. Organizations that use off-site servers can switch practically overnight to a service that provides the latest technology.

Many Internet providers custom-build Web servers on-site. If you hire one, be sure that it offers a range of servers according to your needs and budget. Their server development team should be able to help you select a server that best fits your needs (according to size of documents, processing needs, and the amount of expected traffic).

Firewalls

An on-site Web server invites the world into your system. If your Web server is connected directly to your office LAN, a hacker can gain access to any file on your system. Obviously, this is a risk you cannot take. One security solution is to switch to off-site servers. Another solution is to keep the Web server completely isolated from your network, but this causes problems because it makes it difficult to maintain the Web server, and because almost everyone on your LAN will want Internet access.

Thus, the most common security solution is to have a firewall between your Web server and your office network. Firewalls are computers that filter Internet traffic to prevent unauthorized access into your local network. (See chapter 12, Internet Security.) Once a firewall is in place, the dirty net (Internet) is on one side and the clean, filtered net (your LAN) is on the other.

Firewalls come in two basic varieties: turn-key systems, and add-on software. A turn-key system includes a computer that is installed between your network and your Internet router. Add-on software requires you to install firewall software on an existing computer that is installed between your network and your Internet router.

This is fast-moving technology, so I won't review specific products. In researching this book I found that all of the major firewall products available were easy to install, easy to maintain, had user-friendly graphic interfaces, did not cause any measurable throughput delays, and—best of all—they all passed lab tests with no vulnerabilities. So, as long as you stick with major-brand firewall products, an on-site Web server shouldn't present any major security problems.

In addition to security considerations, your Web servers need to be closely monitored to ensure that all of the documents are being served with speed and efficiency. Every server needs its own backup power supply, a regular, automated backup system, and an assigned technician to make sure that the server remains up and running at all times. If your company can handle these functions on-site, and has the resources for the capital investments, then you won't need to contract for an off-site server.

If you have input into the server purchasing option, I highly recommend that you steer the purchase toward a server that can run Windows NT. The Apple servers, however, also are an excellent choice and make available some very powerful, user-friendly Web server software. The choice of Web server software might directly affect your ability to create, update, and maintain your organization's Web server, so do some research and don't be swayed by marketing hype.

Web server software

In the early days of the Web, putting up a Web server required the computer expertise of a professional. The learning curve required to create a Web site was too great for mainstream users. Fortunately, an explosion of Windows-based Web server software has dramatically simplified Web site creation. For further information you can rely upon the Continuing Education section at the end of this chapter, but here I'll give you an overview of a couple of user-friendly Web servers.

FastTrack Server 2.0

Netscape sells an entry-level Web server called FastTrack Server 2.0. Naturally it's not as feature-laden as applications like WebSite (see review below), but it costs less and might satisfy the needs of a smaller organization with limited computing expertise. Check in the Continuing Education section for more information on Netscape Web servers.

WebSite

O'Reilly Associates' WebSite (see Figure 17-5) is a powerful Web server tool for small companies (and even for individuals) who want to create a Web site. All your organization needs to become part of the World Wide Web is a full-time Internet connection, a dedicated PC, and the WebSite software! The advent of Windows NT and Windows 95 has ushered in the era of mainstream Web servers.

Because of applications such as WebSite, you don't have to be a UNIX expert to put your organization on the Web. Now, using a drag-and-drop interface and familiar Windows functions, any savvy computer user can create and put up a Web site. WebSite includes CGI features that enable your site to display up-to-the-second information from databases, spreadsheets, or just about any document on your site. With WebSite you might easily be able to put up a high-quality Web site that includes text, graphics, and sound.

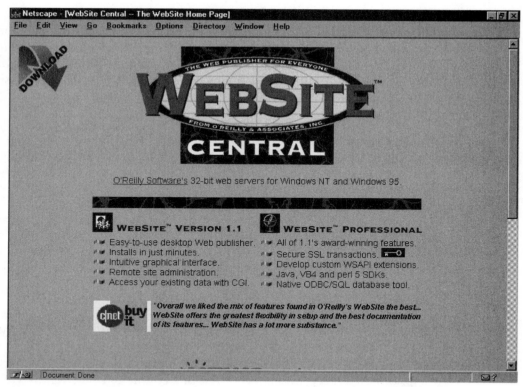

Figure 17-5

Internet Connections

Client-server technology is worthless without a connection between the client and the server. In your office, the connection is provided by a LAN. In cyberspace, the connection is provided by the Internet. Unlike LANs, however, Internet connections come in a wide variety of speeds, with enormous differences between the extremes.

About the slowest Internet connection speed you'll see is 14.4Kbps (kilobits per second) via a modem over a standard phone line. The fastest commonly used Internet connection speed is about 1.54 Mbps (megabits per second) via a T-1 line. Providing a fast Internet connection to visitors with slow modems won't help them much, but you'll increasingly find visitors using ISDN, satellite links, T-1 lines, and cable modems. These users are going to be very quick to abandon a slow, unresponsive site, so a slow Internet connection could cost you customers.

If your organization maintains its own on-site Web servers, then you might not have much control over the speed your site offers to visitors. Still, it's a good idea to check with your system administrator. Connection prices have dropped dramatically and continue to drop. Getting your organization to shop around could give you an enormously faster line for the same fee you're currently paying. For example, T-1 lines have come into the reach of many organizations that could only have afforded a 56Kbps line a year earlier.

If you're renting off-site server space, then find out what kind of Internet connection your Web provider is using. Be prepared and willing to switch if you find they're lagging behind the competition. Insist on multiple T-1 lines as a minimum, and move your site if they give you excuses instead of increased speed.

Establishing your own domain name

Once all the elements are in place—the server, the software, and an Internet connection—your site must become registered on the Internet so visitors can find it easily.

If your Web URL uses the name of your Internet service provider, then your success depends on that provider's continued success. For example, let's say you use fly-by-night.com. They would create a directory for you on their server so that your Web URL would be www.fly-by-night.com/~yourcompany. Your clients, customers, associates, and friends might have difficulty finding you if fly-by-night.com goes out of business, is bought out, or if you get an on-site server.

However, if you register your own domain name, then your Web URL always will be www.yourcompany.com regardless of what server you use. As long as your site remains within the same country, your URL will never have to be changed.

Getting your own domain name registered takes several weeks, and your Internet provider might charge you for the service (typically between $25–$100), but it's a wise business investment. The InterNIC also charges a registration fee—currently $100 for the first two years, then $50 per year after that. Some people have paid their service provider $100, and then received a bill from the InterNIC for $100 that made them believe they'd been struck by a cyberspace scam. It's no scam. Both fees are legitimate charges by two separate entities that both must perform work to register your domain name.

An important business tool

The Internet actually exchanges messages using cryptic, numbered addresses that consist of four numbers separated by periods. They're called dotted quads because they look like a quad of numbers separated by dots: 198.137.240.100.

Because none of us want to remember dotted-quad addresses, the Internet ties these numbers to plain-language addresses and stores them as matched sets. For example, the dotted-quad in the last paragraph represents whitehouse.gov (see Figure 17-6), which is much easier to remember. When you use a domain name address, the Internet converts it to its associated dotted-quad, and then uses the dotted-quad address. Computers are comfortable calling the White House 198.137.241.100.

Figure 17-6

Today a tailored domain name is practically expected if your business's Internet presence is to be taken seriously; so you need one for the good of your business image.

Any dotted quad can be assigned to any domain name, and that's the secret to having a long-lived Web address; only the dotted quad points to a specific computer. If you switch service providers, you can get your domain name reassigned to the dotted quad of the new system, and your Web address and e-mail addresses won't change. Only the Internet look-up table will change and no one sees that anyway, so your company can have the same e-mail addresses forever even if you change servers and get a different dotted-quad.

Creating your Web site on a rented server

You don't have to worry about understanding dotted quads. Your Web service provider will handle the technical details. They will register your domain, set up your Web server, and create an empty root directory into which you can upload your files. Once you're notified that the site exists, you can use the FTP software to create, rename, and delete sub-directories as often as you desire and then to upload files when you're ready.

Your Web server space will be protected by a password, so the public only will have access to download Web pages. Your Web service provider most likely will also set up a password-protected FTP site for you that you can use to exchange and distribute files privately over the Internet. Most providers also include a public FTP site that you can use to let visitors use anonymous FTP to download files from you.

Maintaining an off-site Web server

Once everything is in place, it's time to transfer your HTML Web pages onto your Web server. If your server is on-site and attached to your local network, then this will be a breeze. You might need to observe some firewall precautions, but even then uploading your Web pages will be a snap.

Uploading files to an off-site Web server is a little bit trickier. You'll have to establish an Internet connection between the server and the computer on which you developed your Web site. Fortunately, making such a connection also is a snap. And once the connection is established, the actual transfer process is equally simple.

Overview of FTP

The backbone of file transfers on the Internet is the File Transfer Protocol (FTP). Many Internet users have used FTP to download an incredibly vast collection of computer files. But FTP is a two-way street, so you also can use it to upload files such as your Web pages.

FTP can consume large amounts of Internet bandwidth and contribute to slowing down the system for everyone. If you plan to transfer a lot of large files, consider the time of day. Try to avoid site maintenance during the peak of business days— from about noon on the East Coast until about 1 p.m. on the West Coast. In the early morning, late at night, or over weekends, the Internet is less busy.

It's getting better all the time

HotDog Pro includes a built-in FTP feature that automatically publishes an entire Web site project in a single process (see Figure 17-7). HotDog lets you organize your work into units called *projects* that consist of HTML pages and graphics. A single button launches the FTP process and lets you choose to upload one file, all open files, or an entire project (including all of its directories). If you use HotDog, you might not need a stand-alone FTP client to transfer documents to your Web site.

Transferring documents to your Web site

Some Web service providers, especially the full-service variety, will handle the uploading of your Web pages. Often providers place restrictions on how many times uploading can be performed—some only permit one update per month! Others limit you to a few updates each month, and only permit those updates during slow traffic periods. I do not recommend such a restricted service. Things change so fast on the Internet that you need to have unlimited, instant update access.

If you've got a reliable Internet connection, you'll be able to maintain your off-site Web space as easily as if it were on a local network, and you won't need to wait for your service provider to do it on their schedule. Once the FTP connection is established, you can upload files, test the site, edit the files, upload

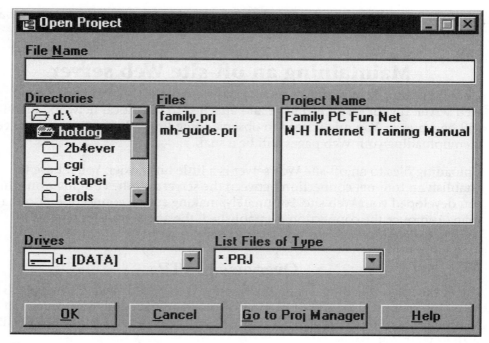

Figure 17-7

them again, and retest—all during the same session. It will appear almost as if it's all happening on your local computer.

WS_FTP

The Netscape Navigator 2.0 has an FTP upload feature, but it's best for occasional use. If you're maintaining a Web site, you'll want a full-featured FTP application (see Figure 17-8). You can download for free the best FTP client available by entering *ftp://ftp.csra.net* into Netscape. Once you're connected, change the host directory to *pub/win3*, then download the file *ws_ftp.zip* (the 16-bit version for Win 3.x), or change the directory to *pub/win32* and download the file *ws_ftp32a.zip* (the 32-bit version for Windows 95 or Windows NT). You then will have to use pkunzip to uncompress the required files.

WS_FTP can be used with the same Winsock connection that you use with Netscape. For example, if you were using Netscape and wanted to use FTP to upload some files, you can leave Netscape connected. Simply use **ALT+TAB** to change to the Program Manager and start WS_FTP. When you're finished with your FTP activity, close WS_FTP and use **ALT+TAB** to return to Netscape. The following Hands-On lesson shows you exactly how this would be done.

FTP Update techniques

You quickly will be able to learn the pattern to editing, updating, and testing your Web pages. It's a simple process that will become nearly automatic because you probably will repeat it countless times. I'll show you the basic process in a Hands-On exercise format. Even though you're not likely to do this exercise now, reading the steps will give you a good overview.

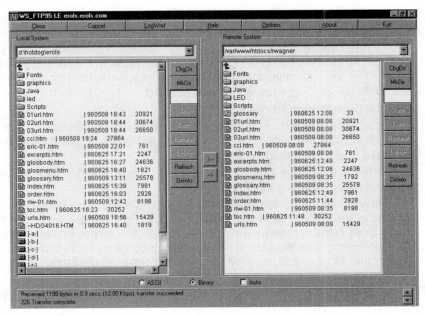

Figure 17-8

Hands On

Objective: **Learn to update a Web site via the FTP.**

❏ Establish an Internet TCP/IP connection.

❏ Start Netscape.

❏ Start WS_FTP.

❏ Start an HTML editor.

❏ Open or create an HTML Web page.

   If you edit the page, be sure you save the changes before moving on to the preview stage.

❏ Preview the Web page with Netscape.

   NOTE: On dedicated HTML editors this involves no more than clicking a preview button that automatically loads the current Web page into your browser.

   If you use WordPerfect's Internet Publisher or Word's Internet Assistant, you'll have to use their preview procedures. Use **ALT+TAB** to switch to Netscape.

   If you see a need for more editing, switch back to your HTML editor, then make and save the changes. Return to Netscape to preview the changes.

   Repeat the process of switching between your browser and your HTML editor until you're finished editing. You now are ready to upload the page (or pages).

❏ Use **ALT+TAB** to switch to WS_FTP.

❏ Click on **Connect** to open the Session Profile dialog box.

   This might open the dialog box for you automatically.

❏ Enter a **Profile Name**.

❏ Enter the **Host Name** address.

   This will be the name of your Web server. If you use an off-site provider, this will not match your domain name.

❏ Set **Host Type** to **automatic detect**.

   Use **automatic detect** unless your provider has given you specific instructions to set it to something else.

Web servers ◀

❑ Enter a **User ID** and a **Password**.

❑ Enter a directory string into **Remote Host** if your provider has given you instructions.

> Many Web service providers have their login software handle the directory switching for you. All you need to do is log in and you'll be taken to the correct directory. If this doesn't happen automatically, then you'll need a specific directory from your provider.

❑ Enter the directory of your home page in **Local PC**.

❑ Check the **Save Password** dialog box.

> If security is a concern, of course you might leave this unchecked. If no one else has access to your computer, you can safely check this box to speed future connections.

❑ Click **Save** to save the setup information.

> In the future you only will need to click on this entry again, then click on **OK**.

❑ Click **OK** to establish the connection.

> You now will be connected via FTP to your Web site. There's a good chance that you will be in a directory above your actual Web site. For example, you might see a list of directories in the right window. Typically the directory on this list called public_html is the location for your Web home page. You might create your own directory structure under this. Most users keep their graphics in a separate directory.

❑ Double-click on **public_html** if you're not already in it.

> Now your Web site is in the right window and your Web pages, saved on your local PC, are in the left window.

❑ Click on your home page in the left window.

> The file you want is typically called *index.htm*. You can transfer several files in one pass if you'll hold down a CTRL key and click on multiple files in the left window.

❑ Click on the **right arrow** between the two windows.

> Wait for the transfer to complete. After the last file transfers, you'll see the directory in the right window be updated.

> NOTE: Compare the file sizes in the left and right windows because sometimes files are truncated during transfer. If all file sizes match exactly, then you can be pretty sure you've had a clean transfer.

❑ Use **ALT+TAB** to switch to Netscape.

❑ Load your home page.

> If you see a need for changes at this point, you'll have to make them, upload the new pages, then retest them in your browser. Let's do that now.

❑ Use **ALT+TAB** to switch to your HTML editor.

❑ Edit your home page as needed.

❑ Click **File, Save** or click the **Save** button to save the changes.

❑ Use **ALT+TAB** to switch to WS_FTP.

❑ Click the **Refresh** button next to the left window.

❑ Highlight the changed file in the left window.

❑ Click on the **right arrow** between the two windows.

> Wait for the transfer to complete. After the file transfers, you'll see the updated directory in the right window. Compare the two file sizes.

❑ Use **ALT+TAB** to return to Netscape.

❑ Press **CTRL+R** or click **View, Reload** to reload the page.

> This is necessary even if you had navigated to another page before doing the update, because Netscape caches pages you visit each session and loads the cached pages if you return during the same session. Thus, if you return to the page you just changed, you won't see the changes because Netscape will be displaying its cached copy. Because Netscape doesn't know you just changed the page, you'll have to use the Reload command to force Netscape to download the page again.

Once you get the pattern of it you'll be able to freely edit, load, and test your Web site by using **ALT+TAB** to switch between your HTML editor, WS_FTP, and your Web browser. Remember to use the reload command every time you return to your browser after uploading files to the site via the FTP.

Distributing files from your Web server

FTP is a two-way street on the information highway. This means you can let users download files from your site. You might make available via FTP such items as spreadsheets with your prices or rates, brochures, instructions, maps and directions, or product specification sheets. HTML makes this process simple on both ends. It will be easy for you to implement in HTML, and your users can get your files by clicking a standard hypertext link.

You will give your visitors access to selected file by using an *anonymous FTP*. With anonymous FTP, your visitors will use a login ID of "Anonymous" and their password will be their e-mail address. Of course, this isn't actually a password, because any e-mail address will work and your system will not know if a user enters a bogus address. Most visitors, however, will use their correct e-mail address.

Check the HTML specifications or the instructions with your HTML editor to find out how to include an FTP hyperlink in a Web page. Check with your Web service provider for the exact location of your site's anonymous before you write the HTML code. Then note the exact names of the files you make available. This is important, because when you include an FTP hyperlink, every character must be exactly correct; your visitors will not be browsing in your FTP directory. Thus, they will not be able look around and figure out what you meant to say. If the directory or the filename is wrong in the link, then the transfer will fail.

FTP filenames

Most Web servers will handle files that cannot be used by a standard IBM PC clone running Microsoft Windows 3.x or DOS. Remember that Windows 3.x and DOS are limited to filenames of eight-dot-three. Windows 95, Windows NT, and UNIX can handle much longer filenames. When downloaded to the older systems, the filenames will be truncated, and they might have odd character substitutions. Limiting the names of your FTP-downloadable files to the eight-dot-three pattern will help your visitors who have older systems.

Well, I've taken you from start to finish. Thanks for coming the whole way. Your patience, diligence, and hard work will pay off many times over as your work and your personal life become evermore enmeshed with the Internet—or will the Internet become more enmeshed with you? Probably both will happen at the same time. The bottom line is that nearly everything you do from now on will be affected in some way by the Internet, and you now understand it well enough to be a productive citizen of cyberspace. I'll see you on-line.

Continuing Education

Criteria for choosing a Web service provider
http://www.digex.net/papers/webhost

This site is subtitled "What You Should Know Before Renting Space on the Web." It was created by Joe Peck, Internet Server Product Manager at Digital Express Group, Inc. (DIGEX). Joe covers all aspects of making a Web server decision, including designing, converting, and creating the information content for your Web site. He discusses installing and operating the Web server that will allow your visitors to access your Web site content. It's written in a context that will help you choose the right option for your organization. One page is a checklist of important factors in the Web server decision-making process that you can use to be sure you've considered all of the appropriate angles.

Netscape
http://home.netscape.com/home/how-to-create-web-services.html

You might find all the help you need with Web servers right inside your familiar Netscape Navigator Web browser. Simply click on **Help**, then on **How to Create Web Services**. Netscape will automatically take you to the location on its own site that discusses setting up and maintaining a Web site. Of course it's got a definite slant toward you using Netscape services, but the principles are as solid as you'll find.

WebTrends
http://www.WebTrends.com

WebTrends is a Web traffic analysis tool that can create log files on your server and automatically produce reports with statistical information and color graphs. It can show you user activity by market, interest level, browser type, and local, national, or international scope. WebTrend's report generation is flexible and can be tailored extensively to filter the information it captures to suit your organization's needs. It's compatible with nearly all Web servers and operating systems.

O'Reilly and Associates
http://website.ora.com

O'Reilly and Associates has emerged as a powerhouse of technology on the Internet. They've published a library of more than 80 excellent technical reference guides that delve into details far more deeply that I have in this book. Actually, mainstream users might find the topics covered in this site to be too technical, but if you are performing or managing the hands-on work involved in publishing your organization's Web site, then you absolutely *must* place O'Reilly's URL on your Bookmark List.

Top 10 copyright myths

HERE'S AN ANSWER to common myths about copyrights as applied to the Internet. It was created by Brad Templeton, the publisher for ClariNet Communications Corporation's news service and covers issues related to e-mail, news, research, and Usenet posting. ClariNet, founded in 1989, is the Internet's first and largest electronic newspaper.

Please note that while most of the principles covered here are universal in Berne copyright signatory nations, some are derived from Canadian and U.S. law. Brad created this document to clear up some common misconceptions about intellectual property law that often are seen on the Internet. It is not intended to be a complete treatise on all the nuances of the subject.

Another note: **do not e-mail Brad Templeton for legal advice**—use other resources or consult a lawyer. You can, however, check out Brad's personal Web page at ClariNet: *www.clari.net/brad* (see Figure A-1).

Copyright myths

Here's the text of Brad's 10 Big Copyright Myths, followed by a summary of the main points. Be sure and check out the Continuing Education section at the end of the chapter, in which we point you to some other Internet sources on copyright issues.

1. If it doesn't have a copyright notice, it's not copyrighted

This was true in the past, but today almost all major nations follow the Berne copyright convention. For example, in the U.S., almost everything created privately and originally after April 1, 1989 is copyrighted and protected whether it has a notice or not. The default you should assume for other people's works is that they are copyrighted and may not be copied unless you *know* otherwise. There are some old works that lost protection without notice, but frankly you should not risk it unless you know for sure.

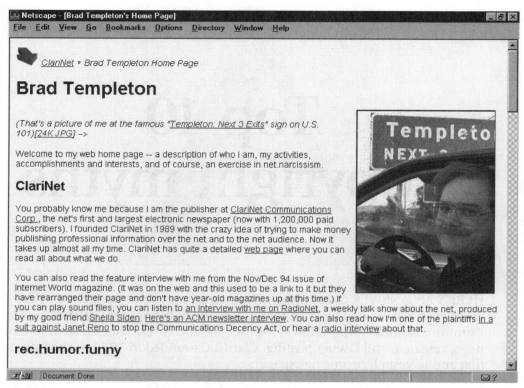

Figure A-1

It is true that a notice strengthens the protection, by warning people and by allowing one to get more and different damages, but it is not necessary. If it looks copyrighted, you should assume it is.

This applies to pictures, too. You may not scan pictures from magazines and post them to the Internet, and if you come upon something unknown, you shouldn't post that either.

The correct form for a copyright notice is:

Copyright (dates) by (copyright holder).

You can use the copyright symbol instead of the word Copyright, but (C) has never been given legal force. The phrase All Rights Reserved used to be required in some nations, but is now not needed.

2. If I don't charge for it, it's not a violation

Absolutely false. Whether you charge can affect the damages awarded in court, but that's essentially the only difference. It's still a violation if you give it away—and there can still be heavy damages if you hurt the commercial value of a protected property.

3. If it's posted to Usenet, it's in the public domain

False. Nothing is in the public domain anymore unless the owner explicitly puts it in the public domain. Explicitly, as in you have a note from the copyright holder stating "I grant this to the public domain." If not those exact words, then words very much like them.

Some argue that posting to the Usenet implicitly grants permission to everybody to copy the posting within fairly wide bounds, and others feel that Usenet is an automatic store-and-forward network where all the thousands of copies made are done at the command (rather than the consent) of the poster. This is a matter of some debate, but even if the former is true (and in this writer's opinion we should all pray it isn't true) it simply would suggest posters are implicitly granting permissions for the sort of copying one might expect when one posts to Usenet, and in no case is this a placement of material into the public domain. Furthermore, it is very difficult for an implicit licence to supersede an explicitly stated licence of which the copier was aware.

Note that all this assumes that the poster had the right to post the item in the first place. If the poster didn't, then all the copies are pirated, and no implied license or theoretical reduction of the copyright can take place.

Copyrights can expire after a long time, putting something into the public domain, and there are some fine points on this issue regarding older copyright law versions. However, none of this applies to an original article posted to Usenet.

Note that granting something to the public domain (PD) is a complete abandonment of all rights. You can't make something PD for non-commercial use. If your work is PD, other people can even modify one byte and put their name on it.

4. My posting was just fair use!

The fair use exemption to copyright law was created to allow things such as commentary, parody, news reporting, research, and education about copyrighted works without the permission of the author. Intent and damage to the commercial value of the work are important considerations. Are you reproducing an article from the New York Times because you needed to in order to criticize the quality of the New York Times, because you couldn't find time to write your own story, or because you didn't want your readers to have to pay to log onto the on-line services with the story or buy a copy of the paper? The first probably is fair use; the others are not.

Fair use is almost always restricted to a short excerpt and is almost always attributed. (One should not use more of the work than is necessary to make the commentary.) It should not harm the commercial value of the work—in the sense of people no longer needing to buy it (which is another reason why reproduction of the entire work generally is forbidden).

Note that most inclusion of text in Usenet follow-ups is for commentary and reply, and it doesn't damage the commercial value of the original posting (if it has any) and as such it is fair use. Fair use isn't an exact doctrine, either. The court decides if the right to comment overrides the copyright on an individual basis in each case.

There have been cases that go beyond the bounds of what's been covered here, but in general they don't apply to the typical Internet misclaim of fair use. It's a risky defense to attempt.

5. If you don't defend your copyright, you lose it

False. Copyright is effectively never lost these days, unless explicitly given away. You may be thinking of trademarks, which can be weakened or lost if not defended.

6. Somebody has that name copyrighted

You can't copyright a name or anything short like a name. Titles usually don't qualify, but you could not write a song titled "Everybody's got something to hide except for me and my monkey" (J. Lennon/P. McCartney).

You can't copyright words, but you can trademark them, generally by using them to refer to your brand of a generic type of product or service, like an Apple computer. Apple Computer owns that word as it is applied to computers, even though it is also an ordinary word. Apple Records owns it when applied to music. Neither owns the word on its own, only in context, and owning a mark doesn't mean complete control—see a more detailed treatise on this law for details.

You can't use somebody else's trademark in a way that would unfairly hurt the value of the mark, or in a way that might make people confuse you with the real owner of the mark, or in a way that might allow you to profit from the mark's good name. For example, if I were giving advice on music videos, I would be very wary of trying to label my works with a name like MTV.

7. They can't get me, defendants in court have powerful rights!

Copyright law is mostly civil law. If you violate a copyright you usually would get sued, not charged with a crime. Innocent until proven guilty, is a principle of criminal law, as is proof beyond a reasonable doubt. In copyright suits, these don't apply the same way or at all. It's mostly which side and set of evidence the judge or jury accepts or believes more, though the rules vary based on the type of infringement. In civil cases you can even be made to testify against your own interests.

8. Copyright violation isn't a crime

Actually, recently in the U.S., commercial copyright violation involving more than 10 copies and value of more than $2500 was made a felony, so use caution (at least you get the protections of criminal law.) On the other hand, don't think you're going to get people thrown in jail for posting your e-mail. The courts have much better things to do than that. This is a fairly new, untested statute.

9. It doesn't hurt anybody—in fact it's free advertising

It's up to the owner to decide if they want the free ads or not. If they want them, they will be sure to contact you. Don't rationalize whether it hurts the owner or not; ask them. Usually that's not too hard to do. In times past, ClariNet published the very funny Dave Barry column to a large and appreciative Usenet audience for a fee, but some person didn't ask, forwarded it to a mailing list, got caught, and the newspaper chain that employs Dave Barry pulled the column from the Internet. Even if you can't think of how the author or owner gets hurt, think about the fact that piracy on the Internet hurts everybody who wants a chance to use this wonderful new technology to do more than read other people's flamewars.

10. They e-mailed me a copy, so I can use it

To have a copy is not to have the copyright. All the e-mail you write is copyrighted. However, e-mail is not, unless previously agreed, secret. So you can certainly report on what e-mail you are sent, and reveal what it says. You can even quote parts of it to demonstrate. Frankly, somebody who sues over an ordinary message might well get no damages, because the message has no commercial value, but if you want to stay strictly within the law, you should seek permission.

On the other hand, don't go nuts if somebody posts your e-mail. If it was an ordinary nonsecret personal letter of minimal commercial value with no copyright notice (like 99.9 of all e-mail), you probably won't get any damages if you sue.

In summary

Almost everything written today is copyrighted the moment it's written, and no copyright notice is required.

Copyright is still violated whether you charged money or not, though damages usually increase if you charge money.

Postings to the Internet are not granted to the public domain, and don't grant you any permission to do further copying except perhaps the sort of copying the poster might have expected in the ordinary flow of the Internet.

Fair use is a complex doctrine meant to allow certain valuable social purposes. Ask yourself why you are republishing what you are posting and why you didn't rewrite it in your own words.

Copyright is not lost because you don't defend it; that's a concept from trademark law. The ownership of names is also from trademark law, so don't say somebody has a name copyrighted.

Copyright law is mostly civil law where the special rights of criminal defendants you hear so much about don't apply. Watch out, however, as new laws are moving copyright violation into the criminal realm.

Don't rationalize that you are helping the copyright holder; the Internet has made it easier than ever to secure permission.

Posting e-mail is technically a violation, but revealing facts from e-mail isn't; for almost all typical e-mail, nobody could wring any damages from you for posting it.

Continuing Education

Brad Cox on Electronic Property
http://www.virtualschool.edu/mon/ElectronicProperty.html

Brad Cox is a professor at George Mason University in Fairfax, Virginia. He's the author of *Superdistribution: Objects as Property on the Electronic Frontier*, an in-depth study of the problems of product distribution in the electronic age (see Figure A-2). On the Web home page listed here, Brad covers four different aspects of our cyberspace world: Electronic Commerce, Electronic Money, Electronic Goods, and Electronic Property.

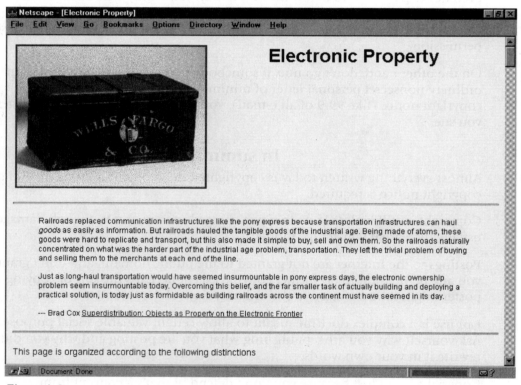

Figure A-2

U.S. Copyright Office Automated Information Service
gopher://marvel.loc.gov/11/copyright

Actual connection to a directory listing within the U.S. copyright office in Washington, D.C. Begin by clicking on the first document on the list, entitled, Introduction to the Copyright Office. After reading it, return to the first page and click on any of the directory folders that you need to access.

The United States Patent and Trademark Office (USPTO) 5

http://www.uspto.gov

The USPTO provides a Web page (see Figure A-3) entitled, Basic Facts About Registering A Trademark. Topics include securing trademark rights, submitting applications, who may apply, how to search for conflicting previously registered trademarks, and rules for using (tm), (SM), and circled R symbols. Some of the information here can help your organization sort out the relationship (or lack thereof) between Internet domain names and registered trademarks.

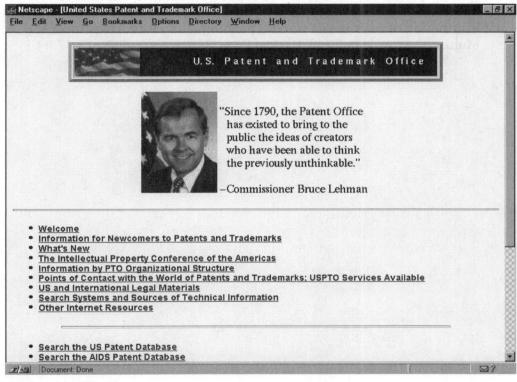

Figure A-3

Cornell University

http://www.law.cornell.edu/topics/copyright.html

This is a comprehensive Web page with hypertext links to just about every aspect of intellectual property law you could ask for. It includes a hypertext version of U.S. copyright law from the Legal Information Institute (LII) and a hypertext version of the Berne international copyright convention.

Copyright Clearance Center Online

http://www.copyright.com

The on-line version of the Copyright Clearance Center, a non-profit organization that provides collective copyright licensing services. They help ease the permissions burdens and consolidate payments rights for organizations of all sizes and types.

Ohio State

http://www.cis.ohio-state.edu/hypertext/faq/usenet/Copyright-FAQ/top.html

A detailed listing of copyright Frequently-Asked-Questions (FAQs), covering many issues including compilation copyright, the intricacies of fair use, and international copyright issues.

Electronic Freedom Frontier's intellectual property law primer

http://www.eff.org/pub/CAF/law/ip-primer

This is a primer written by J. Diane Brinson and Mark F. Radcliffe to help you understand intellectual property law issues as they apply to the development and distribution of multimedia works. The information was derived from the Multimedia Law Handbook (Ladera Press, 340 pages, 1-800-523-3721).

High-speed Internet service

ISDN (Integrated Services Digital Network) is a digital phone service that offers greatly increased speed compared to standard analog phone service. For example, before I got ISDN, the highest speed connection I ever got with my 28.8kbps modem was 21.6kbps. During storms I often connected at only 16.2kbps. With ISDN, I get 115.2kbps every time.

ISDN service may not be available in your area, so check with your local phone company. Remember, even if they say "yes" they might mean "no," because ISDN requires extremely high-quality phone lines and switching equipment. When I got my ISDN service, there was a two-month delay because the phone company discovered that the equipment in my area couldn't handle the rigorous demands of ISDN. They had to perform some major upgrades and system maintenance in my area before ISDN could be installed, and this is not some remote, rural area: This was in the high-tech center of Northern Virginia just outside Washington, D.C., in the same neighborhood with the headquarters of MCI, Sprint, InterNIC, the Internet Society, America On Line, PSI Net, and a host of other cyberspace companies.

Fortunately, everyone I met who was involved in the ISDN program was extremely helpful and very customer-friendly. The local phone company (Bell Atlantic) has a toll-free number to top-notch technical support and configuration help. The hardware vendors have good technical support. Even Microsoft has a section of its Web site dedicated to ISDN (see Figure B-1) at *www.microsoft.com/windows/maps/home.map*.

This chapter will get even a computer novice into using ISDN with Windows 95 pretty easily, but there's a catch: Microsoft only supports ISDN in Windows 95 and Windows NT. If you're using Windows 3.x, you'll need to get the software from a third-party vendor. Your Internet service provider may have the required software and may even bundle it with your ISDN account.

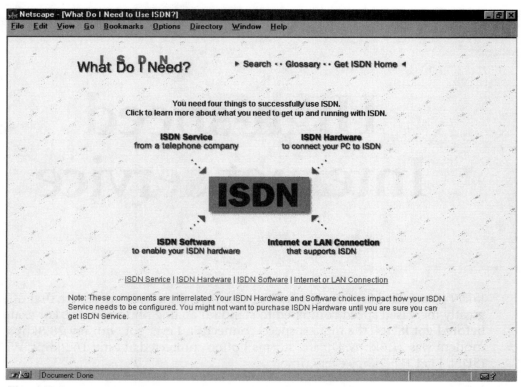

Figure B-1

Bonus speed benefit

Upgrading to ISDN had an unexpected effect on my regular phone line that I still use for my 28.8kbps modem. When Bell Atlantic agreed to set up an ISDN line at my house, it discovered that my area needed a lot of equipment upgrading. After the ISDN service was installed I could see a difference even on my other, analog phone line. Instead of getting connected at 21.6kbps, I now regularly connect at 24.0 or 26.4kbps. So, if your connection speeds fall far short of the 28.8kbps that you expect, have your local phone company check your lines and its equipment to see if some repairs are due.

In case you're wondering why you should care about analog connect speeds after you get ISDN, it's because ISDN service charges by the minute: typically from 2 cents to 4 cents per minute during normal hours. If you're just casually surfing or checking e-mail, there's no reason to waste ISDN connect time. I recommend that you keep your old analog modem and get a switch box to select between the two. Then use the analog modem for routine tasks or for when you expect to be lingering around Web sites, mostly reading and browsing. Save the ISDN charges for when you're doing heavy research or downloading large files.

If you're using Windows 95 and an external terminal adapter, you'll find ISDN an easy and worthwhile switch. Regardless of your equipment and service options, you'll also need to coordinate four different components to be able to surf the Net over an ISDN line:

- ISDN service from your local phone company
- ISDN account with an Internet service provider
- ISDN terminal adapter (TA)
- ISDN software setup

I recommend an external terminal adapter because it will have visible status lights and switches that permit you to recycle the unit off-and-on without shutting down your computer. It's extremely annoying and inefficient to have to shut down all of your software, turn off your computer, and restart everything just because your modem is hung up. With an external modem, you're only delayed a few seconds while you recycle the modem power and log back on. Sure, the external box creates a little more clutter on your desk, but it's well worth the added information and efficiency.

ISDN setup in Windows 95

Windows 95 permits you to easily set up multiple icons for dialing different on-line services. This allows you to set up one icon that dials your analog modem and connects to a low-cost analog account and another icon that dials your ISDN terminal adapter and connects to your ISDN account.

In fact, you probably will create two icons for ISDN because ISDN can use either one channel or two channels over the same phone line. Each channel will get you a data exchange rate of 64kbps and your local phone company will charge you a per-minute fee for each 64kbps channel. Thus, if you use both channels, you connect at 128kbps, but you'll pay a double fee. So, you'll want to create an icon for both 1-channel and 2-channel ISDN.

I'll show you how to create one of each type, using the now-familiar Hands-On format. Before completing these steps, you'll need a terminal adapter connected to your computer and to a working ISDN phone line. These steps are for setting up a Motorola BitSURFR Pro terminal adapter. Windows 95 can handle this installation automatically once the terminal is configured.

Configuring a BitSURFR Pro

One of the biggest setup problems reported by telephone company support staff is that people don't enter the right settings while configuring their BitSURFR. The BitSURFR Pro comes with an application called SURFR Setup, an icon-based, menu-driven utility that simplifies configuration by prompting for all necessary configuration strings in Windows 3.x and Windows 95 (see Figure B-2).

Before installation you'll need to know both of the phone numbers assigned to your ISDN line and your Service Profile Identifiers (SPIDs). During installation, make sure you enter these numbers into yours (assume your new ISDN phone numbers are 555-1234 and 555-1235):

Switch Type: National ISDN

Switch Version: NI-1

SPID for Data Port: 015551234000 (line 1 SPID)

SPID for Voice Port 1: same as above

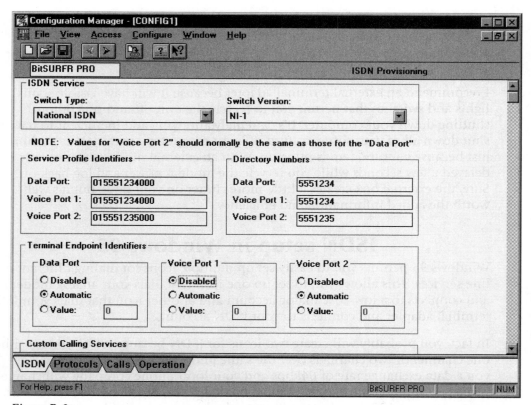

Figure B-2

SPID for Voice Port 2: 015551235000 (line 2 SPID)

Directory Number for Data Port: 5551234

Directory Number for Voice Port 1: 5551234

Directory Number for Voice Port 2: 5551235

TEI for Data Port: Automatic

TEI for Voice Port 1: Disabled

TEI for Voice Port 2: Automatic

When you've entered these numbers, click **Configure, Update Parameters.** After the BitSURFR's lights are through flashing, your configuration is complete. Exit the Configuration Manager and save the configuration settings to a file as prompted. The terminal adapter is now configured for your system, and you're ready to install an ISDN dialer in Windows.

Hands On

Objective: Create a one-channel ISDN dial-up icon.

❏ Begin at your Windows 95 desktop.

Stop! The remaining steps won't work if you *have not* properly configured your BitSURFR using the steps in the sidebar above. If your terminal adapter is configured, then proceed.

❏ Double-click the **My Computer** icon.

❏ Double-click the **Dial-Up Networking** icon.

❏ Double-click the **Make New Connection** icon.

❏ Type *ISDN 1-Channel*.

❏ Select the Motorola BitSURFR Pro from the modem drop-list.

❏ Click **Configure**.

❏ Select the correct Port.

❏ Change the **Maximum speed** window to 115200.

❏ Click the **Connection** tab.

❏ Set **Data bits** to **8**.

❏ Set **Parity** to **None**.

❏ Set **Stop bits** to **1**.

❏ Click **Advanced**.

❏ Check **Use flow control**.

❏ Check **Hardware (RTS/CTS)**.

❏ Click in **Extra Settings**.

> This is the key to making your BitSURFR Pro work. If you have a different terminal adapter, you must get the correct string from the manufacturer or from your ISDN provider's technical support. Without this string, your ISDN won't work.

❏ Type *AT1&C1&D2\Q3A4=0A2=95@BO=1<CR>*

❏ Click **OK, OK, Next.**

> This will take you to the phone number entry screen.

❏ Enter the dial-in phone number for your **ISDN** account.

❏ Click **Finish**.

You now have a one-channel ISDN dial-up icon. This icon will get you a 64kbps ISDN connection.

The next exercise will guide you through creating a 2-channel ISDN dial-up icon. The actual steps are the same, except that in two places (Extra Settings and the phone number) you'll enter slightly modified strings.

Hands On

Objective: **Create a 2-channel ISDN dial-up icon.**

❏ Double-click the **My Computer** icon.

❏ Double-click the **Dial-Up Networking** icon.

❏ Double-click the **Make New Connection** icon.

❏ Type *ISDN 2-Channel*.

❏ Select the Motorola BitSURFR Pro from the modem drop-list.

❏ Click **Configure**.

❏ Select the correct Port.

❏ Change the **Maximum Speed** window to 115200.

❏ Click the **Connection** tab.

❏ Set **Data bits** to **8**.

❑ Set **Parity** to **None**.

❑ Set **Stop bits** to **1**.

❑ Click **Advanced**.

❑ Check **Use flow control**.

❑ Check **Hardware (RTS/CTS)**.

❑ Click in **Extra Settings**.

> In the next step you'll enter a slightly different string to enable the 2-channel mode.

❑ Type *AT1&C1&D2\Q3A4=0A2=95A\@B0=2<CR>*

> The only difference in the two strings is the last character before the <CR>. A 1" is for 1-channel, a 2" is for 2-channel. But there's more. In a couple of steps, you'll need to enter a suffix after the phone number.

❑ Click **OK, OK, Next**.

> This will take you to the phone number entry screen.

❑ Enter the dial-in phone number for your **ISDN** account.

❑ Type *&* (ampersand) after the phone number.

❑ Type the last digit of your dial-in account phone number.

> For example, if your ISDN dial-in account phone number is 555-2468, you would enter 555-2468&8 on this line.

❑ Click **Finish**.

That's it. This icon will get you a 128kbps ISDN connection.

Now you can double-click either of your new ISDN icons and enjoy surfing like you've never seen before, if you've been using only an analog modem. The Web is a lot more fun at ISDN speeds!

Special thanks

My research efforts for this book were blessed by a large number of helpful professionals.

- Motorola set me up with their public relations company, LNS Communications, and sent me a BitSURFR Pro terminal adapter.
- Bell Atlantic in Norfolk, Virginia, worked long hours to bring me a flawless ISDN line.
- Erol's Internet and Computers in Springfield, Virginia, provided a free ISDN Internet account.

Motorola and LNS Communications

My quest for ISDN service began with Bob Clinton in Huntsville, Alabama, when I contacted him about getting me a terminal adapter. From there, the process went on to Motorola's public relations company, LNS Communications, where I got some fabulous help from Jennie Svitaski. No wonder the Motorola BitSURFR has emerged as the industry leader in ISDN terminal adapters. Thanks, Jennie.

Erol's Internet and Computers

In just one phone call I reached Kevin Dugan, in the Springfield, Virginia, office, who set up a free ISDN account right away. Even when I used the account with an analog 28.8kbps modem, I got faster connections than I ever had seen from other local service providers. When my ISDN line was ready—this is no surprise—I couldn't get it to work. So I called their technical support number and instantly reached Eric Nathan, who was a wizard with Windows 95 and ISDN. He quickly confirmed that everything on their end was working fine and that I needed to call Bell Atlantic.

Bell Atlantic

After Erol's confirmed that my account there was working, I called technical support at Bell Atlantic and quickly reached Marty Melton. Marty knows Windows 95 inside and out and confirmed that both my Erol's account and my ISDN line were working properly. After that, he knew the problem was in my setup and he knew right where to look. I built the Hands-On exercises above from Marty's expert guidance.

Marty says that he sees two common problems with new ISDN installations:

- Users fail to get the string entered into the **Extra 8 Settings** window (see the exercises).
- Users don't configure the terminal adapter correctly, especially having trouble entering the Service Provider Identification (SPID) numbers.

Marty expertly outlined the steps that I turned into the exercises you see here. Follow these and you'll be enjoying ISDN in no time.

Long before I needed technical support, I got professional service from Bell Atlantic. It began with Tony Price in the Washington metro area, who authorized my installation and three months of free service while researching this book. After approving the installation, Tony handed me off to Ed Lamb in the Norfolk, Virginia, office who handled everything smoothly, with friendly assistance from Vonda Majette.

 # Continuing Education

Motorola

http://www.motorola.com

Motorola's home page (see Figure B-3) will keep you up to date with their ISDN products. They also include several links to other sites that deal with telecommunications issues. You'll find a helpful FAQs file that might answer some of your ISDN questions and you can use the survey and comments link to tell them what you think about your ISDN service.

Erol's Internet and Computers

http://www.erols.com

A national leader in providing Internet services, Erol's serves the mid-Atlantic region (see Figure B-4). As this book was written, they are the only service provider in this area that uses a T-3 line. That power combined with an ISDN account gives me some incredible surfing speed.

High-speed Internet service ◀

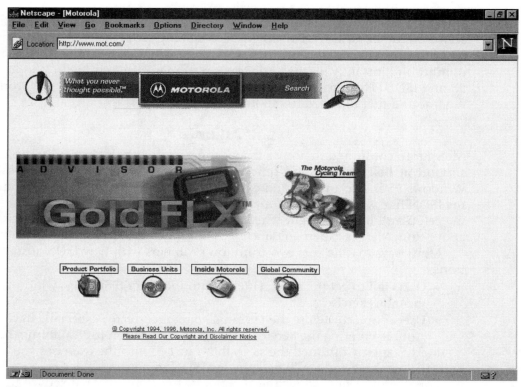

Figure B-3

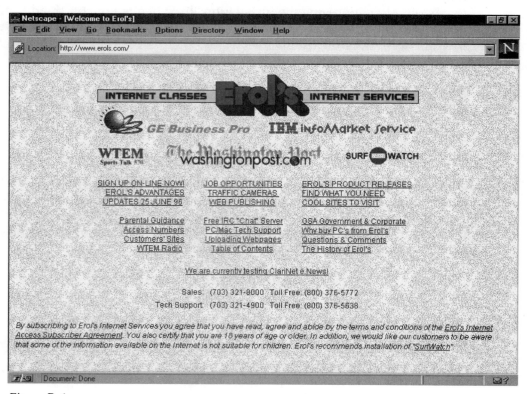

Figure B-4

They have a couple of other fabulous benefits. First, they set up *one* account and *one* dial-in number that handles both analog usage and ISDN usage. Some providers want you to abandon your original account or set up a second account for ISDN. Even if they let you use the same account, they'll have different phone numbers. Erol's has automatic detection equipment that connects with either analog or ISDN service on-the-fly. Second, Erol's has excellent prices, charging only $29.95 per month for a dual account. In contrast, another local provider wanted $89.95 per month for a separate ISDN account.

Bell Atlantic

http://www.bell-atl.com

Check out this home page and you won't miss the What's Hot link to their ISDN pages (see Figure B-5). Finding the answers to everything you need to know about ISDN can start here. Of course this office serves the mid-Atlantic region, so you may need to track down your own phone company's Web page.

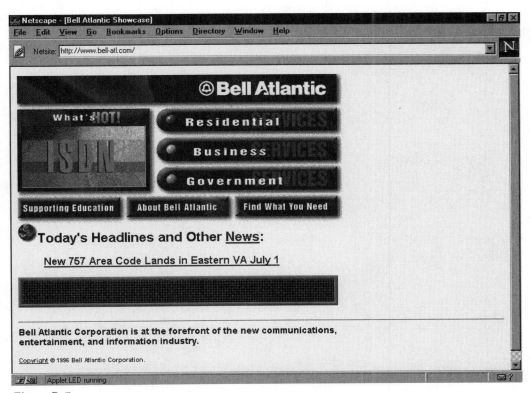

Figure B-5

Glossary

NET TIP This glossary is available on-line at the book's Web site: *www.marketing-coach.com/mh-web*. From the home page, click on the **Glossary** link. The on-line glossary includes a link to Yahoo! that will help you find other Internet glossaries. You can download the on-line version, save it, and use it on your own network or Intranet, provided you keep the title and copyright information intact.

anonymous FTP Using the FTP function of the Internet anonymously by not logging in with an actual, secret login ID and password. Often permitted by large host computers who are willing to share openly some of the files on their system to outside users who otherwise would not be able to log in.

Archie An ancient Internet search tool, not used much since way back in 1994. It's an archive of filenames maintained at Internet FTP sites. Don't pine its passing; you didn't miss anything fun—the Web is much more fun.

bandwidth The transmission capacity of the lines that carry the Internet's electronic traffic. Historically it has imposed severe limitations on the ability of the Internet to deliver all that we are demanding it deliver, but fiber optic cables will ensure that bandwidth soon will be essentially limitless and free.

browser Software that enables users to browse through the cyberspace of the World Wide Web. Netscape is the primary Internet browser today.

ClariNet A commercial news service that provides tailored news reports via the Internet. You can access ClariNet news within Usenet newsgroups. There is a whole series of them, dedicated to a wide range of broad topics. In general, you can find them on news servers at clari.*.

client/server Computer technology that separates computers and their users into two categories: clients or servers. When you want information from a computer on the Internet, you are a client. The computer that delivers the information is the server. A server both stores information and makes it available to any authorized client who requests the information. You may hear this one frequently, especially if someone says "You can't contact us today because our Web server is down."

dial-in An Internet account that can connect any stand-alone PC directly to the Internet. The account is used by having a PC-based (most often, Windows-based) software application dial in to an Internet service provider (ISP). The software connects with the ISP and establishes a TCP/IP link to the Internet that enables your software to access Internet information. The PC that accesses a dial-in connection needs either a modem to connect via a regular phone line or a terminal adapter (TA) to connect via an ISDN phone line.

e-mail (Electronic mail) Messages transmitted over the Internet from user to user. E-mail can contain text, but also can carry with it files of any type as attachments.

FAQs (Frequently Asked Questions) Files that commonly are maintained at Internet sites to answer frequently asked questions so that experienced users don't have to bear the annoying burden of hearing newbies repeatedly ask the same questions. It's good netiquette to check for FAQs and read them. It's extremely poor netiquette—and a good way to get flamed—to post questions that already are answered in the FAQ.

Finger An Internet function that enables one user to query (finger) the location of another Internet user. Finger can be applied to any computer on the Internet, if set up properly. For example, the most famous finger site of all was a Coke machine at Carnegie-Mellon that students wired to the Internet so they could finger it and track such important information as how many bottles of which beverage remained and how long the bottom bottle in each stack had been in the machine—so they wouldn't walk all the way to the machine and find it empty, or purchase a warm soda. You won't use this, but it was fun while it lasted. Most sites on which you could use Finger are shutting it down because it helps hackers crack a system.

firewall A combination of hardware and software that protects a local area network (LAN) from Internet hackers. It separates the network into two or more parts and restricts outsiders to the area outside the firewall. Private or sensitive information is kept inside the firewall.

flames Insulting, enraged Internet messages. The equivalent of schoolyard brawls in cyberspace. Unfortunately, a good schoolyard brawl would be preferable, because at least then the only people who suffer are the dummies who fight. On the Internet, everyone suffers as resources are squandered on ridiculous, infantile behavior. As a representative of a business organization, you won't be using flames, of course.

FQDN (Fully Qualified Domain Name) The official name assigned to a computer. Organizations register names, such as ibm.com or utulsa.edu. They then assign unique names to their computers, such as watson5.ibm.com or hurricane.cs.utulsa.edu.

FTP (File Transfer Protocol) The basic Internet function that enables files to be transferred between computers. You can use it to download files from a remote host computer, as well as to upload files from your computer to a remote host computer. (See Anonymous FTP.)

gateway A host computer that connects networks that communicate in different languages. For example, a gateway connects a company's local area network to the Internet.

GIF (Graphics Interchange Format) A graphics file format that is commonly used on the Internet to provide graphics images in Web pages.

Gopher An organizing tool that was the primary means for obtaining Internet resources before the World Wide Web became popular. Gopher now is buried under mountains of WWW pages—don't bother learning how to use this directly. You sometimes will find a Web link that takes you to a Gopher site, but at that point, if you're using Netscape, its usage will be obvious and actually will look a great deal like the Web.

host A computer that hosts computer users by providing files, providing services, or otherwise sharing its resources.

HTML (Hypertext Markup Language) The basic language that is used to build hypertext documents on the World Wide Web. It is used in plain ASCII-text documents, but when those documents are interpreted (called rendering) by a Web browser such as Netscape, the document can display formatted text, color, a variety of fonts, graphic images, special effects, hypertext jumps to other Internet locations, and information forms.

HTTP (Hypertext Transfer Protocol) The protocol (rules) computers use to transfer hypertext documents.

hypertext Text in a document that contains a hidden link to other text. You can click a mouse on a hypertext word and it will take you to the text designated in the link. Hypertext is used in Windows help programs and CD encyclopedias to jump to related references elsewhere within the same document. The wonderful thing about hypertext, however, is its ability to link using http over the World Wide Web to any Web document in the world, yet still require only a single mouse click to jump clear around the world.

IP (Internet Protocol) The rules that support basic data delivery functions. (See TCP/IP).

IP Address An Internet address that is a unique number consisting of 4 parts separated by dots, sometimes called a "dotted quad." For example, 198.204.112.1. Every Internet computer has an IP address and most computers also have one or more Domain Names that are substitutes for the dotted quad.

IRC (Internet Relay Chat) Currently an Internet tool with a limited use that lets users join a chat channel and exchange typed, text messages. Few people have used IRC, but it is going to create a revolution in communication when the Internet can provide the bandwidth to carry full-color, live-action video and audio. Once that occurs, the IRC will provide full video-conferencing. Even today, while limited for all practical purposes only to text, the IRC can be a valuable business conferencing tool, already providing adequate voice communication.

ISDN (Integrated Services Digital Network) A set of communications standards that enable a single phone line or optical cable to carry voice, digital network services and video. ISDN is intended to eventually replace our standard telephone system.

JPEG (Joint Photographic Experts Group) The name of the committee that designed the photographic image-compression standard. JPEG is optimized for compressing full-color or gray-scale photographic-type, digital images. It doesn't work well on drawn images such as line drawings, and it does not handle black-and-white images or video images.

kbps (kilobits per second) A speed rating for computer modems that measures (in units of 1,024 bits) the maximum number of bits the device can transfer in one second under ideal conditions.

kBps (kilobytes per second). Remember, one byte is eight bits.

leased line A leased phone line that provides a full-time, dedicated, direct connection to the Internet.

listserv An Internet application that automatically serves mailing lists by sending electronic newsletters to a stored database of Internet user addresses. Users can handle their own subscribe/unsubscribe actions without requiring anyone at the server location to personally handle the transaction.

mailing list An e-mail based discussion group. Sending one e-mail message to the mailing list's list server, sends mail to all other members of the group. Users join a mailing list by subscribing. Subscribers to a mailing list receive messages from all other members. Users have to unsubscribe from a mailing list to stop receiving messages forwarded from the group's members.

MIME (Multipurpose Internet Mail Extensions) A set of Internet functions that extends normal e-mail capabilities and enables computer files to be attached to e-mail. Files sent by MIME arrive at their destination as exact copies of the original so that you can send fully-formatted word processing files, spreadsheets, graphics images and software applications to other users via simple e-mail.

modem An electronic device that lets computers communicate electronically using regular phone lines. The name is derived from modulator-demodulator because of their function in processing data over analog phone lines.

netiquette Internet etiquette, good netiquette will keep you out of trouble in newsgroups.

newsgroup An electronic, community bulletin board that enables Internet users all over the world to post and read messages that are public to other users of the group.

NNTP (Network News Transfer Protocol) An Internet protocol that handles Usenet newsgroups at most modern Internet service providers.

POP (Post Office Protocol) An Internet protocol that enables a single user to read e-mail from a mail server.

PoP (Point of Presence) A site that has an array of telecommunications equipment: modems, digital, leased lines, and Internet routers. An Internet access provider may operate several regional PoPs to provide Internet connections within local phone service areas. An alternative is for access providers to employ virtual PoPs (virtual Points of Presence) in conjunction with third party provider.

protocols Computer rules that provide uniform specifications so that computer hardware and operating systems can communicate. It's similar to the way that mail, in countries around the world, is addressed in the same basic format so that postal workers know where to find the recipient's address, the sender's return address and the postage stamp. Regardless of the underlying language, the basic protocols remain the same.

router A network device that enables the network to reroute messages it receives that are intended for other networks. The network with the router receives the message and sends it on its way exactly as received.

shell account A software application that lets you use someone else's Internet connection. It's not the same as having your own, direct Internet connection, but pretty close. Instead, you connect to a host computer and use the Internet through the host computer's connection.

signature file An ASCII text file, maintained within e-mail programs, that contains a few lines of text for your signature. The programs automatically attach the file to your messages so you don't have to repeatedly type a closing.

SLIP/PPP (Serial Line Internet Protocol/Point-to-Point Protocol) Two different, basic rule sets that enable computers to connect, usually by dial-up modem, directly to other computers that provide Internet services.

SMTP (Simple Mail Transfer Protocol) The simple, classic protocol used to handle the Internet's e-mail functions.

spam Anything that nobody wants. Applies primarily to commercial messages posted across a large number of Internet Newsgroups, especially when the ad contains nothing of specific interest to the posted Newsgroup.

T1 An Internet backbone line that carries up to 1.536 million bits per second (1.536Mbps).

T3 An Internet line that carries up to 45 million bits per second (45Mbps).

TA See Terminal Adapter.

TCP/IP (Transmission Control Protocol/Internet Protocol) The basic programming foundation that carries computer messages around the globe via the Internet. Co-created by Vinton G. Cerf, former president of the Internet Society, and Robert E. Kahn.

Telnet An Internet protocol that lets you connect your PC as a remote workstation to a host computer anywhere in the world and to use that computer as if you were logged on locally. You often have the ability to use all of the software and capability on the host computer, even if it's a huge mainframe.

Terminal Adapter (TA) An electronic device that interfaces a PC with an Internet host computer via an ISDN phone line. Often called "ISDN modems." However, because they are digital, TAs are not modems at all. (See modem definition.)

UNIX The computer operating system that was used to write most of the programs and protocols that built the Internet. The need for UNIX is rapidly waning and mainstream users will never need to use a UNIX command-line prompt. The name was created by the programmers who wrote the operating system because they realized that while they were developing the operating system they essentially had become eunuchs.

URL (Uniform Resource Locator) A critical term. It's your main access channel to Internet sites. Equivalent to having the phone number of a place you want to call. You constantly will use URLs with your Internet software applications to

Usenet Another name for Internet Newsgroups. A distributed bulletin board system running on news servers.

Veronica Archie's companion—not really, because Veronica actually helps you find information on Gopher menus. It's an acronym for Very Easy Rodent-Oriented Net-wide Index to Computerized Archives. You probably never will use it, because Web searches are faster and more extensive.

World Wide Web (WWW) (W3) (the Web) An Internet client-server distributed information and retrieval system based upon the hypertext transfer protocol (http) that transfers hypertext documents across a varied array of computer systems. The Web was created by the CERN High-Energy Physics Laboratories in Geneva, Switzerland, in 1991. CERN boosted the Web into international prominence on the Internet.

Continuing Education

McGraw-Hill World Wide Web Training Manual
http://www.marketing-coach.com/mh-web

The on-line version of this book's glossary (see Figure G-1). It has an index at the top of the home page that lets you jump to different terms. Be sure to read the directions on how to use the Netscape Find feature (**CTRL+F**) to find specific words on the page. Hit the search button to automatically search Yahoo! for other indexed Internet glossaries.

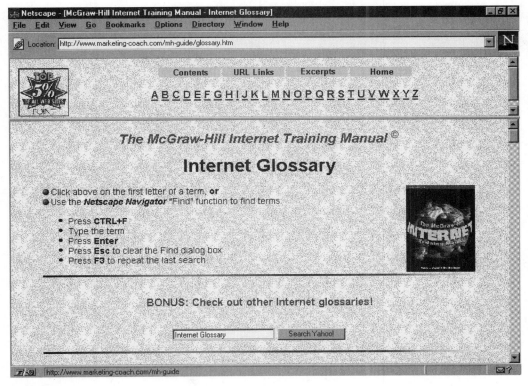

Figure G-1

Index

About the Author

This is Ron Wagner's tenth book. His first two were computer guide books, one on Turbo Pascal and one on Electric Desk (later called LotusWorks). Ron also wrote three software applications for Software Express/Direct that were advertised nationally in *PC Magazine*. That same year—1986, the first year he owned a PC—Ron also wrote a column for a computer magazine called *Uptime*.

Ron switched in 1989 from programming to training and became WordPerfect Corporation's 129th Certified Instructor. PC training and writing have been his primary revenue source since then. Before 1989, Ron spent 16 years as a professional pilot, flying VIP transports for the U.S. Air Force in the Presidential Wing at Andrews AFB in Washington and flying Boeing 727s for Eastern Air Lines out of Washington National.

In 1991, Ron became an international trainer for Group1 Software's ArcList and AccuMail packages, which got him back in the air again, training coast-to-coast in the U.S. and overseas to London, Madrid, Mexico City, Buenos Aires, and Johannesburg. Ron wrote four books in 1991—all were ghost-writing projects for people such as founders of well-known (but nameless here) corporations.

In 1993, he co-authored *The Weather Sourcebook* with Bill Adler, Jr. It sold out its first printing in four months and has gone into its third printing.

Ron expanded his computer business again with Internet training and consulting and now is working with Dick Connor to develop their "Client-centered Interneting" system. They are planning to co-author a book titled *Net Profit: Client-centered Interneting* and to develop the supporting software Your Marketing Coach (see *http://www.marketing-coach.com*).